Tyson Kopczynski
Pete Handley
Marco Shaw

Windows® PowerShell™

UNLEASHED

SAMS | 800 East 96th Street, Indianapolis, Indiana 46240 USA

Windows® PowerShell™ Unleashed

Copyright © 2009 by Pearson Education, Inc.

All rights reserved. No part of this book shall be reproduced, stored in a retrieval system, or transmitted by any means, electronic, mechanical, photocopying, recording, or otherwise, without written permission from the publisher. No patent liability is assumed with respect to the use of the information contained herein. Although every precaution has been taken in the preparation of this book, the publisher and author assume no responsibility for errors or omissions. Nor is any liability assumed for damages resulting from the use of the information contained herein.

ISBN-13: 978-0-672-32988-3

Library of Congress Cataloging-in-Publication Data:

Windows PowerShell unleashed / Tyson Kopczynski, Pete Handley, Marco Shaw.

1. Windows PowerShell (Computer program language) I. Handley, Pete. II. Shaw, Marco. III. Title.

Printed in the United States of America

First Printing December 2008

Trademarks

All terms mentioned in this book that are known to be trademarks or service marks have been appropriately capitalized. Sams Publishing cannot attest to the accuracy of this information. Use of a term in this book should not be regarded as affecting the validity of any trademark or service mark.

Warning and Disclaimer

Every effort has been made to make this book as complete and as accurate as possible, but no warranty or fitness is implied. The information provided is on an "as is" basis. The authors and the publisher shall have neither liability nor responsibility to any person or entity with respect to any loss or damages arising from the information contained in this book.

Bulk Sales

Sams Publishing offers excellent discounts on this book when ordered in quantity for bulk purchases or special sales. For more information, please contact:

U.S. Corporate and Government Sales

1-800-382-3419

corpsales@pearsontechgroup.com

For sales outside of the U.S., please contact

International Sales

international@pearson.com

Editor-in-Chief
Karen Gettman

Executive Editor
Neil Rowe

Development Editor
Mark Renfrow

Managing Editor
Kristy Hart

Project Editor
Jovana San Nicolas-Shirley

Copy Editor
Deadline Driven Publishing

Indexer
Erika Millen

Proofreader
Kathy Ruiz

Technical Editor
Tony Bradley

Publishing Coordinator
Cindy Teeters

Cover Designer
Gary Adair

Compositor
Nonie Ratcliff

Contents at a Glance

Table of Contents

Part III   Managing Microsoft Technologies with PowerShell

About the Authors

With more than nine years of experience in the information technology sector, **Tyson Kopczynski** has become a specialist in Active Directory, Group Policy, Windows scripting, Windows Rights Management Services, PKI, and information technology security practices. Tyson has been a contributing author for such books as *Microsoft Internet Security and Acceleration (ISA) Server 2004 Unleashed* and *Microsoft Windows Server 2003 Unleashed (R2 Edition)*. In addition, he has written detailed technical papers and guides covering various in-the-field technologies he works with extensively. As a consultant at Convergent Computing (CCO), Tyson has been able to work with the next generation of Microsoft technologies since their inception and played a key role in expanding scripting and development practices at CCO. Tyson also holds the SANS Security Essentials Certification (GSEC), Microsoft Certified Systems Engineer (MCSE) Security certification, CompTIA Security+ certification, and SANS Certified Incident Handler (GCIH) certification.

Pete Handley has more than 15 years of experience in IT, including extensive knowledge of Active Directory, Microsoft Exchange, Novell GroupWise messaging, and Novell Directory Services. He has been a contributing author for *Microsoft Exchange 2003 Unleashed*, and *Windows PowerShell Unleashed*. Pete specializes in Visual Basic and PowerShell scripting and is a subject matter expert on the integration and migration of Novell technologies to Microsoft technologies. Pete holds the Microsoft Certified Systems Engineer 2003 (MCSE) certification, the Microsoft Certified Information Technology Professional (MCITP) certification, the Novell Certified Directory Engineer (CDE) certification, and the Certified Information Systems Security Professional (CISSP) certification.

Marco Shaw is an IT system analyst for a Canadian telecommunications company. He has been working in the IT industry for more than ten years, and he recently received a Microsoft Most Valuable Professional (MVP) award for his involvement in the Windows PowerShell community. He is the assistant community director of the new PowerShell Community Web site at http://www.powershellcommunity.org. His primary blog site is http://marcoshaw.blogspot.com. Marco holds a RedHat Certified Engineer (RHCE) certification, Microsoft Certified Professional (MCP) certification, and a bachelor of science degree from the Université de Moncton in New Brunswick, Canada.

Dedication

I dedicate this book to my mom, dad, brother, and sister.
Thanks for putting up with me all these years.

— Tyson Kopczynski

I dedicate this book to my wonderful and supportive wife Melissa.
You really do make it all worthwhile.

— Pete Handley

For Joanne, Gabrielle, Samuel, and Sébastien. I love you all
and thank you for always being so supportive.

— Marco Shaw

Acknowledgments

For the first of many acknowledgments, we would like to thank Neil Rowe from Sams Publishing for his continued support with this series. Thanks to his support and guidance, we were able to put together this new edition to the series. We are also grateful to our contributing authors Chris Amaris and Michael Sneeringer for their assistance in putting together this release of the series. To the editing team, Mark Renfrow and Jovana San Nicolas-Shirley, we are deeply indebted to you for the fantastic suggestions and your meticulous work editing this book. Also, we can't forget to thank all of our families, friends, and co-workers who have been very understanding while we continued our quest to finish the book. Writing a book takes time, and we appreciate everyone's support while we plugged away on another one.

Last, but not least, a personal thanks to all of the Tokyo taxi drivers who helped Tyson Kopczynski many times as he wandered the streets of Tokyo lost in a sea of Kanji and confusing street layouts. You guys rock!

We Want to Hear from You!

As the reader of this book, *you* are our most important critic and commentator. We value your opinion and want to know what we're doing right, what we could do better, what areas you'd like to see us publish in, and any other words of wisdom you're willing to pass our way.

You can email or write me directly to let me know what you did or didn't like about this book—as well as what we can do to make our books stronger.

Please note that I cannot help you with technical problems related to the topic of this book, and that due to the high volume of mail I receive, I might not be able to reply to every message.

When you write, please be sure to include this book's title and author as well as your name and phone or email address. I will carefully review your comments and share them with the author and editors who worked on the book.

E-mail: feedback@samspublishing.com

Mail: Neil Rowe
            Executive Editor
            Sams Publishing
            800 East 96th Street
            Indianapolis, IN 46240 USA

Reader Services

Visit our website and register this book at informit.com/register for convenient access to any updates, downloads, or errata that might be available for this book.

Introduction

Well, we are back for yet another *PowerShell Unleashed* book. However, unlike just a simple revision of the existing book, which most likely would have resulted in only just a few updated chapters, I decided to instead treat this release in the series as almost a completely new book. Granted, the Community Technology Release (CTP) of PowerShell 2.0 did help drive the need to update all aspects of this edition. Nonetheless, there was also a lot of feedback (some positive and some negative) about how the first book could be improved.

So, based on this feedback and the looming PowerShell 2.0 feature list, I set about making a major revision to the book. To start off right, I decided to address how the PowerShell language was covered in the series. After all, the first book in the series was script heavy, but lacking when it came to explaining some of the basics about the PowerShell language. Additionally, we wanted to go into greater detail about how PowerShell could be used to manage Windows resources while further addressing some of the finer technical details of PowerShell's architecture. Needless to say, all of these changes required a reorganization to not only the layout of the book, but also its size.

The bottom line, in this new edition, there are six completely new chapters with the rest of the existing chapters either being extensively rewritten or updated. With all this extra content, the book needed additional authors to jump on board and help pound out the book's technical prose. Thus, joining me on this book as coauthors were Marco Shaw (PowerShell MVP) and Peter Handley (contributing author from the first book). Together, Marco and Peter made great additions to this book and infused fantastic ideas together with even better content—all while writing their chapters.

Finally, the primary goal of this book was to start down the path of explaining the features found in the future 2.0 release of PowerShell. After all, with the 2.0 CTP release late last year, the PowerShell product team ignited our imaginations with the possibilities for what might come down the road (remoting). So, we simply had to do our best to explain the new features. However, given that the 2.0 version is still just a CTP and not a beta, we also walked down a slippery slope, considering that some of these features may not exist in the PowerShell 2.0 RTM. Naturally, like a good reporter might do, we did our best. In the end, we tried to include 2.0 content where applicable while also dedicating an entire chapter to only 2.0 features deemed too important to ignore or voted most likely to survive the beta.

We hope our efforts result in a more comprehensive PowerShell book that can act as both a reference for the current PowerShell 1.0 release while also providing insight into where PowerShell might go with the 2.0 release.

Who Is This Book's Intended Audience?

This *Unleashed* book is intended for an intermediate level of systems administrators who have invested time and energy learning Windows scripting and want to translate those skills into PowerShell skills while learning how it can meet their real-world needs. This book has been written so that anyone with a scripting background can understand what PowerShell is and how to use it, but by no means is it meant to be a complete PowerShell reference. Instead, think of it as a resource for learning how PowerShell can be applied in your own environment. Therefore, the structure of this book reflects that focus by including numerous command examples and working scripts.

How This Book Is Organized

The book is divided into the following three parts:

- Part I, "Introduction to PowerShell"—In this section, you are introduced to PowerShell and some of its internal workings. Topics covered include items such as why PowerShell came into existence, general concepts about PowerShell and how it is constructed, and an in-depth review of PowerShell security.

- Part II, "Using PowerShell"—In this section, you learn more about the PowerShell scripting language, how to use PowerShell to manage Windows resources, and important best practices to follow when using PowerShell. Specific topics covered range from working with the Windows file system, the Registry, permissions, strings, and Windows Management Instrumentation (WMI) to understanding PowerShell language concepts such as loops, functions, arrays, and so on.

- Part III, "Managing Microsoft Technologies with PowerShell"—In this section, you learn how PowerShell can be used to manage Microsoft technologies. Topics covered include using PowerShell to manage Active Directory, Exchange Server 2007, and Systems Center Operations Manager 2007. Additionally, you learn how to programmatically use PowerShell to manage systems and gain insight and understanding into important PowerShell 2.0 features.

Conventions Used in This Book

Commands, scripts, and anything related to code are presented in a special `monospace` computer typeface. Bold indicates key terms being defined, and italic is used to indicate variables or for emphasis. Great care has been taken to be consistent in letter case, naming, and structure, with the goal of making command and script examples more readable. In addition, you might find instances in which commands or scripts haven't been fully optimized. This lack of optimization is for your benefit, as it makes those code samples more intelligible and follows the practice of writing code for others to read.

Other standards used throughout this book are as follows:

Black Code Boxes

```
These code boxes contain commands that run in a PowerShell or Bash
shell session.
```

Gray Code Boxes

```
These code boxes contain source code from scripts, configuration files, or
other items that aren't run directly in a shell session.
```

Please note that although PowerShell can display text in multiple colors, all script output from the examples is printed here in black and white. If you run one of the example scripts on your lab system, the text will be displayed in color.

CAUTION

Cautions alert you to actions that should be avoided.

NOTE

Notes give you additional background information about a topic being discussed.

PART I

Introduction to PowerShell

IN THIS PART

Introduction to Shells

Shells are a necessity when using key components of nearly all operating systems, because they make it possible to perform arbitrary actions such as traversing the file system, running commands, or using applications. As such, every computer user has interacted with a shell by typing commands at a prompt or by clicking an icon to start an application. Shells are an ever-present component of modern computing, frequently providing functionality that is not available anywhere else when working on a computer system.

In this chapter, you take a look at what a shell is and see the power that can be harnessed by interacting with a shell. To do this, you walk through some basic shell commands, and then build a shell script from those basic commands to see how they can become more powerful via scripting. Next, you take a brief tour of how shells have evolved over the past 35 years. Finally, you learn why PowerShell was created, why there was a need for PowerShell, what its inception means to scripters and system administrators, and what some of the differences between PowerShell 1.0 and PowerShell 2.0 CTP2 are.

What Is a Shell?

A shell is an interface that enables users to interact with the operating system. A shell isn't considered an application because of its inescapable nature, but it's the same as any other process that runs on a system. The difference between a shell and an application is that a shell's purpose is to enable users to run other applications. In some operating systems (such as UNIX, Linux, and VMS), the shell is a command-line interface (CLI); in other operating systems (such as Windows and Mac OS X), the shell is a graphical user interface (GUI).

In addition, two types of systems in wide use are often neglected in discussions of shells: networking equipment and kiosks. Networking equipment usually has a GUI shell (mostly a Web interface on consumer-grade equipment) or a CLI shell (in commercial-grade equipment). Kiosks are a completely different animal; because many kiosks are built from applications running atop a more robust operating system, often kiosk interfaces aren't shells. However, if the kiosk is built with an operating system that serves only to run the kiosk, the interface is accurately described as a shell. Unfortunately, kiosk interfaces continue to be referred to generically as shells because of the difficulty in explaining the difference to nontechnical users.

Both CLI and GUI shells have benefits and drawbacks. For example, most CLI shells allow powerful command chaining (using commands that feed their output into other commands for further processing, this is commonly referred to as the pipeline). GUI shells, however, require commands to be completely self-contained and generally do not provide a native method for directing their output into other commands. Furthermore, most GUI shells are easy to navigate, whereas CLI shells do not have an intuitive interface and require a preexisting knowledge of the system to successfully complete automation tasks. Your choice of shell depends on what you're comfortable with and what's best suited to perform the task at hand.

Even though GUI shells exist, the term "shell" is used almost exclusively to describe a command-line environment, not a task you perform with a GUI application, such as Windows Explorer. Likewise, shell scripting refers to collecting commands normally entered on the command line or into an executable file.

As you can see, historically there has been a distinction between graphical and nongraphical shells. An interesting development in PowerShell 2.0 CTP2 is the introduction of an alpha version of Graphical PowerShell, which provides a CLI and a script editor in the same window. Although this type of interface has been available for many years in IDE (Integrated Development Environment) editors for programming languages such as C, this alpha version of Graphical PowerShell gives a sense of the direction from the PowerShell team on where they see PowerShell going in the future—a fully featured CLI shell with the added benefits of a natively supported GUI interface.

Basic Shell Use

Many shell commands, such as listing the contents of the current working directory, are simple. However, shells can quickly become complex when more powerful results are required. The following example uses the Bash shell to list the contents of the current working directory.

```
$ ls
apache2 bin      etc     include lib     libexec man    sbin     share    var
```

However, often seeing just filenames isn't enough and so a command-line argument needs to be passed to the command to get more details about the files.

> **NOTE**
>
> Please note that the Bash examples shown here are included only to demonstrate the capabilities of a command-line shell interface. Although it may be helpful, knowledge of the Bash shell will not be needed to understand any of the scripts or examples in this book.

The following command gives you more detailed information about each file using a command-line argument.

```
$ ls -l
total 8
drwxr-xr-x    13 root    admin     442 Sep 18 20:50 apache2
drwxrwxr-x    57 root    admin    1938 Sep 19 22:35 bin
drwxrwxr-x     5 root    admin     170 Sep 18 20:50 etc
drwxrwxr-x    30 root    admin    1020 Sep 19 22:30 include
drwxrwxr-x   102 root    admin    3468 Sep 19 22:30 lib
drwxrwxr-x     3 root    admin     102 Sep 18 20:11 libexec
lrwxr-xr-x     1 root    admin       9 Sep 18 20:12 man -> share/man
drwxrwxr-x     3 root    admin     102 Sep 18 20:11 sbin
drwxrwxr-x    13 root    admin     442 Sep 19 22:35 share
drwxrwxr-x     3 root    admin     102 Jul 30 21:05 var
```

Now you need to decide what to do with this information. As you can see, directories are interspersed with files, making it difficult to tell them apart. If you want to view only directories, you have to pare down the output by piping the ls command output into the grep command. In the following example, the output has been filtered to display only lines starting with the letter d, which signifies that the file is a directory.

```
$ ls -l | grep '^d'
drwxr-xr-x    13 root    admin     442 Sep 18 20:50 apache2
drwxrwxr-x    57 root    admin    1938 Sep 19 22:35 bin
drwxrwxr-x     5 root    admin     170 Sep 18 20:50 etc
drwxrwxr-x    30 root    admin    1020 Sep 19 22:30 include
drwxrwxr-x   102 root    admin    3468 Sep 19 22:30 lib
drwxrwxr-x     3 root    admin     102 Sep 18 20:11 libexec
drwxrwxr-x     3 root    admin     102 Sep 18 20:11 sbin
drwxrwxr-x    13 root    admin     442 Sep 19 22:35 share
drwxrwxr-x     3 root    admin     102 Jul 30 21:05 var
```

However, now that you have only directories listed, the other information such as date, permissions, size, and so on is superfluous because only the directory names are needed. So in this next example, you use the awk command to print only the last column of output shown in the previous example.

```
$ ls -l | grep '^d' | awk '{ print $NF }'
apache2
bin
etc
include
lib
libexec
sbin
share
var
```

The result is a simple list of directories in the current working directory. This command is fairly straightforward, but it's not something you want to type every time you want to see a list of directories. Instead, we can create an alias or command shortcut for the command that we just executed.

```
$ alias lsd="ls -l | grep '^d' | awk '{ print \$NF }'"
```

Then, by using the lsd alias, you can get a list of directories in the current working directory without having to retype the command from the previous examples.

```
$ lsd
apache2
bin
etc
include
lib
libexec
sbin
share
var
```

As you can see, using a CLI shell offers the potential for serious power when you're automating simple, repetitive tasks.

Basic Shell Scripts

Working in a shell typically consists of typing each command, interpreting the output, deciding how to put that data to work, and then combining the commands into a single, streamlined process. Anyone who has gone through dozens of files, manually adding a single line at the end of each one, will agree that scripting this type of manual process is a much more efficient approach than manually editing each file, and the potential for data entry errors is greatly reduced. In many ways, scripting makes as much sense as breathing.

You've seen how commands can be chained together in a pipeline to manipulate output from the preceding command, and how a command can be aliased to minimize typing. Command aliasing is the younger sibling of shell scripting and gives the command line some of the power of shell scripts. However, shell scripts can harness even more power than aliases.

Collecting single-line commands and pipelines into files for later execution is a powerful technique. Putting output into variables for further manipulation and reference later in the script takes the power to the next level. Wrapping any combination of commands into recursive loops and flow control constructs takes scripting to the same level of sophistication as programming.

Some may say that scripting isn't programming, but this distinction is quickly becoming blurred with the growing variety and power of scripting languages these days. With this in mind, let's try developing the one-line Bash command from the previous section into something more useful.

The lsd command alias from the previous example (referencing the Bash command ls -l | grep '^d' | awk '{ print $NF }') produces a listing of each directory in the current working directory. Now, suppose you want to expand this functionality to show how much space each directory uses on the disk. The Bash utility that reports on disk usage does so on a specified directory's entire contents or a directory's overall disk usage in a summary. It also reports disk usage amounts in bytes by default. With all that in mind, if you want to know each directory's disk usage as a freestanding entity, you need to get and display information for each directory, one by one. The following examples show what this process would look like as a script.

Notice the command line you worked on in the previous section. The for loop parses through the directory list the command returns, assigning each directory name to the DIR variable and executing the code between the do and done keywords.

```
#!/bin/bash

for DIR in $(ls -l | grep '^d' | awk '{ print $NF }'); do
    du -sk ${DIR}
done
```

Saving the previous code as a script file named directory.sh and then running the script in a Bash session produces the following output.

```
$ big_directory.sh
17988    apache2
5900     bin
72       etc
2652     include
82264    lib
0        libexec
0        sbin
35648    share
166768   var
```

Initially, this output doesn't seem especially helpful. With a few additions, you can build something considerably more useful. In this example, we add an additional requirement to report the names of all directories using more than a certain amount of disk space. To achieve this requirement, modify the directory.sh script file as shown in this next example.

```
#!/bin/bash

PRINT_DIR_MIN=35000

for DIR in $(ls -l | grep '^d' | awk '{ print $NF }'); do
    DIR_SIZE=$(du -sk ${DIR} | cut -f 1)
    if [ ${DIR_SIZE} -ge ${PRINT_DIR_MIN} ];then
        echo ${DIR}
    fi
done
```

One of the first things that you'll notice about this version of directory.sh is that we have started adding variables. PRINT_DIR_MIN is a value that represents the minimum number of kilobytes a directory uses to meet the printing criteria. This value could change fairly regularly, so we want to keep it as easily editable as possible. Also, we could reuse this value elsewhere in the script so that we don't have to change the amount in multiple places when the number of kilobytes changes.

You might be thinking the find command would be easier to use. However, although find is terrific for browsing through directory structures, it is too cumbersome for simply viewing the current directory, so the convoluted ls command is used instead. If we were looking for files in the hierarchy, the find command would be the most appropriate choice. However, because we are simply looking for directories in the current directory, the ls command is the best tool for the job in this situation.

The following is an example of the output rendered by the script so far.

```
$ big_directory.sh
lib
share
var
```

This output can be used in a number of ways. For example, systems administrators might use this script to watch user directories for disk usage thresholds if they want to notify users when they have reached a certain level of disk space. For this purpose, knowing when a certain percentage of users reaches or crosses the threshold would be useful.

NOTE

Keep in mind that plenty of commercial products on the market notify administrators of overall disk thresholds being met, so although some money can be saved by writing a shell script to monitor overall disk use, it's not necessary. The task of finding how many users have reached a certain use threshold is different, as it involves proactive measures to prevent disk use problems before they get out of control. The solution is notifying the administrator that certain users should be offloaded to new disks because of growth on the current disk. This approach isn't foolproof, but is an easy way to add a layer of proactive monitoring to ensure that users don't encounter problems when using their systems. Systems administrators could get creative and modify this script with command-line parameters to serve several functions, such as listing the top disk space users and indicating when a certain percentage of users have reached the disk threshold. That kind of complexity, however, is beyond the scope of this chapter.

In our next Bash scripting example, we modify the directory.sh script to display a message when a certain percentage of directories are a specified size.

```
#!/bin/bash

DIR_MIN_SIZE=35000
DIR_PERCENT_BIG_MAX=23

DIR_COUNTER=0
BIG_DIR_COUNTER=0

for DIR in $(ls -l | grep '^d' | awk '{ print $NF }'); do
    DIR_COUNTER=$(expr ${DIR_COUNTER} + 1)
```

```
    DIR_SIZE=$(du -sk ${DIR} | cut -f 1)
    if [ ${DIR_SIZE} -ge ${DIR_MIN_SIZE} ];then
        BIG_DIR_COUNTER=$(expr ${BIG_DIR_COUNTER} + 1)
    fi
done

if [ ${BIG_DIR_COUNTER} -gt 0 ]; then
    DIR_PERCENT_BIG=$(expr $(expr ${BIG_DIR_COUNTER} \* 100) / ${DIR_COUNTER})
    if [ ${DIR_PERCENT_BIG} -gt ${DIR_PERCENT_BIG_MAX} ]; then
        echo "${DIR_PERCENT_BIG} percent of the directories are larger than
${DIR_MIN_SIZE} kilobytes."
    fi
fi
```

Now, the preceding example barely looks like what we started with. The variable name PRINT_DIR_MIN has been changed to DIR_MIN_SIZE because we're not printing anything as a direct result of meeting the minimum size. The DIR_PERCENT_BIG_MAX variable has been added to indicate the maximum allowable percentage of directories at or above the minimum size. Also, two counters have been added: one (DIR_COUNTER) to count the directories and one (BIG_DIR_COUNTER) to count the directories exceeding the minimum size.

Inside the for loop, DIR_COUNTER is incremented, and the if statement in the for loop now simply increments BIG_DIR_COUNTER instead of printing the directory's name. An if statement has been added after the for loop to do additional processing, figure out the percentage of directories exceeding the minimum size, and then print the message if necessary. With these changes, the script now produces the following output.

```
$ big_directory.sh
33 percent of the directories are larger than 35000 kilobytes.
```

The output shows that 33 percent of the directories are 35MB or more. By modifying the echo line in the script to feed a pipeline into a mail delivery command and tweaking the size and percentage thresholds for the environment, systems administrators can schedule this shell script to run at specified intervals and produce directory size reports easily. If administrators want to get fancy, they can make the size and percentage thresholds configurable via command-line parameters.

As you can see, even a basic shell script can be powerful. With a mere 22 lines of code, we have a useful shell script. Some quirks of the script might seem inconvenient (using the expr command for simple math can be tedious, for example), but every programming language has its strengths and weaknesses. As a rule, some tasks you need to do are convoluted to perform, no matter what language you're using.

The moral of this story is that shell scripting, or scripting in general, can make life much easier. For example, say your company merges with another company. As part of that merger, you have to create 1,000 user accounts in Active Directory or another authentication system. Usually, a systems administrator grabs the list, sits down with a cup of coffee, and starts clicking or typing away. If an administrator manages to get a migration budget, he can hire an intern or consultants to do the work or purchase migration software. But why bother performing repetitive tasks or spending money that could be put to better use (such as a bigger salary)?

Instead, the answer should be to automate those iterative tasks by using scripting. Automation is the purpose of scripting. As a systems administrator, you should take advantage of scripting with CLI shells or command interpreters to gain access to the same functionality developers have when coding the systems you manage. However, scripting tools tend to be more open, flexible, and focused on the tasks that you as an IT professional need to perform, as opposed to development tools that provide a framework for building an entire application from a blank canvas.

A Shell History

The first shell in wide use was the Bourne shell, the standard user interface for the UNIX operating system, which is still required by UNIX systems during the startup sequence. This robust shell provided pipelines and conditional and recursive command execution. It was developed by C programmers for C programmers.

Oddly, however, despite being written by and for C programmers, the Bourne shell didn't have a C-like coding style. This lack of a similarity to the C language drove the invention of the C shell, which introduced more C-like programming structures. While the C shell inventors were building a better mousetrap, they decided to add command-line editing and command aliasing (defining command shortcuts), which eased the bane of every UNIX user's existence: typing. The less a UNIX user has to type to get results, the better.

Although most UNIX users liked the C shell, learning a completely new shell was a challenge for some. So the Korn shell was invented, which added a number of the C shell features to the Bourne shell. Because the Korn shell is a commercially licensed product, the open-source software movement needed a shell for Linux and FreeBSD. The collaborative result was the Bourne Again Shell, or Bash, invented by the Free Software Foundation.

Throughout the evolution of UNIX and the birth of Linux and FreeBSD, other operating systems were introduced along with their own shells. Digital Equipment Corporation (DEC) introduced Virtual Memory System (VMS) to compete with UNIX on its VAX systems. VMS had a shell called Digital Command Language (DCL) with a verbose syntax, unlike that of its UNIX counterparts. Also, unlike its UNIX counterparts, it wasn't case sensitive nor did it provide pipelines.

Somewhere along the line, the PC was born. IBM took the PC to the business market, and Apple rebranded roughly the same hardware technology and focused on consumers. Microsoft made DOS run on the IBM PC, acting as both kernel and shell and including some features of other shells. (The pipeline syntax was inspired by UNIX shells.)

Following DOS was Windows, which quickly evolved from an application to an operating system. Windows introduced a GUI shell, which has become the basis for Microsoft shells ever since. Unfortunately, GUI shells are notoriously difficult to script, so Windows provided a DOSShell-like environment. It was improved with a new executable, cmd.exe instead of command.com, and a more robust set of command-line editing features. Regrettably, this change also meant that shell scripts in Windows had to be written in the DOSShell syntax for collecting and executing command groupings.

Over time, Microsoft realized its folly and decided systems administrators should have better ways to manage Windows systems. Windows Script Host (WSH) was introduced in Windows 98, providing a native scripting solution with access to the underpinnings of Windows. It was a library that enabled scripting languages to use Windows in a powerful and efficient manner. WSH is not its own language, however, so a WSH-compliant scripting language was required to take advantage of it, such as JScript, VBScript, Perl, Python, Kixstart, or Object REXX. Some of these languages are quite powerful in performing complex processing, so WSH seemed like a blessing to Windows systems administrators.

However, the rejoicing was short lived because there was no guarantee that the WSH-compliant scripting language you chose would be readily available or a viable option for everyone. The lack of a standard language and environment for writing scripts made it difficult for users and administrators to incorporate automation by using WSH. The only way to be sure the scripting language or WSH version would be compatible on the system being managed was to use a native scripting language, which meant using DOSShell and enduring the problems that accompanied it. In addition, WSH opened a large attack vector for malicious code to run on Windows systems. This vulnerability gave rise to a stream of viruses, worms, and other malicious programs that have wreaked havoc on computer systems, thanks to WSH's focus on automation without user intervention.

The end result was that systems administrators viewed WSH as both a blessing and a curse. Although WSH presented a good object model and access to a number of automation interfaces, it wasn't a shell. It required using Wscript.exe and Cscript.exe; scripts had to be written in a compatible scripting language, and its attack vulnerabilities posed a security challenge. Clearly, a different approach was needed for systems management; over time, Microsoft reached the same conclusion.

Enter PowerShell

Microsoft didn't put a lot of effort into a CLI shell; instead, it concentrated on a GUI shell, which is more compatible with its GUI-based operating systems. (Mac OS X didn't put any effort into a CLI shell, either; it used the Bash shell.) However, the resulting DOSShell had a variety of limitations, such as conditional and recursive programming structures not being well documented and heavy reliance on goto statements. These drawbacks hampered shell scripters for years, and they had to use other scripting languages or write compiled programs to solve common problems.

The introduction of WSH as a standard in the Windows operating system offered a robust alternative to DOSShell scripting. Unfortunately, WSH presented a number of challenges, as discussed in the preceding section. Furthermore, WSH didn't offer the CLI shell experience that UNIX and Linux administrators had enjoyed for years, which resulted in Windows administrators being made fun of by the other chaps for the lack of a CLI shell and its benefits.

Luckily, Jeffrey Snover (the architect of PowerShell) and others on the PowerShell team realized that Windows needed a strong, secure, and robust CLI shell for systems management. Enter PowerShell. PowerShell was designed as a shell with full access to the underpinnings of Windows via the .NET Framework, Component Object Model (COM) objects, and other methods. It also provided an execution environment that's familiar, easy, and secure. PowerShell is aptly named, as it puts the power into the Windows shell. For users wanting to automate their Windows systems, the introduction of PowerShell was exciting because it combined the power of WSH with the familiarity of a traditional shell.

PowerShell provides a powerful native scripting language, so scripts can be ported to all Windows systems without worrying about whether a particular language interpreter is installed. You might have gone through the rigmarole of scripting a solution with WSH in Perl, Python, VBScript, JScript, or another language, only to find that the next system you worked on didn't have that interpreter installed. At home, users can put whatever they want on their systems and maintain them however they see fit, but in a workplace, that option isn't always viable. PowerShell solves that problem by removing the need for nonnative interpreters. It also solves the problem of wading through Web sites to find command-line equivalents for simple GUI shell operations and coding them into .cmd files. Last, PowerShell addresses the WSH security problem by providing a platform for secure Windows scripting. It focuses on security features such as script signing, lack of executable extensions, and execution policies (which are restricted by default).

For anyone who needs to automate administration tasks on a Windows system, PowerShell provides a much-needed injection of power. Its object-oriented nature boosts the power available to you, too. If you're a Windows systems administrator or scripter, becoming a PowerShell expert is highly recommended.

PowerShell is not just a fluke or a side project at Microsoft. The PowerShell team succeeded at creating an amazing shell and winning support within Microsoft for its creation. For example, the Exchange product team adopted PowerShell as the backbone of the management interface in Exchange Server 2007. That was just the start. Other product groups at Microsoft, such as System Center Operations Manager 2007, System Center Data Protection Manager V2, and System Center Virtual Machine Manager, are being won over by what PowerShell can do for their products. In fact, PowerShell is the approach Microsoft has been seeking for a general management interface to Windows-based systems. Over time, PowerShell could replace current management interfaces, such as cmd.exe, WSH, CLI tools, and so on, and become integrated into the Windows operating system as its backbone management interface. With the introduction of PowerShell, Microsoft has addressed a need for CLI shells. The sky is the limit for what Windows systems administrators and scripters can achieve with it.

New Capabilities in PowerShell 2.0 CTP2

With the release of PowerShell 2.0 CTP2, the PowerShell team has expanded the capabilities of PowerShell 1.0 to include a number of key new features. Although PowerShell 2.0's final feature set is likely to change from the CTP2 release, these features are central to PowerShell 2.0 and are expected to make it into the final release of the product.

The first major new feature of PowerShell 2.0 CTP2 is the addition of **PowerShell Remoting**. In a major step forward from the original release of PowerShell 1.0, PowerShell 2.0 CTP2 provides support for running cmdlets and scripts on a remote machine. The Windows Remote Management Service (WS-Man) is used to accomplish this, and a new cmdlet named Invoke-Expression is used to designate the target machine and the command to be executed. The following code example shows the general usage of the Invoke-Expression cmdlet to run the command get-process powershell on a remote computer named XP1.

```
PS C:\> invoke-expression -comp XP1 -command "get-process powershell"

Handles  NPM(K)   PM(K)    WS(K) VM(M)   CPU(s)    Id ProcessName
-------  ------   -----    ----- -----   ------    -- -----------
    522      12   30652    29076   158     3.70  1168 powershell

PS C:\>
```

Another new feature of PowerShell 2.0 CTP2 is the introduction of background jobs or PSJobs. A PSJob is simply a command or expression that executes asynchronously, freeing up the command prompt immediately for other tasks. A new series of Cmdlets related to PSJobs are included, which enable PSJobs to be started, stopped, paused, and listed. It also enables the results analyzed.

Also included in PowerShell 2.0 CTP2 is a new functionality called ScriptCmdlets. Previously, cmdlets had to be written in a .NET framework programming language such as C#, which made it a challenge for many scripters to create their own cmdlets. In this release of PowerShell, the ScriptCmdlets functionality enables scripters to write their own cmdlets with no more effort than writing a PowerShell function. While ScriptCmdlets are handled differently from compiled cmdlets and have certain limitations in this release of PowerShell (such as lack of support for help files), this functionality makes it far easier for scripters to extend PowerShell to address their specific requirements.

The last new feature of PowerShell 2.0 CTP2 that we discuss in this chapter is the introduction of Graphical PowerShell. Graphical PowerShell is currently in an early alpha version, but includes a number of powerful new capabilities that enhance the features of the basic PowerShell CLI shell. Graphical PowerShell provides an interface with both an interactive shell pane and a multi-tabbed scripting pane, as well as the ability to launch multiple shell processes (also known as runspaces) from within Graphical PowerShell.

All of these new features and more are discussed and demonstrated in more detail in subsequent chapters.

Summary

In summary, this chapter has served as an introduction to what a shell is, where shells came from, how to use a shell, and how to create a basic shell script. While learning these aspects about shells, you have also learned why scripting is so important to systems administrators. As you have come to discover, scripting enables systems administrators to automate repetitive tasks. In doing so, task automation enables systems administrators to perform their jobs more effectively, freeing them to perform more important business-enhancing tasks.

In addition to learning about shells, you have also been introduced to what PowerShell is and why PowerShell was needed. As explained, PowerShell is the replacement to WSH, which, although it was powerful, had a number of shortcomings (security and interoperability being the most noteworthy). PowerShell was also needed because Windows lacked a viable CLI that could be used to easily complete complex automation tasks. The end result for replacing WSH and improving on the Windows CLI, is PowerShell, which is built around the .NET Framework and brings a much needed injection of backbone to the world of Windows scripting and automation. Lastly, the key new features of PowerShell 2.0 CTP2 were reviewed at a high level, with detailed analysis of these new capabilities to be provided in subsequent chapters.

CHAPTER 2

Basic PowerShell Concepts

This chapter brings you up to speed on the technical basics of PowerShell and how to use it, with a focus on the new capabilities offered in PowerShell 2.0 CTP2. You learn how to download and install PowerShell, work with the PowerShell command-line interface (CLI), use cmdlets, access the help features of PowerShell 2.0, and write a basic script. This chapter isn't intended to be a complete getting-started guide; instead, it covers the important concepts you need to understand for later chapters.

Getting Started

The best way to get started with PowerShell is to visit the Windows PowerShell home page, as shown in Figure 2.1.

The URL for the Windows PowerShell home page is http://www.microsoft.com/powershell/.

This site is a great resource for information about PowerShell, and enables you to download documentation, tools, read up on the latest product news, and obtain the latest versions of PowerShell. Your next step is downloading and installing PowerShell. Before diving into the installation process, it's important to clarify which version of PowerShell is most appropriate for your requirements. There are currently two versions of PowerShell available for download from Microsoft: PowerShell 1.0 RTW and PowerShell 2.0 CTP2. Each of these versions is described in the following sections.

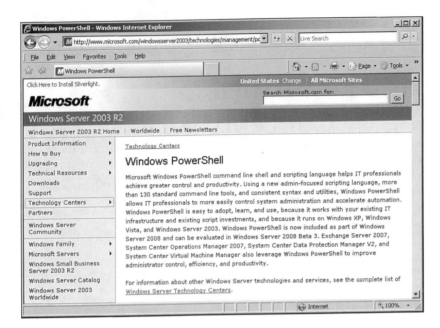

FIGURE 2.1   The Microsoft Windows PowerShell Home Page

PowerShell 1.0 RTW

As of this writing, the current released version of PowerShell is version 1.0 RTW (Release To Web). This version of PowerShell was released to the public in November 2006. Although PowerShell 1.0 RTW does not include the new features of PowerShell 2.0 CTP2 discussed in Chapter 1, "Introduction to Shells," it is the most current stable release of PowerShell and, as of this writing, it is the only version that can be recommended for use in a production environment. PowerShell 1.0 RTW can be downloaded for all supported platforms at the following URL: http://www.microsoft.com/windowsserver2003/technologies/management/powershell/download.mspx.

Enabling PowerShell 1.0 on Windows Server 2008

Windows PowerShell 1.0 is included as a feature of the Windows Server 2008 operating system. However, before PowerShell can be used, it must be added using the ServerManager snap-in. To complete this task, follow these steps:

1. Log on to the desired server with Local Administrator privileges.

2. Click **Start**, and then click **Run**.

3. In the **Run** dialog box, type **ServerManager.msc**, and then click **OK**.

4. In the **Features Summary** section, click the **Add Features** task.

5. On the **Select Feature** page, select the **Windows PowerShell** feature, and then click **Next**.

6. On the **Confirm Installation Selections** page, review the selections made, and then click **Install**.

7. On the **Installation Results** page, review the results, and then click **Close**.

PowerShell 2.0 CTP2

PowerShell 2.0 CTP2 is a Community Technology Preview version of the PowerShell language. This prerelease version of PowerShell 2.0 contains the new language features described in Chapter 1, and is most appropriate for those of us interested in experimenting with the new capabilities of PowerShell 2.0 in a lab or pre-production environment. Prior to installing PowerShell 2.0 CTP2, you need to ensure that your system meets the following minimum installation requirements:

▶ Supported operating systems for PowerShell 2.0 CTP2 include Windows XP with Service Pack 2, Windows Vista with Service Pack 1, Windows Server 2003 with Service Pack 1, and Windows Server 2008.

▶ The Microsoft .NET Framework 2.0 is required for installation of PowerShell 2.0 CTP2.

▶ The Microsoft .NET Framework 3.0 is required to use the new Graphical PowerShell and Out-Gridview cmdlets in PowerShell 2.0 CTP2.

▶ The Get-Event cmdlet works only on Windows Vista and Windows Server 2008 and requires the Microsoft .NET Framework 3.5.

▶ The Windows Remote Management (WinRM) CTP2 component is required to use the new remoting features in PowerShell 2.0 CTP2.

▶ Remoting works only on Windows Vista with Service Pack 1 (SP1) and on Windows Server 2008.

All of the additional components listed can be downloaded from the Microsoft Download Center at http://www.microsoft.com/downloads/ (see Figure 2.2).

Before Installing PowerShell 2.0 CTP2

If you currently have PowerShell 1.0 installed on your system, you need to remove it before installing PowerShell 2.0. The steps that follow describe the procedures you need to follow to uninstall PowerShell 1.0, depending on your operating system.

Uninstalling Windows PowerShell 1.0

▶ **Windows XP-SP2 and Windows Server 2003:** Under **Add/Remove Programs**, select the option to show updates. Remove the PowerShell updates as applicable for your system: **KB926139** (en-us), **KB926140** (localized), and **KB926141** (MUI pack).

▶ **Windows Vista:** Go to **Control Panel> Programs and Features> Installed Updates**. Uninstall the PowerShell update: **KB928439**.

▶ **Windows Server 2008:** In Windows Server 2008, PowerShell 1.0 comes as an optional component. If you have enabled PowerShell 1.0, you must turn the feature off before you can install PowerShell 2.0 CTP2. Launch Server Manager and choose the option to remove features. Select PowerShell from the list and disable the features.

> **NOTE**
>
> Please note that you will *not* be able to install PowerShell 2.0 on a Windows 2008 server that has Exchange 2007 or the Exchange Management Shell installed.

FIGURE 2.2   The Microsoft Download Center

Install and Configure WinRM (Windows Remote Management)

WinRM is Microsoft's implementation of the **WS-Management Protocol**, which is a Simple Object Access Protocol (**SOAP**)-based protocol that provides a common method for systems to access and exchange management information. By default, WinRM uses ports 80 and 443 for its transport; thus, it is compatible with most firewalls. However, WinRM also enables these default ports to be changed if necessary. While WinRM is natively supported in Windows Vista and Windows Server 2008, the **WS-Management 2.0 CTP** component is required to support remoting in the PowerShell 2.0 CTP2 release. The WS-Management 2.0 CTP update for can be downloaded from: https://connect. microsoft.com/site/sitehome.aspx?SiteID=200&wa=wsignin1.0

NOTE

For Windows Vista systems, Windows Vista Service Pack 1 is required to enable WinRM functionality.

Downloading and Installing PowerShell 2.0

After installing .NET Framework 2.0 and .NET Framework 3.0, and after verifying that any necessary WinRM components are installed on your system, your next step is to download the PowerShell 2.0 CTP2 installation package from http://www.microsoft.com/downloads/details.aspx?FamilyId=7C8051C2-9BFC-4C81-859D-0864979FA403& displaylang=en (see Figure 2.3).

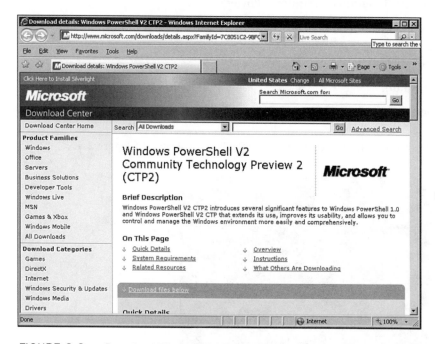

FIGURE 2.3   Download Windows PowerShell 2.0

To install PowerShell, on the download page, find the correct PowerShell installation package for your x86 or x64 version of Windows. Then, download the PowerShell installation package by clicking the appropriate download link. Next, start the PowerShell installation by clicking Open in the download box or double-clicking the installation file. (The filename differs depending on the platform, Windows version, and language pack.) After the installer has started, follow the installation instructions.

Another installation method is a silent installation at the command line, using the /quiet switch with the PowerShell installation filename. This installation method can be useful if you plan to install PowerShell on many different systems and want to distribute the installation via a logon script, Systems Management Server (SMS), or another software management method. To perform a silent installation, follow these steps:

1. Click **Start > Run**.

2. Type **cmd**, and then click **OK** to open a **cmd** command prompt.

3. Type *PowerShell-exe-filename* /**quiet** (replacing the italicized text with the PowerShell installation filename) and press Enter.

After installing PowerShell, you can access it through three different methods. To use the first method of accessing it from the Start menu, follow these steps:

1. Click **Start > All Programs > Windows PowerShell 2.0**.

2. Click **Windows PowerShell**.

To use the second method, follow these steps:

1. Click **Start > Run**.

2. Type **PowerShell** in the **Run** dialog box, and then click **OK**.

Both these methods open the PowerShell console, which is shown in Figure 2.4.

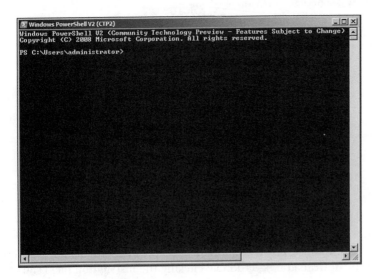

FIGURE 2.4   The PowerShell console

Follow these steps to use the third method from a cmd command prompt:

1. Click **Start > Run**.

2. Type **cmd** and click **OK** to open a cmd command prompt.

3. At the command prompt, type **powershell**, as shown in Figure 2.5, and press Enter.

```
Administrator: C:\Windows\system32\cmd.exe - powershell                    _ □ x
C:\>powershell
Windows PowerShell U2 (Community Technology Preview - Features Subject to Change
)
Copyright (C) 2008 Microsoft Corporation. All rights reserved.

PS C:\>
```

FIGURE 2.5   The PowerShell console launched through the cmd command prompt

Configure WSMan Settings

As mentioned earlier, the PowerShell Remoting and PSJobs features rely on Windows
Remote Management (WinRM) technology. For these features to work, a number of
configuration changes need to be made to the PowerShell 2.0's default WSMan
settings. Fortunately, this process is made simple through a PowerShell script called
Configure-Wsman.ps1 in the $pshome folder. This script configures WS-Man settings. The
following command executes the Configure-WSMan.ps1 script from the $pshome location:

```
& $pshome\Configure-Wsman.ps1
```

Please note: Due to PowerShell 2.0's default script execution policy (initially set to
Restricted), the Configure-WSman.ps1 script will initially not be allowed to run. The
screen shot that follows shows the error that you receive if you attempt to run this script
without modifying the default script execution policy.

```
PS C:\> & $pshome\Configure-Wsman.ps1
File C:\WINDOWS\system32\WindowsPowerShell\v1.0\\Configure-Wsman.ps1
cannot be loaded because the execution of scripts is disabled on this
system. Please see "get-help about_signing" for more details.
At line:1 char:2
+ & <<<< $pshome\Configure-Wsman.ps1
PS C:\>
```

To allow the `Configure-WSMan.ps1` script to execute successfully, you can use the `Set-ExecutionPolicy` cmdlet to set the execution policy to `RemoteSigned`, as shown in the example that follows. After the script completes, you can optionally use the `Set-ExecutionPolicy` cmdlet to return PowerShell to its default script execution policy. The command sequence that follows shows three separate actions: setting the script execution policy to RemoteSigned, executing the `Configure-WSMan.ps1` script, then setting the script execution policy back to Default. (We use the Set-ExecutionPolicy cmdlet again later in this chapter when writing a basic PowerShell script. Chapter 5, "Understanding PowerShell Security," discusses PowerShell security and related best practices in more detail.) The screen shot that follows shows an abbreviated version of the verbose output generated by running the `Configure-WSMan.ps1` script.

```
PS C:\> set-executionpolicy RemoteSigned
PS C:\> & $pshome\Configure-Wsman.ps1
Configuring WSMan
.
.
.
Configuring WSMan Complete
Opening port 80 and port 443
PS C:\> set-executionpolicy Default
PS C:\>
```

After you have completed the steps described previously, PowerShell 2.0 CTP2 is configured and ready for use.

Understanding the Command-Line Interface (CLI)

The syntax for using PowerShell from the CLI is similar to the syntax for other CLI shells. The fundamental component of a PowerShell command is, of course, the name of the command to be executed. In addition, the command can be made more specific by using parameters and arguments for parameters. Therefore, a PowerShell command can have the following formats:

```
[command name]

[command name] -[parameter]
[command name] -[parameter] -[parameter] [argument1]
[command name] -[parameter] -[parameter] [argument1],[argument2]
```

NOTE

In PowerShell, a **parameter** is a variable that can be accepted by a command, script, or function. An **argument** is a value assigned to a parameter. Although these terms are often used interchangeably, remembering these definitions is helpful when discussing their uses in PowerShell.

You can see an example of using a command, a parameter, and an argument by running the `dir` command with the `/w` parameter (which displays the output of `dir` in a wide format) and an argument of `C:\temp\*.txt`, as shown here:

```
[C:\>dir /w C:\temp*.txt
 Volume in drive C is OS
 Volume Serial Number is 1784-ADF9

 Directory of C:\temp

Bad Stuff.txt  mediapc.txt    note.txt     Progress.txt
        4 File(s)        953 bytes
        0 Dir(s) 16,789,958,656 bytes free

C:\>
```

The result of this command is a wide-format directory listing of all the `.txt` files in `C:\temp`. If you use the `dir` command without any parameters or arguments, the outcome is entirely different. The same result happens with PowerShell. For example, here is a basic PowerShell command that gets process information about `explorer.exe`:

```
PS C:\> get-process -Name explorer

Handles NPM(K)   PM(K)   WS(K)  VM(M)  CPU(s)    Id ProcessName
------- ------   -----   -----  -----  ------    -- -----------
   807  20       31672   14068  149    62.95   1280 explorer


PS C:\>
```

In this example, `Get-Process` is the command, `-Name` is the parameter, and `explorer` is the argument. The result of this command is process information about `explorer.exe`. If no parameters or arguments are used, the `Get-Process` command just lists process information about all currently running processes, not information about a specific process. To have control over what a command does or have it perform more than its default action, you need to understand the command's syntax. To use commands effectively in the CLI, use the Get-Help command, discussed later in "Useful Cmdlets," to get detailed information about what a command does and its use requirements.

Navigating the CLI

As with all CLI-based shells, you need to understand how to navigate the PowerShell CLI to use it effectively. Table 2.1 lists the editing operations associated with various keys when using the PowerShell Console.

TABLE 2.1   PowerShell Console Editing Features

Keys	Editing Operation
Left and right arrows	Moves the cursor left and right through the current command line.
Up and down arrows	Move up and down through the list of recently typed commands.
Insert	Switches between insert and overstrike text-entry modes.
Delete	Deletes the character at the current cursor position.
Backspace	Deletes the character immediately preceding the current cursor position.
F7	Displays a list of recently typed commands in a popup window in the command shell. Use the up and down arrows to select a previously typed command, and then press Enter to execute the selected command.
Tab	Auto-completes command-line sequences. Use the Shift+Tab sequence to move backward through a list of potential matches.

Luckily, most of the features in Table 2.1 are native to the cmd command prompt, which makes PowerShell adoption easier for administrators already familiar with the Windows command line. The only major difference is that the Tab key auto-completion is enhanced in PowerShell beyond what's available with the cmd command prompt.

Tab Key Auto-Completion in PowerShell

As with the cmd command prompt, PowerShell performs auto-completion for file and directory names. So, if you enter a partial file or directory name and press Tab, PowerShell returns the first matching file or directory name in the current directory. Pressing Tab again returns a second possible match and enables you to cycle through the list of results. Like the cmd command prompt, PowerShell's Tab key auto-completion can also auto-complete with wild cards, as shown in this example:

```
PS C:\> cd C:\Doc*
<tab>
PS C:\> cd 'C:\Documents and Settings'
PS C:\Documents and Settings>
```

The difference between Tab key auto-completion in cmd and PowerShell is that PowerShell can auto-complete commands. For example, you can enter a partial command name and press the Tab key, and PowerShell steps through a list of possible command matches, as shown here:

```
PS C:\> get-pro
<tab>
PS C:\> get-process
```

PowerShell can also auto-complete parameter names associated with a particular command. Simply enter a command and partial parameter name and press the Tab key, and PowerShell cycles through the parameters for the command you have specified. This method also works for variables associated with a command. In addition, PowerShell performs auto-completion for methods and properties of variables and objects. Take a look at an example using a variable named $Z set to the value "Variable":

```
PS C:\> $Z = "Variable"
PS C:\> $Z.<tab>
```

After you type $Z and press the Tab key, PowerShell cycles through the possible operations that can be performed against the $Z variable. For example, if you select the $Z.Length property and press Enter, PowerShell returns the length of the string in the $Z variable, as shown here:

```
PS C:\> $Z = "Variable"
PS C:\> $Z.
<tab>
PS C:\> $Z.Length
8
PS C:\
```

The auto-complete function for variables distinguishes between **properties** and **methods**. Properties are listed without an open parenthesis (as in the preceding $Z.Length example), and methods are listed with an open parenthesis, as shown in this example:

```
PS C:\> $Z = "Variable"
PS C:\> $Z.con
<tab>
PS C:\> $Z.Contains(
```

When the $Z.Contains(prompt appears, you can use this method to query whether the $Z variable contains the character V by entering the following command:

```
PS C:\> $Z = "Variable"
PS C:\> $Z.Contains("V")
True
PS C:\>
```

PowerShell corrects capitalization for the method or property name to match its definition. For the most part, this functionality is cosmetic because by default, PowerShell is not case sensitive.

Understanding Cmdlets

Cmdlets are a fundamental part of PowerShell's functionality. They are implemented as managed classes (built on the .NET Framework) that include a well-defined set of methods to process data. A cmdlet developer writes the code that runs when the cmdlet is called and compiles the code into a DLL that's loaded into a PowerShell instance when the shell is started.

Cmdlets are always named with the format Verb-Noun where the verb specifies the action and the noun specifies the object to operate on. As you might have noticed, most PowerShell names are singular, not plural, to make PowerShell more universally usable. For example, a command might provide a value or a set of values, and there's no way to know ahead of time whether a cmdlet name should be plural. Also, the English language is inconsistent in dealing with plurals. For example, the word *fish* can be singular or plural, depending on the context. If English isn't your first language, figuring out what's supposed to be plural or the correct plural form could be daunting.

> **NOTE**
>
> The default PowerShell verb is Get, which is assumed if no other verb is given. The effect of this default setting is that the process command produces the same results as Get-Process.

To determine the parameters a cmdlet supports, you can review the help information for the cmdlet by using either of the following commands:

```
PS C:\> cmdletName -?
PS C:\> get-help cmdletName
```

Furthermore, you can use the Get-Command cmdlet to determine what parameters are available and how they are used. Here's an example of the syntax:

```
PS C:\> get-command cmdletName
```

When working with the Get-Command cmdlet, piping its output to the Format-List cmdlet produces a more concise list of the cmdlet's use. For example, to display just the definition information for Get-Process, use the following command:

```
PS C:\> get-command get-process | format-list Definition
Definition : Get-Process [[-Name] <String[]>] [-Verbose] [-Debug] [-ErrorAction
       <ActionPreference>] [-ErrorVariable <String>] [-OutVariable <String>]
       [-OutBuffer <Int32>]
       Get-Process -Id <Int32[]> [-Verbose] [-Debug] [-ErrorAction
       <ActionPreference>] [-ErrorVariable <String>] [-OutVariable <String>]
       [-OutBuffer <Int32>]
       Get-Process -InputObject <Process[]> [-Verbose] [-Debug] [-ErrorAction
       <ActionPreference>] [-ErrorVariable <String>] [-OutVariable <
       String>] [-OutBuffer <Int32>]
PS C:\>
```

Common Parameters

Because cmdlets derive from a base class, a number of **common parameters**, which are available to all cmdlets, can be used to help provide a more consistent interface for PowerShell cmdlets. These common parameters are described in Table 2.2.

TABLE 2.2   PowerShell Common Parameters

Parameter	Data Type	Description
Verbose	Boolean	Generates detailed information about the operation, much like tracing or a transaction log. This parameter is effective only in cmdlets that generate verbose data.
Debug	Boolean	Generates programmer-level detail about the operation. The cmdlet must support the generation of debug data for this parameter to be effective.

TABLE 2.2   Continued

ErrorAction	Enum	Determines how the cmdlet responds when an error occurs. Values are Continue (the default), Stop, SilentlyContinue, and Inquire.
ErrorVariable	String	Specifies a variable that stores errors from the command during processing. This variable is populated in addition to $error.
OutVariable	String	Specifies a variable that stores output from the command during processing.
OutBuffer	Int32	Determines the number of objects to buffer before calling the next cmdlet in the pipeline.
WhatIf	Boolean	Explains what happens if the command is executed but doesn't actually execute the command.
Confirm	Boolean	Prompts the user for permission before performing any action that modifies the system.

NOTE

The last two parameters in Table 2.2, WhatIf and Confirm, are special in that they require a cmdlet to support the .NET method ShouldProcess, which might not be true for all cmdlets. The ShouldProcess method confirms the operation with the user, sending the name of the resource to be changed for confirmation before performing the operation.

Getting Help

When you're getting started with PowerShell, the Get-Help and Get-Command cmdlets are useful. These two cmdlets, described in the following sections, help you explore what PowerShell does and help you learn more about the commands you can run.

Get-Help

As you might expect, you use the Get-Help cmdlet to retrieve help information about cmdlets and other topics. To display a list of all help topics, enter Get-Help * at the PowerShell command prompt, as shown in the example that follows. Please note that due to space limitations, the example shows only a subset of the available topics returned by Get-Help.

```
PS C:\> get-help *

Name                Category            Synopsis
----                --------            --------
ac                  Alias               Add-Content
```

```
asnp            Alias            Add-PSSnapin
clc             Alias            Clear-Content
cli             Alias            Clear-Item
clp             Alias            Clear-ItemProperty
clv             Alias            Clear-Variable
cpi             Alias            Copy-Item
cpp             Alias            Copy-ItemProperty
cvpa            Alias            Convert-Path
diff            Alias            Compare-Object
epal            Alias            Export-Alias
epcsv           Alias            Export-Csv
fc              Alias            Format-Custom
fl              Alias            Format-List
foreach         Alias            ForEach-Object
...
PS C:\>
```

To narrow down the list of entries returned by Get-Help, you can shorten it by filtering
on topic name and category. For example, to get a list of all cmdlets starting with the verb
Get, try the command shown in the following example:

```
PS C:\> get-help -Name get-* -Category cmdlet

Name                 Category             Synopsis
----                 --------             --------
Get-Command          Cmdlet               Gets basic information...
Get-Help             Cmdlet               Displays information a...
Get-History          Cmdlet               Gets a list of the com...
Get-PSSnapin         Cmdlet               Gets the Windows Power...
Get-EventLog         Cmdlet               Gets information about...
Get-ChildItem        Cmdlet               Gets the items and chi...
Get-Content          Cmdlet               Gets the content of th...
...

PS C:\>
```

After you have selected a help topic, you can retrieve the help information by using the
topic name as the parameter to the Get-Help cmdlet. For example, to retrieve help for the
Get-Content cmdlet, enter the following command:

```
PS C:\> get-help get-content
```

> **NOTE**
>
> PowerShell has two parameters for the `get-help` cmdlet: `-detailed` and `-full`. The `-detailed` parameter displays additional information about a cmdlet, including descriptions of parameters and examples of using the cmdlet. The `-full` parameter displays the entire help file for a cmdlet, including technical information about parameters.

Cmdlet Help Topics

PowerShell help is divided into sections for each cmdlet. Table 2.3 describes the help details for each cmdlet.

TABLE 2.3   **PowerShell Help Sections**

Help Section	Description
Name	The name of the cmdlet.
Synopsis	A brief description of what the cmdlet does.
Detailed Description	A detailed description of the cmdlet's behavior, usually including usage examples.
Syntax	Specific usage details for entering commands with the cmdlet.
Parameters	Valid parameters that can be used with this cmdlet.
Input Type	The type of input this cmdlet accepts.
Return Type	The type of data that the cmdlet returns.
Terminating Errors	If present, identifies any errors that result in the cmdlet terminating prematurely.
Non-Terminating Errors	Identifies noncritical errors that might occur while the cmdlet is running but don't cause the cmdlet to terminate its operation.
Notes	Additional detailed information on using the cmdlet, including specific scenarios and possible limitations or idiosyncrasies.
Examples	Common usage examples for the cmdlet.
Related Links	References other cmdlets that perform similar tasks.

Get-Command

Another helpful cmdlet is `Get-Command`, used to list all available cmdlets in a PowerShell session:

```
PS C:\> get-command

CommandType      Name                    Definition
-----------      ----                    ----------
Cmdlet           Add-Content             Add-Content [-Path] <String[...
Cmdlet           Add-History             Add-History [[-InputObject] ...
Cmdlet           Add-Member              Add-Member [-MemberType] <PS...
Cmdlet           Add-PSSnapin            Add-PSSnapin [-Name] <String...
Cmdlet           Clear-Content           Clear-Content [-Path] <Strin...
Cmdlet           Clear-Item              Clear-Item [-Path] <String[]...
Cmdlet           Clear-ItemProperty      Clear-ItemProperty [-Path] <...
Cmdlet           Clear-Variable          Clear-Variable [-Name] <Stri...
Cmdlet           Compare-Object          Compare-Object [-ReferenceOb...
...

PS C:\>
```

The Get-Command cmdlet is more powerful than Get-Help because it lists all available commands (cmdlets, scripts, aliases, functions, and native applications) in a PowerShell session, as shown in this example:

```
PS C:\ get-command note*

CommandType      Name                 Definition
-----------      ----                 ----------
Application      NOTEPAD.EXE          C:\WINDOWS\NOTEPAD.EXE
Application      notepad.exe          C:\WINDOWS\system32\notepad.exe


PS C:\>
```

When using Get-Command with elements other than cmdlets, the information returned is different from information you see for a cmdlet. For example, with an existing application, the value of the Definition property is the path to the application. However, other information about the application is also available, as shown here:

```
PS C:\> get-command ipconfig | format-list *
FileVersionInfo : File:          C:\WINDOWS\system32\ipconfig.exe
        InternalName:    ipconfig.exe
        OriginalFilename: ipconfig.exe
        FileVersion:    5.1.2600.2180 (xpsp_sp2_rtm.040803-2158)
        FileDescription: IP Configuration Utility
        Product:        Microsoftr Windowsr Operating System
        ProductVersion:  5.1.2600.2180
        Debug:          False
        Patched:        False
        PreRelease:     False
        PrivateBuild:   False
        SpecialBuild:   False
        Language:       English (United States)


Path        : C:\WINDOWS\system32\ipconfig.exe
Extension   : .exe
Definition  : C:\WINDOWS\system32\ipconfig.exe
Name        : ipconfig.exe
CommandType : Application
```

With a function, the Definition property is the body of the function:

```
PS C:\> get-command Prompt

CommandType    Name         Definition
-----------    ----         ----------
Function       prompt       Write-Host ("PS " + $(Get-Lo...


PS C:\>
```

With an alias, the Definition property is the aliased command:

```
PS C:\> get-command write

CommandType    Name         Definition
-----------    ----         ----------
Alias          write        Write-Output


PS C:\>
```

With a script file, the Definition property is the path to the script. With a non-PowerShell script (such as a .bat or .vbs file), the information returned is the same as other existing applications.

Understanding Variables

A **variable** is a storage place for data. In most shells, the only data that can be stored in a variable is text data. In advanced shells and programming languages, data stored in variables can be almost anything, from strings to sequences to objects. Similarly, PowerShell variables can be just about anything.

To define a PowerShell variable, you must name it with the $ prefix, which helps delineate variables from aliases, cmdlets, filenames, and other items a shell operator might want to use. A variable name is case sensitive and can contain any combination of alphanumeric characters (A–Z and 0–9) and the underscore (_) character. Although PowerShell variables have no set naming convention, using a name that reflects the type of data the variable contains is recommended, as shown in this example:

```
PS C:\> $MSProcesses = get-process | where {$_.company -match
".*Microsoft*"}
PS C:\> $MSProcesses

Handles  NPM(K)    PM(K)     WS(K) VM(M)    CPU(s)     Id ProcessName
-------  ------    -----     ----- -----    ------     -- -----------
     68       4     1712      6496    30      0.19   2420 ctfmon
    715      21    27024     40180   126     58.03   3620 explorer
    647      19    23160     36924   109     18.69   1508 iexplore
    522      11    31364     30876   151      6.59   3268 powershell
    354      17    28172     47612   482     36.22   2464 WINWORD


PS C:\>
```

As you can see from the previous example, the information that is contained within the $MSProcesses variable is a collection of Microsoft processes that currently run on the system.

> **NOTE**
>
> A variable name can consist of any characters, including spaces, provided the name is enclosed by braces ({ and } symbols). However, if you use a nonstandard variable name, PowerShell warns you this practice is not recommended.

Built-In Variables

When a PowerShell session is started, a number of variables are defined automatically, as shown in this example:

```
PS C:\> set-location variable:
PS Variable:\> get-childitem


Name                             Value
----                             -----
Error                            {CommandNotFoundException}
DebugPreference                   SilentlyContinue
PROFILE                          \\bob'shosting.com\homes\tyson\My Documents\P...
HOME                             U:\
Host                             System.Management.Automation.Internal.Host.In...
MaximumHistoryCount              64
MaximumAliasCount                4096
input                            System.Array+SZArrayEnumerator
StackTrace                             at System.Management.Automation.CommandDis...
ReportErrorShowSource            1
ExecutionContext                 System.Management.Automation.EngineIntrinsics
true                             True
VerbosePreference                SilentlyContinue
ShellId                          Microsoft.PowerShell
false                            False
null
MaximumFunctionCount             4096
ConsoleFileName
ReportErrorShowStackTrace        0
FormatEnumerationLimit           4
?                                True
PSHOME                           C:\Program Files\Windows PowerShell\v1.0
MyInvocation                     System.Management.Automation.InvocationInfo
PWD                              Variable:\
^                                set-location

_
ReportErrorShowExceptionClass    0
ProgressPreference               Continue
ErrorActionPreference            Continue
args                             {}
MaximumErrorCount                256
NestedPromptLevel                0
WhatIfPreference                 0
$                                variable:
```

```
=ReportErrorShowInnerException   0
ErrorView                        NormalView
WarningPreference                Continue
PID                              3124
ConfirmPreference                High
MaximumDriveCount                4096
MaximumVariableCount             4096


PS C:\>
```

These built-in shell variables are divided into two types. The first type has a special meaning in PowerShell because it stores configuration information for the current PowerShell session. Of these special variables, the following should be considered noteworthy because they're used often throughout this book:

- $_—Contains the current pipeline object
- $Error—Contains error objects for the current PowerShell session

```
PS C:\> get-service | where-object {$_.Name -match "W32Time"}

Status   Name                   DisplayName
------   ----                   -----------
Running  W32Time                Windows Time


PS C:\>
```

```
PS C:\> $Error
Unexpected token 'Name' in expression or statement.
PS C:\>
```

The second type of built-in variable consists of preference settings used to control the behavior of PowerShell. Table 2.4 describes these variables, based on the *PowerShell User Guide*.

> **NOTE**
>
> A command policy can be one of the following strings: `SilentlyContinue`, `NotifyContinue`, `NotifyStop`, or `Inquire`.

TABLE 2.4   PowerShell Preference Settings

Name	Allowed Values	Description
`$DebugPreference`	Command policy	Action to take when data is written via `Write-Debug` in a script or `WriteDebug()` in a cmdlet or provider.
`$ErrorActionPreference`	Command policy	Action to take when data is written via `Write-Error` in a script or `WriteError()` in a cmdlet or provider.
`$MaximumAliasCount`	Int	Maximum number of aliases.
`$MaximumDriveCount`	Int	Maximum number of allowed drives.
`$MaximumErrorCount`	Int	Maximum number of errors held by `$Error`.
`$MaximumFunctionCount`	Int	Maximum number of functions that can be created.
`$MaximumVariableCount`	Int	Maximum number of variables that can be created.
`$MaximumHistoryCount`	Int	Maximum number of entries saved in the command history.
`$ShouldProcessPreference`	Command policy	Action to take when `ShouldProcess` is used in a cmdlet.
`$ProcessReturnPreference`	Boolean	`ShouldProcess` returns this setting.
`$ProgressPreference`	Command policy	Action to take when data is written via `Write-Progress` in a script or `WriteProgress()` in a cmdlet or provider.
`$VerbosePreference`	Command policy	Action to take when data is written via `Write-Verbose` in a script or `WriteVerbose()` in a cmdlet or provider.

Understanding Aliases

Unfortunately, using PowerShell requires a lot of typing unless you're running a script. For example, open a PowerShell console and try to type the following command:

```
PS C:\> get-process | where-object {$_.Company -match ".*Microsoft*"}
| format-table Name, ID, Path —Autosize
```

That's a long command to type. Luckily, like most shells, PowerShell supports aliases for cmdlets and executables. So, if you want to cut down on the typing in this command, you can use PowerShell's default aliases. Using these aliases, the Get-Process example looks like this:

```
PS C:\> gps | ? {$_.Company -match ".*Microsoft*"} | ft Name, ID, Path
-Autosize
```

This example isn't a major reduction in the amount of typing, but aliases can save you some time and prevent typos. To get a list of the current PowerShell aliases supported in your session, use the Get-Alias cmdlet as shown in the following example. Please note that due to space limitations, the example shows only a small subset of the available PowerShell aliases; the complete list is returned when you actually execute the Get-Alias cmdlet.

```
PS C:\> get-alias

CommandType      Name              Definition
-----------      ----              ----------
Alias            ac                Add-Content
Alias            asnp              Add-PSSnapin
Alias            clc               Clear-Content
Alias            cli               Clear-Item
Alias            clp               Clear-ItemProperty
Alias            clv               Clear-Variable
Alias            cpi               Copy-Item

PS C:\>
```

Discovering Alias Cmdlets

Several alias cmdlets enable you to define new aliases, export aliases, import aliases, and display existing aliases. By using the following command, you can get a list of all related alias cmdlets:

```
PS C:\> get-command *-Alias

CommandType      Name              Definition
-----------      ----              ----------
Cmdlet           Export-Alias      Export-Alias [-Path] <String...
Cmdlet           Get-Alias         Get-Alias [[-Name] <String[]...
Cmdlet           Import-Alias      Import-Alias [-Path] <String...
Cmdlet           New-Alias         New-Alias [-Name] <String> [...
Cmdlet           Set-Alias         Set-Alias [-Name] <String> [...
```

You've already seen how to use the Get-Alias cmdlet to produce a list of aliases available in the current PowerShell session. The Export-Alias and Import-Alias cmdlets are used to export and import alias lists from one PowerShell session to another. Finally, the New-Alias and Set-Alias cmdlets enable you to define new aliases for the current PowerShell session.

NOTE

The alias implementation in PowerShell is limited. As mentioned earlier, an alias works only for cmdlets or executables, *not* for cmdlets and executables used with a parameter. However, there are methods to work around this limitation. One method is defining the command in a variable and then calling the variable from other commands. The problem with this approach is that the variable can be called only in the current PowerShell session, unless it's defined in the profile.ps1 file. The second (preferred) method is to place your command in a function.

Creating Persistent Aliases

The alises created when you use the New-Alias and Set-Alias cmdlets are valid only in the current PowerShell session. Exiting a PowerShell session discards any existing aliases. To have aliases persist across PowerShell sessions, you must define them in the profile.ps1 file, as shown in this example:

```
set-alias new new-object
set-alias time get-date
...
```

Although command shortening is appealing, the extensive use of aliases isn't recommended. One reason is that aliases aren't very portable to scripts. For example, if you use a lot of aliases in a script, you must include a Set-Aliases sequence at the start of the script to make sure those aliases are present, regardless of machine or session profile, when the script runs.

However, a bigger concern than portability is that aliases can often confuse or obscure the true meaning of commands or scripts. The aliases you define might make sense to you, but not everyone shares your logic in defining aliases. So if you want others to understand your scripts, you must be careful about using too many aliases. Instead, look into creating reusable functions.

NOTE

When creating aliases for scripts, use names that other people can understand. For example, there's no reason, other than to encode your scripts, to create aliases consisting of only two letters.

Creating Your First Script

Most of the commands covered in this chapter are interactive, meaning you enter commands at the PowerShell prompt, and output is returned. Although using PowerShell interactively is helpful for tasks that need to be done only once, it's not an effective way to perform repetitive automation tasks. Fortunately, PowerShell has the capability to read in files containing stored commands, which enables you to compose, save, and recall a sequence of commands when needed. These sequences of stored commands are commonly referred to as **scripts**.

PowerShell scripts are simply text files stored with a .ps1 extension. You can use any text editor (such as Notepad) to create a text file containing commands that make up a PowerShell script. For example, open Notepad and type the following command:

```
get-service | where-object {$_.Status -eq "Stopped"}
```

Next, save this file with the name ListStoppedServices.ps1 in a directory of your choice. For this example, the C:\Scripts directory is used.

Before you can run this script, you need to adjust PowerShell's execution policy because the default setting doesn't allow running scripts for protection against malicious scripts. To change this setting, you use the Set-ExecutionPolicy cmdlet, as shown in the following example. You can also use the Get-ExecutionPolicy cmdlet to verify the current execution policy. (Chapter 5 discusses PowerShell security and best practices in more detail.)

```
PS C:\> set-executionpolicy RemoteSigned
PS C:\> get-executionpolicy
RemoteSigned
PS C:\>
```

The RemoteSigned policy enables scripts created locally to run without being digitally signed, but still requires scripts downloaded from the Internet to be digitally signed. These settings give you the flexibility to run unsigned scripts from your local machine, yet, they provide some protection against unsigned external scripts.

After changing PowerShell's execution policy to RemoteSigned, you can run the script in any PowerShell session by simply typing the script's full directory path and filename. In the following example, entering the C:\Scripts\ListStoppedServices.ps1 command produces this output:

```
PS C:\> C:\Scripts\ListStoppedServices.ps1

Status   Name              DisplayName
------   ----              -----------
Stopped  Alerter           Alerter
Stopped  AppMgmt           Application Management
Stopped  aspnet_state      ASP.NET State Service
Stopped  BITS              Background Intelligent Transfer Ser...
Stopped  Browser           Computer Browser


PS C:\>
```

Although this basic one-line script is simple, it stills serves to illustrate how to write a script and use it in PowerShell. If needed, you can include more commands to have it perform the automation task. The following is an example:

```
param ([string] $StartsWith)

$StopServices = get-service | where-object {$_.Status -eq "Stopped"}

write-host "The following $StartsWith services are stopped on" `
  "$Env:COMPUTERNAME:" -Foregroundcolor Yellow

$StopServices | where-object {$_.Name -like $StartsWith} | `
  format-table Name, DisplayName
```

The script then displays this output:

```
PS C:\> C:\Scripts\ListStoppedServices.ps1 N*
The following N* services are stopped on PLANX:

Name              DisplayName
----              -----------
NetDDE            Network DDE
NetDDEdsdm        Network DDE DSDM
NtLmSsp           NT LM Security Support Provider
NtmsSvc           Removable Storage


PS C:\>
```

This script is a little more complex because it can filter the stopped services based on the provided string to make the output cleaner. This script isn't a complicated piece of automation, but it does serve to illustrate just some of the power that PowerShell has. To use that power, you just need to gain a better understanding of PowerShell's features so that you can write more complex and meaningful scripts.

Summary

This chapter served as an introduction to the use of PowerShell 2.0, including downloading and installing PowerShell 2.0 CTP2, getting familiar with and using the PowerShell CLI, and learning about PowerShell cmdlets, with a focus on the new cmdlets and features included in PowerShell 2.0. In addition, this chapter covered the use of PowerShell variables and aliases, and provided examples of how to include these techniques. Finally, this chapter walked you through creating a basic PowerShell script that lists all of the stopped services on a machine.

Advanced PowerShell Concepts

Most shells operate in a text-based environment. Being text-based, these types of shells require an administrator to manipulate the text-based data from commands to complete an automation task. For example, if you need to pipe data from one command to the next, usually the output from the first command must be reformatted to meet the second command's requirements. While this method does work, and has so for years, it means that working with text-based shells can be difficult, time-consuming, and frustrating without the use of custom tools to complete an automation task (awk is a good example of this).

Luckily, Microsoft took note of this frustration when it set out to develop the next generation command-line interface (CLI) and scripting language (PowerShell). In doing so, it made an architectural decision to build PowerShell on top of the .NET Framework. The result from this decision is that PowerShell retrieves data from commands in the form of .NET Framework objects. Treating data as objects is different than most other shells that operate purely in a text-based environment. Instead of transporting data as plain text, an object allows commands (or cmdlets) to access object properties and methods directly, simplifying an administrator's interaction with the shell and scripting language. Instead of modifying text data, you can just refer to the required data by name. Similarly, instead of writing code or using a tool to transform data into a usable format, you can simply refer to objects and manipulate them as needed. For example:

```
PS > get-service

Status     Name                   DisplayName
------     ----                   -----------
Running    AeLookupSvc            Application Experience
Stopped    ALG                    Application Layer Gateway Service
Stopped    Appinfo                Application Information
Stopped    AppMgmt                Application Management
Running    Ati External Ev...     Ati External Event Utility
Running    AudioEndpointBu...     Windows Audio Endpoint Builder
...
```

When the Get-Service cmdlet is executed it collects information about all of the services that exist on the local computer. Each service is then passed as an object to the next cmdlet in the pipeline. In this case, another cmdlet is not waiting in the pipeline to process the stream of objects; instead, information is just redirected to the console. The result is a list of services where each row in the displayed table directly relates to an object that was created and passed through the pipeline by PowerShell.

Because the Get-Service cmdlet creates a collection of objects, you can just as easily put the members of these objects to work. For example:

```
PS > (get-service)[0].Status
Running
```

In the previous command, the Status property of the first object that is returned by the Get-Service cmdlet is examined. If you wanted to, you could also use the object's methods to complete a task, such as:

```
PS > (get-service)[0].Stop()
PS > (get-service)[0].Status
Stopped
```

Or, you could also pass the object to another command to complete the task:

```
PS > (get-service)[0] | Start-Service
PS > (get-service)[0].Status
Running
```

In either case, there is an object, and that object is accessed and manipulated directly from the command line. In many respects, interfacing with an object in this manner is the power that the .NET Framework brings to PowerShell. Additionally, because PowerShell is based on the .NET self-describing object model, you also have access to the extensive libraries that are available in the .NET Framework. Just imagine, you now have easy access to all of the pre-coded goodies that programmers have had for years. However, to truly appreciate what using a self-describing object model can bring to your command line and script activities, you need to first understand how easy it is to explore and use the objects that are created in PowerShell.

Working with the .NET Framework

Although it was touched upon briefly in the beginning of this chapter, the importance of Powershell's .NET Framework integration cannot be stressed enough. By using PowerShell, an administrator now has direct CLI access to the .NET Framework's thousands and thousands of classes, interfaces, and value types. By definition, each of these .NET Framework "types" is an abstract description of a programmable component that can be used to complete a wide range of automation tasks. In other words, directly from the CLI, an administrator now has access to the same type of reusable programmatic objects that programmers have enjoyed for years.

To an administrator, the obvious question might be: "Why is this so exciting?" Simply put, the answer is that access to the .NET Framework's class library has the power to make administrators extremely productive in relation to the management tasks that they need to complete. Examples of tasks (but not limited to) that fall under this category are as follows:

▶ Retrieving data from a Web service or centralized data store

▶ Interacting with users using Windows Forms without creating an application

▶ Managing Active Directory (configuration) via a reusable script

▶ Automating complex account provisioning and deprovisioning activities

▶ Remotely changing local administrator passwords on thousands of machines

▶ Synchronizing information between Active Directory and Active Directory Application Mode (ADAM)

▶ Performing online Volume Shadow Copy Service (VSS) snap-shots of data across many systems

To better understand how these benefits are derived, you must first remember that most of the power is realized through the usage of .NET objects. At a basic level, PowerShell uses a .NET object to drastically reduce the amount of effort to complete a task. This reduction may be in the form of fewer commands issued in the CLI or in a script.

However, to truly gain insight into how a class and its resulting .NET object can provide these benefits, it helps to first investigate what comprises these somewhat abstract entities.

To start this explorative process, you need to first understand that a .NET Framework type contains a group of members. These members consist of properties, methods, fields, events, and constructors. An explanation for each member type is as follows:

▶ **Property and Field**—Both are attributes that describe something about the object. For example, a System.String typed object has a Length property. As its name suggests, examining this property will tell you the length of the string.

▶ **Method**—An action that an object can complete. An example of a method is the ToUpper method for System.String typed object. You can use this method to convert a string to uppercase characters.

▶ **Event**—An occurrence that can be reacted to. For example, in the System.Process class, there is an event named Exited. By using this event, you can monitor for when a process has shut down and exited.

▶ **Constructer**—A unique member in that it is used to create a new object. For example, when PowerShell creates a new instance of an object based on a .NET class, it uses the Constructor method to complete this task.

These members consist of two basic types: **static** or **instance**. **Static** members are shared across all instances of a class and don't require a typed object to be created before being used. Instead, static members are accessed simply by referring to the class name as if it were the name of the object followed by the static operator (::). For example:

```
PS > [System.DirectoryServices.ActiveDirectory.Forest]::GetCurrentForest()
```

In the previous example, the DirectoryServices.ActiveDirectory.Forest class is used to retrieve information about the current forest. To complete this task the class name is enclosed within the two square brackets ([…]). Then the GetCurrentForest method is invoked by using the static operator (::).

NOTE

To retrieve a list of static members for a class, use the Get-Member cmdlet: get-member -inputObject ([System.String]) -static. The Get-Member cmdlet is explained in more detail later in this chapter.

The second member type, **instance**, is a member that can be accessed only when an instance of a class already exists. This means that you need to first create the object instance before an instance member can be put to use. For example:

```
PS > $ps = new-object System.Diagnostics.Process
```

In the preceding command, the New-Object cmdlet is used to create an instance of the System.Diagnostics.Process class. The resulting Process object, which resides in the $PS variable, consists of instance members from the System.Diagnostics.Process class. In addition to using the New-Object cmdlet, as previously shown, an object instance or collection that is created using a cmdlet also consists of instance members that are based on a .NET class. For example:

```
PS > $ps = get-process powershell
```

The resulting object from the Get-Process cmdlet consists of the same instance members found with the object that was generated using the New-Object cmdlet. In other words, the object is a .NET object that is based on the System.Diagnostics.Process class and inherits instance members from that type. However, in this case, the cmdlet not only creates a System.Diagnostics.Process typed object, but also binds that object to the powershell process.

> **NOTE**
>
> Throughout the remainder of this chapter, you will see the usage of the word "type" in relation to the usage of the word "object." In object-oriented programming (OOP), a type refers to the structure that makes up an object. Thus, a type determines the standard set of properties, methods, and so on an object is to consist of after it is created.

Using the New-Object Cmdlet

The New-Object cmdlet is used to both create .NET and COM objects. To create an instance of a .NET object, you simply provide the fully qualified name of the .NET class you want to use, as shown here:

```
PS > $Ping = new-object Net.NetworkInformation.Ping
```

By using the New-Object cmdlet, you now have an instance of the Ping class that enables you to detect whether a remote computer can be reached via Internet Control Message Protocol (ICMP). Therefore, you have an object-based version of the Ping.exe command-line tool, which can be manipulated just like any other PowerShell object. For example:

```
PS > $Ping.Send("scl-dc01")

Status        : Success
Address       : 192.168.0.11
RoundtripTime : 2 ms
BufferSize    : 32
Options       : TTL=128, DontFragment=False
```

To create an instance of a COM object, the comObject switch parameter is used. To use this parameter, define its argument as the COM object's programmatic identifier (ProgID), as shown here:

```
PS > $IE = new-object -comObject InternetExplorer.Application
```

In the previous example, the comObject switch parameter is used to create an instance of Internet Explorer which is then dumped into the $IE parameter. Then, like the $Ping example, the $IE COM instance can be manipulated just like any other PowerShell object:

```
PS > $IE.Visible=$True
PS > $IE.Navigate("www.cnn.com")
```

Understanding Assemblies

The physical manifestation of the .NET Framework is called a .NET assembly. A .NET assembly is a partially compiled code library that can be used for execution. By using this library, developers are able to quickly create and deploy applications without impacting other applications that reside on a system. In addition, a .NET assembly can easily be shared among other applications, reducing the amount of effort needed to manage and deploy code across applications.

The assembly itself can consist of either a dynamic link library (DLL) or an EXE file. Additionally, in some cases, an assembly may consist of many files: code, resources, images, and so on, making it a multifile assembly. In either case, all assemblies can consist of the following four elements:

▶ An assembly manifest, which contains metadata describing the assembly: name, files, security requirements, version information, references to resources, and so on.

▶ Type metadata (describes the types that are implemented).

▶ Partially compiled code in the MS intermediate language (MISL). This code is used to implement the defined types in an assembly.

▶ Any related resources (images and other nonexecutable data).

NOTE

Oddly enough, the only required element is the assembly manifest. All other elements are optional depending on what the assembly is being used for.

PowerShell is, by definition, a .NET application. Being a .NET application, it is linked to a number of different common .NET assemblies. As such, most of the common classes (types) are readily available from within a PowerShell session. However, there might be cases where certain assemblies are not loaded into PowerShell's AppDomain and thus not available. For example, if you try to create a Windows Forms object using the New-Object cmdlet, you get the following error:

```
PS > $Form = new-object System.Windows.Forms.Form
New-Object : Cannot find type [System.Windows.Forms.Form]: make sure
the assembly containing this type is loaded.
At line:1 char:19
+ $Form = new-object  <<<< System.Windows.Forms.Form
```

If you encounter this error, there is no reason to be alarmed. The error is PowerShell's subtle way of informing the operator about a failed attempt to use an assembly that has not been loaded. To load additional assemblies into a PowerShell session, use the System.Reflection.Assembly class shown here:

```
PS > [System.Reflection.Assembly]::LoadWithPartialName("System.Windows.Forms")
```

In the previous example, the LoadWithPartialName method is used to load the System.Windows.Forms assembly from the Global Assembly Cache (GAC) using what is called a partial name (or simple text name). Using a partial name is an easy way to load additional .NET assemblies; however, Microsoft has now made the LoadWithPartialName method obsolete. The replacement is the Load method, which is meant to prevent partial binds when .NET assemblies are loaded. Using the Load method requires more work. However, if you don't mind the implications of a partial bind (such as your script failing), you can continue using the LoadWithPartialName method until it is removed from the .NET Framework.

To use the Load method, you need the full name (also known as a strong name) of the assembly that is loaded. An assembly's full name consists of its simple text name, the version number, its culture definition, and its public key. For example:

```
System.Windows.Forms, Version=2.0.0.0, Culture=neutral,
PublicKeyToken=b77a5c561934e089
```

To get this information, you can look at the assembly's properties using Windows Explorer. By default all .NET assemblies are located in the `%systemroot%\assembly` folder. Or, you can use a third-party tool such as `GACView` to review the assemblies loaded into the GAC.

> **NOTE**
>
> The Global Assembly Cache (GAC) in the .NET Framework acts as the central place for registered assemblies. As mentioned, the `%systemroot%\assembly` folder contains all globally available assemblies. These assemblies have mangled filenames so that the version and public key tokens can be included. To view and manipulate the contents of the global assembly cache using Windows Explorer, a shell extension (Assembly Cache Viewer–Shfusion.dll) is added when the .NET Framework is installed.

In addition to the `LoadWithPartialName` and `Load` methods, you can also load assemblies using the `LoadFrom` and `LoadFile` methods. Typically, these methods are used for .NET-based DLLs included with Microsoft SDKs, from third-party vendors, or your own custom assemblies. For example, say you develop a .NET assembly to manage **xyz** application. To load that assembly into a PowerShell session, you might use the following command:

```
PS > [System.Reflection.Assembly]::LoadFrom("C:\Really_Cool_Stuff\
myfirstdll.dll")
```

Understanding Reflection

Reflection is a feature in the .NET Framework that enables developers to examine objects and retrieve their supported methods, properties, fields, and so on. Because PowerShell is built on the .NET Framework, it provides this feature, too, with the `Get-Member` cmdlet. This cmdlet analyzes an object or collection of objects you pass to it via the pipeline. For example, the following command analyzes the objects returned from the `Get-Process` cmdlet and displays their associated properties and methods:

```
PS > get-service | get-member -MemberType property
```

Developers often refer to this process as "interrogating" an object. This method of accessing and retrieving information about an object can be useful in understanding its methods and properties without referring to Microsoft's MSDN documentation, or searching the Internet.

Using the Get-Member Cmdlet

The only way to truly understand the power of the `Get-Member` cmdlet is to use it to discover what an object can do. In this section, you step through the process of using the `Get-Member` cmdlet to discover how a `DirectorySearcher` object can be used to search for objects in Active Directory. The first step in this process is to create a `DirectorySearcher` object using the following command:

```
PS > $Searcher = new-object System.DirectoryServices.DirectorySearcher
```

In the previous command, a `DirectorySearcher` object was created using the `New-Object` cmdlet. The resulting object is then dumped into the $Searcher variable. The goal of using the `DirectorySearcher` class is to retrieve user information from Active Directory, but you do not yet know what members the returned object supports. To retrieve this information, run the `Get-Member` cmdlet against a variable containing your mystery object. For example:

```
PS > $Searcher | get-member


   TypeName: System.DirectoryServices.DirectorySearcher

Name               MemberType  Definition
----               ----------  ----------
add_Disposed       Method      System.Void add_Disposed(EventHandler
                               value)
CreateObjRef       Method      System.Runtime.Remoting.ObjRef
                               CreateObjRef(Type requestedType)
Dispose            Method      System.Void Dispose()
Equals             Method      System.Boolean Equals(Object obj)
FindAll            Method      System.DirectoryServices.
                               SearchResultCollection FindAll()
FindOne            Method      System.DirectoryServices.SearchResult
                               FindOne()
...
```

The information that is returned by the `Get-Member` cmdlet is a list of members that the object supports. Within that list, you will find that the `DirectorySearcher` object has a number of methods and properties that will allow you to conduct a search against an Active Directory domain. To conduct a search, the first step is to define the filter that will be used to limit information that is returned from Active Directory to just the objects you want. To do this, use the `DirectorySearcher`'s `Filter` property; this takes a Lightweight Directory Access Protocol (LDAP) search filter statement. For example, if you wanted to search only for user accounts that are disabled, the following filter statement would be used:

```
PS > $Searcher.Filter = `
"(&((sAMAccountType=805306368)(userAccountControl:1.2.840.113556.1.4.8
03:=2)))"
```

After the filter is defined, the next step is to execute the search using the `FindAll` method:

```
PS > $Searcher.FindAll()


Path                                                        Properties
----                                                        ----------
LDAP://CN=Erica,OU=Sales,DC=companyabc,DC=com
{samaccounttype, objectsid, whencreated, primarygroupid...}
LDAP://CN=Bill,OU=IT,DC=companyabc,DC=com                   {samaccounttype,
objectsid, whencreated, primarygroupid...}
LDAP://CN=Miro,OU=Spore,DC=companyabc,DC=com
{samaccounttype, objectsid, whencreated, primarygroupid...}
LDAP://CN=Yelena,OU=Spore,DC=companyabc,DC=com
{samaccounttype, objectsid, whencreated, primarygroupid...}
...
```

In the results that are returned from the search, you will find a collection of user accounts that are disabled. Using this collection, you can then further explore what members the resulting objects support by again using the Get-Member cmdlet. For example, to return the methods supported by the first object in the collection, use the following command:

```
PS > ($Searcher.FindAll())[0] | get-member -MemberType method
```

Or if you wanted, you could dump the entire collection into a variable, and then interrogate it using the Get-Member cmdlet to understand what properties are supported. For example:

```
PS > $Users = $Searcher.FindAll()
PS > $Users | gm -MemberType property


   TypeName: System.DirectoryServices.SearchResult

Name         MemberType Definition
----         ---------- ----------
Path         Property   System.String Path {get;}
Properties   Property   System.DirectoryServices.
                        ResultPropertyCollection Properties {get;}
```

Either way, based on the results from the Get-Member cmdlet, you gain insight into what an object or collection of objects can be used for. In the previous example, the

Get-Member cmdlet provided you with information about the properties that are supported. In this case, the object collection supports the Properties and Path properties. The Properties property contains a list of attributes for each user account, whereas the Path property contains the ADsPath. Using the ADsPath, you can then use the [ADSI] type accelerator (explained later in this chapter) to bind to a user account and continue your exploration using the Get-Member cmdlet, as shown in the following example:

```
PS > [ADSI]$Users[1].Path | gm


   TypeName: System.DirectoryServices.DirectoryEntry

Name                 MemberType Definition
----                 ---------- ----------
accountExpires       Property   System.DirectoryServices.
                                PropertyValueCollection accountExpires {get;set;}
adminCount           Property   System.DirectoryServices.PropertyValueCollection
                                adminCount {get;set;}
cn                   Property   System.DirectoryServices.PropertyValueCollection
                                cn {get;set;}
...
```

At this point, you should now have an appreciation for how the Get-Member cmdlet works. Using this cmdlet, you can understand how a DirectorySearcher object can be used to conduct an Active Directory search. After completing the search, you used the ADsPath that was returned within the search results to bind to an Active Directory object. Once again, you then used the Get-Member cmdlet to gain insight into what members are suppored by the resulting DirectoryEntry object. In both cases, you learned to use the resulting object(s) from the .NET Framework DirectorySearcher and DirectoryEntry classes without referring to any documention. Instead, you used Reflection and the Get-Member cmdlet to gather the information that you needed to complete the automation task on hand. Together, these are two powerful tools, and by now, having a working knowledge of these tools, your PowerShell sessions should be many times more productive.

Understanding the Pipeline

The use of objects gives you a more robust method for dealing with data. In the past, data was transferred from one command to the next by using the pipeline, which makes it possible to string a series of commands together to gather information from a system. However, as mentioned previously, most shells have a major disadvantage: The information gathered from commands is text-based. In such cases, raw text needs to be parsed (transformed) into a format the next command can understand before being piped. To see how this parsing works, review the following Bash shell example:

```
$ ps -ef | grep "bash" | cut -f2
```

The goal in the previous example is to get the process ID (PID) for the bash process. To complete this task, a list of currently running processes is gathered with the ps command and then piped to the grep command and filtered on the string bash. Next, the remaining information is piped to the cut command, which returns the second field containing the PID based on a tab delimiter.

> **NOTE**
>
> A **delimiter** is a character used to separate data fields. The default delimiter for the cut command is a tab. If you want to use a different delimiter, use the -d parameter.

Based on the man information for the grep and cut commands, it seems as though the ps command should work. However, the PID isn't returned or displayed in the correct format.

The command doesn't work because the Bash shell requires you to manipulate text data to display the PID. The output of the ps command is text-based, so transforming the text into a more usable format requires a series of other commands, such as grep and cut. Manipulating text data makes this task more complicated. For example, to retrieve the PID from the data piped from the grep command, you need to provide the field location and the delimiter for separating text information to the cut command. To find this information, run the first part of the ps command:

```
$ ps -ef | grep "bash"
  bob    3628      1 con  16:52:46 /usr/bin/bash
```

The field you need is the second one, 3628. Notice that the ps command doesn't use a tab delimiter to separate columns in the output; instead, it uses a variable number of spaces or a whitespace delimiter, between fields.

> **NOTE**
>
> A **whitespace delimiter** consists of characters, such as spaces or tabs, that equate to a blank space.

The cut command has no way to tell that variable number spaces should be used as a field separator, which is why the command doesn't work. To get the PID, you need to use the **awk** scripting language. The command and output in that language would look like this:

```
$ ps -ef | grep "bash" | awk '{print $2}'
3628
```

The point is that although most UNIX and Linux shell commands are powerful, using them can be complicated and frustrating. Because these shells are text-based, often commands lack functionality or require using additional commands or tools to perform tasks. To address the differences in text output from shell commands, many utilities and scripting languages have been developed to parse text.

The result of all this parsing is a tree of commands and tools that make working with shells unwieldy and time-consuming, which is one reason for the proliferation of management interfaces that rely on GUIs. This trend can be seen among tools Windows administrators use, too, as Microsoft has focused on enhancing the management GUI at the expense of the CLI.

Luckily, for Windows administrators, this trend is now changing with the introduction of PowerShell. They now not only have access to the same automation capabilities as their UNIX and Linux counterparts, but PowerShell and its use of objects fill the automation need Windows administrators have had since the days of batch scripting and WSH in a more usable and less parsing intense manner. To illustrate this, the following command completes the same type of task that you reviewed in the Bash shell example:

```
PS > get-process powershell | format-table id -AutoSize

   Id
   --
3628
```

On the surface, the command doesn't necessarily look any shorter or less complex then the Bash shell example. But, underneath something special is happening in the PowerShell pipeline. When the command is executed, a pipeline processor is generated to manage the entire pipeline execution. To start things off, the pipeline processor binds values to the parameters as command-line input for the first cmdlet in the pipeline. In this case, the value is powershell, which is being bound to the Get-Process name parameter by its position within the command. Next, the pipeline processor starts the command processing, gathers the results as a base .NET object, wraps that object within a specifically typed PowerShell object called a PSObject (explained later in this chapter), and then finally passes that object to the next cmdlet in the pipeline.

Like the first cmdlet, the pipeline processor again performs the value to parameter binding. However, in this case, the pipeline processor attempts to perform the binding to parameters that accept pipeline input. For example, if you were to review the full help information for the Format-Table cmdlet, you will find that the inputObject parameter accepts pipeline input.

```
PS > get-help format-table
-inputObject <psobject>
...

     Accept pipeline input?          true (ByValue)
...
```

After the passed value (PSObject) has been bound to the correct parameter, the pipeline processor again starts the command processing, gathers the results as a base .NET object, wraps that object in a PSObject, and then finally passes that object to the next cmdlet in the pipeline. This process then continues until the end of the pipeline has been reached. The pipeline processor then (by default) pipes the resulting object to the Out-Default cmdlet. The Out-Default cmdlet is a special non-interactive cmdlet that is responsible for figuring out how to format and output the object to the PowerShell Console. All pipelines, by default, end with this cmdlet.

In summary, a PowerShell pipeline is a command-processing factory. In this factory, there are a series of commands (cmdlets) that are separated by the pipe operator ("|"). When the factory is put to work, PowerShell attempts to ensure that data from one command is piped correctly to the next command without the need to perform any type of parsing. An example of this is shown in Figure 3.1.

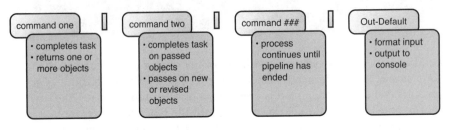

FIGURE 3.1   A simplistic view of the PowerShell pipeline

The previously shown figure is a simplistic view of the PowerShell pipeline. If this was a book written purely for an audience of developers, there would be number of additional concepts that would need to be discussed about the PowerShell pipeline. Most important of these concepts is the fact that the previous example explains only the pipeline in reference to a single object being passed through. As such, the question must be asked, "What happens when there are numerous objects that are returned by the first cmdlet?" An example of this is shown in the following command:

```
PS > get-process | format-table name, id -AutoSize
```

Here, the Get-Process cmdlet returns a collection of objects. This is different from the first pipeline example where the Get-Process cmdlet returned only one object (unless you had multiple PowerShell Console sessions running at once). If PowerShell were like a conventional programming environment, the results from the pipeline would be returned to the console session only after the entire object collection had finished being processed by each cmdlet. However, like most other shell languages, PowerShell processes objects one at a time within the pipeline. By streaming the objects, PowerShell is able to start outputting data from the pipeline as soon as it is available.

As you might have guessed, being able to stream results back to the interactive console as soon as they are available is important. If this didn't happen, and the command was data-intensive, then you might be sitting with a blank console session for some time until the pipeline has finished executing. A perfect example of where streaming might be beneficial is shown with the following command:

```
PS > get-childitem -Path hklm: -Recurse
```

Here, the command issued is a recursive dump of the entire HKLM PSDrive. If PowerShell didn't perform pipeline streaming, then it might take minutes before any information is returned to the console session. Instead, when the command is issued, results are displayed almost immediately within the console.

Powerful One-Liners

At this point, you may still be wondering what makes the PowerShell pipeline so powerful. While reading through the previous examples, you might have seen several clues. However, it isn't until you have put these clues together can you then gain a full appreciation for what can be accomplished with PowerShell from the CLI. The following is a summary of some key concepts that have been reviewed so far:

- ▶ PowerShell is an object-based shell.

- ▶ Data in PowerShell is in the form of .NET objects that are then encapsulated in a generic PSObject.

- ▶ The PowerShell pipeline processor attempts to ensure that objects in the pipeline can be passed successfully to the next cmdlet.

- ▶ The pipeline processor also streams objects through the pipeline.

- ▶ Pipelines, by default, end with the Out-Default cmdlet, which figures out how to format the output to the console.

Putting these concepts all together, you are empowered with the tools needed to construct a complex pipeline that can complete any number of automation tasks. This concept of completing tasks via a single complex pipeline is often referred to as a PowerShell one-liner. To illustrate this concept, the three following examples show a PowerShell one-liner in increasing complexity. In the first example, the object collection returned by the Get-Process cmdlet is piped into the Where-Object cmdlet. Then, by using the Match conditional operator, the object collection is filtered so that only objects with a value that contains Microsoft in the Company property are returned:

```
PS > get-process | where-object {$_.Company -match ".*Microsoft*"}
```

In the next example, the one-liner is expanded such that the Select-Object is used to return only a process's Name, ID, and Path:

```
PS > get-process | where-object {$_.Company -match ".*Microsoft*"} |
select Name, ID, Path
```

In the last example, the resulting object collection from the Select-Object cmdlet is then piped to the ConvertTo-Html cmdlet. The HTML that is generated from this cmdlet is then finally redirected into a file named report.html:

```
PS > get-process | where-object {$_.Company -match ".*Microsoft*"} |
select Name, ID, Path | convertto-html > report.html
```

While stepping through these examples, you can see how the pipeline continues to become more and more complex. In the first example, the results from the pipeline just dumped Microsoft-related process information to the Out-Default cmdlet. By the third example, the results were refined and exported into an HTML-based report. The entire automation task for creating this report is done using a single line of code. In comparison, if you were to use WSH to complete this task, it would take many lines of code and several different automation interfaces.

To further demonstrate this, here is a more compelling example of a complex one-liner:

```
PS > import-csv .\users.csv | foreach {get-adobject -filter
"(&(samAccountName=$($_.employeeID)))"} | select
@{name='Name';Expression={$_.cn} },@{ name='Accountname';
Expression={$_.sAMAccountName} },@{ name='Mail'; Expression={$_.mail}}
| export-csv results.csv
```

This one-liner makes use of the Get-ADObject cmdlet, which is available after installing the **PowerShell Community Extensions** package. By utilizing this cmdlet, the one-liner is able to complete an Active Directory search for users based on information that is imported from a CSV file. Then, using the Select-Object cmdlet, information about each user found is exported to a results CSV file. In other words, a user report that would have taken many lines of code to complete using WSH is instead completed using one long line of code (a one-liner). Needless to say, one-liners can be powerful to an administrator who seeks to perform complex automation tasks.

NOTE

PowerShell Community Extensions (PSCX) is a community-based project that is focused on providing a number of different useful cmdlets, providers, aliases, filters, functions, and scripts. This package can be freely downloaded from the following site: `www.codeplex.com/PowerShellCX`.

The Extended Type System (ETS)

For the most part, PowerShell is a typeless language in that an administrator rarely needs to specify or think about the type of object that they happen to be working with. However, just because you don't see it, doesn't mean PowerShell is typeless. Instead PowerShell is type-driven. After all, it is object-based, and it has to interface with many different types of objects from the less than perfect .NET to Windows Management Instrumentation (WMI), Component Object Model (COM), ActiveX Data Objects (ADO), Active Directory Service Interfaces (ADSI), Extensible Markup Language (XML), and even custom objects. To handle these many different types of objects (both programmatically and logically) while ensuring that they can be passed through the Pipeline, PowerShell adapts to different object types and then produces its interpretation of an object for you. To do this, PowerShell uses the **Extended Type System (ETS)**, which provides an interface that enables administrators to manipulate and change objects as needed.

The ETS was designed to overcome three basic problems that are encountered in PowerShell. First, there can be cases where a .NET object doesn't behave in a default manner, which then can prevent data from flowing between cmdlets. For example, when working with WMI, ADO, and XML objects, their members describe only the data that they contain. Nonetheless, the goal of PowerShell is to work with the data that is referenced by these objects. To get around this predicament, the ETS provides the notion of adapters, which allow an underlying object to be adapted to meet the expected default semantics. Secondly, there might be cases where a .NET object just doesn't provide the capabilities that are required to complete the task at hand. Using the ETS, these objects can be extended with additional members. Lastly, PowerShell attempts to always interact with an operator by presenting itself as a typeless scripting language. In other words, a variable rarely needs to be declared as a particular type despite the fact that PowerShell is type-driven.

To accomplish these feats the ETS uses a common object that has the capability to state its type dynamically, add members dynamically, and make interactions with all objects consistent. The name for this abstraction layer is the PSObject, a common object used for all object access in PowerShell. The PSObject can encapsulate any base object (.NET, custom, and so on), any instance members, and implicit or explicit access to adapted and type-based extended members, depending on the type of base object.

By wrapping an existing object (base object), the PSObject can be used to show an adapted view of an object or as a vehicle to extend that object. An adapted view of an object will expose only a view of an object that contains a selected set of members that can then be directly accessible. To better understand the relationship between a base object and the resulting PSObject, refer to Figure 3.2.

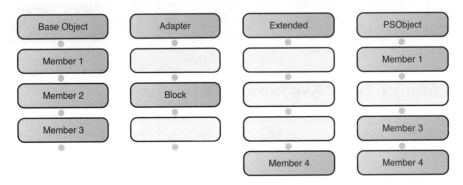

FIGURE 3.2   How an object is adapted and the resulting PSObject

In the event that the resulting PSObject does not expose the needed functionality, PowerShell has several different object views that can be used to access blocked members from the base object and gain insight into how the PSObject was constructed. These views are explained as follows:

▶ **PSBase**—Used to access the base object (a list of the original properties of the .NET object without extension or adaptation).

▶ **PSAdapted**—A view of the adapted object.

▶ **PSExtended**—Provides a list of extended elements (properties and methods that were added in the Types.ps1xml files or by using the Add-Member cmdlet).

▶ **PSObject**—Describes the adapter that converts the base object to a PSObject.

▶ **PSTypeNames**—A list of object types that describe an object.

In certain cases, you might encounter issues with the behavior of a cmdlet's interpretation of an object. A perfect example of such a scenario can be found with how PowerShell interacts with the DirectoryEntry class. Details about this interaction are explained in Chapter 13, "PowerShell as a Management Interface." Many of the more useful base object members are not exposed in a PowerShell-based DirectoryEntry object. When this type of scenario is encountered, you can use PSBase view to review the base object and make use of its members. For example:

```
PS > $OU = new-object
DirectoryServices.DirectoryEntry("LDAP://OU=Accounts,DC=companyabc,DC=com")
PS > $OU.PSBase | gm
```

By default, the Get-Member cmdlet returns only information from the PSObject, PSExtended, and PSTypeNames views. As shown in the previous example, the PSBase view is used in conjunction with the Get-Member cmdlet to expose the members of the base object. To interact with the base object's members, you use the PSBase view and PowerShell's "." notation, as shown in the following command:

```
PS > $OU.PSBase.Properties
```

After the previous command is issued, you are presented with a formatted table that contains all of the specified Active Directory object's attributes and their associated values.

Understanding the Add-Member Cmdlet

As mentioned before, the ETS can also be used to extend objects. So, in addition to PSObject blocking useful members, there might be cases where you will want to extend an object to include additional members. To extend objects in PowerShell, there are two different interfaces. The first interface is to programmatically extend an object by using a custom Types.ps1xml file. The second interface is to use the Add-Member cmdlet and extend the object directly from the command line. For example:

```
PS > $ProcList = get-process "Power*"
PS > $ProcList | add-member -Type scriptProperty "RunTime" {return
((date) - ($this.starttime))}
```

In the preceding example, a scriptProperty is added to a collection of process objects. In the property that is added, a ScriptBlock is defined that is used to calculate the time in minutes that the process has been running. The formatted results from the added scriptPoperty are shown in the next example:

```
PS > $Proclist | select Name, @{name='RunTime';
Expression={"{0:n0}" -f $_.RunTime.TotalMinutes}}

Name                                                              RunTime
----                                                              -------
powershell                                                        63
```

In the examples that you have just reviewed, it is important to understand that two object collections are actually created. The first object collection is generated when the Get-Process cmdlet is executed. The second object collection is generated when the Add-Member cmdlet is executed. Why does this happen? Well, when the Add-Member cmdlet is used, it actually wraps the original object in a new PSObject instance.

Understanding the `types.ps1xml` **File**

Be default, all object types that are used by PowerShell cmdlets, providers, and the `powershell.exe` are defined via an XML file named `types.ps1xml`. This file is part of the default PowerShell installation. However, the framework within this file represents the method by which you can define a new object type or extend an existing object type. In other words, you create your own `types.ps1xml` file and then load it into your PowerShell session using the `Update-TypeData` cmdlet.

NOTE

Do not modify the default `types.ps1xml` file because doing so may put PowerShell into an unusable state.

Working with Types

In PowerShell, there are several different ways to cast an object as a certain type. The first method is to use PowerShell's built-in capability to determine basic types: strings, numbers, arrays, and hash tables. To use these basic types, you just define the data as it might be when typed. For example, to define an object that is typed as a string, you use the following format:

```
PS > $mystring = "This is a string"
PS > $mystring.GetType()


IsPublic IsSerial Name                                      BaseType
-------- -------- ----                                      --------
True     True     String                                    System.Object


PS >
```

Or, to define an object that is typed as an integer, you use the following format:

```
PS > $mynumber = 123456
PS > $mynumber.GetType()


IsPublic IsSerial Name                                      BaseType
-------- -------- ----                                      --------
True     True     Int32                                     System.ValueType


PS >
```

To define an object that is typed as an array, you use the following format:

```
PS > $myarray = "1","2","3","4"
PS > $myarray.GetType()

IsPublic IsSerial Name                                    BaseType
-------- -------- ----                                    --------
True     True     Object[]                                System.Array

PS >
```

Lastly, to define an object that is typed as a hash table, you use the following format:

```
PS > $mytable= @{name = "Bob Barker"; job = "TV Guy"}
PS > $mytable.GetType()

IsPublic IsSerial Name                                    BaseType
-------- -------- ----                                    --------
True     True     Hashtable                               System.Object

PS >
```

The other method to define a type in PowerShell is to use something that is called a literal type. As the name suggests, a literal type is used in PowerShell to specify a particular type either during a cast, during the declaration of a variable, or as the object itself. The following command shows how to case series of numbers into an array:

```
PS > $myarray = [System.Array]"1","2","3"
```

In the previous example, you see a string that is enclosed within a set of square brackets ([]). When used, square brackets ([]) denote that the term enclosed is a .NET Framework reference. A reference can be:

▶ **A Fully Qualified Class Name**—[System.Diagnostics.Process]

▶ **A Class under the System Namespace**—[Diagnostics.Process]

▶ **A Type Accelerator**—[ADSI], [WMI], [Regex], and so on

In this case, the string that is enclosed is a full type name (Fully Qualified Class Name) that denotes that the resulting object is to be of the specific type (System.Array). Keep in mind, however, that when working with classes under the System namespace, you don't need to include "System" in the full typed name. Instead, in an effort to reduce typing, PowerShell always appends "System" to a type name if it's invalid and tries again to perform the type conversion. For example:

```
PS > $myarray = [Array]"1","2","3"
```

In cases where a type conversion cannot be performed, an error will always be thrown:

```
PS > $mynumber = [int]"this will not work"
Cannot convert value "this will not work" to type "System.Int32".
Error: "Input string was not in a correct format."
At line:1 char:18
+ $mynumber = [int]" <<<< this will not work"
```

To declare a variable as a particular type, you place the type name, enclosed in brackets, in front of the variable name. For example:

```
PS > [array]$myarray = "1","2","3"
```

Lastly, you can also use a type as an object itself, as shown in the following example:

```
PS > [System.Array] | gm –static

   TypeName: System.Array

Name            MemberType  Definition
----            ----------  ----------
AsReadOnly      Method      static   AsReadOnly(T[] array)
BinarySearch    Method      static System.Int32 BinarySearch(T[] array,
                            T value), static System.Int32
                            BinarySearch(T[...
Clear           Method      static System.Void Clear(Array array, Int32
                            index, Int32 length)
ConstrainedCopy Method      static System.Void ConstrainedCopy(Array
                            sourceArray, Int32 sourceIndex, Array
                            destinatio...
...
Reverse         Method      static System.Void Reverse(Array array),
                            static System.Void Reverse(Array array,
                            Int32 in...
...
```

In the previous example, you use the Get-Member cmdlet to retrieve the methods that are supported by an object that is typed as a System.Array. To actually use one of these static methods, you need to use the ":::" operator, as shown in the next example:

```
PS > [System.Array]::Reverse($myarray)
PS > $myarray
3
2
1
PS > [System.Array]::Reverse($myarray)
PS > $myarray
1
2
3
```

Type Accelerators

A **type accelerator**, also known as a **type shortcut**, is simply an alias for specifying a .NET type. Without a type accelerator, defining a variable type requires entering a fully qualified class name, as shown here:

```
PS > $User = [System.DirectoryServices.DirectoryEntry]"LDAP://CN=Fujio
Saitoh,OU=Accounts,OU=Managed Objects,DC=companyabc,DC=com"
PS > $User

distinguishedName
-----------------
{CN=Fujio Saitoh,OU=Accounts,OU=Managed Objects,DC=companyabc,DC=com}
...
```

Instead of typing the entire class name, you can just use the [ADSI] type accelerator to define the variable type, as shown in the following example:

```
PS > $User = [ADSI]"LDAP://CN=Fujio Saitoh,OU=Accounts,OU=Managed
Objects,DC=companyabc,DC=com"
```

Type accelerators have been included in PowerShell mainly to cut down on the amount of typing to define an object type. However, for some reason, a definitive list of supported type accelerators isn't provided within the PowerShell documentation, even though the [WMI], [ADSI], and other common type accelerators are referenced on numerous Web blogs. Regardless of the lack of documentation, type accelerators are a fairly useful feature of PowerShell. Table 3.1 lists some of the more commonly used type accelerators.

TABLE 3.1   Type Accelerators in PowerShell

Type Accelerator	TypeOf
[int]	Int32
[long]	Int64
[string]	String
[char]	Char
[bool]	Boolean
[byte]	Byte
[double]	Double
[decimal]	Decimal
[float]	Single
[single]	Single
[regex]	Text.RegularExpressions.Regex
[array]	Array
[xml]	Xml.XmlDocument
[scriptblock]	Management.Automation.ScriptBlock
[switch]	Management.Automation.SwitchParameter
[hashtable]	Collections.Hashtable
[type]	Type
[ref]	Management.Automation.PSReference
[psobject]	Management.Automation.PSObject
[wmi]	Management.ManagementObject
[wmisearcher]	Management.ManagementObjectSearcher
[wmiclass]	Management.ManagementClass
[adsi]	DirectoryServices.DirectoryEntry
[adsisearcher]	DirectoryServices.DirectorySearcher

Summary

This chapter's primary focus was to delve deeper into what PowerShell is and how it works. Among the many key concepts that were reviewed, the most important of these is to understand that PowerShell is an object-based shell that is built on top of the .NET Framework. In addition, because of PowerShell's relationship with the .NET Framework, it exposes the power of that framework's object model and a .NET feature called Reflection directly from within a command-line console (or script file).

While an object-based shell is not necessarily a new concept, the PowerShell product team wanted to design a shell that would empower its users, not frustrate them. The end result is a shell that meets this objective by attempting to abstract all objects into a common form (PSObject) that can be used without modification (parsing) in your commands and scripts. This feature combined with a robust command pipeline, the concept of cmdlets, and the capability to be adapted as needed, make PowerShell a tool that facilitates the ability to complete tasks.

CHAPTER 4

Other Key PowerShell Concepts

Although previous chapters in this book have emphasized PowerShell's ease of use for scripters familiar with other scripting languages such as Bash and VBScript, the PowerShell language introduces a number of key new concepts that enable scripters to take their automation tasks to a new level of capability, organization, and clarity. The goal of this chapter is to explore these new concepts, provide specific examples to demonstrate each concept, and to illustrate the underlying principle behind each concept to help take your understanding of the inner workings of PowerShell to the next level.

Formatting Output

As you are getting started with PowerShell, you will probably make use of PowerShell's **formatting cmdlets** almost from the beginning. The formatting cmdlets are a key part of PowerShell's functionality, as they enable you to organize the output of other cmdlets in a useful manner. This section provides an overview of the native PowerShell formatting cmdlets and their capabilities, explores how the formatting cmdlets actually perform their work, and discusses how to customize the output of the formatting cmdlets to meet your own requirements.

The Formatting Cmdlets

There are four native PowerShell cmdlets that deal specifically with formatting the output of commands:

▶ **Format-List**—The Format-List cmdlet formats the output of a command as a list of properties in which each property is displayed on a separate line. You can use Format-List to format and display all or selected properties of an object as a list (Format-List *).

▶ **Format-Table**—The Format-Table cmdlet formats the output of a command as a table with a selected properties of the object in each column. The object type determines the default layout and properties that are displayed in each column, but you can use the Property parameter to select the properties that you want to see.

▶ **Format-Wide**—The Format-Wide cmdlet formats objects as a wide table that displays only one property of each object. You can use the Property parameter to determine which property is displayed.

▶ **Format-Custom**—The Format-Custom cmdlet formats the output of a command as defined in an alternate view. Format-Custom is designed to display views that are not just tables or just lists. You can use the views defined in the *format.PS1XML files \ in the Windows PowerShell directory or you can create your own views in new PS1XML files and use the Update-FormatData cmdlet to add them to Windows PowerShell.

PowerShell's Formatting under the Hood

As you are first getting used to working with PowerShell, it is easy to type a command such as get-process | format-list and appreciate the ease of getting results from PowerShell without needing to have a detailed understanding of exactly how PowerShell is displaying these results. This section takes a look at the mechanics of the formatting cmdlets and describes how to customize the output of PowerShell's formatting cmdlets to meet your own requirements.

As we discussed in Chapter 3, "Advanced PowerShell Concepts," the Extended Type System (ETS) enables existing .NET objects to be assigned new behaviors by PowerShell. PowerShell uses ETS to include detailed formatting information for the objects that it uses. This formatting information is stored in a series of files with a .ps1xml extension that reside in the PowerShell home directory. In PowerShell 2.0 CTP2, the PowerShell home directory is **C:\WINDOWS\system32\WindowsPowerShell\v1.0**; this value is also stored in the PowerShell variable $PSHOME. The command that follows shows a list of the .ps1xml files that are part of the current release of PowerShell 2.0 CTP2.

```
PS C:\> dir $PSHOME/*format* | ft name

Name
----
```

```
Certificate.Format.ps1xml
DotNetTypes.Format.ps1xml
FileSystem.Format.ps1xml
Help.Format.ps1xml
PowerShellCore.format.ps1xml
PowerShellTrace.format.ps1xml
Registry.format.ps1xml


PS C:\>
```

The function of each of these seven formatting files is described in the following:

▶ `Certificate.Format.ps1xml`—Provides formatting guidelines for objects such as X.509 certificates and certificate stores.

▶ `DotNetTypes.Format.ps1xml`—Formats .NET types not covered by the other formatting files, such as CultureInfo, FileVersionInfo, and EventLogEntry objects.

▶ `FileSystem.Format.ps1xml`—Contains formatting information for file system objects such as files and directories.

▶ `Help.Format.ps1xml`—Describes the views that PowerShell uses to display help file content, such as detailed and full views, parameters, and examples.

▶ `PowerShellCore.format.ps1xml`—Formats objects that are created by the PowerShell core cmdlets, such as `Get-Member` and `Get-ExecutionPolicy`.

▶ `PowerShellTrace.format.ps1xml`—Controls the appearance of trace objects, such as those generated by the `Trace-Command` cmdlet.

▶ `Registry.format.ps1xml`—Instructs PowerShell on the formatting and appearance of registry objects, such as keys and entries.

CAUTION

Although you are welcome to take a look at any of the formatting files listed previously, these files should *not* be edited directly, or PowerShell's basic functionality may be impacted. Each of these files is digitally signed to prevent modification.

Customizing Output Formats

As you continue to use PowerShell for your scripting automation tasks, you will likely run into situations where it would be really helpful to be able to add an additional property to a `PSObject`. For example, you might want to create a new alias property to make it easier to reference a property in an existing `PSObject`. There are two different ways to approach this kind of task. If you just need to add a property temporarily, you can use the Add-Member cmdlet to add an additional property to an existing PSObject. The sequence of commands that follows shows how to add a NoteProperty System.String property called Status with a value of done to the type name System.IO.DirectoryInfo:

```
PS C:\> $a = (get-childitem)[0]
PS C:\> $a | add-member -membertype noteproperty -name Status -value
done
PS C:\> $a | get-member -membertype noteproperty


   TypeName: System.IO.DirectoryInfo

Name            MemberType    Definition
----            ----------    ----------
PSChildName     NoteProperty  System.String PSChildName=Documents and
                              Settings
PSDrive         NoteProperty  System.Management.Automation.PSDriveInfo
                              PSDrive=C
PSIsContainer   NoteProperty  System.Boolean PSIsContainer=True
PSParentPath    NoteProperty  System.String
                              PSParentPath=Microsoft.PowerShell.Core\FileSystem::C:\
PSPath          NoteProperty  System.String
                              PSPath=Microsoft.PowerShell.Core\FileSystem::C:\
                              Documents and Settings
PSProvider      NoteProperty  System.Management.Automation.ProviderInfo
                              PSProvider=Microsoft.PowerShell.Core\FileSystem
Status          NoteProperty  System.String status=done


PS C:\>
```

The limitation of adding properties to PSObjects interactively is that the properties persist only for the duration of your PowerShell session. After you close PowerShell, any custom properties that you have added are destroyed and need to be manually recreated in subsequent sessions if you want to use the properties again. If you find that you are making regular use of custom properties and would like to have these properties automatically loaded every time PowerShell is launched, the best solution is to create a custom .ps1xml file that can be loaded as part of your PowerShell profile. The steps that follow describe how to create your own custom .ps1xml file and add it to your Windows PowerShell console.

To create a new .ps1xml file, you can begin with a blank template similar to the one shown in the following. You should save this file in your PowerShell user profile directory with the name `Types.Custom.ps1xml`. To obtain the path for your PowerShell user profile, you can enter the command $profile at any PowerShell prompt. The value that is returned is similar to `C:\Documents and Settings\<username>\My Documents\WindowsPowerShell\Microsoft.PowerShell_profile.ps1`. Thus, this file should be saved as `C:\Documents and Settings\<username>\My Documents\WindowsPowerShell\Types.Custom.ps1xml`.

```
<?xml version="1.0" encoding="utf-8" ?>
<Types>
</Types>
```

The previous example is a valid `.ps1xml` file, but it contains no data. To configure PowerShell to load this `Types.Custom.ps1xml` file when PowerShell starts, you can add the following lines to your PowerShell profile:

```
$typeFile = (join-path (split-path $profile) "Types.Custom.ps1xml")
Update-TypeData -PrependPath $typeFile
```

At this point, you have configured PowerShell to load a custom `.ps1xml` file named `Types.Custom.ps1xml` for your user profile when PowerShell is launched. The next step is to add some customizations to `Types.Custom.ps1xml`. The example that follows demonstrates adding an `AliasProperty` named `BytesFree` to the `System.IO.DriveInfo` PSObject, which references the existing property `AvailableFreeSpace`:

```
<?xml version="1.0" encoding="utf-8" ?>
<Types>
    <Type>
      <Name>System.IO.DriveInfo</Name>
        <Members>
                <AliasProperty>
                  <Name>BytesFree</Name>
                  <ReferencedMemberName>AvailableFreeSpace</ReferencedMemberName>
                </AliasProperty>
        </Members>
      </Type>
</Types>
```

After you have saved the `Types.Custom.ps1xml` file in your PowerShell user profile directory as described previously, exit PowerShell and restart it to allow the new custom types file to be included. The example that follows shows the output of [System.IO.DriveInfo]::getdrives() pipelined to Format-List (aliased here as fl) with the properties Name, DriveType, VolumeLabel, and BytesFree. Note that PowerShell now accepts BytesFree as a valid property for System.IO.DriveInfo and returns the value for AvailableFreeSpace, even though the BytesFree label is displayed by Format-List.

```
PS C:\> $a = [System.IO.DriveInfo]::getdrives()
PS C:\> $a | fl Name, DriveType, VolumeLabel, BytesFree


Name         : C:\
DriveType    : Fixed
VolumeLabel  : IBM_PRELOAD
BytesFree    : 51519315968

Name         : D:\
DriveType    : Fixed
VolumeLabel  : 60 GB
BytesFree    : 19784757248

Name         : E:\
DriveType    : Fixed
VolumeLabel  : Data
BytesFree    : 36199202816

Name         : F:\
DriveType    : CDRom
VolumeLabel  :
BytesFree    :

PS C:\>
```

Although the example shown is a relatively straightforward demonstration of adding an alias for an existing PSObject property, it is possible to perform much more detailed customizations in a .ps1xml file, such as including script blocks to assign a scripted action to a PSObject property. The following abbreviated example comes from PowerShell's default types.ps1xml file and illustrates how the DateTime property of the System.DateTime type is populated using a series of scripted commands to parse the input and return a value:

```
<?xml version="1.0" encoding="utf-8" ?>
<Types>
    <Type>
```

```
        <Name>System.DateTime</Name>
        <Members>
            <ScriptProperty>
                <Name>DateTime</Name>
                <GetScriptBlock>
                    if ($this.DisplayHint -ieq  "Date")
                    {
                        "{0}" -f $this.ToLongDateString()
                    }
                    elseif ($this.DisplayHint -ieq "Time")
                    {
                        "{0}" -f  $this.ToLongTimeString()
                    }
                    else
                    {
                        "{0} {1}" -f $this.ToLongDateString(),
$this.ToLongTimeString()
                    }
                </GetScriptBlock>
            </ScriptProperty>
        </Members>
    </Type>
</Types>
```

NOTE

If you plan to make extensive customizations to your own `.ps1xml` file, and especially if you plan to distribute your customizations to other users, it is a best practice to digitally sign your `.ps1xml` file. Please review Chapter 5, "Understanding PowerShell Security," for more information on digitally signing PowerShell files.

Providers

Most computer systems are used to store data, often in a structure such as a file system. Because of the amount of data stored in these structures, processing and finding information can be unwieldy. Most shells have interfaces, or **providers**, for interacting with data stores in a predictable, set manner. PowerShell also has a set of providers for presenting the contents of data stores through a core set of cmdlets. You can then use these cmdlets to browse, navigate, and manipulate data from stores through a common interface. To get a list of the core cmdlets, use the following command:

```
PS C:\> help about_core_commands
...
    ChildItem CMDLETS
    Get-ChildItem

    CONTENT CMDLETS
    Add-Content
    Clear-Content
    Get-Content
    Set-Content

    DRIVE CMDLETS
    Get-PSDrive
    New-PSDrive
    Remove-PSDrive

    ITEM CMDLETS
    Clear-Item
    Copy-Item
    Get-Item
    Invoke-Item
    Move-Item
    New-Item
    Remove-Item
    Rename-Item
    Set-Item

    LOCATION CMDLETS
    Get-Location
    Pop-Location
    Push-Location
    Set-Location

    PATH CMDLETS
    Join-Path
    Convert-Path
    Split-Path
    Resolve-Path
    Test-Path

    PROPERTY CMDLETS
    Clear-ItemProperty
    Copy-ItemProperty
    Get-ItemProperty
```

```
    Move-ItemProperty
    New-ItemProperty
    Remove-ItemProperty
    Rename-ItemProperty
    Set-ItemProperty

    PROVIDER CMDLETS
    Get-PSProvider



PS C:\>
```

To view built-in PowerShell providers, use the following command:

```
PS C:\> get-psprovider

Name                 Capabilities              Drives
----                 ------------              ------
Alias                ShouldProcess             {Alias}
Environment          ShouldProcess             {Env}
FileSystem           Filter, ShouldProcess     {C, D, E, F...}
Function             ShouldProcess             {Function}
Registry             ShouldProcess             {HKLM, HKCU}
Variable             ShouldProcess             {Variable}
Certificate          ShouldProcess             {cert}


PS C:\>
```

The preceding list displays not only built-in providers, but also the drives each provider currently supports. A **drive** is an entity that a provider uses to represent a data store through which data is made available to the PowerShell session. For example, the Registry provider creates a PowerShell drive for the HKEY_LOCAL_MACHINE and HKEY_CURRENT_USER Registry hives.

To see a list of all current PowerShell drives, use the following command:

```
PS C:\> get-psdrive

Name            Provider         Root
----            --------         ----
```

```
Alias        Alias
C            FileSystem      C:\
cert         Certificate     \
D            FileSystem      D:\
E            FileSystem      E:\
Env          Environment
F            FileSystem      F:\
Function     Function
G            FileSystem      G:\
HKCU         Registry        HKEY_CURRENT_USER
HKLM         Registry        HKEY_LOCAL_MACHINE
U            FileSystem      U
Variable     Variable


PS C:\>
```

Accessing Drives and Data

One way to access PowerShell drives and their data is with the Set-Location cmdlet. This cmdlet, shown in the following example, changes the working location to another specified location that can be a directory, subdirectory, location stack, or Registry location:

```
PS C:\> set-location hklm:
PS HKLM:\> set-location software\microsoft\windows
PS HKLM:\software\microsoft\windows>
```

Next, use the Get-ChildItem cmdlet to list the subkeys under the Windows key:

```
PS HKLM:\software\microsoft\windows> get-childitem


   Hive: Microsoft.PowerShell.Core\Registry::HKEY_LOCAL_MACHINE\
software\microsoft\windows

SKC  VC Name                    Property
---  -- ----                    --------
 55  13 CurrentVersion          {DevicePath, MediaPathUnexpanded, SM_...
  0  16 Help                    {PINTLPAD.HLP, PINTLPAE.HLP, IMEPADEN...
  0  36 Html Help               {PINTLGNE.CHM, PINTLGNT.CHM, PINTLPAD...
  1   0 ITStorage               {}
```

```
  0    0 Shell                     {}


PS HKLM:\software\microsoft\windows>
```

Note that with a Registry drive, the Get-ChildItem cmdlet lists only the subkeys under a
key, not the actual Registry values. This is because Registry values are treated as properties
for a key rather than a valid item. To retrieve these values from the Registry, you use the
Get-ItemProperty cmdlet, as shown in this example:

```
PS HKLM:\software\microsoft\windows> get-itemproperty currentversion


PSPath                        :
Microsoft.PowerShell.Core\Registry::HKEY_LOCAL_MACHI

NE\software\microsoft\windows\currentversion
PSParentPath                  :
Microsoft.PowerShell.Core\Registry::HKEY_LOCAL_MACHI
                                NE\software\microsoft\windows
PSChildName                   : currentversion
PSDrive                       : HKLM
PSProvider                    : Microsoft.PowerShell.Core\Registry
DevicePath                    : C:\WINDOWS\inf
MediaPathUnexpanded           : C:\WINDOWS\Media
SM_GamesName                  : Games
SM_ConfigureProgramsName      : Set Program Access and Defaults
ProgramFilesDir               : C:\Program Files
CommonFilesDir                : C:\Program Files\Common Files
ProductId                     : 76487-OEM-0011903-00101
WallPaperDir                  : C:\WINDOWS\Web\Wallpaper
MediaPath                     : C:\WINDOWS\Media
ProgramFilesPath              : C:\Program Files
SM_AccessoriesName            : Accessories
PF_AccessoriesName            : Accessories
(default)                     :


PS HKLM:\software\microsoft\windows>
```

As with the Get-Process command, the data returned is a collection of objects. You can
modify these objects further to produce the output you want, as this example shows:

```
PS HKLM:\software\microsoft\windows> get-itemproperty currentversion |
select ProductId

ProductId
---------
76487-OEM-XXXXXXX-XXXXX


PS HKLM:\software\microsoft\windows>
```

Accessing data from a FileSystem drive is just as simple. The same type of command logic is used to change the location and display the structure:

```
PS HKLM:\software\microsoft\windows> set-location c:
PS C:\> set-location "C:\WINDOWS\system32\windowspowershell\v1.0"
PS C:\WINDOWS\system32\windowspowershell\v1.0> get-childitem about_a*


    Directory: Microsoft.PowerShell.Core\FileSystem::C:\WINDOWS\system32\
window spowershell\v1.0


Mode       LastWriteTime        Length    Name
----       -------------        ------    ----
-----      9/8/2006             2:10 AM   5662 about_alias.help.txt
-----      9/8/2006             2:10 AM   3504 about_arithmetic_operators.help.txt
-----      9/8/2006             2:10 AM   8071 about_array.help.txt
-----      9/8/2006             2:10 AM   15137 about_assignment_operators.help.txt
-----      9/8/2006             2:10 AM   5622 about_associative_array.help.txt
-----      9/8/2006             2:10 AM   3907 about_automatic_variables.help.txt
...

PS C:\WINDOWS\system32\windowspowershell\v1.0>
```

What's different is that data is stored in an item instead of being a property of that item. To retrieve data from an item, use the Get-Content cmdlet, as shown in this example:

```
PS C:\WINDOWS\system32\windowspowershell\v1.0> get-content
about_Alias.help.txt
TOPIC
    Aliases
```

```
SHORT DESCRIPTION
    Using pseudonyms to refer to cmdlet names in the Windows
PowerShell

LONG DESCRIPTION
    An alias is a pseudonym, or "nickname," that you can assign to a
    cmdlet so that you can use the alias in place of the cmdlet name.
    The Windows PowerShell interprets the alias as though you had
    entered the actual cmdlet name. For example, suppose that you want
    to retrieve today's date for the year 1905. Without an alias, you
    would use the following command:

        Get-Date -year 1905
...


PS C:\WINDOWS\system32\windowspowershell\v1.0>
```

NOTE

Not all drives are based on a hierarchical data store. For example, the Environment, Function, and Variable PowerShell providers aren't hierarchical. Data accessed through these providers is in the root location on the associated drive.

Mounting a Drive

PowerShell drives can be created and removed, which is handy when you're working with a location or set of locations frequently. Instead of having to change the location or use an absolute path, you can create new drives (also referred to as "mounting a drive" in PowerShell) as shortcuts to those locations. To do this, use the New-PSDrive cmdlet, shown in the following example:

```
PS C:\> new-psdrive -name PSScripts -root D:\Dev\Scripts -psp FileSystem

Name        Provider      Root                        CurrentLocation
----        --------      ----                        ---------------
PSScripts   FileSystem    D:\Dev\Scripts


PS C:\> get-psdrive

Name        Provider      Root                        CurrentLocation
```

```
----           --------     ----                                  ----------------
Alias          Alias
C              FileSystem   C:\
cert           Certificate  \
D              FileSystem   D:\
E              FileSystem   E:\
Env            Environment
F              FileSystem   F:\
Function       Function
G              FileSystem   G:\
HKCU           Registry     HKEY_CURRENT_USER                     software
HKLM           Registry     HKEY_LOCAL_MACHINE                    ...crosoft\windows
PSScripts      FileSystem   D:\Dev\Scripts
U              FileSystem   U:\
Variable       Variable


PS C:\>
```

To remove a drive, use the Remove-PSDrive cmdlet, as shown here:

```
PS C:\> remove-psdrive -name PSScripts
PS C:\> get-psdrive

Name           Provider     Root                                  CurrentLocation
----           --------     ----                                  ----------------
Alias          Alias
C              FileSystem   C:\
cert           Certificate  \
D              FileSystem   D:\
E              FileSystem   E:\
Env            Environment
F              FileSystem   F:\
Function       Function
G              FileSystem   G:\
HKCU           Registry     HKEY_CURRENT_USER                     software
HKLM           Registry     HKEY_LOCAL_MACHINE                    ...crosoft\windows
U              FileSystem   U:\
Variable       Variable


PS C:\>
```

Profiles

A PowerShell **profile** is a saved collection of settings for customizing the PowerShell environment. There are four types of profiles, loaded in a specific order each time PowerShell starts. The following sections explain these profile types, where they should be located, and the order in which they are loaded.

The All Users Profile

The All Users profile is located in `%windir%\system32\windowspowershell\v1.0\profile.ps1`. Settings in the All Users profile are applied to all PowerShell users on the current machine. If you plan to configure PowerShell settings across the board for users on a machine, then this is the profile to use.

The All Users Host-Specific Profile

This profile is located in `%windir%\system32\windowspowershell\v1.0\`*`ShellID`*`_profile.ps1`. Settings in the All Users host-specific profile are applied to all users of the current shell (by default, the PowerShell Console). PowerShell supports the concept of multiple shells or hosts. For example, the PowerShell Console is a host and the one most users use exclusively.

> **NOTE**
>
> While the word **host** is colloquially used to refer to a physical computer system that provides services to users, in the context of the PowerShell language, the word **host** signifies an instance of the PowerShell console host program, which provides PowerShell services to users of PowerShell. Many of the native PowerShell cmdlets reflect this frame of reference, such as **Read-Host** and **Write-Host**, which both provide text processing functionality within an existing PowerShell session.

However, other applications can call an instance of the PowerShell runtime to access and run PowerShell commands and scripts. An application that does this is called a **hosting application** and uses a host-specific profile to control the PowerShell configuration. The host-specific profile name is reflected by the host's `ShellID`. In the PowerShell Console, the `ShellID` is the following:

```
PS C:\ $ShellId
Microsoft.PowerShell
PS C:\
```

Putting this together, the PowerShell Console's All Users host-specific profile is named `Microsoft.PowerShell_profile.ps1`. For other hosts, the `ShellID` and All Users host-specific profile names are different. For example, the PowerShell Analyzer (www.powershellanalyzer.com) is a PowerShell host that acts as a rich graphical interface for the PowerShell environment. Its `ShellID` is `PowerShellAnalyzer.PSA`, and its All Users host-specific profile name is `PowerShellAnalyzer.PSA_profile.ps1`.

The Current User's Profile

This profile is located in `%userprofile%\My Documents\WindowsPowerShell\profile.ps1`. Users who want to control their own profile settings can use the current user's profile. Settings in this profile are applied only to the user's current PowerShell session and don't affect any other users.

The Current User's Host-Specific Profile

This profile is located in `%userprofile%\My Documents\WindowsPowerShell\`
`ShellID_profile.ps1`. Like the All Users host-specific profile, this profile type loads settings for the current shell. However, the settings are user-specific.

NOTE

When you start the shell for the first time, you might see a message indicating that scripts are disabled and no profiles are loaded. You can modify this behavior by changing the PowerShell execution policy, discussed in Chapter 5.

Scopes

A **scope** is a logical boundary in PowerShell that isolates the use of functions and variables. Scopes can be defined as global, local, script, and private. They function in a hierarchy in which scope information is inherited downward. For example, the local scope can read the global scope, but the global scope can't read information from the local scope. Scopes and their use are described in the following sections.

The Global Scope

As the name indicates, a **global scope** applies to an entire PowerShell instance. Global scope data is inherited by all child scopes, so any commands, functions, or scripts that run make use of variables defined in the global scope. However, global scopes are *not* shared between different instances of PowerShell.

The following example shows the `$Processes` variable being defined as a global variable in the `ListProcesses` function. Because the `$Processes` variable is being defined globally, checking `$Processes.Count` after `ListProcesses` completes returns a count of the number of active processes at the time `ListProcesses` was executed.

```
PS C:\> function ListProcesses {$Global:Processes = get-process}
PS C:\> ListProcesses
PS C:\> $Processes.Count
37
```

> **NOTE**
>
> In PowerShell, you can use an explicit scope indicator to determine the scope a variable resides in. For instance, if you want a variable to reside in the global scope, you define it as $Global:*variablename*. If an explicit scope indicator isn't used, a variable resides in the current scope for which it's defined.

The Local Scope

A **local scope** is created dynamically each time a function, filter, or script runs. After a local scope has finished running, information in it is discarded. A local scope can read information from the global scope but can't make changes to it.

The following example shows the locally scoped variable $Processes being defined in the ListProcesses function. After ListProcesses finishes running, the $Processes variable no longer contains any data because it was defined only in the ListProcesses function. As you can see, checking $Processes.Count after the ListProcesses function is finished produces no results.

```
PS C:\> function ListProcesses {$Processes = get-process}
PS C:\> ListProcesses
PS C:\> $Processes.Count
PS C:\>
```

The Script Scope

A **script scope** is created whenever a script runs and is discarded when the script finishes running. To see an example of how a script scope works, create the following script and save it as ListProcesses.ps1:

```
$Processes = get-process
write-host "Here is the first process:" -Foregroundcolor Yellow
$Processes[0]
```

After you have created the script file, run it from a PowerShell session. Your output should look similar to this example:

```
PS C:\> .\ListProcesses.ps1
Here is the first process:

Handles  NPM(K)    PM(K)     WS(K) VM(M)   CPU(s)     Id ProcessName
-------  ------    -----     ----- -----   ------     -- -----------
    105       5     1992      4128    32            916 alg


PS C:\> $Processes[0]
Cannot index into a null array.
At line:1 char:12
+ $Processes[0 <<<< ]
PS C:\>
```

Notice that when the ListProcesses.ps1 script runs, information about the first process object in the $Processes variable is written to the console. However, when you try to access information in the $Processes variable from the console, an error is returned because the $Processes variable is valid only in the script scope. When the script finishes running, that scope and all its contents are discarded.

The Private Scope

A **private scope** is similar to a local scope, with one key difference: Definitions in the private scope aren't inherited by any child scopes.

The following example shows the privately scoped variable $Processes defined in the ListProcesses function. Notice that during execution of the ListProcesses function, the $Processes variable isn't available to the child scope represented by the script block enclosed by { and } in lines 6–9.

```
PS C:\> function ListProcesses {$Private:Processes = get-process
>>      write-host "Here is the first process:" -Foregroundcolor Yellow
>>      $Processes[0]
>>      write-host
>>
>>      &{
>>          write-host "Here it is again:" -Foregroundcolor Yellow
>>          $Processes[0]
>>      }
>> }
>>
PS C:\> ListProcesses
```

```
Here is the first process:

Handles   NPM(K)      PM(K)        WS(K) VM(M)    CPU(s)      Id ProcessName
-------   ------      -----        ----- -----    ------      -- -----------
    105        5       1992         4128    32                916 alg

Here it is again:
Cannot index into a null array.
At line:7 char:20
+           $Processes[0 <<<< ]


PS C:\>
```

This example works because it uses the '&' call operator. With this call operator, you can execute fragments of script code in an isolated local scope. This technique is helpful for isolating a script block and its variables from a parent scope or, as in this example, isolating a privately scoped variable from a script block.

Dot Sourcing

What if you want to use a script in a pipeline or access it as a library file for common functions? Normally, this isn't possible because PowerShell discards a script scope whenever a script finishes running. Luckily, PowerShell supports the **dot sourcing** technique, a term that originally came from UNIX. Dot sourcing a script file tells PowerShell to load a script scope into the calling parent's scope, rather than creating a new local scope for the execution of the script.

To dot source a script file, simply prefix the script name with a period (dot) when running the script, as shown here:

```
PS C:\> . c:\scripts\myscript.ps1
```

Library Files

In PowerShell, library files are groups of cmdlets that are used to perform related functions. In most cases, library files that are used in PowerShell are implemented in a **dynamic link library (DLL)**, which is then registered with PowerShell to provide access to the cmdlet functionality implemented in the DLL. This section walks through the process of registering a new PowerShell library file, adding the snapin to the console, and confirming that the new library file is providing the expected functionality.

By default, a number of PSSnapins are included with PowerShell. These PSSnapins contain the built-in cmdlets used by PowerShell. You can display a list of these cmdlets by entering the command Get-PSSnapin at the PowerShell command prompt as shown in the following:

```
PS C:\> get-pssnapin


Name        : Microsoft.PowerShell.Core
PSVersion   : 2.0
Description : This Windows PowerShell snap-in contains Windows
              PowerShell management cmdlets used to manage components
              of Windows PowerShell.

Name        : Microsoft.PowerShell.Host
PSVersion   : 2.0
Description : This Windows PowerShell snap-in contains cmdlets used by
              the Windows PowerShell host.

Name        : Microsoft.PowerShell.Management
PSVersion   : 2.0
Description : This Windows PowerShell snap-in contains management
              cmdlets used to manage Windows components.

Name        : Microsoft.PowerShell.Security
PSVersion   : 2.0
Description : This Windows PowerShell snap-in contains cmdlets to
              manage Windows PowerShell security.

Name        : Microsoft.PowerShell.Utility
PSVersion   : 2.0
Description : This Windows PowerShell snap-in contains utility Cmdlets
              used to manipulate data.


PS C:\>
```

You can also use the Get-PSSnapin command to return a list of all the registered PSSnapins outside of the default PowerShell snapins listed in the previous example. Entering the command Get-PSSnapin -Registered on a newly installed PowerShell system will return nothing, as shown in the following:

```
PS C:\> get-pssnapin -registered
PS C:\>
```

To register a third-party library, the .NET utility InstallUtil.exe is used. In the example below, InstallUtil.exe is used to install a third-party library file called nivot. powershell.eventing.dll. This DLL is part of the third-party PowerShell Eventing library, which can be freely downloaded from http://www.codeplex.com/PSEventing:

```
PS C:\pseventing> &
"$env:windir\Microsoft.NET\Framework\v2.0.50727\InstallUtil.exe "
nivot.powershell.eventing.dll
Microsoft (R) .NET Framework Installation utility Version
2.0.50727.1433
Copyright (c) Microsoft Corporation.  All rights reserved.


Running a transacted installation.

Beginning the Install phase of the installation.
See the contents of the log file for the
C:\pseventing\nivot.powershell.eventing.dll assembly's progress.
The file is located at
C:\pseventing\nivot.powershell.eventing.InstallLog.
Installing assembly
'C:\pseventing\nivot.powershell.eventing.dll'.
Affected parameters are:
   logtoconsole =
   assemblypath = C:\pseventing\nivot.powershell.eventing.dll
   logfile = C:\pseventing\nivot.powershell.eventing.InstallLog

The Install phase completed successfully, and the Commit phase is
beginning.
See the contents of the log file for the
C:\pseventing\nivot.powershell.eventing.dll assembly's progress.
The file is located at
C:\pseventing\nivot.powershell.eventing.InstallLog.
Committing assembly
'C:\pseventing\nivot.powershell.eventing.dll'.
Affected parameters are:
   logtoconsole =
   assemblypath = C:\pseventing\nivot.powershell.eventing.dll
   logfile = C:\pseventing\nivot.powershell.eventing.InstallLog

The Commit phase completed successfully.

The transacted install has completed.
PS C:\pseventing>
```

4

NOTE

The version of the `InstallUtil` program that you must use varies depending on whether you are installing on a 32-bit or 64-bit platform.

To install 32-bit registry information, use: **%systemroot%\Microsoft.NET\Framework\ v2.0.50727\installutil.exe.**

To install 64-bit registry information, use: **%systemroot%\Microsoft.NET\ Framework64\v2.0.50727\installutil.exe.**

After the DLL library file has been registered with PowerShell, the next step is to register the DLL's snapin with PowerShell, so that the cmdlets contained in the DLL are made available to PowerShell. In the case of the PowerShell Eventing library, the snapin is registered by using the command `Add-PSSnapin` `pseventing` as shown in the following:

```
PS C:\> add-pssnapin pseventing
PS C:\>
```

Now that the `pseventing` snapin has been registered, you can enter the command `Get-Help` `pseventing` as shown in the following to review the usage information for the PSEventing cmdlets:

```
PS C:\pseventing> get-help pseventing
TOPIC
    PowerShell Eventing Library (version 1.0)


SHORT DESCRIPTION
    Describes the Windows PowerShell Eventing (PSEventing) snapin and
    how to use the contained cmdlets and scripts that ship with
    PSEventing.


LONG DESCRIPTION
    PowerShell Eventing is a PowerShell Snapin that opens a new door
    for scripters into the powerful world of .NET events. Previously
    thought shut tight given the nature of the command-line driven
    prompt, this library provides the tools to automatically capture
    events in real-time, but lets you deal with them in your time.
```

```
CMDLETS
    The current PSEventing cmdlets are listed below:


    Get-Event
        Retrieve one or more PSEvent objects representing tracked .NET
        events that have been raised since the last invocation of this
        command.


    New-Event
        Create a custom PSEvent with an optional associated object
        payload. This can be used for inter-runspace communication, or
        simple notification inside a loop.

    Get-EventBinding
        Shows information about currently bound and/or
        unbound events on one or more .NET objects, accessible through
        PowerShell variables.

    Connect-EventListener
        Allows PowerShell to sink events for a given .NET object.

    Disconnect-EventListener
        Disconnects one or more event sinks for a given .NET object.

    Start-KeyHandler
        Allows PowerShell to transparently intercept keypresses and
        breaks (ctrl+c) converting them into PSEvent objects to be
        added to the queue.

    Stop-KeyHandler
        Stop all keypress handling activity.
```

4

Now that the registration of the PSEventing library DLL is complete and the associated snapin has been added to the console, you can enter the command Get-PSSnapin -registered again and see that the PSEventing snapin has been added to the console.

```
PS C:\> get-pssnapin -registered


Name        : PSEventing
PSVersion   : 2.0
Description : PowerShell Eventing Library 1.0



PS C:\>
```

NOTE

The PSEventing library actually uses an installation script to complete the DLL registration and snapin tasks described previously. These tasks are listed out here simply to illustrate the process.

Now that you have registered the third-party library file and added its snapin to the console, you may find that the library does not meet your needs, and you want to remove it. The removal process is basically a reversal of the installation steps listed previously. First, you remove the snapin from the console using the command Remove-PSSnapin pseventing, as shown in the following:

```
PS C:\> Remove-PSSnapin pseventing
PS C:\>
```

After the third-party snapin has been unregistered, you will once again use InstallUtil.exe with a /U switch to unregister the DLL, as shown in the following:

```
PS C:\pseventing> & "$env:windir\Microsoft.NET\Framework\v2.0.50727\
InstallUtil.exe " /U nivot.powershell.eventing.dll
Microsoft (R) .NET Framework Installation utility Version
2.0.50727.1433
Copyright (c) Microsoft Corporation. All rights reserved.

The uninstall is beginning.
See the contents of the log file for the
C:\pseventing\nivot.powershell.eventing.dll assembly's progress.
The file is located at
C:\pseventing\nivot.powershell.eventing.InstallLog.
Uninstalling assembly 'C:\pseventing\nivot.powershell.eventing.dll'.
```

```
Affected parameters are:
   logtoconsole =
   assemblypath = C:\pseventing\nivot.powershell.eventing.dll
   logfile = C:\pseventing\nivot.powershell.eventing.InstallLog

The uninstall has completed.
PS C:\pseventing>
```

After the uninstall has completed, you can verify that the library file was successfully unregistered by entering the command Get-PSSnapin –registered and verifying that no third-party libraries are listed.

```
PS C:\> get-pssnapin –registered
PS C:\>
```

As you can see from the examples above, PowerShell's implementation of library files provides a straightforward method for extending PowerShell's functionality, and is currently used by many third-party vendors to register their cmdlets. Although developing your own library files is beyond the scope of this chapter, there are many resources available online to assist you with this type of project. A good starting point for PowerShell development work is the *Windows PowerShell Programmer's Guide* at http://msdn.microsoft.com/en-us/library/cc136167(VS.85).aspx.

Summary

This chapter covered a number of key PowerShell concepts that are useful as your knowledge of PowerShell increases. We discussed PowerShell's formatting cmdlets and went into detail about how these cmdlets do their work, including a walkthrough of the Add-Member cmdlet and creating a customized .ps1xml file to load customized alias properties when PowerShell starts up. This chapter also covered PowerShell's implementation of providers, which enable access to the contents of data stores through a core set of cmdlets. The provider cmdlets enable users to browse, navigate, and manipulate data from stores such as file systems, the Windows registry, certificate stores, and PowerShell variables. We reviewed PowerShell's hierarchy of profiles and provided details on the functionality provided by each of the four profile types. The behavior of PowerShell scopes was documented with particular attention to the limits imposed by global, local, script, and private scopes. The dot sourcing technique was reviewed as a way to run a script in the current scope instead of creating a local scope. Finally, PowerShell's use of library files was discussed, including a walkthrough of the process of registering a new third-party DLL with PowerShell and adding the associated snapin to the console, then removing the snapin and unregistering the DLL to return the system to its original state.

CHAPTER 5

Understanding PowerShell Security

With today's growing emphasis on security in all areas of the IT enterprise, it is becoming more critical than ever to ensure that the automation tools used to manage the enterprise can be operated in a secure manner. The Windows Scripting Host (WSH) introduced with Windows 98 provided some welcome new automation functionality for systems administrators, but at the same time, it introduced a new attack vector for virus writers. The fundamental issue with WSH is that it executes any script that is presented to it, regardless of whether the script contains a legitimate administrative command or a piece of malicious code. There is also no easy way to identify a beneficial or malicious script, or even to determine if the contents of a script have been modified. Because of these concerns, WSH quickly gained a reputation as a security vulnerability, despite its many benefits as a Windows automation tool.

One of the goals of the PowerShell team was to design an automation language that was secure by default, and also to provide the extensibility necessary to allow PowerShell to be used in an enterprise environment without compromising security. This is accomplished through a combination of several methods:

- **Secure behavior by default**—PowerShell implements a number of default behaviors such as requiring a full path to a script, and not automatically associating .ps1 files (the default PowerShell script extension) with PowerShell.

- **Execution policies**—PowerShell includes four levels of execution policy security, which provide complete control over the scripts that are run on a system with PowerShell installed. Out of the box, the Restricted execution policy is in force, which prevents any scripts from being run at all until the policy is updated to permit scripts to run.

- **Code signing**—PowerShell includes functionality to digitally sign scripts, which can be used in conjunction with PowerShell's execution policies to allow only signed scripts to run.

Each of these topics is covered in detail in a subsequent section. In addition, this chapter also covers best practices for PowerShell security and specific examples on securely integrating PowerShell into your environment.

PowerShell Default Security

One of the key security issues with the Windows Scripting Host's handling of scripts is that a user can simply use Windows Explorer to navigate to a folder, double-click on a script, and potentially wreak havoc on the system. This is because by default, certain file extensions such as .vbs or .js are associated with the Windows Scripting Host. When a file with one of these extensions is double-clicked in Explorer, WSH runs the script. To ensure that PowerShell scripts cannot be automatically invoked by clicking on the script, PowerShell's .ps1 script files are associated by default with the Notepad application. In other words, you can't just double-click a .ps1 file to run it. Instead, PowerShell scripts must run from a PowerShell session by using the relative or absolute path or through the cmd command prompt by using the PowerShell executable.

Another default PowerShell security measure is that to run or open a file in the current directory from the PowerShell console, you must prefix the command with .\ or ./. This feature prevents PowerShell users from accidentally running a command or PowerShell script without explicitly specifying the script to be executed.

Execution Policies

An **execution policy** defines restrictions on how PowerShell allows scripts to run or what configuration files can be loaded. PowerShell has four execution policies, discussed in more detail in the following sections: Restricted, AllSigned, RemoteSigned, and Unrestricted.

Restricted

By default, PowerShell is configured to run under the Restricted execution policy. This execution policy is the most secure because it allows PowerShell to operate only in an interactive mode. This means no scripts can be run, and only configuration files digitally signed by a trusted publisher are allowed to run or load.

AllSigned

The AllSigned execution policy is a notch under Restricted. When this policy is enabled, only scripts or configuration files that are digitally signed by a publisher you trust can be run or loaded. Here's an example of what you might see if the AllSigned policy has been enabled:

```
PS C:\Scripts> .\evilscript.ps1

The file C:\Scripts\evilscript.ps1 cannot be loaded. The file
C:\Scripts\evilscript.ps1 is not digitally signed. The script will not
execute on the system. Please see "get-help about_signing" for more
details.
At line:1 char:16
+ .\evilscript.ps1 <<<<

PS C:\Scripts>
```

Signing a script or configuration file requires a code-signing certificate. This certificate can come from a trusted certificate authority (CA), or you can generate one with the Certificate Creation Tool (Makecert.exe). Usually, however, you want a valid code-signing certificate from a well-known trusted CA, such as Verisign, Thawte, or your corporation's internal public key infrastructure (PKI). Otherwise, sharing your scripts or configuration files with others might be difficult because your computer isn't a trusted CA by default.

NOTE

The "Code Signing" section of this chapter explains how to obtain a valid trusted code-signing certificate. Reading this section is strongly recommended because of the importance of digitally signing scripts and configuration files.

RemoteSigned

The RemoteSigned execution policy is designed to prevent remote PowerShell scripts and configuration files that aren't digitally signed by a trusted publisher from running or loading automatically. Scripts and configuration files that are locally created can be loaded and run without being digitally signed, however.

A remote script or configuration file can be obtained from a communication application, such as Microsoft Outlook, Internet Explorer, Outlook Express, or Windows Messenger. Running or loading a file downloaded from any of these applications results in the following error message:

```
PS C:\Scripts> .\interscript.ps1

The file C:\Scripts\interscript.ps1 cannot be loaded. The file
C:\Scripts\interscript.ps1 is not digitally signed. The script will
not execute on the system. Please see "get-help about_signing" for
more details..
At line:1 char:17
+ .\interscript.ps1 <<<<

PS C:\Scripts>
```

To run or load an unsigned remote script or configuration file, you must specify whether to trust the file. To do this, right-click the file in Windows Explorer and click Properties. In the General tab, click the Unblock button (see Figure 5.1).

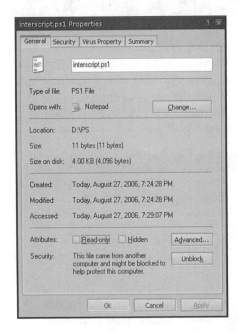

FIGURE 5.1   Trusting a remote script or configuration file

After you trust the file, the script or configuration file can be run or loaded. If it's digitally signed, but the publisher isn't trusted, however, PowerShell displays the following prompt:

```
PS C:\Scripts> .\signed.ps1

Do you want to run software from this untrusted publisher?
File C:\Scripts\signed.ps1 is published by CN=companyabc.com, OU=IT,
O=companyabc.com, L=Oakland, S=California, C=US and is not trusted on
your system. Only run scripts from trusted publishers.

[V] Never run  [D] Do not run  [R] Run once  [A] Always run  [?] Help
(default is "D"):
```

In this case, you must choose whether to trust the file content.

NOTE

Please see the section "Code Signing" section for more details on the options presented at this prompt.

Unrestricted

As the name suggests, the Unrestricted execution policy removes almost all restrictions for running scripts or loading configuration files. All local or signed trusted files can run or load, but for remote files, PowerShell prompts you to choose an option for running or loading that file, as shown here:

```
PS C:\Scripts> .\remotescript.ps1

Security Warning
Run only scripts that you trust. While scripts from the Internet can
be useful, this script can potentially harm your computer. Do you want
to run
C:\Scripts\remotescript.ps1?

[D] Do not run  [R] Run once  [S] Suspend  [?] Help (default is "D"):
```

Setting the Execution Policy

To change the execution policy, you use the Set-ExecutionPolicy cmdlet, shown here:

```
PS C:\> set-executionpolicy AllSigned

PS C:\>
```

If you want to know the current execution policy, use the Get-ExecutionPolicy cmdlet:

```
PS C:\> get-executionpolicy

AllSigned

PS C:\>
```

By default, when PowerShell is first installed, the execution policy is set to Restricted. As you know, default settings never stay default for long. In addition, if PowerShell is installed on many machines, the likelihood of its execution policy being set to Unrestricted increases. Fortunately, Microsoft has provided a Group Policy Administrative Template called PowerShellExecutionPolicy.adm to enable Active Directory administrators to centrally control the PowerShell execution policy at a domain level. This is accomplished by creating a Group Policy Object (GPO) to define the desired execution policy setting, which is then applied by all machines in the domain where PowerShell is installed. To create a new GPO to centrally administer the PowerShell execution policy for workstations in your domain, follow these steps:

1. Log on to a GPO management machine as the GPO administrator.

2. Download and install the Administrative Templates for Windows PowerShell. Visit www.microsoft.com and search for "Administrative Templates for Windows PowerShell," and then download the file from the link provided.

3. Using the Group Policy MMC, create a GPO named **PowerShell Script Execution Policy**.

4. In the console tree, click to expand **Computer Configuration** and then **Administrative Templates**.

5. Right-click **Administrative Templates** and click **Add/Remove Templates** in the shortcut menu.

6. Navigate to the folder with the PowerShellExecutionPolicy.adm file. By default, this file is located in C:\Program Files\Microsoft Group Policy. Select the file, click **Open**, and then click **Close**. The PowerShell node is then displayed under the Administrative Templates node.

7. Click the **Administrative Templates** node, and then click **View**, **Filtering** from the Group Policy MMC menu. Click to clear the **Only show policy settings that can be fully managed** checkbox. Clearing this option enables you to manage preference settings.

8. Next, click the **PowerShell** node under **Administrative Templates**.

9. In the details pane, right-click **Security Settings** and click **Properties** in the shortcut menu.

10. Click **Enabled**.

11. Set the **Execution Policy** to one of these values: Restricted, AllSigned, RemoteSigned, or Unrestricted.

12. Close the PowerShell Script Execution Policy GPO.

13. Link the **PowerShell Script Execution Policy** GPO at the domain level, and then close the Group Policy MMC.

Controlling the execution policy through a GPO preference setting might seem like a less than perfect solution. After all, a preference setting doesn't offer the same level of security as an execution policy setting, so users with the necessary rights can modify it easily. This lack of security is probably why Microsoft removed the original ADM file from PowerShell. A future release of PowerShell might allow controlling the execution policy with a valid GPO policy setting.

Code Signing

In an effort to learn how to sign PowerShell scripts and configuration files, you have searched the Internet, read several blogs about code signing, reviewed the PowerShell documentation, and even browsed through some PowerShell books. Yet the more you read about code signing, the more confused you are. Finally, in frustration, you open your PowerShell console and enter the following command:

```
set-executionpolicy unrestricted
```

Before you enter this command, remember what you learned about execution policies earlier in this chapter. Using the Unrestricted setting negates an important security layer that was designed to prevent malicious code from running on your system. Code signing is another essential component of PowerShell security, but many people believe it's too complicated to learn and set their execution policies to Unrestricted to avoid having to use it. In response to an entry on script signing at Scott Hanselman's blog (www.hanselman.com/blog), one person commented that "Handling code signing certificates is way over the head of most users, including average developers and admins." This statement indicates a real need that should be addressed, hence this section devoted to code signing. Code signing seems complicated on the surface, but with some clear instructions, the process is easy to understand. Scripters, developers, and administrators should be familiar with it as an important part of their overall security efforts.

What Is Code Signing?

In short, **code signing** is the process of digitally signing scripts, executables, dynamic link libraries (DLLs), and so forth to establish a level of trust for the code. The trust granted to digitally signed code is based on two assumptions. One, a signed piece of code ensures that the code hasn't been altered or corrupted since being signed. Two, the digital signature serves to prove the identity of the code's author, which helps you determine whether the code is safe for execution.

These two assumptions are a way to ensure the integrity and authenticity of code. However, these assumptions alone are no guarantee that signed code is safe to run. For these two assumptions to be considered valid, you need the digital signature and the infrastructure that establishes a mechanism for identifying the digital signature's originator.

A digital signature is based on public key cryptography, which has algorithms used for encryption and decryption. These algorithms generate a key pair consisting of a private key and a public key. The private key is kept secret so that only the owner has access to it, but the public key can be distributed to other entities. Some form of secure interaction is then required between other entities and the key pair owner. Depending on the type of interaction, one key is used to lock (encrypt) the communication, and the other key is used to unlock (decrypt) the communication. In digital signatures, the private key is used to generate a signature, and the public key is used to validate the generated signature. The process is as follows:

1. A one-way hash of the content (documents, code, and so forth) being signed is generated by using a cryptographic digest.

2. The hash is then encrypted with the private key, resulting in the digital signature.

3. Next, the content is transmitted to the recipient.

4. The recipient then creates another one-way hash of the content and decrypts the hash by using the sender's public key.

5. Finally, the recipient compares the two hashes. If both hashes are the same, the digital signature is valid and the content hasn't been modified.

NOTE

A one-way hash (also known as a message digest, fingerprint, or compression function) is a cryptographic algorithm that turns data into a fixed-length binary sequence. The term one-way comes from the fact that it is difficult to derive the original data from the resulting sequence.

To associate an entity, such as an organization, a person, or a computer, with a digital signature, a digital certificate is used. A digital certificate consists of the public key and identifying information about the key pair owner. To ensure a digital certificate's integrity, it's also digitally signed. A digital certificate can be signed by its owner or a trustworthy third party called a **certificate authority (CA).**

The act of associating code with the entity that created and published it removes the anonymity of running code. Furthermore, associating a digital signature with a code-signing certificate is much like using a brand name to establish trust and reliability. Armed with this information, users of PowerShell scripts and configuration files can make informed decisions about running a script or loading a configuration file. This, in a nutshell, is why code signing is an important aspect of the PowerShell security framework.

Obtaining a Code-Signing Certificate

There are two methods for obtaining a code-signing certificate: generating self-signed certificates and using a CA from a valid public key infrastructure (PKI).

Generating a self-signed certificate for signing your PowerShell scripts and configuration files is simpler and quicker and has the advantage of not costing anything. However, no independent third party verifies the certificate's authenticity, so it doesn't have the same level of trust that's expected from code signing. As a result, no other entity would trust your certificate by default. To distribute your PowerShell script or configuration file to other machines, your certificate would have to be added as a trusted root CA and a trusted publisher.

Although changing what an entity trusts is possible, there are two problems. One, entities outside your sphere of control might not choose to trust your certificate because there's no independent method for verifying who you are. Two, if the private key associated with your self-signed certificate becomes compromised or invalid, there's no way to manage your certificate's validity on other entities. Given these problems, limiting the use of self-signed certificates to a local machine or for testing purposes is recommended.

If you plan to digitally sign your scripts and configuration files so that they can be used in an enterprise or even the public realm, you should consider the second method of obtaining a code-signing certificate: a CA from a valid PKI. A valid PKI can mean a well-known and trusted commercial organization, such as www.globalsign.net, www.thawte.com, `www.verisign.com`, or an internal PKI owned and operated by your organization. Obtaining a code-signing certificate from an external PKI can be quick and easy, as long as you keep a few caveats in mind.

First, a certificate must be purchased from the owner of the external PKI. Second, because you're purchasing the certificate from an outside entity, you're placing a lot of trust in the organization's integrity. For these reasons, code-signing certificates from commercial PKIs should be limited to certificates used to sign scripts and configuration files for public distribution.

Therefore, an internal PKI should be used for scripts and configuration files not meant for public consumption. Keep in mind that deploying and managing an internal PKI takes planning, effort, and money (Hardware Security Modules [HSM], security consultants, and so forth can be expensive). Most organizations tend to shy away from the effort required to set up a PKI. Instead, they bring up CAs ad hoc, purchase certificates from commercial PKIs, or ignore PKI requirements. A commercial PKI might not provide the level of trust your organization needs, and the ad-hoc approach isn't recommended because it reduces trust of certificates generated by rogue CAs which are CAs that have a low level of assurance around their integrity. Having no valid PKI infrastructure can make internal distribution of digitally signed files difficult. Finally, organizations that ignore PKI requirements illustrate another drawback of using an internal PKI: time.

If there's no PKI in your organization, obtaining a code-signing certificate might take an extended period of time. PKIs do not materialize overnight. If you have identified a PKI requirement for your scripts, there are probably additional PKI requirements in your organization. These requirements need to be identified and considered before a PKI is deployed. Trying to drive a PKI deployment around your needs alone isn't the best approach for an infrastructure service that needs to meet the needs of an entire organization. After you have presented the PKI requirement to your organization, you might have to wait for the services to be provided. However, after the PKI is in place, you can obtain code-signing certificates knowing that the infrastructure fully supports the distribution of your signed PowerShell scripts and configuration files.

Method One: Self-Signed Certificate

This method of creating a self-signed certificate is based on using the makecert utility, which is part of the .NET Framework Software Development Kit (SDK). Follow these steps:

1. Download the latest Microsoft .NET Framework SDK by visiting www.microsoft.com and searching for "Microsoft .NET Framework SDK." At the time of this writing, the current .NET Framework SDK version is 2.0.

2. Install the SDK on the machine where you want to generate the self-signed certificate.

3. Locate the **makecert** utility on your system. The default location is C:\Program Files\Microsoft.NET\SDK\v2.0\Bin.

4. Open a cmd command prompt and change the working directory to the location of the makecert utility using the cd command.

5. Create a self-signed certificate by using the following command:

```
makecert -r -pe -n "CN=CertificateCommonName" -b 01/01/2000 -e 01/01/2099 –eku
1.3.6.1.5.5.7.3.3 -ss My
```

You should see output similar to the following:

```
C:\Program Files\Microsoft Visual Studio 8\SDK\v2.0\Bin>makecert -r -
pe -n "CN= Turtle Code Signing" -b 01/01/2000 -e 01/01/2099 -eku
1.3.6.1.5.5.7.3.3 -ss My
Succeeded
```

6. Finally, use the following PowerShell command to verify that the certificate was installed:

```
PS C:\> get-childitem cert:\CurrentUser\My —codesign
    Directory:
Microsoft.PowerShell.Security\Certificate::CurrentUser\My
Thumbprint                                 Subject
----------                                 -------
944E910757A862B53DE3113249E12BCA9C7DD0DE   CN=Turtle Code Signing
PS C:\>
```

Method Two: CA Signed Certificate

This method is based on obtaining a code-signing certificate from a Microsoft Windows CA. These steps assume a PKI has been deployed at your organization. If not, installing Windows Certificate Services to meet your immediate need isn't recommended. Follow these steps to set up a code-signing certificate:

1. Request that your PKI administrator create and enable a code-signing certificate template for your PowerShell scripts and configuration files.

2. Use Internet Explorer to access the Certificate Services Web Enrollment site at https://*CAServerName*/certsrv (replacing *CAServerName* with the name of your server).

3. Click the **Request a Certificate** link.

4. On the Request a Certificate page, click the **Advanced certificate request** link.

5. On the Advanced Certificate Request page, click the **Create and submit a request to this** CA link.

6. In the Certificate Template section, click to select the code-signing certificate your PKI administrator created.

7. Enter the rest of the identifying information and certificate request options according to your organization's certificate policy. You can use Figure 5.2 as a guideline.

FIGURE 5.2   Example of requesting a code signing certificate

8. Click the **Submit** button.

9. In the **Potential Scripting Violation** dialog box that opens (see Figure 5.3), click **Yes** to continue.

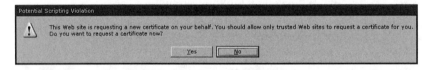

FIGURE 5.3   Potential Scripting Violation message box

10. Next, if applicable, set the private key security level based on your organization's certificate policy (see Figure 5.4), and then click **OK**.

11. If your organization's certificate policy requires approval from a certificate manager, then ask your certificate manager to approve the certificate request you just submitted. If approval isn't required, go to step 16.

12. After the certificate request has been approved, use Internet Explorer to access the Certificate Services Web Enrollment site at `https://CAServerName/certsrv` (replacing *CAServerName* with the name of your server).

FIGURE 5.4   Creating a new RSA signature key dialog box

13. Click the **View the status of a pending certificate request** link.

14. On the next page, click the appropriate certificate request link.

15. On the Certificate Issued page, click the **Install this certificate** link.

16. In the **Potential Scripting Violation** dialog box that opens (see Figure 5.5), click **Yes** to continue.

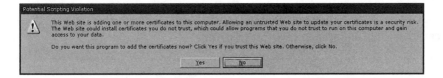

FIGURE 5.5   Potential Scripting Violation message box

17. Finally, the Certificate Services Web Enrollment site states that the certificate was installed successfully. Use the following PowerShell command to verify the certificate installation status:

```
PS C:\> get-childitem cert:\CurrentUser\My -codesign

    Directory:
Microsoft.PowerShell.Security\Certificate::CurrentUser\My
Thumbprint                                Subject
----------                                -------
5CBCE258711676061836BC45C1B4ACA6F6C7D09E
E=Richard.Stallman@goodcode.com, C...
PS C:\>
```

The PVK Digital Certificate Files Importer

When a digital certificate is generated, sometimes the private key is stored in a PVK (private key) file, and the corresponding digital certificate is stored in a Software Publishing Certificate (SPC) file. When a code-signing certificate has been obtained from Verisign or Thawte, for example, the digital certificate is issued to you as a SPC and PVK file combination. If you want to use the code-signing certificate to digitally sign PowerShell scripts or configuration files, you must import the SPC and PVK file combination into your personal certificate store.

> **NOTE**
>
> A **certificate store** is a location that resides on a computer or device that is used to store certificate information. In Windows, you can use the Certificates MMC snapin to display the certificate store for a user, a computer, or a service. Your personal certificate store is referring to your own "user" certificate store.

To import the SPC+PVK, you use the Microsoft utility called PVK Digital Certificate Files Importer. To download it, visit www.microsoft.com and search for "PVK Digital Certificate Files Importer."

Next, enter the following command to import the SPC+PVK, substituting your own filenames:

```
pvkimprt -IMPORT "mycertificate.spc" "myprivatekey.pvk"
```

Signing PowerShell Scripts

When signing a PowerShell script, you use the Set-AuthenticodeSignature cmdlet, which takes two required parameters. The first parameter, filePath, is the path and file-name for the script or file to be digitally signed. The second parameter, certificate, is the X.509 certificate used to sign the script or file. To obtain the X.509 certificate in a format the Set-AuthenticodeSignature cmdlet understands, you retrieve the certificate as an object with the Get-ChildItem cmdlet, as shown in this example:

```
PS C:\> set-authenticodesignature —filePath signed.ps1 —certificate
@(get-childitem cert:\CurrentUser\My —codeSigningCert)[0] —
includeChain "All"
    Directory: C:\
SignerCertificate                              Status         Path
-----------------                              ------         ----
5CBCE258711676061836BC45C1B4ACA6F6C7D09E       Valid          signed.ps1
PS C:\>
```

To retrieve the certificate you want from the user's certificate store, you use the Get-ChildItem cmdlet with the codeSigningCert SwitchParameter. This SwitchParameter can be used only with the PowerShell Certificate provider and acts as a filter to force the Get-ChildItem cmdlet to retrieve only code-signing certificates. Last, to ensure that the entire certificate chain is included in the digital signature, the includeChain parameter is used.

After the Set-AuthenticodeSignature cmdlet has been executed successfully, the signed file has a valid digital signature block containing the digital signature. A signature block in a PowerShell script or configuration file is always the last item in the file and can be found easily because it's enclosed between SIG # Begin signature block and SIG # End signature block, as shown here:

```
write-host ("This is a signed script!") -Foregroundcolor Green
# SIG # Begin signature block
# MIIIHQYJKoZIhvcNAQcCoIIIDjCCCAoCAQExCzAJBgUrDgMCGgUAMGkGCisGAQQB
# gjcCAQSgWzBZMDQGCisGAQQBgjcCAR4wJgIDAQAABBAfzDtgWUsITrck0sYpfvNR
# AgEAAgEAAgEAAgEAAgEAMCEwCQYFKw4DAhoFAAQUOBxWZ+ceVCY8SKcVLl/3iq2F
# w0OgggYVMIIGETCCBPmgAwIBAgIKcsuBWwADAAAAIzANBgkqhkiG9w0BAQUFADBE
...
# KwYBBAGCNwIBCzEOMAwGCisGAQQBgjcCARUwIwYJKoZIhvcNAQkEMRYEFG+QcdwH
# dHiuftHilhdyHCeSl0UgMA0GCSqGSIb3DQEBAQUABIGAZxItZJ+uo1E/cVhOCFex
# 9hinxULa3s0urQi362qa+NQ7yV3XczQOAPl0/kBIrEcwFN6YyS7PPm0wkCAPnfib
# 4J3uKxZK+4l9iHTiEVmp1ZO5G+P3KrqUS9ktFs7v9yTgqc8JLznxsRLvMwZpAMB0
# R2792YGWH5Jy4AwDYeljQ6Y=
# SIG # End signature block
```

NOTE

This process for digitally signing scripts also applies to PowerShell configuration files. Configuration files, depending on the execution policy setting, might also need to be signed before they are loaded into a PowerShell session.

Verifying Digital Signatures

To verify the digital signature of PowerShell scripts and configuration files, you use the Get-AuthentiCodeSignature cmdlet. It returns a valid status or an invalid status, such as HashMismatch, indicating a problem with the file.

Valid status:

```
PS C:\> get-authenticodesignature signed.ps1


    Directory: C:\
SignerCertificate                           Status              Path
-----------------                           ------              ----
5CBCE258711676061836BC45C1B4ACA6F6C7D09E    Valid               signed.ps1


PS C:\> .\signed.ps1

This is a signed script!

PS C:\>
```

Invalid status:

```
PS C:\> Get-AuthenticodeSignature signed.ps1


    Directory: C:\
SignerCertificate                           Status              Path
-----------------                           ------              ----
5CBCE258711676061836BC45C1B4ACA6F6C7D09E    HashMismatch        signed.ps1

PS C:\ .\signed.ps1

File C:\signed.ps1 cannot be loaded. The contents of file
D:\signed.ps1 may have been tampered because the hash of the file does
not match the hash stored in the digital signature. The script will
not execute on the system. Please see "get-help about_signing" for
more details.

At line:1 char:12
+ .\signed.ps1 <<<<

PS C:\>
```

Based on the error in the preceding example, the script has been modified or tampered with or is corrupt. If the script has been modified by its owner, it must be signed again before it can be used. If the script has been tampered with or is corrupt, it should be discarded because its validity and authenticity can no longer be trusted.

Signed Code Distribution

Distributing signed PowerShell scripts and configuration files requires the user to determine whether to trust code from a particular publisher. The first step is to validate the publisher's identity based on a chain of trust. To establish a chain of trust, the user uses the publisher's code-signing certificate associated with the digital signature to verify that the certificate owner is indeed the publisher. For example, Figure 5.6 shows an unbroken path (or chain) of valid certificates from the publisher's certificate to a trusted root certificate (or trust anchor).

FIGURE 5.6   The certificate path

When a well-known trusted public root CA or internally trusted root CA is the trust anchor for the publisher's certificate, the user explicitly trusts that the publisher's identity claims are true.

For Windows users, if a root CA is considered trusted, that CA's certificate resides in the Trusted Root Certification Authorities certificate store (see Figure 5.7).

When a root CA is not a valid trust anchor or the certificate is self-signed, the user needs to decide whether to trust a publisher's identity claim. If the user determines the identity claim to be valid, the root CA's certificate or the self-signed certificate should be added to the Trusted Root Certification Authorities certificate store to establish a valid chain of trust.

After the publisher's identity has been verified or trusted, the next step is deciding whether the signed code is safe for execution. If a user has previously decided that code from a publisher is safe for execution, the code (PowerShell script or configuration file) runs without further user action.

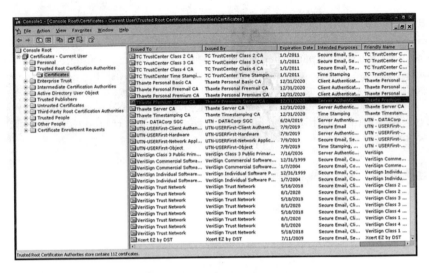

FIGURE 5.7   Trusted Root Certification Authorities certificate store

For Windows users, if a publisher is considered trusted, its code-signing certificate resides in the Trusted Publishers certificate store (see Figure 5.8).

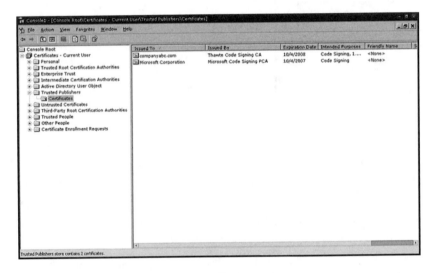

FIGURE 5.8   Trusted Publishers certificate store

If a publisher is not trusted, PowerShell prompts the user to decide whether to run signed code from that publisher, as shown in this example:

```
PS C:\> .\signed.ps1

Do you want to run software from this untrusted publisher?
File C:\signed.ps1 is published by CN=companyabc.com, OU=IT,
O=companyabc.com, L=Oakland, S=California, C=US and is not trusted on
your system. Only run scripts from trusted publishers.

[V] Never run  [D] Do not run  [R] Run once  [A] Always run  [?] Help
(default is "D"):
```

The following list explains the available options:

- *[V] Never run*—This option places the publisher's certificate in the user's Untrusted Certificates certificate store. After a publisher's certificate has been determined to be untrusted, PowerShell never allows code from that publisher to run unless the certificate is removed from the Untrusted Certificates certificate store or the execution policy is set to Unrestricted or RemoteSigned.

- *[D] Do not run*—This option, which is the default, halts execution of the untrusted code.

- *[R] Run once*—This option allows one-time execution of the untrusted code.

- *[A] Always run*—This option places the publisher's certificate in the user's Trusted Publishers certificate store. Also, the root CA's certificate is placed in the Trusted Root Certification Authorities certificate store, if it isn't already there.

Enterprise Code Distribution

You might be wondering how to control what code is considered trusted in your organization. Obviously, having users or machines decide what to trust defeats the purpose of distributing signed code in a managed environment. If your environment is managed, your PKI deployment should have methods for controlling what's trusted in an organization. If your organization is a Windows environment, the most common method is through GPO. For example, you can define trusted publishers by using a Certificate Trust List (CTL) or manage them through the Internet Explorer Maintenance extension.

Public Code Distribution

Determining trust in the public realm is entirely different. When establishing trust between two private entities, they are able to define what is and isn't trusted. When dealing with public entities, you don't have this level of control. It is up to those public entities to determine what they do or do not trust.

PowerShell Security Best Practices

Security has often been an area that was not considered during the development of software. Unfortunately, this has frequently been true for scripting as well. This type of approach is no longer feasible in today's security-focused business environments. A failure of technology security in a business today can have a lasting impact on the financial health of a business, damage its reputation in the business community, and even expose the customers of the business to such threats as identity theft. For these reasons, the next three sections may be the most important sections in this chapter because they deal with PowerShell script security best practices.

Digitally Sign PowerShell Scripts and Configuration Files

As emphasized earlier in this chapter, you should always digitally sign your PowerShell scripts and configuration files so that users and machines that run your scripts can trust that the code is actually from you and hasn't been tampered with or corrupted. Adhering to this practice also means you can keep the PowerShell execution policy on your machine and others in your organization set to AllSigned.

> **NOTE**
>
> Code signing doesn't apply just to PowerShell scripts and configuration files. You can apply the principles of code signing to other items, such as executables, macros, DLLs, other scripts, device drivers, firmware images, and so forth. Other code can benefit from the security of digital signatures, and you can further limit the possibility of untrusted code running in your environment.

Never Set Execution Policies to Unrestricted

Setting your execution policy to Unrestricted is like leaving an open door for malicious code to run on your systems. Because of this risk, you should set your execution policy to RemoteSigned at a minimum. This setting still allows you to run scripts and load configuration files created locally on your machine, but it prevents remote code that hasn't been signed and trusted from running. However, the RemoteSigned setting isn't foolproof and could allow some remote code to run through PowerShell.

Following these guidelines and becoming proficient in code signing are crucial to guaranteeing that your PowerShell environment doesn't become a target for malicious code. Setting your execution policy to AllSigned increases security even more because it requires that all scripts and configuration files be signed by a trusted source before running or loading them.

Try to Run Scripts with the Minimum Required Rights

IT security practices include following the principle of least privileges, which ensures that entities such as users, processes, and software are granted only the minimum rights needed to perform a legitimate action. For example, if a user doesn't need administrative rights to run a word-processing program, there's no reason to grant that user the administrative level of privileges.

The principle of least privileges also applies to scripting. When you're developing a script, make an effort to code in a manner that requires the minimum rights to run the script. In addition, document the required rights to run your script in case they aren't apparent to users. If users don't know the required rights to run a script, they might try running it with administrative rights, which increases the possibility of causing unwanted and possibly damaging changes to your environment.

PowerShell 2.0 CTP2 and Windows Remote Management (WinRM)

With the introduction of PowerShell 2.0 CTP2, the PowerShell team has introduced the concept of **remoting**, which allows PowerShell commands to be executed against remote machines by leveraging the capabilities of a protocol called **WinRM**. As described in Chapter 2, "Basic PowerShell Concepts," WinRM is Microsoft's implementation of the **WS-Management Protocol**, which is a **Simple Object Access Protocol (SOAP)**-based protocol that provides a common method for systems to access and exchange management information. Although the addition of remoting is a major step forward in the capabilities of PowerShell, it also introduces a whole new range of potential security concerns. Fortunately, it is possible to centrally manage and configure WinRM to ensure that these powerful new remoting capabilities can be implemented securely in an enterprise. This section provides an overview of the tools and techniques needed to accomplish this.

Configuring WinRM

The primary utility used to manage WinRM settings is called winrm.cmd. After you have installed WinRM using the procedures described in Chapter 2, you can enter the command winrm from a PowerShell prompt to get an overview of the syntax and available commands as shown in the following:

```
PS C:\> winrm

Windows Remote Management Command Line Tool
Windows Remote Management (WinRM) is the Microsoft implementation of
the WS-Management protocol which provides a secure way to communicate
with local and remote computers using web services.

Usage:
  winrm OPERATION RESOURCE_URI [-SWITCH:VALUE [-SWITCH:VALUE] ...]
        [@{KEY=VALUE[;KEY=VALUE]...}]
For help on a specific operation:
...
```

After WinRM is first installed, remote functionality is disabled by default. To perform an initial default setup of WinRM, enter the command `winrm quickconfig` at the PowerShell command prompt. This command performs several tasks:

- Sets the WinRM service to automatically start.
- Starts the WinRM service.
- Creates a WinRM listener to accept WS-Man requests.
- Enables the WinRM firewall exception.

Following is an example of the output of the `winrm quickconfig` command:

```
PS C:\> winrm quickconfig

WinRM is not set up to allow remote access to this machine for
management.
The following changes must be made:

Set the WinRM service type to auto start.
Start the WinRM service.
Create a WinRM listener on HTTP://* to accept WS-Man requests to any
IP on this machine.
Enable the WinRM firewall exception.

Make these changes [y/n]? y

WinRM has been updated for remote management.
WinRM service type changed successfully.
WinRM service started.
Created a WinRM listener on HTTP://* to accept WS-Man requests to any
IP on this machine.
WinRM firewall exception enabled.

PS C:\>
```

After the initial configuration of WinRM has been performed, additional customization of the WinRM service on the machine can be performed using the `winrm` command-line utility, such as changing the listener ports from the default of 80 and 443.

Working with Windows Remote Shell (WinRS)

WinRM also includes a component known as Windows Remote Shell (WinRS). WinRS is a tool that can be used to remotely execute programs and scripts on a remote machine. WinRS is also used extensively by PowerShell 2.0 CTP2's remoting functions. Here's an example of running a WinRS command on a Windows XP computer named **XP1** to obtain the IP configuration information from a remote computer named **XP2**:

```
PS C:\> winrs -r:XP2.companyabc.com ipconfig /all
Windows IP Configuration
        Host Name . . . . . . . . . . . . : xp2
        Primary Dns Suffix  . . . . . . . : companyabc.com
        Node Type . . . . . . . . . . . . : Hybrid
        IP Routing Enabled. . . . . . . . : No
        WINS Proxy Enabled. . . . . . . . : No
        DNS Suffix Search List. . . . . . : companyabc.com
Ethernet adapter Local Area Connection:
        Connection-specific DNS Suffix  . : companyabc.com
        Description . . . . . . . . . . . : VMware Accelerated AMD
                                            PCNet Adapter
        Physical Address. . . . . . . . . : 00-0C-29-B8-42-7D
        Dhcp Enabled. . . . . . . . . . . : Yes
        Autoconfiguration Enabled . . . . : Yes
        IP Address. . . . . . . . . . . . : 10.1.0.61
        Subnet Mask . . . . . . . . . . . : 255.255.0.0
        Default Gateway . . . . . . . . . : 10.1.0.1
        DHCP Server . . . . . . . . . . . : 10.1.0.50
        DNS Servers . . . . . . . . . . . : 10.1.0.50
        Lease Obtained. . . . . . . . . . : Wednesday, April 30, 2008
                                            5:13:22 PM
        Lease Expires . . . . . . . . . . : Thursday, May 08, 2008
                                            5:13:22 PM
PS C:\>
```

5

Although this command looks straightforward, there are a number of things going on in the background that may not be immediately apparent. Notice that the command winrs -r:XP2.companyabc.com ipconfig /all does not specify credentials to be used to connect to the XP2 computer, yet the command succeeds in returning the IP configuration information from XP2. This command works because both XP1 and XP2 are members of the **companyabc.com** Active Directory domain, and WinRS automatically attempts to authenticate to a remote machine using Kerberos authentication if no credentials are specified in the winrs command. In this case, the account that was used to run the command on XP1 was a member of the **Domain Admins** group in the **companyabc. com** domain, so WinRS was able to authenticate to the **companyabc.com** domain via Kerberos and access the XP2 machine using the logged-in credentials of the current user account on XP1. For situations where a remote machine may not support pass-through authentication via Kerberos, as shown in the example (such as workgroup machines or machines belonging to an untrusted Active Directory domain), WinRS also supports Basic authentication, Digest authentication, and Negotiate authentication. If none of these authentication methods are available, WinRS also provides support for maintaining a static list of trusted hosts. Finally, by default, all communication between the WinRS client and the WinRM service are encrypted.

NOTE

Although it is possible to use WinRS to run commands against a target machine that does not belong to the same Active Directory domain as the source machine, doing so lowers the effective security of WinRM on both machines, and should be done *only* in a lab environment to ensure that the machines are not compromised. Here is an example of how to do this using the WinRM command to allow a domain workstation to run remote commands against a workgroup server:

On the workstation, enter the following commands:

```
WinRM set winrm/config/service/auth @{Basic="true"}
WinRM set winrm/config/client @{TrustedHosts="<local>"}
WinRM set winrm/config/client @{TrustedHosts="ServerName"}
```

On the server, enter the following commands:

```
WinRM set winrm/config/service/auth @{Basic="true"}

WinRM set winrm/config/client @{TrustedHosts="<local>"}

WinRM set winrm/config/client @{TrustedHosts="WorkstationName"}
```

These commands enable the use of Basic authentication between the workstation and the server, allow the use of a local TrustedHosts file, and specify that the workstation explicitly trust the server and the server explicitly trust the workstation for WinRM traffic. You can now enter the following command on the workstation, specifying the appropriate credentials for the server, and run a remote ipconfig /all command against the server:

```
Winrs -r:ServerName -u:ServerUserName -p:ServerUserPassword ipconfig /all
```

Configuring WinRM and WinRS Settings Through Group Policy

As you can see from the WinRS example, WinRM and WinRS support many different authentication options, which if improperly configured can reduce the effective security of your environment and leave machines vulnerable to attack. Although WinRM and WinRS are generally secure when the installation defaults are left in place, it is easy for a locally privileged user to change these settings. To ensure that WinRM and WinRS configuration settings are consistently applied to machines that belong to an Active Directory domain, WinRM and WinRS configuration can be performed through Active Directory Group Policy.

When WinRM is installed on a machine, two new administrative template files are copied to **C:\WINDOWS\system32\GroupPolicy\Adm**. These files are named **windowsremotemanagement.adm** and **windowsremoteshell.adm**, and are used to manage Group Policy settings for the WinRS client and WinRM service.

To create a new GPO to centrally administer the WinRM configuration settings for machines in your domain, follow the steps:

1. Install WinRM on a GPO management machine, as described in Chapter 2.

2. Log on to a GPO management machine as the GPO administrator.

3. Using the Group Policy MMC, create a GPO named **WinRM Configuration Policy**.

4. Right-click the **WinRM Configuration Policy** and choose **Edit.**

5. In the console tree, click to expand **Computer Configuration > Administrative Templates > Windows Components**.

6. You will see two nodes named **Windows Remote Management (WinRM)** and **Windows Remote Shell**, as shown in Figure 5.9.

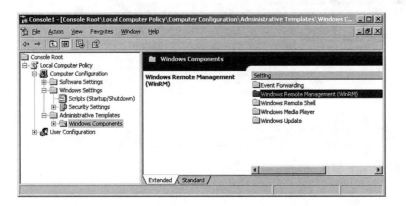

FIGURE 5.9   Windows Remote Management GPO Settings Nodes

7. The **Windows Remote Management (WinRM)** node contains configuration settings for the WinRM Client and the WinRM Service. The **Windows Remote Shell** node contains settings that apply to the WinRS Client.

8. Review the available configuration settings under WinRM Client and WinRM Service, as shown in Figures 5.10 through 5.12.

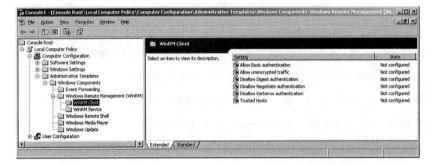

FIGURE 5.10   WinRM Client GPO Settings

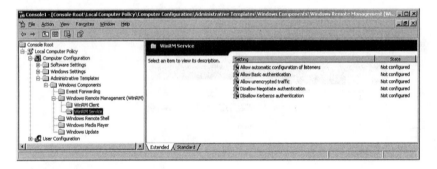

FIGURE 5.11   WinRM Service GPO Settings

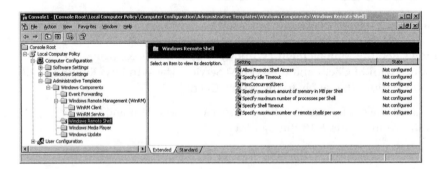

FIGURE 5.12   Windows Remote Shell GPO Settings

9. Depending on the security requirements of your environment, you may want to disable certain functionality globally. For example, both the WinRM Client and WinRM Service support the option to disallow Basic authentication as well as disallow unencrypted traffic. The WinRM Client also supports disallowing trusted hosts.

After you have configured the settings that you want, close the **WinRM Configuration Policy** GPO.

Link the **WinRM Configuration Policy** GPO at the domain level, and then close the Group Policy MMC.

Summary

This chapter provided an in-depth exploration into PowerShell security. Although this chapter covered a wide range of security topics and technical concepts, the key thing to remember is that PowerShell 2.0 CTP2 was designed to be secure by default, and it provides a number of powerful mechanisms to ensure that it can be integrated into any Windows environment while adhering to security best practices. However, as you begin to work with PowerShell and create your own scripts, it is crucial to have a clear understanding of code signing and to always sign any scripts that are used in a production environment. Although code signing is a new concept for many scripters, and the concepts involved may seem arcane at first, code signing is a key defense against malicious or even just erroneous code that can easily damage your environment.

Just as Active Directory Group Policy can be used to establish a baseline of settings for PowerShell and WinRM in your environment, PKI also allows you to develop a framework of trust that allows your signed scripts to be distributed throughout your enterprise and used with a high degree of confidence. Although this chapter discusses PKI primarily in the context of signing code, PKI is an extremely powerful and capable set of tools that provides the technical means to accurately establish a trust level in almost any set of circumstances. Although PKI is a complex topic, there can be tremendous benefits for your organization if your interests lead you to extend the lessons learned in this chapter to your enterprise at large.

PART II

Using PowerShell

IN THIS PART

The PowerShell Language

This chapter focuses on performing traditional programming operations with PowerShell. Although many discussions of PowerShell emphasize the new features and capabilities of the language, the designers of the PowerShell language also drew extensively on existing programming and scripting languages to ensure that this new language encompassed the most useful features of these earlier languages. If you are already familiar with the concepts in this chapter, you can use your existing knowledge to become proficient that much more quickly. If you are just getting started with scripting and programming, you can be confident that the effort you put into understanding these language concepts will be applicable to working with PowerShell and can help you create a broader understanding of how programs and scripts accomplish their work. Regardless of your previous level of experience, the examples and discussions covered in this chapter help to illustrate how PowerShell can be used to efficiently accomplish your programming and scripting tasks.

Expressions and Operators

An **expression** in PowerShell can be understood as a calculation that evaluates an equation and returns a result. An **operator** in PowerShell is the element of an expression that actually performs the calculation (such as an addition or subtraction operand). Although expressions and operators are closely linked in their usage in PowerShell, this section discusses the implementation details of each of these elements and provides examples to illustrate how operators and expressions work together in PowerShell.

Expressions

The three general categories of expressions that are used in PowerShell are **arithmetic expressions** (expressions that return a numerical result), **assignment expressions** (expressions which are used to set, display, and modify variables), and **comparison expressions** (expressions which use Boolean logic to compare two values and return a True or False result).

Here is a simple example of an arithmetic expression being evaluated by PowerShell:

```
PS C:\> 1 + 1
2
```

The following example shows the use of an assignment expression to set the variable $a to the value Example Text String:

```
PS C:\> $a = "Example Text String"
PS C:\> $a
Example Text String
```

In this next example of a comparison expression, the variable $a is set to the value Example Text String, and the variable $b is set to the value Second Example Text String. The expressions $a -eq $b and $a -ne $b are then evaluated and return a True or False value, as shown in the following:

```
PS C:\> $a = "Example Text String"
PS C:\> $b = "Second Example Text String"
PS C:\> $a -eq $b
False
PS C:\> $a -ne $b
True
```

Operators

The PowerShell language contains a substantial number of **operators**, which are used to construct **expressions** that return information from PowerShell. Because of the large number of operators that are available in PowerShell, we first review a group of basic operators and then spend time looking at PowerShell's advanced operators in more detail.

Basic Operators

The six types of basic operators in PowerShell include arithmetic operators, assignment operators, comparison operators, pattern matching operators, regular expression operators, and logical and bitwise operators. One key characteristic of operators in PowerShell is that they can work against many different types of objects (such as numbers, strings, and arrays). For example, the arithmetic operator + can be used to concatenate two text strings into a third string as shown in the following example:

```
PS C:\> $a = "This string was concatenated "
PS C:\> $b = "using the addition operator."
PS C:\> $c = $a + $b
PS C:\> $c
This string was concatenated using the addition operator.
```

Table 6.1 describes the arithmetic operators and provides an example of their usage.

TABLE 6.1   PowerShell Arithmetic Operators

Operator Type	Operator	Description
Arithmetic	+	Adds two values together. (1 + 1 = 2)
Arithmetic	*	Multiplies the first value by the second value. (2 * 2 = 4)
Arithmetic	-	Subtracts the second value from the first value. (10 − 8 = 2)
Arithmetic	/	Divides the first value by the second value. (24 / 6 = 4)
Arithmetic	%	Returns the remainder of dividing the first value by the second value. (13 % 3 = 1)

PowerShell's **assignment operators** operate similarly to the arithmetic operators described in Table 6.1, but instead of working with two values on the left side of the equation and returning a result on the right side of the equation, assignment operators take a single variable on the left side of the equation, perform an operation against this variable, and then replace the contents of the original variable with the results of the operation (see Table 6.2).

TABLE 6.2   PowerShell Assignment Operators

Operator Type	Operator	Description
Assignment	=	Sets the variable to the value specified. ($a = 10)
Assignment	+=	Adds the specified value to the variable. ($a+=2, equivalent to $a=$a + 2)
Assignment	-=	Subtracts the specified value from the variable. ($a -=2, equivalent to $a=$a - 2)

TABLE 6.2   Continued

Operator Type	Operator	Description
Assignment	*=	Multiplies the variable by the specified value. ($a*=2, equivalent to $a=$a * 2)
Assignment	/=	Divides the variable by the specified value. ($a/=2, equivalent to $a=$a / 2)
Assignment	%=	Divides the variable by the specified value and sets the variable to be the value of the remainder. ($a%=3, equivalent to $a=$a % 3)

The **comparison operators** in PowerShell are used to compare a pair of variables and return a Boolean True or False result (see Table 6.3). Notice that for each comparison operator (such as -eq), two related operators begin with the letters C and I (such as -ceq and ieq). The prefix C on a comparison operator indicates case sensitivity (for instance, Hello is different from hello), and the I prefix indicates explicit case insensitivity (for instance, Hello and hello are treated the same way). By default, PowerShell's comparison operators are case insensitive when comparing two strings.

TABLE 6.3   PowerShell Comparison Operators

Operator Type	Operator	Description
Comparison	-eq (also -ceq and -ieq)	Compares the first variable to the second variable and returns a value of True if the variables match or False if they do not.
Comparison	-ne (also -cne and -ine)	Compares the first variable to the second variable and returns a value of False if the variables match or True if they do not.
Comparison	-gt (also -cgt and -igt)	Compares the first variable to the second variable and returns a value of True if the first variable is greater than the second variable or False if it is not.
Comparison	-ge (also -cge and -ige)	Compares the first variable to the second variable and returns a value of True if the first variable is greater than or equal to the second variable, False if it is not.
Comparison	-lt (also -clt and -ilt)	Compares the first variable to the second variable and returns a value of True if the first variable is less than the second variable or False if it is not.
Comparison	-le (also -cle and -ile)	Compares the first variable to the second variable and returns a value of True if the first variable is less than or equal to the second variable or False if it is not.

TABLE 6.3   Continued

Operator Type	Operator	Description
Comparison	-contains (also -ccontains and -icontains)	Compares the values on the left side of -contains to the values on the right side and returns a value of True if the value on the right is present in the values on the left or False if it is not.
Comparison	-notcontains (also -cnotcontains and -inotcontains)	Compares the values on the left side of -notcontains to the values on the right side and returns a value of False if the value on the right is present in the values on the left or True if it is not.

The **pattern matching operators** used in PowerShell also use Boolean logic to compare two strings of text and return a result. To provide more granular comparison abilities, the pattern matching operators work in conjunction with a set of **wildcards** to create patterns for matching. Four wildcard operators can be used in conjunction with the pattern matching operators -like and -notlike to perform comparisons. The pattern matching operators and their associated wildcards are described in the following two tables.

TABLE 6.4   PowerShell Pattern Matching Operators

Operator Type	Operator	Description
Pattern Matching	-like (also -clike and -ilike)	Compares the values on the left side of -like to the values on the right side and returns a value of True if the value on the right is present in the values on the left or False if it is not.
Pattern Matching	-notlike (also -cnotlike and -inotlike)	Compares the values on the left side of -notlike to the values on the right side and returns a value of False if the value on the right is present in the values on the left or True if it is not.

TABLE 6.5   Characters Used with PowerShell Pattern Matching Operators

Character	Description	Example
*	Matches any pattern; can also be used as part of a search string to match subsequent characters in the original string.	"apple" -like "a*" returns True
?	Used to specify a wildcard value for a single character in a string.	"apple" -like "a?p?e" returns True
[x-y]	Matches a range of characters in sequential order.	"apple" -like "[a-c]pple" returns True
[xy]	Matches any one of the specified characters.	"apple" -like "[a][p][p][l][e]" returns True

The **regular expression operators** are closely related to the pattern matching operators, and will be a familiar concept to users of VBScript or Perl. However, the regular expression operators (`-match`, `-notmatch`, and `-replace`) are more flexible than pattern matching operators. Regular expression operators support the same type of syntax and wildcards as the pattern matching operators, but the characters used with regular expressions are different from the pattern matching wildcards. These characters are described in the following tables.

TABLE 6.6   PowerShell Regular Expression Operators

Operator Type	Operator	Description
Regular Expression	`-match` (also `-cmatch` and `-imatch`)	Compares the values on the left side of `-match` to the values on the right side and returns a value of `True` if the value on the right matches the values on the left or `False` if it does not.
Regular Expression	`-notmatch` (also `-cnotmatch` and `-inotmatch`)	Compares the values on the left side of `-notmatch` to the values on the right side and returns a value of `False` if the value on the right matches the values on the left or `True` if it does not.
Regular Expression	`-replace` (also `-creplace` and `-ireplace`)	Compares the value on the left side of `-replace` with the first value on the right side. If the first value on the right matches all or part of the value on the left, replace the matching value on the left with the second value on the right.

TABLE 6.7   Characters Used with PowerShell Regular Expressions

Character	Description	Example
None	Matches exact characters or character sequence anywhere in the original value.	`"apple" -match "pl"` returns True
.	Matches any single character.	`"apple" -match "a...e"` returns True
[value]	Matches at least one of the characters between the brackets.	`"apple" -match "[pear]"` returns True
[range]	Matches at least one of the characters within the specified range.	`"apple" -match "a[a-z]ple"` returns True
[^]	Matches any characters except those in the brackets.	`"apple" -match "[^fig]"` returns True
^	Performs a match of the specified characters starting at the beginning of the original value.	`"apple" -match "^app"` returns True
$	Performs a match of the specified characters starting at the end of the original value.	`"apple" -match "ple$"` returns True
*	Matches any pattern; can also be used as part of a search string to match subsequent characters in the original string.	`"apple" -match "a*"` returns True

TABLE 6.7   Continued

Character	Description	Example
?	Matches a single character in a string.	"apple" –match "a?ple" returns True
+	Matches repeating instances of the preceding characters.	
\	Denotes the character following the backslash as an escaped character.	"apple$" -match "apple\$" returns True
\p(name)	Matches any character in the named character class specified by (name). Supported names are Unicode groups and block ranges.	"abcd defg" -match "\p{Ll}+" returns True
\P(name)	Matches text not included in groups and block ranges specified in (name).	1234 -match "\P{Ll}+" returns True
\w	Matches any word character. Equivalent to the Unicode character categories [\p{Ll} \p{Lu}\p{Lt}\p{Lo}\p{Nd}\p{Pc}]. If ECMAScript-compliant behavior is specified with the ECMAScript option, \w is equivalent to [a-zA-Z_0-9].	"abcd defg" -match "\w+" matches abcd
\W	Matches any nonword character. Equivalent to the Unicode categories [^\p{Ll}\p{Lu}\p{Lt}\p{Lo}\p{Nd}\p{Pc}].	"abcd defg" -match "\W+" matches the space
\s	Matches any white-space character. Equivalent to the Unicode character categories [\f\n\r\t\v\x85\p{Z}].	"abcd defg" -match "\s+" returns True
\S	Matches any non-white-space character. Equivalent to the Unicode character categories [^\f\n\r\t\v\x85\p{Z}].	"abcd defg" -match "\S+" returns True
\d	Matches any decimal digit. Equivalent to \p{Nd} for Unicode and [0-9] for non-Unicode behavior.	12345 -match "\d+" returns True
\D	Matches any nondigit. Equivalent to \P{Nd} for Unicode and [^0-9] for non-Unicode behavior.	"abcd" -match "\D+" returns True
{n}	Specifies exactly n matches; for example, (pizza){2}.	"abc" -match "\w{2}" returns True
{n,}	Specifies at least n matches; for example, (abc){2,}.	"abc" -match "\w{2,}" returns True
{n,m}	Specifies at least n, but no more than m, matches.	"abc" -match "\w{2,3}" returns True

The last category of operators that we cover in this section is the PowerShell **logical and bitwise operators**. These operators support only **integer** values in the current release of PowerShell, so they are used exclusively for numerical calculations. The logical and bitwise operators available in PowerShell 2.0 CTP are listed in Table 6.8.

TABLE 6.8   PowerShell Logical and Bitwise Operators

Operator Type	Operator	Description
Logical and Bitwise	-and	Performs a logical **and** of the left and right values.
Logical and Bitwise	-or	Performs a logical **or** of the left and right values.
Logical and Bitwise	-xor	Performs a logical **exclusive-or** of the left and right values.
Logical and Bitwise	-not	Returns the logical **complement** of the argument value.
Logical and Bitwise	-band	Performs a **binary and** of the bits in the left and right values.
Logical and Bitwise	-bor	Performs a **binary or** of the bits in the left and right values.
Logical and Bitwise	-bxor	Performs a **binary exclusive-or** of the bits in the left and right values.
Logical and Bitwise	-bnot	Return the **bitwise complement** of the argument value.

Advanced Operators

In addition to the basic operators described in the previous section, PowerShell also supports several advanced operators. These advanced operators include **type operators**, **unary operators**, **grouping operators**, **array operators**, **property and method operators**, **format operators**, and **redirection operators**. This section describes each of these operators and provides examples of how they are used in PowerShell operations.

Type operators serve as a method to compare the types of two different objects and return a Boolean True or False value. There is also a type operator to change the type of an object to another type. The following example shows the use of the -is, -isnot, and -as type operators to verify the type of a string, and then it displays a second numerical string as an integer.

```
PS C:\> $a = "This is an example string"
PS C:\> $a -is [string]
True
PS C:\> $a -isnot [string]
False
PS C:\> $b = "256"
PS C:\> $b -as [int]
256
```

Unary operators are similar to the **arithmetic operators** discussed in the section on basic operators. The unary operators include +, -, ++, --, |<type>|, and , (the comma). Unary operators can change a number into a positive or negative number, increment or decrement a number, change the type of a variable, or create a single element array. The following example shows each of these unary operators in use:

```
PS C:\> $a = 3 * 6
PS C:\> -$a
-18
PS C:\> $b = "256"
PS C:\> +$b
256
PS C:\> --$a
PS C:\> $a
17
PS C:\> ++$a
PS C:\> $a
18
PS C:\> [int] "0xDEADBEEF"
-559038737
PS C:\> ,(3*7)
21
PS C:\>
```

Grouping operators are used in PowerShell to bring together a set of terms and perform an operation against these terms. The three types of grouping operators include **parentheses** (used to group expression operators), the **subexpressions grouping operator** (the $ symbol, used to group together collections of statements), and the **array subexpressions operator** (the @ symbol, used to group together collections of statements and insert the results into an array). Each of these grouping operators is demonstrated in the following example:

```
PS C:\> (3 * 7) + 4
25
PS C:\> $($a = "s*";get-process $a)
Handles  NPM(K)    PM(K)      WS(K) VM(M)   CPU(s)     Id ProcessName
-------  ------    -----      ----- -----   ------     -- -----------
    332       8     2224       5312    37   562.27    800 services
     21       1      164        372     4     0.04    644 smss
    156       6     3608       5756    48     0.89   1924 spoolsv
    301       9     3860       7600    49     0.81   1644 svchost
    632       0        0        264     2   124.16      4 System

PS C:\> @(get-date;get-executionpolicy)
Monday, June 30, 2008 5:14:11 PM
RemoteSigned
```

The **array operators** are a set of PowerShell operators that enable arrays to be created, modified, and reordered. Array operators can work with arrays that are one-dimensional or multidimensional. Because the use of array operators is so closely linked to working with arrays, we discuss the use of array operators in the section on arrays later in this chapter.

Property and method operators are some of the most commonly used operators in PowerShell. The basic property operator is the **period** (.), which is used to access properties of a variable. In the following example, the string $a is set to 12345, and then the period operator is used to access the Length property of the variable $a using the syntax $a.Length.

```
PS C:\> $a = "12345"
PS C:\> $a.Length
5
```

> **NOTE**
>
> When you are working with properties of a variable, one of the helpful features of PowerShell is the **tab completion** feature. Tab completion enables you to enter the variable name, the period property operator, and then press the **Tab** key to cycle through the available properties for that variable. Try setting a variable in a PowerShell session, enter just the variable name and a period (as in $a.), and then press the **Tab** key repeatedly to view the property options for the variable.

The PowerShell **method operators** are frequently used in conjunction with the property operators to provide finer control over the data that is returned from a property query. The basic syntax for using method operators with the period property operator is as follows:

```
<variable-name>.<method-name>(method-argument1,method-argument2…)
```

The next example shows the string variable $b being set to 1234567890, and then shows the SubString method being called with an argument of (0,4) to return the first four characters of the $b string.

```
PS C:\> $b = "1234567890"
PS C:\> $b.substring(0,4)
1234
```

A second frequently used PowerShell method operator is the **double colon** (::). The double colon is used to access members of a specific class of objects, and it is technically referred to as a **static member accessor**. Because the double colon method operator is working with members of a class, the argument on the left side of the double colon must be a valid type name, and the argument on the right side must be a valid member name for the class on the left, as in the example [string]::Equals. To obtain a list of valid methods for a given type, you can use the command [<type-name>] | Get-Member -static, replacing **<type-name>** with the specific type in which you are interested. The following example shows the available static methods for the char type using the command [char] | Get-Member -static.

```
PS C:\> [char] | get-member -static
   TypeName: System.Char
Name                   MemberType Definition
----                   ---------- ----------
ConvertFromUtf32       Method     static System.String ConvertFromUtf32(Int32
                                  utf32)
ConvertToUtf32         Method     static System.Int32 ConvertToUtf32(Char
                                  highSurrogate, Char lowSurrogate), static Syst...
Equals                 Method     static System.Boolean Equals(Object objA, Object
                                  objB)
GetNumericValue        Method     static System.Double GetNumericValue(Char c),
                                  static System.Double GetNumericValue(Str...
GetUnicodeCategory     Method     static System.Globalization.UnicodeCategory
                                  GetUnicodeCategory(Char c), static System....
IsControl              Method     static System.Boolean IsControl(Char c), static
                                  System.Boolean IsControl(String s, Int...
IsDigit                Method     static System.Boolean IsDigit(Char c), static
                                  System.Boolean IsDigit(String s, Int32 i...
IsHighSurrogate        Method     static System.Boolean IsHighSurrogate(Char c),
                                  static System.Boolean IsHighSurrogate(S...
IsLetter               Method     static System.Boolean IsLetter(Char c), static
                                  System.Boolean IsLetter(String s, Int32...
IsLetterOrDigit        Method     static System.Boolean IsLetterOrDigit(Char c),
                                  static System.Boolean IsLetterOrDigit(S...
IsLower                Method     static System.Boolean IsLower(Char c), static
                                  System.Boolean IsLower(String s, Int32 i...
IsLowSurrogate         Method     static System.Boolean IsLowSurrogate(Char c),
                                  static System.Boolean IsLowSurrogate(Str...
IsNumber               Method     static System.Boolean IsNumber(Char c), static
                                  System.Boolean IsNumber(String s, Int32...
IsPunctuation          Method     static System.Boolean IsPunctuation(Char c),
                                  static System.Boolean IsPunctuation(Strin...
IsSeparator            Method     static System.Boolean IsSeparator(Char c), static
                                  System.Boolean IsSeparator(String s,...
IsSurrogate            Method     static System.Boolean IsSurrogate(Char c), static
                                  System.Boolean IsSurrogate(String s,...
```

6

```
IsSurrogatePair      Method      static System.Boolean IsSurrogatePair(String s,
                                  Int32 index), static System.Boolean Is...
IsSymbol             Method      static System.Boolean IsSymbol(Char c), static
                                  System.Boolean IsSymbol(String s, Int32...
IsUpper              Method      static System.Boolean IsUpper(Char c), static
                                  System.Boolean IsUpper(String s, Int32 i...
IsWhiteSpace         Method      static System.Boolean IsWhiteSpace(Char c),
                                  static System.Boolean IsWhiteSpace(String ...
Parse                Method      static System.Char Parse(String s)
ReferenceEquals      Method      static System.Boolean ReferenceEquals(Object
                                  objA, Object objB)
ToLower              Method      static System.Char ToLower(Char c, CultureInfo
                                  culture), static System.Char ToLower(Ch...
ToLowerInvariant     Method      static System.Char ToLowerInvariant(Char c)
ToString             Method      static System.String ToString(Char c)
ToUpper              Method      static System.Char ToUpper(Char c, CultureInfo
                                  culture), static System.Char ToUpper(Ch...
ToUpperInvariant     Method      static System.Char ToUpperInvariant(Char c)
TryParse             Method      static System.Boolean TryParse(String s, Char&
                                  result)
MaxValue             Property    static System.Char MaxValue {get;}
MinValue             Property    static System.Char MinValue {get;}


PS C:\>
```

After you have identified the available methods for a particular type, you can select the particular method that you want for that type, and then access it using the double colon operator. The next example shows the variable $c being set to A (capital letter A), and then the char type method ToLower being called against the $c variable to convert the variable from upper case to lower case. The second example shows the variable $d being set to a (lower case A), and then the char method ToUpper being called to convert this variable from lower to upper case.

```
PS C:\> $c = "A"
PS C:\> [char]::ToLower($c)
a
PS C:\> $d = "a"
PS C:\> [char]::ToUpper($d)
A
```

The **format operator** in PowerShell is used to provide more granular control over PowerShell's output. The basic structure of a format operator statement includes a **format string** on the left and an array of values on the right, as shown in the following example:

```
'{0} {1} {2}' - f 1,2,3
```

> **NOTE**
>
> Note that the values on the right side of a format operator statement are not limited to being numeric (character and string values are also supported). However, most of the advanced format string arguments operate primarily against numerical values.

The following formatting examples show a list of three fruit names being output in reverse order (apples bananas cherries becomes cherries bananas apples) and three sets of numbers being displayed in a different order than they were originally entered (123 456 789 becomes 123 789 456). The last example shows a list of three items (Item1, Item2, and Item3) and the resulting output when the format string includes only the second element of the array.

```
PS C:\> '{2} {1} {0}' -f "apples","bananas","cherries"
cherries bananas apples
PS C:\> '{0} {2} {1}' -f "123","456","789"
123 789 456
PS C:\> '{1}' -f "Item1","Item2","Item3"
Item2
PS C:\>
```

So, at a basic level, the format operator can be used to control the order in which elements of an array are displayed, or which elements are displayed at all. However, the format operator can also provide a tremendous number of other output options, simply by applying different arguments to the format strings. The general syntax for format string arguments is {0:<argument>}, where 0 is replaced by the array element that you are interested in, and <argument> is replaced by the format string argument that you want to apply to the data in the array element. Table 6.9 illustrates some of the possible arguments for format strings, describes what each of them does, and provides a usage example for each argument.

TABLE 6.9   Selected Format String Arguments

Format String Element	Description	Example
{0}	General format string argument; displays the specified element exactly as entered.	'{0}' -f "MyTextString returns MyTextString
{0:x}	Displays the specified element in hexadecimal format, with alpha-numeric characters displayed in lower case.	'{0:x}' -f 12345678 returns bc614e
{0:p}	Displays the specified element as a percentage.	'{0:p}' -f .372 returns 37.20 %
{0:C}	Displays the specified element in currency format.	'{0:C}' -f 14.78 returns $14.78
{0:hh}, {0:mm}	Returns the two-digit hour and two-digit minute value from a Get-DateTime command.	"{0:hh}:{0:mm}" -f (get-date) returns 08:35

Although the number of possible format operators is too great to be covered in the scope of this chapter, MSDN provides a comprehensive reference on the syntax for the use of arguments in .NET Framework formatting strings in the .NET Framework Developer's Guide in the section on Formatting Types. This guide can be found by visiting msdn.microsoft.com and searching on the keywords "Formatting Types." Through the use of these and other format operators, a wide variety of format string elements can be created to meet your formatting requirements.

The final advanced operators that we cover in this section are the **redirection operators**. The redirection operators are used to direct command output to another location, such as a file. The next example shows the output of the PowerShell command Get-Process s* being redirected to the text file C:\S-Processes.txt. The file C:\S-Processes.txt is then displayed at the command line using the Get-Content command.

```
PS C:\> get-process s* > c:\S-Processes.txt
PS C:\> get-content c:\S-Processes.txt
Handles  NPM(K)    PM(K)     WS(K) VM(M)   CPU(s)     Id ProcessName
-------  ------    -----     ----- -----   ------     -- -----------
    332       8     2224      5312    37   638.45    800 services
     21       1      164       372     4     0.04    644 smss
    158       6     3660      5780    48     1.01   1924 spoolsv
    301       9     3860      7600    49     0.86   1644 svchost
    630       0        0       264     2   171.28      4 System
PS C:\>
```

NOTE

One major difference in PowerShell's redirection operators versus other shells is that the < (input redirection) operator is currently not implemented as of PowerShell 2.0 CTP2. A syntax error is returned if you attempt to use an input redirection operator in a PowerShell command.

Table 6.10 describes each of the redirection operators available in PowerShell 2.0 CTP2 and provides examples of their usage.

TABLE 6.10   PowerShell Redirection Operators

Redirection Operator	Description	Example
>	Redirects the output of a command to the specified file. The specified file is overwritten	`get-process s* > c:\SProcesses.txt`
>>	Redirects the output of a command to the specified file. If the specified file exists, the output of the command is appended to the existing file.	`get-process s* >> c:\SProcesses.txt`
2>	Redirects any errors generated by a command to the specified file. The specified file is overwritten if it exists.	`dir c:\nosuchfile.txt 2> c:\filenotfound.txt`
2>>	Redirects any errors generated by a command to the specified file. If the specified file exists, any errors generated by the command are appended to the specified file.	`dir c:\missingfile.txt 2>> c:\filenotfound.txt`
2>&1	Redirects any errors generated by a command to the output pipe (displaying the errors at the console) instead of redirecting the errors to a file.	`dir c:\missingfile.txt 2>&1`
<	Not currently supported as of PowerShell 2.0 CTP.	The input redirection operator is currently not supported in PowerShell 2.0 CTP.

Escape Sequences

The grave-accent or backtick (`) acts as the PowerShell escape character. Depending on when this character is used, PowerShell interprets characters immediately following it in a certain way.

If the backtick character is used at the end of a line in a script, it acts as a continuation character. In other words, ` acts the same way & does in VBScript, enabling you to break long lines of code into smaller chunks, as shown here:

```
$Reg = get-wmiobject -Namespace Root\Default -computerName `
    $Computer -List | where-object `
    {$_.Name -eq "StdRegProv"}
```

If the backtick character precedes a PowerShell variable, the characters immediately following it should be passed on without substitution or processing:

```
PS C:\> $String = "Does this work?"
PS C:\> write-host "The question is: $String"
The question is: Does this work?
PS C:\> write-host "The question is: `$String"
The question is: $String
PS C:\>
```

If the backtick character is used in a string or interpreted as part of a string, that means the next character should be interpreted as a special character. For example, if you want to place a TAB in your string, you use the `t escape character sequence, as shown here:

```
PS C:\> $String = "Look at the tab:`t [TAB]"
PS C:\> write-host $string
Look at the tab:         [TAB]
PS C:\>
```

Table 6.11 lists the escape character sequences supported by PowerShell.

TABLE 6.11 PowerShell Escape Sequences

Character	Meaning
`'	Single quotation mark
`"	Double quotation mark
`0	Null character
`a	Alert (bell or beep signal to the computer speaker)
`b	Backspace
`f	Form feed (used for printer output)
`n	Newline
`r	Carriage return
`t	Horizontal tab (8 spaces)
`v	Vertical tab (used for printer output)

Error Handling

PowerShell errors are divided into two types: terminating and nonterminating.
Terminating errors, as the name implies, stop a command. **Nonterminating errors** are
generally just reported without stopping a command. Both types of errors are reported in
the $Error variable, which is a collection of errors that have occurred during the current
PowerShell session. This collection contains the most recent error, as indicated by
$Error[0] up to $MaximumErrorCount, which defaults to 256.

Errors in the $Error variable can be represented by the ErrorRecord object. It contains
error exception information and several other properties that are useful for understanding
why an error occurred

The next example shows the information that is contained in InvocationInfo property of
an ErrorRecord object:

```
PS C:\> $Error[0].InvocationInfo


MyCommand         : Get-ChildItem
ScriptLineNumber  : 1
OffsetInLine      : -2147483648
ScriptName        :
Line              : dir z:
PositionMessage   :
                    At line:1 char:4
                    + dir  <<<< z:
InvocationName    : dir
PipelineLength    : 1
PipelinePosition  : 1



PS C:\>
```

Based on this information, you can determine a number of details about $Error[0],
including the command that caused the error to be thrown. This information is crucial to
understanding errors and handling them effectively.

Use the following command to see a full list of ErrorRecord properties:

```
PS C:\> $Error[0] | get-member -MemberType Property


   TypeName: System.Management.Automation.ErrorRecord
```

```
Name                     MemberType  Definition
----                     ----------  ----------
CategoryInfo             Property    System.Management.Automation.ErrorCategoryI...
ErrorDetails             Property    System.Management.Automation.ErrorDetails E...
Exception                Property    System.Exception Exception {get;}
FullyQualifiedErrorId    Property    System.String FullyQualifiedErrorId {get;}
InvocationInfo           Property    System.Management.Automation.InvocationInfo...
TargetObject             Property    System.Object TargetObject {get;}


PS C:\>
```

Table 6.12 shows the definitions for each of the ErrorRecord properties that are listed in the preceding example:

TABLE 6.12   ErrorRecord Property Definitions

Property	Definition
CategoryInfo	Indicates under which category an error is classified
ErrorDetails	Can be null, but when used provides additional information about the error
Exception	The error that occurred
FullyQualifiedErrorId	Identifies an error condition more specifically
InvocationInfo	Can be null, but when used explains the context in which the error occurred
TargetObject	Can be null, but when used indicates the object being operated on

Methods for Handling Errors in PowerShell

Methods for handling errors in PowerShell can range from simple to complex. The simple method is to allow PowerShell to handle the error. Depending on the type of error, the command or script might terminate or continue. However, if the default error handler doesn't fit your needs, you can devise a more complex error-handling scheme by using the methods discussed in the following sections.

Method One: cmdlet Preferences

In PowerShell, **ubiquitous parameters** are available to all cmdlets. Among them are the ErrorAction and ErrorVariable parameters, used to determine how cmdlets handle *nonterminating* errors, as shown in this example:

```
PS C:\> get-childitem z: -ErrorVariable Err -ErrorAction
SilentlyContinue
PS C:\> if ($Err){write-host $Err -Foregroundcolor Red}
Cannot find drive. A drive with name 'z' does not exist.
PS C:\>
```

The ErrorAction parameter defines how a cmdlet behaves when it encounters a *nonterminating* error. In the preceding example, ErrorAction is defined as SilentlyContinue, meaning the cmdlet continues running with no output if it encounters a *nonterminating* error. Other options for ErrorAction are as follows:

▶ Continue—Print error and continue (default action)

▶ Inquire—Ask users whether they want to continue, halt, or suspend

▶ Stop—Halt execution of the command or script

NOTE

The term *nonterminating* has been emphasized in this section because a terminating error bypasses the defined ErrorAction and is delivered to the default or custom error handler.

The ErrorVariable parameter defines the variable name for the error object generated by a *nonterminating* error. As shown in the previous example, ErrorVariable is defined as Err. Notice the variable name doesn't have the $ prefix. However, to access ErrorVariable outside a cmdlet, you use the variable's name with the $ prefix ($Err). Furthermore, after defining ErrorVariable, the resulting variable is valid for the current PowerShell session or associated script block. This means other cmdlets can append error objects to an existing ErrorVariable by using a + prefix, as shown in this example:

```
PS C:\> get-childitem z: -ErrorVariable Err -ErrorAction
SilentlyContinue
PS C:\> get-childitem y: -ErrorVariable +Err -ErrorAction
SilentlyContinue
PS C:\> write-host $Err[0] -Foregroundcolor Red
Cannot find drive. A drive with name 'z' does not exist.
PS C:\> write-host $Err[1] -Foregroundcolor Red
Cannot find drive. A drive with name 'y' does not exist.
PS C:\>
```

Method Two: Trapping Errors

When encountering a terminating error, PowerShell's default behavior is to display the error and halt the command or script execution. If you want to use custom error handling for a terminating error, you must define an exception trap handler to prevent the terminating error (ErrorRecord) from being sent to the default error-handling mechanism. The same holds true for *nonterminating* errors as PowerShell's default behavior is to just display the error and continue the command or script execution.

To define a trap, you use the following syntax:

```
trap ExceptionType {code; keyword}
```

The first part is *ExceptionType*, which specifies the type of error a trap accepts. If no *ExceptionType* is defined, a trap accepts all errors. The *code* part can consist of a command or set of commands that run after an error is delivered to the trap. Defining commands to run by a trap is optional. The last part, *keyword*, is what determines whether the trap allows the statement block where the error occurred to execute or terminate.

Supported keywords are as follows:

▶ Break—Causes the exception to be rethrown and stops the current scope from executing

▶ Continue—Enables the current scope execution to continue at the next line where the exception occurred

▶ Return [*argument*]—Stops the current scope from executing and returns the argument, if specified

If a keyword isn't specified, the trap uses the keyword Return [*argument*]; *argument* is the ErrorRecord that was originally delivered to the trap.

Trap Examples

The following two examples show how traps can be defined to handle errors. The first trap example shows a trap being used in conjunction with a *nonterminating* error that is produced from an invalid DNS name being given to the System.Net.Dns class. The second example shows a trap being again used in conjunction with a *nonterminating* error that produced from the Get-Item cmdlet. However, in this case, because the ErrorAction parameter has been defined as Stop, the error is a terminating error that is then handled by the trap.

Example one: `errortraps1.ps1`

```
$DNSName = "www.-baddnsname-.com"

trap [System.Management.Automation.MethodInvocationException]{
    write-host ("ERROR: " + $_) -Foregroundcolor Red; Continue}

write-host "Getting IP address for" $DNSName
write-host ([System.Net.Dns]::GetHostAddresses("www.$baddnsname$.com"))
write-host "Done Getting IP Address"
```

The `$_` parameter in this example represents the `ErrorRecord` that was delivered to the trap.

Output:

```
PS C:\> .\errortraps1.ps1
Getting IP address for www.-baddnsname-.com
ERROR: Exception calling "GetHostAddresses" with "1" argument(s): "No
such host
is known"
Done Getting IP Address
PS C:\>
```

Example two: `errortraps2.ps1`

```
write-host "Changing drive to z:"

trap {write-host("[ERROR] " + $_) -Foregroundcolor Red; Continue}

get-item z: -ErrorAction Stop
$TXTFiles = get-childitem *.txt -ErrorAction Stop

write-host "Done getting items"
```

NOTE

A cmdlet doesn't generate a terminating error unless there's a syntax error. This means a trap doesn't catch nonterminating errors from a cmdlet unless the error is transformed into a terminating error by setting the cmdlet's `ErrorAction` to `Stop`.

Output:

```
:\> .\errortraps2.ps1
Changing drive to z:
[ERROR] Command execution stopped because the shell variable
"ErrorActionPrefere
nce" is set to Stop: Cannot find drive. A drive with name 'z' does not
exist.
Done getting items
PS C:\>
```

Trap Scopes

A PowerShell scope determines how traps are executed. Generally, a trap is defined and executed within the same scope. For example, you define a trap in a certain scope; when a terminating error is encountered in that scope, the trap is executed. If the current scope doesn't contain a trap and an outer scope does, any terminating errors encountered break out of the current scope and are delivered to the trap in the outer scope.

Method Three: The Throw Keyword

In PowerShell, you can generate your own terminating errors. This doesn't mean causing errors by using incorrect syntax. Instead, you can generate a terminating error on purpose by using the throw keyword, as shown in the next example if a user doesn't define the argument for the MyParam parameter when trying to run the MyParam.ps1 script. This type of behavior is useful when data from functions, cmdlets, data sources, applications, and so on is not what is expected and can prevent the script or set of commands from executing correctly further into the execution process.

Script:

```
param([string]$MyParam = $(throw write-host "You did not define MyParam" -
Foregroundcolor Red))

write-host $MyParam
```

Output:

```
PS C:\ .\MyParam.ps1
You did not define MyParam
ScriptHalted
At C:\MyParam.ps1:1 char:33
+ param([string]$MyParam = $(throw  <<<< write-host "You did not
define MyParam
" -Foregroundcolor Red))
PS C:\>
```

Managing Elements with Arrays

Arrays are a frequently used construct in all programming languages and PowerShell. At its simplest level, an **array** is just a collection of objects. In programming terms, an array can be seen as a data structure that consists of a group of elements. These elements are indexed and accessed by referencing the index number of the element. Arrays can be **one-dimensional** (a collection of elements that can be accessed individually by specifying a single index value, such as a single column of numbers) or **multidimensional** (a collection of elements that require multiple index values to specify a particular element, such as a table of numbers).

PowerShell has a set of operators specifically for working with arrays and collections. The most frequently used array operator is the **comma** (,). The comma operator is used to separate elements in a one-dimensional array. The next example shows the integers 0,1,2,3,4,5 being stored as a one-dimensional array in the variable $a.

```
PS C:\> $a = 0,1,2,3,4,5
PS C:\> $a
0
1
2
3
4
5
```

Unlike many other programming languages, PowerShell does not contain a specific syntax for defining an array (also known as an **array literal**). Instead, the PowerShell array operators are used to create collections of elements, which can then be accessed by assigning the collection to a variable. In the previous example, the PowerShell command $a=0,1,2,3,4,5 creates a one-dimensional array assigned to the variable $a. A slightly different syntax is used to create multidimensional arrays, which are discussed later in this section.

Another way to create a one-dimensional array in PowerShell is through the use of the **array subexpression operator,** discussed earlier in this chapter in the "Advanced Operators" section. The array subexpression operator follows the syntax @(element1,element2) and inserts the elements in parentheses into an array. The following example shows the variable $a being populated with the contents of the subexpression operator @(1,2,3,4,5).

```
PS C:\> $a=@(1,2,3,4,5)
PS C:\> $a
1
2
3
4
5
```

As with all the PowerShell array operators, the array subexpression operator is not restricted to working with integers. For example, it is possible to store the output of PowerShell cmdlets as elements in an array using the array subexpression operator. However, it might be necessary to use the **semicolon** as a separator in this instance (which PowerShell recognizes as a command terminator), which is not the case when using the comma. The following example shows the results of running the command `$a=@(get-process s*,get-date,get-service D*)`, which attempts to run three separate PowerShell commands that list all processes beginning with the letter S, list the current date, and list all services beginning with the letter D. When this command is run, the parser interprets the second two commands as parameters of the Get-Process command and returns an error, as shown here:

```
PS C:\> $a=@(get-process s*,get-date,get-service D*)
Get-Process : A parameter cannot be found that matches parameter name
'D*'.
At line:1 char:17
+ $a=@(get-process <<<< s*,get-date,get-service D*)
```

To ensure that PowerShell correctly interprets the sequence of commands and is able to store each of the commands as elements in the array, the command can be reentered as `$a=@(get-process s*;get-date;get-service D*)`. This is the same command as in the previous example, but the semicolon is used as a separator here instead of the comma. As you can see from the next example, the command is successful and the output of the three PowerShell commands is stored in the variable $a using the array subexpression operator.

```
PS C:\> $a=@(get-process s*;get-date;get-service D*)
PS C:\> $a
Handles  NPM(K)    PM(K)    WS(K) VM(M)    CPU(s)     Id ProcessName
-------  ------    -----    ----- -----    ------     -- -----------
    331       8     2220     4464    37    625.35    800 services
     21       1      164      372     4      0.06    644 smss
    158       6     3652     5776    48      0.93   1948 spoolsv
     92       6     1704     3612    37      0.05   1692 svchost
    629       0        0      264     2    103.29      4 System
```

```
Date            : 7/1/2008 12:00:00 AM
Day             : 1
DayOfWeek       : Tuesday
DayOfYear       : 183
Hour            : 16
Kind            : Local
Millisecond     : 972
Minute          : 57
Month           : 7
Second          : 35
Ticks           : 633505282559727193
TimeOfDay       : 16:57:35.9727193
Year            : 2008


Status          : Running
Name            : DcomLaunch
DisplayName     : DCOM Server Process Launcher

Status          : Running
Name            : Dhcp
DisplayName     : DHCP Client

Status          : Stopped
Name            : dmadmin
DisplayName     : Logical Disk Manager Administrative Service

Status          : Stopped
Name            : dmserver
DisplayName     : Logical Disk Manager

Status          : Running
Name            : Dnscache
DisplayName     : DNS Client
```

6

NOTE

An interesting point about the previous array subexpression operator command that captures the output of three PowerShell cmdlets is that each returned value is stored as its own element in the array. For example, the **services** process is the first element of the array, and the **DNS Client** service is the last element of the array. The number of elements in the array is determined dynamically by PowerShell based on the number of values returned from the three cmdlets.

After an array has been created, you can access elements of the array by referring to the variable containing the array and specifying the element you want using the element's index value enclosed in **square brackets** ([ ]). The next example shows an one-dimensional array $b being created with the elements "apricots","blueberries", "cranberries","dates","elderberries", "figs", and then a second command $b[2] is used to retrieve the third element of the array. (Array element numbering begins at 0, so the six elements of our example array $b have an index value ranging from 0 to 5.)

```
PS C:\> $b =
"apricots","blueberries","cranberries","dates","elderberries","figs"
PS C:\> $b[2]
Cranberries
```

PowerShell also includes operators to work with a range of array elements and to work with array elements in reverse order. The PowerShell **range operator** (..) is used to specify a range of elements, and the **hyphen** (-) is used to indicate a **negative index**, which accesses array elements starting from the end of the array instead of the beginning. We go through a couple of examples to show how these operators work.

The first example defines an array of fruit names in the variable $b, then issues the command $b[3..5], which displays the elements of array $b with an index value between 3 and 5 (dates, elderberries, and figs). Next, the command $b[-1] is issued to display the last element of the array (figs), and you can also see that the command $b[-2] displays the second-to-last element of the array (elderberries). The final example shown combines the range operator and the hyphen in the command $b[-1..-3], which displays the last three elements of the array in reverse order (figs, elderberries, and dates).

```
PS C:\> $b =
"apricots","blueberries","cranberries","dates","elderberries","figs"
PS C:\> $b[3..5]
dates
elderberries
figs

PS C:\> $b[-1]
figs

PS C:\> $b[-2]
elderberries

PS C:\> $b[-1..-3]
figs
elderberries
dates
```

Another technique for working with array elements in PowerShell is known as **array slicing**. Array slicing is similar to using the range operator, but it is possible to select array elements that are not sequential. Assuming that the array $b exists and has at least five elements, the syntax for using the array slicing technique is as follows:

```
$b[0,2,4]
```

Executing this command will return the array elements in array $b with the index values of 0,2,4. The next example defines an array of six fruit names in the variable $b, uses array slicing to return the array elements in array $b with the index values of 0, 2, and 4, and then uses the elements with the index values of 1, 3, and 5.

```
PS C:\> $b =
"apricots","blueberries","cranberries","dates","elderberries","figs"
PS C:\> $b[0,2,4]
apricots
cranberries
elderberries

PS C:\> $b[1,3,5]
blueberries
dates
figs
```

As you can see from the previous examples, it is possible to use the comma operator to create arrays containing numeric or text elements without needing to specify the type of data that the array will contain. Although it is possible to restrict the type of data that can be stored in an array, by default, PowerShell allows any type of data to be contained in an array element, and it can even store different data types in elements contained within the same array. The following example shows the array $c being created with the elements 1,3.1416,0xF,"text"," ","string". Note that when the array elements are listed, PowerShell converts the hexadecimal value for 0xF to the decimal value 15. You can also use any of the PowerShell operators described earlier in this chapter to work with array elements, such as addition or division, as shown in the following examples. However, your array elements must be type-compatible for the operation to be successful. The final example shows the results of attempting to add a numeric value to a string.

```
PS C:\> $c = 1,3.1416,0xF,"text"," ","string"
PS C:\> $c
1
3.1416
15
```

```
text

string
PS C:\> $d = $c[3] + $c[4] + $c[5]
PS C:\> $d
text string
PS C:\> $e = $c[2] / $c[1]
PS C:\> $e
4.7746371275783
PS C:\> $f = $c[0] + $c[5]
Cannot convert value "string" to type "System.Int32". Error: "Input
string was not in a correct format."
At line:1 char:13
+ $f = $c[0] + <<<<  $c[5]
```

A **multidimensional array** is a collection of elements that require multiple index values to identify a particular element. The following grid represents a simple multidimensional array that contains nine elements. When referring to a particular array element in a multidimensional array, the convention is to specify the **row** index value first, and then the **column** index value. For example, the index value pair 1,0 returns a value of 4 when applied to the example array shown here. The index value pair 2,1 returns a value of 8.

Index	Column 0	Column 1	Column 2
Row 0	1	2	3
Row 1	4	5	6
Row 2	7	8	9

PowerShell handles multidimensional arrays somewhat differently from one-dimensional arrays. Whereas a one-dimensional array can be constructed simply by the use of the comma operator, a multidimensional array must be created using the New-Object cmdlet using the following syntax:

```
$a = new-object 'object[,]' number_of_rows,number_of_columns
```

The next example creates a two-dimensional array identical to the one shown in the previous grid. You can see that as in the previous grid, the element stored at row 1, column 0 has a value of 4, whereas the element stored at row 2, column 1 has a value of 8.

```
PS C:\> $2_dimensional_array = new-object 'object[,]' 3,3
PS C:\> $2_dimensional_array[0,0] = 1
PS C:\> $2_dimensional_array[0,1] = 2
```

```
PS C:\> $2_dimensional_array[0,2] = 3
PS C:\> $2_dimensional_array[1,0] = 4
PS C:\> $2_dimensional_array[1,1] = 5
PS C:\> $2_dimensional_array[1,2] = 6
PS C:\> $2_dimensional_array[2,0] = 7
PS C:\> $2_dimensional_array[2,1] = 8
PS C:\> $2_dimensional_array[2,2] = 9
PS C:\> $2_dimensional_array[1,0]
4
PS C:\> $2_dimensional_array[2,1]
8
PS C:\>
```

Other than the need to refer to elements of a multidimensional array using multiple index values, multidimensional arrays function the same way as one-dimensional arrays and can be managed using the same operators and techniques that apply to one-dimensional arrays.

Creating Functions

In PowesrShell, **functions** are one of four categories of commands. (The other three categories are **cmdlets**, **scripts**, and **native commands**.) A function is a uniquely named piece of script code that resides in memory while PowerShell is running, but is deleted from memory when PowerShell closes.

At its most basic level, a PowerShell function can be defined at the command line using the following syntax:

```
function <function-name> (function-parameters) {function-statements}
```

When defining a function, all the elements shown in the previous example are required except for the **function-parameters** argument, which is optional.

The next example shows a simple function called my-function being created at the PowerShell command line to illustrate the basic syntax of creating a function.

```
PS C:\> function my-function { "This is a function."}
PS C:\> my-function
This is a function.
PS C:\>
```

PowerShell also enables more complex functions to be created at the command line. You can demonstrate this functionality by entering the following syntax at the PowerShell command prompt:

```
function <function-name> {
```

After you press Enter after the curly brace, the prompt changes to >> and you can enter your function statements on multiple lines. After you have completed entering your function, you can enter a closing curly brace (}) on a line by itself, and then press Enter to return to the standard PowerShell command prompt. The following example shows this technique being used to create a function named multiline-function.

```
PS C:\> function multiline-function {
>> $a = 1
>> $b = 2
>> $c = 3
>> $a
>> $b
>> $c
>> $a + $b + $c
>> }
>>
PS C:\> multiline-function
1
2
3
6
PS C:\>
```

Although creating these simple functions can be instructive, they aren't particularly useful for day-to-day work in PowerShell. One of the most powerful capabilities that PowerShell provides is the use of the **pipeline** to direct the output of one command into another. Let's take a look at a slightly more complex function that is designed to accept input from the PowerShell pipeline.

```
PS C:\> function add-numbers {
>> $sum_of_numbers = 0;
>> foreach ($number in $input) {$sum_of_numbers += $number}
>> $sum_of_numbers
>> }
>>
PS C:\> 1,2,3 | add-numbers
```

```
6
PS C:\> 1,3,5,7,9 | add-numbers
25
PS C:\> 1..10 | add-numbers
55
PS C:\> 1..100 | add-numbers
5050
PS C:\>
```

The previous function is named Add-Numbers. The first thing this function does is to initialize the variable $sum_of_numbers to 0. It stores any data that it receives in a variable called $input, and then takes each data element in $input and adds it to $sum_of_numbers. After it has completed parsing the data in $input, it returns the current value of $sum_of_numbers to the command line.

In the examples of using the Add-Numbers function, you can see that the function can accept numerical input separated by commas or operate against a range of numbers using the **range operator**, as we discussed in the section on arrays. In all cases, the Add-Numbers function takes the data provided, adds each element to the $sum_of_numbers variable, and displays the total.

The next type of function that we focus on in this section is a function that can perform the same type of actions that a cmdlet does. Because compiled cmdlets follow a specific order of operations, functions that act like cmdlets must operate in the same way. The following diagram shows the general structure that this type of function must follow:

```
function <function-name> (function-parameter-list)
{
  begin {
        <begin-statement-list>
        }
process {
        <process-statement-list>
        }
end {
        <end-statement-list>
        }
}
```

This function template defines three categories of actions that are performed by the function: begin actions, process actions, and end actions. Statements specified in the begin section are executed before any objects in the pipeline are evaluated by the function. The statements in the process section are executed once for each object in the pipeline.

Finally, the statements in the end section are executed after the process section has completed and no more objects are present in the pipeline. The next example function follows this template and helps to illustrate how this sequence of events unfolds:

```
PS C:\> function example-cmdlet ($a) {
>> begin {$p=0; "Begin Phase: Process iteration count is $p, cmdlet
argument is $a"}
>> process {$p++; "Process Phase: Process iteration count is $p,
pipeline element is $_, cmdlet argument is $a"}
>> end {"End Phase: Process iteration count is $p, cmdlet argument is
$a"}
>> }
```

This function is configured to accept a single command-line parameter, which is the variable $a. It can also receive and process input from the pipeline. In the following example, a list of five numbers is entered and piped to the example-cmdlet function that has a parameter of 7, as shown here:

```
PS C:\> 2,4,6,8,10 | example-cmdlet 7
```

When this command is executed, the example-cmdlet function goes through its three phases and reports on the values for process iteration count, the cmdlet argument, and the element in the pipeline during the process phase.

```
PS C:\> 2,4,6,8,10 | example-cmdlet 7
Begin Phase: Process iteration count is 0, cmdlet argument is 7
Process Phase: Process iteration count is 1, pipeline element is 2,
cmdlet argument is 7
Process Phase: Process iteration count is 2, pipeline element is 4,
cmdlet argument is 7
Process Phase: Process iteration count is 3, pipeline element is 6,
cmdlet argument is 7
Process Phase: Process iteration count is 4, pipeline element is 8,
cmdlet argument is 7
Process Phase: Process iteration count is 5, pipeline element is 10,
cmdlet argument is 7
End Phase: Process iteration count is 5, cmdlet argument is 7
PS C:\>
```

This next example does a better job of demonstrating the capabilities of this type of function. In the following command, the output of the command `get-process s*` is piped to the `example-cmdlet` function, which has a parameter of `(get-process explorer).CPU`, as shown here:

```
PS C:\> (get-process s*) | example-cmdlet (get-process explorer).CPU
```

When this command executes, the `example-cmdlet` function again goes through its three phases, but both the pipeline ($p) and the function argument ($a) are dynamically obtained from the PowerShell environment instead of being statically assigned, as in the first example.

```
PS C:\> (get-process s*) | example-cmdlet (get-process explorer).CPU
Begin Phase: Process iteration count is 0, cmdlet argument is
389.409944
Process Phase: Process iteration count is 1, pipeline element is
System.Diagnostics.Process (services), cmdlet argument
 is 389.409944
Process Phase: Process iteration count is 2, pipeline element is
System.Diagnostics.Process (smss), cmdlet argument is
389.409944
Process Phase: Process iteration count is 3, pipeline element is
System.Diagnostics.Process (spoolsv), cmdlet argument
is 389.409944
Process Phase: Process iteration count is 4, pipeline element is
System.Diagnostics.Process (svchost), cmdlet argument
is 389.409944
Process Phase: Process iteration count is 5, pipeline element is
System.Diagnostics.Process (svchost), cmdlet argument
is 389.409944
Process Phase: Process iteration count is 6, pipeline element is
System.Diagnostics.Process (svchost), cmdlet argument
is 389.409944
Process Phase: Process iteration count is 7, pipeline element is
System.Diagnostics.Process (svchost), cmdlet argument
is 389.409944
Process Phase: Process iteration count is 8, pipeline element is
System.Diagnostics.Process (svchost), cmdlet argument
is 389.409944
Process Phase: Process iteration count is 9, pipeline element is
System.Diagnostics.Process (svchost), cmdlet argument
is 389.409944
```

6

```
Process Phase: Process iteration count is 10, pipeline element is
System.Diagnostics.Process (svchost), cmdlet argument
 is 389.409944
Process Phase: Process iteration count is 11, pipeline element is
System.Diagnostics.Process (System), cmdlet argument
is 389.409944
End Phase: Process iteration count is 11, cmdlet argument is
389.409944
PS C:\>
```

After you work with functions and create some functions that are useful for you, you will most likely want to use them again in future. PowerShell provides a simple way to accomplish this by saving functions as text files. The following example shows the example-cmdlet function that we previously worked with saved as a PowerShell script file named MyFunctions.ps1:

```
#
# MyFunctions.ps1
#
function global:example-cmdlet ($a) {
begin {$p=0; "Begin Phase: Process iteration count is $p, cmdlet argument is $a"}
process {$p++; "Process Phase: Process iteration count is $p, cmdlet argument is
$a"}
end {"End Phase: Process iteration count is $p, cmdlet argument is $a"}
}
```

There are a couple of items to note about the previous script. The first three lines of the script are preceded by the # symbol, which is used to add comments to a script. Also, on line 4 of the script, you will notice that a global: keyword has been prefixed to the function name. This is done to ensure that the example-cmdlet function is added to PowerShell's global scope. Additional functions can be added to the MyFunctions.ps1 script following the standard function syntax and adding the global: prefix to the function name. Finally, it is important to note that the only thing that MyFunctions.ps1 does is to define a global function named example-cmdlet—it does not generate any output of its own or perform any other tasks. Let's take a look at how to use MyFunctions.ps1 to load a function into memory.

In the next example, the script file MyFunctions.ps1 has been saved to the folder C:\scripts. The script is executed by entering the full path to the script file at the PowerShell command prompt. After the MyFunctions.ps1 script is run, you can confirm that the example-cmdlet function was loaded into memory by using PowerShell's **function provider**. (More details on PowerShell's providers are available in the section on providers in Chapter 4, "Other Key PowerShell Concepts.")

```
PS C:\> C:\scripts\MyFunction.ps1
PS C:\> dir function:/example-cmdlet

CommandType      Name                              Definition
-----------      ----                              ----------
Function         example-cmdlet                    param($a) begin {...
```

After the `example-cmdlet` function has been loaded into memory, it can be used just as if it had been entered from the command line. If you find that you need to have a certain function available every time PowerShell starts, the function can be added to a PowerShell profile script such as `%UserProfile%\\My Documents\WindowsPowerShell\Microsoft.PowerShell_profile.ps1` so that it will be loaded automatically at startup. (For more information on PowerShell profiles, please consult the section on profiles in Chapter 4.)

Understanding Filters

Filters in PowerShell are similar to functions. The primary difference between filters and functions is that although a function in a pipeline runs once after all the input has been gathered, a filter runs once for **each** element in the pipeline. As with a function, a PowerShell filter is defined using the following syntax:

```
filter <filter-name> (filter-parameters) {filter-statements}
```

The key functional difference between functions and filters is the way that data from the pipeline is handled. Because filters are designed to process a single pipeline element at a time, they are ideal for evaluating a large amount of data from the pipeline and returning a subset of the pipeline data. Filters use a special variable $_ to operate on the current element in the pipeline. The following example shows the basic layout of a PowerShell filter:

```
filter <filter-name> (filter-parameter-list)
{
process {
        <process-statement-list>
      }
}
```

Looking at the previous example, one way to understand a PowerShell filter is to think of it as a function with only a process clause (that is, no `begin` or `end` clauses). The next example shows the creation of a simple filter named add-one that increments the current value of each number in the pipeline by one:

```
PS C:\> filter add-one {$_+1}
PS C:\> 1,2,3,4,5 | add-one
2
3
4
5
6
PS C:\>
```

Controlling Script Flow with Loops

A **loop** in PowerShell is a method for controlling the logical flow and code execution within a script. Several different types of loops are available in PowerShell. These loops include the while loop, the do/while loop, the for loop, and the foreach loop. This section covers each of these methods and provides usage examples for each method.

A while loop in PowerShell executes a set of statements as long as a given condition is true. The syntax of the while loop is shown here:

```
while (condition) {action}
```

An example of a while loop in operation is shown in the following example. The variable $myvar is initially set to 2 and is multiplied by 2 with each iteration of the while loop. The loop continues as long as the value of the variable $myvar is not equal to 32.

```
PS C:\> $myvar=2; while ($myvar -ne 32){$myvar*=2; "The value of
`$myvar is $myvar"}
The value of $myvar is 4
The value of $myvar is 8
The value of $myvar is 16
The value of $myvar is 32
PS C:\>
```

A do/while loop in PowerShell is similar to a while loop. The main difference between these two types of loop is that in a do/while loop, an action is performed before a condition is checked. The syntax of the do/while loop is shown here:

```
do {action} while (condition)
```

The following example shows a do/while version of the previous while loop example:

```
PS C:\> $myvar=2; do {$myvar*=2; "The value of `$myvar is $myvar"}
while ($myvar -ne 32)
The value of $myvar is 4
The value of $myvar is 8
The value of $myvar is 16
The value of $myvar is 32
PS C:\>
```

for loops in PowerShell are generally used for counting or iterating through a collection of objects one by one. This can be useful when it is necessary to know the exact element you are working with in a list or collection. The general syntax for a for loop is shown here:

```
for (loop_counter_initial_value;loop_counter_evaluation;increment_loop_counter)
{action}
```

The three values between the parentheses (loop_counter_initial_value, loop_counter_evaluation, and increment_loop_counter) define the behavior of the for loop. The next example shows the initial value of the loop counter ($z) being set to 0, the loop counter evaluation being set to continue if $z does not equal 10, and the loop counter incrementing $z by 1 during each iteration. As long as $z does not equal 10, a message is printed out indicating the current value of $z.

```
PS C:\> for ($z=0; $z -ne 10; $z++) {"The value of `$z is $z."}
The value of $z is 0.
The value of $z is 1.
The value of $z is 2.
The value of $z is 3.
The value of $z is 4.
The value of $z is 5.
The value of $z is 6.
The value of $z is 7.
The value of $z is 8.
The value of $z is 9.
PS C:\>
```

Another type of loop provided by PowerShell is the foreach loop. As with a for loop, a foreach loop is most frequently used to operate on collections of objects. However, a foreach loop has the advantage of not requiring a separate counter to manage the iteration of the loop. The general syntax for a foreach loop is shown here:

```
foreach (<element> in <pipeline>) {action}
```

This syntax provides more flexibility than a standard for loop for several reasons. First, the **element** and the pipeline do not have to be numerical values—they can be any valid PowerShell data type. Second, the foreach loop does not require a specific range of data to be defined before the foreach loop executes. In this sense, the foreach loop can operate more like a query than a loop. The next example uses a foreach loop to count the number of *.ps1 files in a directory named c:\scripts and uses the number of files returned to govern how many times the foreach loop iterates. While it runs, the loop accumulates the number of files returned in the variable $number and accumulates the total size of the returned files in the variable $size.

```
PS C:\> $number=0;$size=0;foreach ($file in dir c:\scripts\*.ps1)
{$number += 1; $size += $file.length}
PS C:\> $number
4
PS C:\> $size
1372
PS C:\> dir c:\scripts\*.ps1


        Directory: Microsoft.PowerShell.Core\FileSystem::C:\scripts


Mode                LastWriteTime         Length Name
----                -------------         ------ ----
-a---          6/18/2008     3:16 PM         211 ListNouns.ps1
-a---          6/18/2008     2:08 PM         211 ListVerbs.ps1
-a---          7/14/2008    11:32 AM         310 myfunction.ps1
-a---          7/14/2008    11:23 AM         640 testps1.ps1


PS C:\>
```

Using Logic and Making Decisions

PowerShell provides several different options for using logic to make decisions within functions and scripts. In addition to the basic if/else loops that are familiar to users of other programming languages, PowerShell enables scripters to implement decision making in their scripts using **labels** and keywords, such as break and continue, to control script behavior. PowerShell also implements a construct known as the switch statement for use in decision making, which is similar to the VBScript SELECT CASE statement but provides more functionality because of its highly flexible matching options. This section describes each of these methods and gives usage examples.

The if/else loop is the most basic conditional statement in PowerShell and is most likely familiar to most users of other programming languages. The general syntax for if/else loops in PowerShell is as follows:

```
if (condition1) {action1} elseif (condition2) {action2} else {action3}
```

The following example uses the if, elseif, and else keywords in conjunction with the **-gt** comparison operator to evaluate a variable named $mynum:

```
if ($mynum -gt 1000)
{
"The variable mynum is greater than 1000."
}
elseif ($mynum -gt 100)
{
"The variable mynum is greater than 100."
}
else
{
"The variable mynum is less than 100."
}
```

Scripts in PowerShell can also use **labels** to make decisions about script flow. Labels can be used in any of the loop types that have been discussed thus far, but are most commonly used in while loops to enable script execution to halt when a certain condition is met. Labels are frequently used in conjunction with the break and continue keywords to direct script execution to a particular point in the script. The following example shows the break keyword being used to direct the script execution from within a nested loop to the :exit label:

```
:outerloop while (condition)
{
    while (condition)
    {
    break exit:
    }
}
:exit {}
```

Another construct used for decision making in PowerShell is the switch statement. The switch statement is used to perform a selection based on a value, and then it executes an action based on the value returned. The following is the syntax for the switch statement:

```
switch -options (<pipeline>)
{
<pattern> {statement-list}
<pattern> {statement-list}
<default> {statement-list}
}
```

The -options argument for the switch statement can support wildcards and regular expressions, in addition to enabling the user to specify case sensitivity in matches, exact matches only, or to scan a file instead of a set of objects. The following example shows a basic usage of the switch statement to identify a specific type of fruit based on an input value:

```
$fruit = 7

switch ($fruit)
    {
        1 {"The fruit is an apple."}
        2 {"The fruit is a banana."}
        3 {"The fruit is a cherry."}
        4 {"The fruit is a date."}
        5 {"The fruit is an elderberry."}
        6 {"The fruit is a fig."}
        7 {"The fruit is a grape."}
        default {"The type of fruit could not be determined."}
    }
```

In the previous example, the variable $fruit is set to 7, so the switch statement matches on the statement "The fruit is a grape". If the value of $fruit were set to a number that was not between 1 and 7, the **default** choice would be returned because the value passed to the switch statement did not match any of the available options.

A more complex usage of the switch statement is shown next. In this case, the variable $fruit is set to date, and the –wildcard option is added to the switch statement to enable string matching against the $fruit argument. To allow the wildcard match to succeed, the patterns preceding the seven fruit names have been modified to follow the syntax a*, which allows matching on the first letter of the $fruit variable.

```
$fruit = "date"

switch -wildcard ($fruit)
    {
        "a*" {"The fruit is an apple."}
        "b*" {"The fruit is a banana."}
        "c*" {"The fruit is a cherry."}
        "d*" {"The fruit is a date."}
        "e*" {"The fruit is an elderberry."}
        "f*" {"The fruit is a fig."}
        "g*" {"The fruit is a grape."}
        default {"The type of fruit could not be determined."}
    }
```

The other commonly used option for the switch statement is the -regex option, which matches based on regular expressions. In this example, the variable $fruit is set to G32790 to represent a product code for a particular type of fruit. The patterns for the seven fruit names have been changed to include a range of letters that allow matching on the first letter of the product code stored in the $fruit variable.

```
$fruit = "G32790"

switch -regex ($fruit)
    {
        "[a-g]" {"The fruit is an apple."}
        "[h-k]" {"The fruit is a banana."}
        "[l-n]" {"The fruit is a cherry."}
        "[m-p]" {"The fruit is a date."}
        "[q-v]" {"The fruit is an elderberry."}
        "[w-y]" {"The fruit is a fig."}
        "[z]" {"The fruit is a grape."}
        default {"The type of fruit could not be determined."}
    }
```

Building Scripts with Scriptblocks

In PowerShell, a **scriptblock** is a construct that groups statements and commands into a single block of code. Scriptblocks are always contained between a set of braces ({ }). In this respect, scriptblocks are nearly identical to functions, with the notable exception that scriptblocks do not have names. Instead of having names, scriptblocks are assigned to variables to work with them. Many of the programming examples in this chapter have made use of scriptblocks, but this section covers their usage in detail.

In PowerShell, scriptblocks are functions without names, and functions are scriptblocks with names. You can demonstrate this at any PowerShell command prompt by obtaining the full name of any of the built-in PowerShell functions. In the following example, the command `$function:help.gettype().Fullname` is used to return the full type name of the built-in PowerShell `help` function, which is reported as `System.Management.Automation.ScriptBlock`.

```
PS C:\> $function:help.gettype().Fullname
System.Management.Automation.ScriptBlock
PS C:\>
```

At its most basic level, a PowerShell scriptblock can be defined using the following syntax:

```
{ keyword (parameter list) <statement-list>}
```

The only required information to create a scriptblock is the `statement-list` parameter—all other information is optional. Referring back to our earlier discussion on functions, it is possible to create a scriptblock that acts like a cmdlet by including the `begin`, `process`, and `end` clauses, as shown in the following example:

```
{keyword (parameter list)
  begin {
        <begin-statement-list>
        }
process {
         <process-statement-list>
        }
end {
        <end-statement-list>
        }
}
```

Because scriptblocks in PowerShell do not have names, they must be assigned to variables in order to work with them. To execute a scriptblock that is assigned to a variable, the **call operator** or & symbol is used. The following example shows a scriptblock of {Write-Host $file.fullname $file.length} being assigned to the variable $a. After the scriptblock has been assigned to the variable $a, a foreach loop is invoked to operate against all of the *.ps1 files in the c:\scripts directory. The statement list for the foreach loop is set to &$a, which executes the command {Write-Host $file.fullname $file.length} for each of the $file objects in the pipeline.

```
PS C:\>  $a = {Write-Host $file.fullname $file.length}
PS C:\> foreach ($file in Get-ChildItem c:\scripts\*.ps1) {&$a}
C:\scripts\ListNouns.ps1 211
C:\scripts\ListVerbs.ps1 211
C:\scripts\myfunction.ps1 310
C:\scripts\testps1.ps1 640
PS C:\>
```

Another powerful use for scriptblocks is to pass them as parameters to cmdlets. In the following example, a dir command is issued with the parameter c:\scripts*.ps1, which produces a list of all the *.ps1 files in c:\scripts. The output of this command is pipelined to the Copy-Item cmdlet, and a scriptblock of {"C:\text\" + $_.Name + ".TXT"} is provided as an argument for the -Destination parameter. This enables the Copy-Item cmdlet to take each item in the pipeline, append a .TXT extension to the filename that it is passed, and then copy the resulting file to the c:\text directory.

```
PS C:\> Dir c:\scripts\*.ps1 | Copy-Item –Destination {"C:\text\" +
$_.Name + ".TXT"}
PS C:\> dir c:\scripts\


    Directory: Microsoft.PowerShell.Core\FileSystem::C:\scripts


Mode                LastWriteTime     Length Name
----                -------------     ------ ----
-a---         6/18/2008   3:16 PM        211 ListNouns.ps1
-a---         6/18/2008   2:08 PM        211 ListVerbs.ps1
-a---         7/14/2008  11:32 AM        310 myfunction.ps1
-a---         7/14/2008  11:23 AM        640 testps1.ps1


PS C:\> dir c:\text
```

```
    Directory: Microsoft.PowerShell.Core\FileSystem::C:\text


Mode                LastWriteTime        Length Name
----                -------------        ------ ----
-a---          6/18/2008    3:16 PM         211 ListNouns.ps1.TXT
-a---          6/18/2008    2:08 PM         211 ListVerbs.ps1.TXT
-a---          7/14/2008   11:32 AM         310 myfunction.ps1.TXT
-a---          7/14/2008   11:23 AM         640 testps1.ps1.TXT


PS C:\>
```

Summary

This chapter focused on the component elements of PowerShell programming and provided an overview of each of these elements. PowerShell includes a large number of expressions and operators that provide the underlying logic for almost all PowerShell operations, which were documented and demonstrated in several examples. The PowerShell escape sequences were reviewed and their usage discussed. Several different techniques for error handling in PowerShell scripts were documented, including using ubiquitous parameters, trapping errors, and the throw keyword to generate terminating errors. The construction and use of arrays in PowerShell were covered, focusing on using PowerShell's native operators to create and manipulate one-dimensional and multidimensional arrays without the use of an array literal keyword. PowerShell's implementation of functions was discussed in detail, including a step-by-step process to build a function that includes the same clauses as a cmdlet, in addition to storing functions in script files for later reuse. The use of filters in PowerShell was discussed in the context of providing more granular control over objects passed to a pipeline. Four different types of loops were reviewed, and the capabilities and benefits of each type of loop were enumerated. PowerShell's mechanisms for implementing decision logic were discussed, including if/else statements, the use of labels in conjunction with the break and continue keywords, and the switch statement. Finally, the use of scriptblocks in PowerShell was reviewed, with a focus on the relationship between scriptblocks and functions, methods for assigning scriptblocks to variables and invoking scriptblocks using the call operator, and passing scriptblocks to cmdlets as arguments to enhance the capabilities of built-in PowerShell commands. Although the sheer number of commands, parameters, and options provided by the PowerShell language might be overwhelming at first glance, each of these elements is an integrated part of a logical, flexible, and extraordinarily capable shell that will quickly reward your efforts at learning and add many new possibilities to your scripting skill set.

## CHAPTER 7

PowerShell and Strings

T his chapter explains how PowerShell can be used to deal with strings, and we use examples to help illustrate this important concept.

We examine how strings are handled in the .NET Framework and we look at the [string] type accelerator.

We then move on to the Select-String cmdlet. A brief overview is given of basic operations that can be done with strings.

We go back to the .NET Framework features and look at the members of a string object, and then we discuss wildcards, regular expressions, and the kinds of operators that can be found in PowerShell.

Finally, we talk about two new operators that are in the 2.0 CTP and the format operator.

System.String

A string is typically a series of alphabetical characters, but it can also include numbers and non-alphanumeric characters, such as a space or a tab. A simple string that most people encounter when they are new to a scripting or programming language is "Hello World!" Because PowerShell is based on the .NET Framework, even a simple string is actually still an object.

PowerShell does a lot of things automatically when dealing with strings. Let's show the "long" way to create a string from within PowerShell by calling the appropriate .NET Framework classes.

```
PS > $mystring=new-object System.String "testing"
PS >
```

We use the New-Object cmdlet with the System.String class to define our object. We pass the argument "testing" to the class. Technically, this isn't an argument, but a constructor.

If we were using a programming language such as C#, declaring a string wouldn't be so easy.

It's easier with PowerShell because we can let PowerShell do all the work for us. With PowerShell, the following code is exactly the same as the previous code.

```
PS > $mystring2="testing"
PS >
```

Just to prove both are actually string objects, we could have used Get-Member to list out the class and members of the object, but we are going to use a little shortcut to get to the object type quicker.

```
PS > $mystring.gettype().fullname
System.String
PS > $mystring2.gettype().fullname
System.String
PS >
```

The previous is just another way for us to get the type of object with which we are dealing.

[String] **Type Accelerator**

We showed how easy it is to create a string object in PowerShell. However, there are some occasions when we want to create a string, but we might end up with an integer or an array.

```
PS > get-content array.txt
111
222
333
PS > $test=get-content array.txt
PS > $test.gettype().fullname
System.Object[]
```

```
PS > $test.gettype()
IsPublic IsSerial Name                                    BaseType
-------- -------- ----                                    --------
True     True     Object[]                                System.Array

PS > [string]$test2=get-content array.txt
PS > $test2.gettype().fullname
System.String
PS > $test2
111 222 333
PS >
```

Something similar can be done if we need to force an integer to be a string:

```
PS > $var=5
PS > $var.gettype().fullname
System.Int32
PS > [string]$var2=5
PS > $var2.gettype().fullname
System.String
PS >
```

Select-String Cmdlet

PowerShell provides the Select-String cmdlet to work with strings. One big bonus for this cmdlet is that it supports wildcards, which we look at in more detail later. This cmdlet comes with many more features in the 2.0 CTP, and we'll look at a few of these new features.

Let's provide some examples of how we can pipe a list of elements to the cmdlet.

```
PS > "test","testing"|select-string -pattern "test"

test
testing


PS > "test","testing"|select-string -pattern "test$"

test
```

```
PS > "test","testing"|select-string -notmatch -pattern "test"
PS > "test","testing","foo"|select-string -notmatch -pattern "test"

foo


PS >
```

The previous example uses a wildcard character to make sure we match on the exact string "test" only, in contrast to the example just before it where searching for "test" provided two matches.

We use the NotMatch parameter to get any entries where the string does not exist. We see the first example of using NotMatch returns nothing, because our string "test" matched all the entries passed via the pipeline. In the second example, however, we see we match on "foo."

NOTE

The NotMatch parameter used above is available only with the 2.0 CTP. The CTP also comes with a AllMatches parameter, which we look at next.

Let's provide another example of a new feature included with the CTP: the AllMatches parameter. This cmdlet returns a MatchInfo object with a special Matches property. Using this Matches property provides us with additional information on the matches found.

In PowerShell 1.0, the Select-String cmdlet will only return the first match in a string. In contrast, with 2.0, Select-String provides a new AllMatches parameter that can return all the matches found within a string passed. This is helpful when the string contains multiple occurrences of the substring or pattern we are searching for.

```
PS > $var="foo bar foo"|select-string "foo"
PS > $var2="foo bar foo"|select-string -allmatches "foo"
PS > $var.matches


Groups    : {foo}
Success   : True
Captures  : {foo}
Index     : 0
Length    : 3
Value     : foo
```

```
PS > $var2.matches


Groups    : {foo}
Success   : True
Captures  : {foo}
Index     : 0
Length    : 3
Value     : foo

Groups    : {foo}
Success   : True
Captures  : {foo}
Index     : 8
Length    : 3
Value     : foo



PS >
```

We see in the previous example that when we use the AllMatches parameter, we have a Matches property from the resulting object that lists all the matching strings contained within the original input string.

NOTE

Had we gone with using .NET classes, any of the limitations in 1.0 can be overcome, but the scripting requirements become more involved, and then we possibly need to refer to developer documentation.

Simple Operations

We can do a few simple things when dealing with strings: We can add them together and multiply them by an integer. Although we won't provide examples here, you can also combine these operators together when working with strings.

```
PS > "test"+"ing"
testing
PS > "testing"*10
testingtestingtestingtestingtestingtestingtestingtestingtestingtesting
PS >
```

Let's provide a simple example of multiplying a string. Here's an example that might help you pick your lottery numbers the next time.

```
PS > 1..100|foreach-object{get-random -min 1 -max 11}|group-
object|sort-object name|format-table —autosize
@{label="Number";expression={$_.name}},@{label="Occurences";expression
={"*"*$_.count}}


Number Occurences
------ ----------
1      ***************
10     *******
2      ***********
3      *********
4      ******
5      *********
6      ***********
7      ********
8      ************
9      ********


PS >
```

We use Get-Random, a new cmdlet from the 2.0 CTP, to provide a graphical representation of the number of times that our numbers from 1 to 10 have been generated randomly.

System.String Members

Remembering that we are dealing with .NET objects, and our simple string has a lot of intrinsic properties and methods provided by the .NET Framework. Let's look at each of the supported members and provide a simple example of each of the more commonly used ones.

NOTE

The following output has been truncated on the right-hand side to improve readability.

```
PS > "test"|Get-Member -force


   TypeName: System.String

Name              MemberType    Definition
----              ----------    ----------
pstypenames       CodeProperty
System.Collections.ObjectModel.Collection`1[[Syst
psadapted         MemberSet     psadapted {Chars, Length, get_Chars, get_Length,
psbase            MemberSet     psbase {Chars, Length, get_Chars, get_Length, Ind
psextended        MemberSet     psextended {}
psobject          MemberSet     psobject {Members, Properties, Methods, Immediate
Clone             Method        System.Object Clone()
CompareTo         Method        System.Int32 CompareTo(Object value), System.Int3
Contains          Method        System.Boolean Contains(String value)
CopyTo            Method        System.Void CopyTo(Int32 sourceIndex, Char[] dest
EndsWith          Method        System.Boolean EndsWith(String value), System.Boo
Equals            Method        System.Boolean Equals(Object obj), System.Boolean
GetEnumerator     Method        System.CharEnumerator GetEnumerator()
GetHashCode       Method        System.Int32 GetHashCode()
GetType           Method        System.Type GetType()
GetTypeCode       Method        System.TypeCode GetTypeCode()
get_Chars         Method        System.Char get_Chars(Int32 index)
get_Length        Method        System.Int32 get_Length()
IndexOf           Method        System.Int32 IndexOf(Char value, Int32 startIndex
IndexOfAny        Method        System.Int32 IndexOfAny(Char[] anyOf, Int32 start
Insert            Method        System.String Insert(Int32 startIndex, String val
IsNormalized      Method        System.Boolean IsNormalized(), System.Boolean IsN
LastIndexOf       Method        System.Int32 LastIndexOf(Char value, Int32 startI
LastIndexOfAny    Method        System.Int32 LastIndexOfAny(Char[] anyOf, Int32 s
Normalize         Method        System.String Normalize(), System.String Normaliz
PadLeft           Method        System.String PadLeft(Int32 totalWidth), System.S
PadRight          Method        System.String PadRight(Int32 totalWidth), System.
Remove            Method        System.String Remove(Int32 startIndex, Int32 coun
Replace           Method        System.String Replace(Char oldChar, Char newChar)
Split             Method        System.String[] Split(Params Char[] separator), S
StartsWith        Method        System.Boolean StartsWith(String value), System.B
Substring         Method        System.String Substring(Int32 startIndex), System
ToCharArray       Method        System.Char[] ToCharArray(), System.Char[] ToChar
ToLower           Method        System.String ToLower(), System.String ToLower(Cu
ToLowerInvariant  Method        System.String ToLowerInvariant()
ToString          Method        System.String ToString(), System.String ToString(
```

7

```
ToUpper            Method        System.String ToUpper(), System.String ToUpper(Cu
ToUpperInvariant Method          System.String ToUpperInvariant()
Trim               Method        System.String Trim(Params Char[] trimChars), Syst
TrimEnd            Method        System.String TrimEnd(Params Char[] trimChars)
TrimStart          Method        System.String TrimStart(Params Char[] trimChars)
Chars            ParameterizedProperty System.Char Chars(Int32 index) {get;}
Length             Property      System.Int32 Length {get;}
```

In the previous example, we pipe a string to the get-member cmdlet. Using a feature named .NET Reflection, we can get a listing of all the members of the object passed along the pipeline (in this case, the members are properties and methods). There are also other types of members like events, but these are not supported in PowerShell version 1.

Let's look at the more commonly used methods and properties provided by a string object.

Contains **Method**

The Contains method provides us a way to determine whether a particular string is contained within the original string.

```
PS > "test_string".contains("test")
True
PS > "test_string".contains("foo")
False
PS >
```

Note that in the previous example, we could have also used variables to determine whether a string contains another string. We are going to provide this example once here, but these examples of using variables apply to all the upcoming examples where we demonstrate other supported methods.

```
PS > $larger="test_string"
PS > $smaller="test"
PS > $larger.contains($smaller)
True
PS >
```

EndsWith **Method**

The EndsWith method provides us with a way to determine whether a string ends with a particular string.

```
PS > "test_string".endswith("test")
False
PS > "test_string".endswith("string")
True
PS >
```

Insert **Method**

The Insert method provides us with a way to insert a string into another string at a certain point in the string. In the following example, we insert the string "foo" starting after the fourth character of the original string.

```
PS > "test_string".insert(4,"foo")
testfoo_string
PS >
```

Using zero as the integer in the first argument passed would result in the string of the second argument being prepended to the original string.

```
PS > "test_string".insert(0,"foo")
footest_string
PS >
```

Remove **Method**

The Remove method provides us with a way to remove a particular string from an original string based on a starting position and length.

```
PS > "test_string".remove(5,1)
test_tring
PS >
```

The length of the string we want to remove is actually optional. If we include only one integer in the argument passed to the method, everything from that point, up to the end of the string, is removed.

```
PS > "test_string".remove(5)
test_
PS >
```

Replace **Method**

The Replace method provides us with some basic functionality to replace a particular string with a new string.

```
PS > "test_string".replace("_string","ing")
testing
PS >
```

Later in this chapter, we see other methods that can be used to replace strings with a new string.

Split **Method**

The Split method provides us a way to split up a string into smaller pieces.

```
PS > "test_string".split("_")
test
string
PS >
```

One useful feature when Split is used is that the results can be referenced similarly to the way individual elements are referenced with an array.

```
PS > "test_string".split("_")[0]
test
PS > "test_string".split("_")[1]
string
PS >
```

StartsWith **Method**

The StartsWith method provides us a way to determine whether a string begins with a particular string.

```
PS > "test_string".startswith("test")
True
PS > "test_string".startswith("foo")
False
PS >
```

SubString **Method**

The SubString method provides us a way to extract a particular string from the original string based on a starting position and length. If only one argument is provided, it is taken to be the starting position, and the remainder of the string is outputted.

```
PS > "test_string".substring(0,4)
Test
PS > "test_string".substring(4)
_string
PS >
```

Another useful feature of the SubString method is when we want to get just a certain part of the ending of a string.

```
PS > "test_string".substring("test_string".length-6)
string
PS >
```

ToLower **Method**

The ToLower method provides us a way to convert an entire string to lowercase letters.

```
PS > "Test_String1".tolower()
test_string1
PS >
```

ToString **Method**

The ToString method provides us a way to attempt to basically extract a string from the current object. When dealing with an actual string, this method is pretty useless, but we can provide an example of where this might actually be useful.

```
PS > $a="The date is: "
PS > $b=get-date
PS > $a + $b
The date is: 06/09/2008 23:13:48
PS > $a + $b.tostring()
The date is: 6/9/2008 11:13:48 PM
PS > $a=get-date
PS > $b=" is today's date"
PS > $a + $b
Cannot convert argument "1", with value: " is today's date", for
"op_Addition" to type "System.TimeSpan": "Cannot convert value " is
today's date" to type "System.TimeSpan". Error: "Input string was not
in a correct format.""
At line:1 char:5
+ $a + <<<<  $b
PS > $a.tostring() + $b
6/9/2008 11:20:27 PM is today's date
PS >
```

We use a string and a DateTime object (what is returned by Get-Date) to demonstrate when ToString can be useful. PowerShell is smart, and if it sees we started a command with a string, it is trying to convert anything we attempt to add to a string also.

Now, when we reverse the order of things and put the DateTime object first, PowerShell can't figure out what to do and spits out an error. To get around this, we use the ToString method for the DateTime object, and then we can use the regular addition symbol to join the strings together.

ToUpper **Method**

The ToUpper method provides us a way to convert an entire string to uppercase letters.

```
PS > "Test_String1".toupper()
TEST_STRING1
PS >
```

Trim **Method**

The Trim method provides us a way to cut off a part of a string.

```
PS > "Test_string1".trim("1")
Test_string
PS >
```

Length **Property**

The Length property, which is the only property supported by the string object, provides us a way to determine the actual number of characters in the string.

```
PS >"test_string".length
11
PS >
```

Wildcards

Often, when dealing with strings, we might need to match a certain part of the string to get the desired results. We have seen some tricks earlier in this chapter, but let's introduce wildcards.

```
PS > get-help about_wildcard
```

Three basic wildcards are supported by PowerShell: * , ?, [ ]. The following table outlines each of these possibilities and explains how the last wildcard ([ ]) can be used in two different scenarios: matching a range or matching a specific set.

Table 7.1 provides several examples of how regular expressions can be used. Each of the different types of wildcards are listed with a description, example usage, and examples where the expression will or will not match against.

TABLE 7.1   Wildcard Examples

Wilcard	Description	Example	Match	No match
*	Matches zero or more characters	t*	T,t,te,testing	Ntesting
?	Matches exactly one character in the specified position	?g	ng,ig	Testing
[]	Matches a range of characters	[a-t]esting	aesting,nesting, testing	zesting
[]	Matches specified characters	[st]esting	sesting,testing	resting

Wildcards are useful in everyday use. For example, we might want to find all the files with the string "file" in the name. We don't just want to match on "file" alone, so here's an example of some possibilities:

▶ We want to match on any extension: "file.*."

▶ We want to match on anything that may be before or after the string: "*file*.*."

▶ We want to match on anything that contains one character after the string:
"*file?.*."

▶ We want to match on anything that contains only one number before the string:
"[0-9]file.*."

We could go on with different possibilities.

Let's provide another example on how wildcards be used as a simple method to locate commands. We are going to use wildcards to help us find the Get-EventLog cmdlet.

> **NOTE**
>
> The following output has been truncated on the right-hand side to improve readability.

```
PS> get-command *eventlog
CommandType      Name              Definition
-----------      ----              ----------
Cmdlet           Get-EventLog      Get-EventLog [-LogName] <String>
PS> get-command *eventlog*
CommandType      Name              Definition
-----------      ----              ----------
Application      eventlog.dll      C:\WINDOWS\system32\eventlog.dll
Cmdlet           Get-EventLog      Get-EventLog [-LogName] <String>
PS > get-command *eventlo?
CommandType      Name              Definition
-----------      ----              ----------
Cmdlet           Get-EventLog      Get-EventLog [-LogName] <String>
PS > get-command *eventlog?
PS >
```

In the previous box, we look at the * and ? wildcards. In the first command, we search for *eventlog, which can be interpreted as us looking for "anything is allowed before we have the string eventlog." We see we get the result we want. Next, we look for *eventlog*, which can be interpreted as looking for "anything is allowed before we have the string eventlog, and anything is allowed after." Those are two examples where we use *.

Our third command, we combine * and ? as *eventlo?, which can be interpreted as us looking for "anything before the string eventlo, then one single character." In this case, ? matches "g." Finally, we look for *eventlog?. Now, this fails because we ended our search string with ?, which means one more character must be there; otherwise, the wildcard doesn't match anything.

Several cmdlets support wildcards like this as values being passed to their parameters. Let's look at the first part of the full help details of the Get-Eventlog cmdlet.

> **NOTE**
>
> The following output has been truncated on the right-hand side to improve readability.

```
PS > get-help get-eventlog -full

NAME
    Get-EventLog

SYNOPSIS
    Gets the events in a specified event log or gets a list of the
event logs on the l

SYNTAX
    Get-EventLog [-logName] <string> [-newest <int>] [-computerName
<string[]>] [<Comm

    Get-EventLog [-list] [-asString] [-computerName <string[]>]
[<CommonParameters>]


DETAILED DESCRIPTION
    The Get-EventLog cmdlet gets information about event logs and
event log entries fr
    mputer.


PARAMETERS
    -logName <string>
        Specifies an event log. Get-Eventlog gets the events from the
specified log. Y
        ch command.

        Required?                     true
        Position?                     1
        Default value
        Accept pipeline input?        false
        Accept wildcard characters?   False
```

We show only the first parameter listed, but want to highlight the last line where we see "Accept wildcard characters?". We see it says "False" after, which means this particular parameter doesn't accept the use of wildcards. That being said, all the parameters supported by Get-EventLog don't support wildcards. Let's use another cmdlet: Get-ChildItem.

> **NOTE**
>
> The following output has been truncated on the right-hand side to improve readability.

```
PS > get-help get-childitem -full


NAME
    Get-ChildItem

SYNOPSIS
    Gets the items and child items in one or more specified locations.

SYNTAX
    Get-ChildItem [[-path] <string[]>] [[-filter] <string>] [-include
<string[]>] [-exc
    rce] [-name] [<CommonParameters>]

    Get-ChildItem [-literalPath] <string[]> [[-filter] <string>] [-include
<string[]>]
        [-force] [-name] [<CommonParameters>]


DETAILED DESCRIPTION
    The Get-Childitem cmdlet gets the items in one or more specified locations.
If the
    items inside the container, known as child items. You can use the Recurse
paramete
    ainers.

    A location can be a file system location, such as a directory, or a
location expose
    registry hive or a certificate store.


PARAMETERS
    -path <string[]>
        Specifies a path to one or more locations. Wildcards are permitted. The
default
        ry (.).

        Required?                       false
        Position?                       1
        Default value                   <NOTE: if not specified uses the Current
location>
        Accept pipeline input?          true (ByValue, ByPropertyName)
        Accept wildcard characters?     True
```

In the previous box, we have another example of using help to list out parameters. For the Get-ChildItem cmdlet, we see that the path parameter accepts a wildcard. We can easily determine this because we see "True" next to "Accept wildcard characters". Let's test it out.

```
PS > get-childitem -path testing.txt

    Directory: Microsoft.PowerShell.Core\FileSystem::C:\demo

Mode                LastWriteTime     Length Name
----                -------------     ------ ----
-a---        1/21/2008   11:41 AM       1012 testing.txt

PS > get-childitem -path testing*

    Directory: Microsoft.PowerShell.Core\FileSystem::C:\demo

Mode                LastWriteTime     Length Name
----                -------------     ------ ----
-a---        1/21/2008   11:41 AM       1012 testing.txt
-a---        1/26/2008   12:06 PM         25 testing1.ps1

PS > get-childitem -path testing.*

    Directory: Microsoft.PowerShell.Core\FileSystem::C:\demo

Mode                LastWriteTime     Length Name
----                -------------     ------ ----
-a---        1/21/2008   11:41 AM       1012 testing.txt

PS > get-childitem -path testing.tx?

    Directory: Microsoft.PowerShell.Core\FileSystem::C:\demo

Mode                LastWriteTime     Length Name
----                -------------     ------ ----
-a---        1/21/2008   11:41 AM       1012 testing.txt

PS >
```

In the previous box, we show a practical example of how we can use wildcards when passing a value to a parameter that supports them.

Comparison Operators

Wildcards can be useful when we need to do string comparisons to possibly determine if a string resembles (or not) another particular string. We can use wildcards to compare strings against more general strings where we just need a particular substring to match, but still have strict guidelines on the matches we will accept or not.

```
PS > get-help about_comparison_operator
```

In Table 7.2, we provide examples outlining the most commonly used comparison operators when dealing with strings.

TABLE 7.2   Examples of Commonly Used Operators

Operator	Description	Example	True/False
-eq	Equals	"abc –eq "abc"	True
-ne	Not equal	"abc" –ne "abc"	False
-like	Wildcard comparison	"abc" –like "a*"	True
-notlike	Wildcard comparison	"abc" –notlike "a*"	False
-match	Regular expression comparison	"abc" –match "[ade]"	True
-notmatch	Regular expression comparison	"abc" –notmatch "[ade]"	False

When dealing with these operators, the result is returned as a Boolean value (either true or false).

The use of the eq and ne operators is also commonly used when dealing with integers, but also equally applies to comparing strings. These two operators don't support wildcards. Wildcards and regular expressions, which we cover in the next section, are supported with the Like/NotLike and Match/NotMatch operators respectively. Although the examples look more like wildcard comparisons, Match/NotMatch can work with more complicated regular expression comparisons.

Let's look at the Like/NotLike operators first because we just provided an overview of wildcards in the previous section.

Here are some simple examples of using Like/NotLike with wildcards.

```
PS > "foo" -like "foo"
True
PS > "foo" -like "f*"
True
PS > "foo" -like "f?"
False
PS > "foo" -like "f??"
True
PS >
```

Remember, when using the * wildcard, it matches anything. In the previous example, we try to determine if "foo" is like "f?". The results returns false, because ? takes the place of a single character. We can confirm this when, in our next example, we compare "foo" with "f??," which returns true. It returns true because of the two ? wildcards, which each match an "o."

Regular Expressions

The topic of regular expressions can usually consist of an entire chapter alone. Complex regular expressions have baffled many people and alluded even intermediate users at times. Nonetheless, it is important to have a basic grasp of the concepts.

```
PS > get-help about_regular_expression
```

We briefly talked about the Match and NotMatch comparison operators earlier in this chapter. Now that we are talking about regular expressions, we are going to talk about these operators and provide examples.

Match/NotMatch **Comparison Operator**

PowerShell supports a number of the regular expression characters. Table 7.3 provides several examples where regular expressions are used wih the Match/NotMatch comparison operators.

TABLE 7.3   Regular Expression Characters

Format	Logic	Example
value	Matches exact characters anywhere in the original value	"test" –match "es"
.	Matches any single character	"test" –match "t..t"
[value]	Matches at least one of the characters in the brackets	"test" –match "t[aeo]st"
[range]	Matches at least one of the characters within the range. The use of a hyphen allows specification of a contiguous character.	"test" –match "[s-u]est"
[^]	Matches any character except those in brackets.	"test" –match "[^abc]est"
^	Matches the beginning characters.	"test" –match "^te"
$	Matches the end characters.	"test" –match "st$"
*	Matches zero or more instances of the preceding character.	"test" –match "t*"
?	Matches zero or one instance of the preceding character.	"test" –match "t?"
+	Matches one or more instances on the preceding character.	"test" –match "e+"
\	Marches the character that follows as an escaped character.	"test$" –match "test\$"

7

PowerShell supports the quantifiers available in .NET regular expressions, and the following are some examples of quantifiers. We provides some examples of quantifiers in Table 7.4.

NOTE

The use of the string "\w" comes from the .NET Framework. Basically it represents any word character which includes all alpha-numeric characters.

TABLE 7.4   Examples of Quantifiers

Format	Logic	Example
*	Specifies zero or more matches.	`"abc" -match "\w*"`
+	Matches repeating instances of the preceding characters.	`"test" -match "\w+"`
?	Specifies zero or one matches.	`"test" -match "\w?"`
{n}	Specifies exactly n matches.	`"test" -match "\w{4}"`
{n,}	Specifies at least n matches.	`"test" -match "\w{4,}"`
{n,m}	Specifies at least n matches, but no more than m matches.	`"test" -match "\w{4,5}"`

NOTE

PowerShell supports the character classes available in .NET regular expressions. Check the built-in help, in particular the command `Get-Help About_Regular_Expression`.

Replace Operators

When dealing with strings, we might need to replace certain parts of a string with another string. We saw earlier that string objects support a replace method. There is also a replace operator. The difference is that the replace operator supports regular expressions, so it is more powerful.

Table 7.5 provides some simple examples of using the replace operator.

TABLE 7.5   Examples of the Replace Operator

Operator	Case	Example	Results
-replace	Insensitive	"testing"–replace "T","R"	Resting
-ireplace	Insensitive	"testing"–replace "T","R"	Resting
-creplace	Sensitive	"testing"–replace "T","R"	testing

Let's provide a more complicated example using a real regular expression. Here, we use the string "`file000.txt`" as an example. We want to replace a string where we find two consecutive decimals.

```
PS > "file000.txt" -replace "\d{2}"
file0.txt
PS > "file000.txt" -replace "\d{2}","YY"
fileYY0.txt
PS >
```

> **NOTE**
>
> The use of the string "\d" comes from the .NET Framework. Basically, it represents any numeric character.

[RegEx] **Type Accelerator**

The .NET Framework provides a class named System.Text.RegularExpressions.Regex that provides powerful capabilities when dealing with regular expressions. As with other .NET classes, we can call this directly from within PowerShell. To make this even better, PowerShell has a type accelerator or shortcut for this class: [RegEx].

Let's look at an example of using this .NET class. We're going to put together a long regular expression that should be able to match any valid email address.

We're going to use [RegEx] to define the type of our variable, and then use it to check a few strings.

```
PS > [regex]$regex="^([0-9a-zA-Z]([-.\w]*[0-9a-zA-Z])*@([0-9a-zA-Z]
[-\w]*[0-9a-zA-Z]\.)+[a-zA-Z]{2,9})$"
PS > ($regex.match("some.user@domain.com")).Success
True
PS > ($regex.match("foo")).Success
False
PS >
```

Let's pick the previous expression apart.

▶ The RegEx starts with "^" and ends with "$". These represent the beginning and the end of a string, respectively.

▶ In a few spots, we have the string "[0-9a-zA-Z]". This basically represents any alpha-numeric character matching all decimals from 0 to 9 and all alphabetical characters, including upper and lowercase letters. In other words, this will match 0, a, and A and any other valid alphabetical or numerical character.

▶ Near the middle, we have the "@" symbol. This basically just represents itself. Every email address has the "@" symbol after the username and before the domain name.

▶ We have this part at the beginning "^([0-9a-zA-Z]([-.\w]*[0-9a-zA-Z])*. This guarantees we have at least a single alpha-numeric character at the beginning of the string. This also guarantees that if we have a character such as "-", ".", or "_", for example, there must be an alpha-numeric character that follows before it can be a valid username.

▶ We have this part at the end ([0-9a-zA-Z][-\w]*[0-9a-zA-Z]\.)+[a-zA-Z]{2,9})$". This guarantees we have at least have a format of something such as "[0-9a-zA-Z] [0-9a-zA-Z]. [a-zA-Z] [a-zA-Z]". Again, if we start off the string with an alpha-numeric character, and then have a character such as "-", ".", or "_", there must be one more alpha-numeric character following this. The "+" indicates that what precedes in parentheses "([0-9a-zA-Z][-\w]*[0-9a-zA-Z]\.)" must occur one or more times to be valid.

2.0 CTP: `Join` and `Split`

As of the 2.0 CTP, two new operators were added for dealing with strings: `Join` and `Split`. Let's look briefly at each and how these can be used to help us to work with string objects more efficiently.

```
PS > get-help about_join
PS > get-help about_split
```

Join Operator

The `join` operator provides the ability to combine strings together into one string. Two different methods can be used with this operator, as shown here:

▶ `-Join <String[]>`

▶ `<String[]> -Join <Delimiter>`

The first method simply joins a bunch of strings together, whereas the second method enables us to define whether we want to use any kind of delimiter when we join our substrings together. Let's provide an example of using each method.

```
PS > -join ("123","456")
123456
PS > "123","456" -join ";"
123;456
```

In the first example, we join two strings together. The second example joins the two strings, but places a semicolon in the resulting string.

Split **Operator**

The Split operator provides the ability to split a string into smaller ones. Three different methods can be used with this operator, as shown here:

▶ -Split <String>

▶ <String> -Split <Delimiter>[,<Max-substrings>[,"<Options>"]]

▶ <String> -Split {<ScriptBlock>} [,<Max-substrings>]

The first method can Split a string into smaller pieces, the second method enables us to define whether we want to use any kind of delimiter when we split the strings into smaller parts, and the third method enables us to provide a more complicated scriptblock to determine how our string will be split up. Let's provide an example of the first two methods. For more examples, please consult the built-in help.

> **NOTE**
>
> You can substitute Split with Csplit for adding case sensitivity to the delimiter rules. Isplit is also valid, but is also case-insentitive like Split. However, this is not valid for our first example provided previously.

```
PS > -split "1 2 3"
1
2
3
PS > "1,2,3" -split ","
1
2
3
PS >
```

In the first example, simply split a string into smaller strings based on splitting the string at each blank space. The second example splits the string into smaller pieces based on using the comma as a delimiter.

Format **Operator**

The Format operator (-f) provides a lot of flexibility when it comes for formatting strings. This operator is based on the .NET Framework's composite formatting (http://msdn. microsoft.com/en-us/library/txafckwd.aspx).

```
PS > get-help about_operator
```

> **NOTE**
>
> The format operator is briefly discussed only in the built-in help.

```
PS > "1,2","3,4"|foreach-object{"{0} {1}" -f $_.split(",")}
1 2
3 4
PS >
```

> **NOTE**
>
> The PowerShell team blog offers a tip on how to determine if an object supports special formatting or not and also provides an example of using different types of formatting for a DateTime object:
>
> http://blogs.msdn.com/powershell/archive/2006/06/16/634575.aspx

Summary

In summary, we looked at how string objects can be created and manipulated within PowerShell. We also spent a bit of time trying to help the reader understand how the .NET Framework can be used within PowerShell.

We looked at wildcards, regular expressions, and the various operators that can be used. We also provided some brief examples on how operators can be useful when dealing with strings.

Near the end of the chapter, we introduce some new operators that are available with the 2.0 CTP.

## CHAPTER 8

PowerShell and the File System

This chapter explains how PowerShell can be used to manage the Windows file system. This chapter provides examples on how to manage the file system using PowerShell. We discuss the core cmdlets; look at file system navigation; manage drives, folders and files; and show how to work with XML and CSV files. In addition, this chapter presents a working file-management script based on a real-world situation.

The goal is to give you a chance to learn how PowerShell scripting techniques can be applied to meet real-world file system automation needs.

Core Cmdlets

PowerShell provides a set of core cmdlets that can be used to manage all the various data stores that are supported via PowerShell Providers, which were discussed in Chapter 4, "Other Key PowerShell Concepts." These core cmdlets can be used to manage all the supported data stores, so a consistent user experience is provided. If you need to create something in the registry or in the file system, the command and its syntax are similar.

NOTE

Some of the parameters to these cmdlets, and even some of the cmdlets themselves, might either require different arguments or possibly not work at all, depending on which provider is currently being used. For example, `Select-String` works differently while in the file system provider versus the registry provider. Unfortunately, there isn't any help currently available that will dynamically update itself to let you know what will and will not work.

The following command retrieves a list of the core cmdlets for manipulating data stores available via PowerShell providers:

```
PS > help about_core_commands
```

Navigating the File System

PowerShell has a built-in provider, the PowerShell FileSystem Provider, for interfacing with the Windows file system. The abstraction layer this provider furnishes between PowerShell and the Windows file system gives the file system the appearance of a hierarchical data store. Therefore, interfacing with the file system is the same as with any other data store that's accessible through a PowerShell provider.

Being able to move around in a file system is one of the most essential tasks in PowerShell. Several core cmdlets deal with file system navigation. For individuals more familiar with either DOS or UNIX/Linux servers, PowerShell offers aliases in most cases that are more familiar to users who are just getting accustomed to using PowerShell. The two key cmdlets when dealing with file system navigation are Set-Location (alias cd) and Get-Location (alias pwd).

Get-Location **Cmdlet**

The Get-Location cmdlet retrieves the current working directory. As you move through the file system, if you have changed your default PowerShell prompt, it can be useful to have a quick reminder of your current location in the file system.

```
PS > get-location
C:\
```

Set-Location **Cmdlet**

The Set-Location cmdlet accepts a parameter that sets the working directory to the value specified. Using Set-Location enables one to move through the file system, and when you might need to access a file or run a script, only the relative file name needs to be used (versus the full path).

```
PS > get-location
C:\
PS > set-location "C:\documents and settings"
PS > get-location
Path
--------------------
C:\documents and settings
PS >
```

> **NOTE**
>
> Tab completion works well with Set-Location. Start off the desired path, and then hit the TAB key. Additionally, one can use tab completion to even complete a path containing subdirectories. For example, if you want to change to the directory "C:\Documents and Settings\userABC\Desktop," you can simply do
>
> set-location "c:\docu*\userA*\desk* [TAB].
>
> As long as the preceding string leads to a unique path, PowerShell auto-completes the entire string.

Push-Location **Cmdlet**

The Push-Location cmdlet, along with the Pop-Location cmdlet reviewed in the next section, are useful when navigating to and from multiple directories. Using Push-Location, we can have PowerShell remember certain directories for later use. Here's a simple example of "pushing" the current directory to a list of locations.

```
PS > get-location

Path
----
C:\Documents and Settings\ma36788


PS > push-location
```

Pop-Location **Cmdlet**

In the previous section, we saw how to push a directory onto a list of locations. Now, we are going to recall the last location remembered using Pop-Location.

```
PS > get-location

Path
----
C:\Documents and Settings\ma36788


PS > push-location
PS > cd c:\temp
PS > get-location
```

8

```
Path
----
C:\temp

PS > pop-location
PS > get-location

Path
----
C:\Documents and Settings\ma36788
```

Managing Drives

PowerShell drives can be created and removed, which is handy when you're working with a location or set of locations frequently. Instead of having to change the location or use an absolute path, you can create new drives (also referred to as "mounting a drive" in PowerShell) as shortcuts to those locations.

Adding a Drive

To add a new drive, or a shortcut in this case, use the New-PSDrive cmdlet, shown in the following example:

```
PS > new-psdrive -name PSScripts -root D:\Dev\Scripts -psp FileSystem
Name          Provider      Root                         CurrentLocation
----          --------      ----                         ---------------
PSScripts     FileSystem    D:\Dev\Scripts
PS > get-psdrive
Name          Provider      Root                         CurrentLocation
----          --------      ----                         ---------------
Alias         Alias
C             FileSystem    C:\
cert          Certificate   \
D             FileSystem    D:\
E             FileSystem    E:\
Env           Environment
F             FileSystem    F:\
Function      Function
G             FileSystem    G:\
HKCU          Registry      HKEY_CURRENT_USER                     software
HKLM          Registry      HKEY_LOCAL_MACHINE            ...crosoft\windows
PSScripts     FileSystem    D:\Dev\Scripts
U             FileSystem    U:\
Variable      Variable
PS > get-location
C:\
```

Removing a Drive

To remove a drive, use the Remove-PSDrive cmdlet, as shown here:

```
PS C:\> remove-psdrive -name PSScripts
PS C:\> get-psdrive
Name            Provider        Root                            CurrentLocation
----            --------        ----                            ---------------
Alias           Alias
C               FileSystem      C:\
cert            Certificate     \
D               FileSystem      D:\
E               FileSystem      E:\
Env             Environment
F               FileSystem      F:\
Function        Function
G               FileSystem      G:\
HKCU            Registry        HKEY_CURRENT_USER                      software
HKLM            Registry        HKEY_LOCAL_MACHINE             ...crosoft\windows
U               FileSystem      U:\
Variable        Variable
PS C:\>
```

Managing Folders

Let's look at how to manage folders in PowerShell. Some cmdlets behave a bit differently depending on the provider. Dealing with folders while in a file system provider is easy to comprehend. In most cases, the arguments passed to the cmdlet are similar when dealing with a folder versus a file. This section examines folder management, and the next section covers file management.

Adding a Folder

To create a new folder, the New-Item cmdlet is used. We pass it a Type parameter with a value of Directory to indicate this will be a directory.

```
PS > new-item -type directory -path testing
    Directory: Microsoft.PowerShell.Core\FileSystem::C:\demo
Mode                LastWriteTime       Length Name
----                -------------       ------ ----
d----         2/7/2008  10:30 PM               testing
PS >
```

Removing a Folder

Removing a folder is just as easy using the Remove-Item cmdlet with the proper parameters and values.

```
PS > new-item -type directory -path testing
    Directory: Microsoft.PowerShell.Core\FileSystem::C:\demo
Mode                LastWriteTime      Length Name
----                -------------      ------ ----
d----         2/7/2008   10:35 PM             testing
PS > new-item -type file -path testing\foo
    Directory: Microsoft.PowerShell.Core\FileSystem::C:\demo\testing
Mode                LastWriteTime      Length Name
----                -------------      ------ ----
-a---         2/7/2008   10:35 PM           0 foo
PS > remove-item -path testing
Confirm
The item at C:\demo\testing has children and the Recurse parameter was
not specified. If you continue, all children
will be removed with the item. Are you sure you want to continue?
[Y] Yes  [A] Yes to All  [N] No  [L] No to All  [S] Suspend  [?] Help
(default is "Y"):
PS >
```

> **NOTE**
>
> When creating a file or a folder, you want to specify the type as either directory or file. We see how to use new-item to create a file later.

The previous example shows what happens when we try to delete a directory that has some contents. If the testing directory were empty, there would be no output.

> **NOTE**
>
> Remember to use whatIf and confirm parameters when available to make any kind of change, such as deleting. You are either presented with the details of what PowerShell would have done had you entered the command as is or be prompted with an "Are you sure?" response before PowerShell continues with the command entered.

Moving a Folder

Let's look at how to move a folder. Moving something consists of actually moving a directory, in this case, from some directory to another. In other words, you won't typically use the `Move-Item` cmdlet to simply move the folder test to test2, which is basically renaming a folder, which we will see just after this.

```
PS > move-item bar c:\temp
PS > get-item c:\temp\bar
    Directory: Microsoft.PowerShell.Core\FileSystem::C:\temp
Mode                LastWriteTime     Length Name
----                -------------     ------ ----
d----         1/15/2008   3:59 PM            bar
PS > get-childitem c:\temp\bar
    Directory: Microsoft.PowerShell.Core\FileSystem::C:\temp\bar
Mode                LastWriteTime     Length Name
----                -------------     ------ ----
-a---         1/29/2008  10:24 PM          6 fooing.txt
PS >
```

In the previous example, we moved a directory to a new location. It's important to check that it has been moved. Notice that we first used `Get-Item`, and then `Get-ChildItem`. `Get-Item` simply lists an item itself, whereas `Get-ChildItem` lists the child items, such as files.

> **NOTE**
>
> When dealing with the `Move-Item` cmdlet, if you want to move directories recursively, especially when wanting to reproduce the directory structure from the source to the destination, it is easier to use the DOS xcopy command. PowerShell can handle this kind of operation, but several lines of scripting are required.

Renaming a Folder

In contrast with actually moving a folder, where it may be moved from one directory to a completely different location, renaming a folder would be more appropriate to use when the location of a folder will remain constant, but we are looking to change the name of the folder.

We say it is more appropriate to use `Rename-Item`, but `Move-Item` would be equally useful.

```
PS > new-item -type directory -path foo
    Directory: Microsoft.PowerShell.Core\FileSystem::C:\demo
Mode                LastWriteTime     Length Name
----                -------------     ------ ----
d----          2/8/2008  12:32 AM            foo
PS > rename-item foo foobar
PS > get-item foobar
```

8

```
        Directory: Microsoft.PowerShell.Core\FileSystem::C:\demo
Mode                    LastWriteTime         Length Name
----                    -------------         ------ ----
d----            2/8/2008   12:32 AM                 foobar
PS >
```

Testing for a Folder

You might need to check whether a directory actually exists, especially in scripts dealing with any kind of file system management task. Using Test-Path returns a Boolean value (either "True" or "False") depending on the result of the test.

```
PS > get-item foobar
        Directory: Microsoft.PowerShell.Core\FileSystem::C:\demo
Mode                    LastWriteTime         Length Name
----                    -------------         ------ ----
d----            2/8/2008   12:32 AM                 foobar


PS > test-path foobar
True
PS > test-path some_invalid_dir
False
PS >
```

A good practical example that we show is checking for the existence of a directory before continuing to run a script. In this case, we create a simple function to show how this works.

```
PS > function test_path {
>> if(!(test-path some_invalid_path)){
>> "Path not found"
>> break
>> }
>> "After if condition"
>> }
>>
PS > test_path
Path not found
PS >
```

We see that our function ended when we test for the existence of a file. If the file doesn't exist, which we determine using "(if(!(",we run that statement block that outputs some text and then the break statement is invoked, which exits the function.

In some cases, you want to make sure you use the pathType parameter. It takes the arguments leaf, for a file, container, for a directory, or any.

Managing Files

We looked at how to manage folders with PowerShell. Now, we look at how to manage files. Because of how PowerShell tries to provide a common experience to users, the cmdlets used will be the same for managing files versus managing folders. The only differences are found in the values passed to the arguments of the cmdlets.

Creating a File

The process to create a new file is basically the same as creating a new folder except a different value for a parameter is used.

```
PS > new-item -type file -path abc

    Directory: Microsoft.PowerShell.Core\FileSystem::C:\demo

Mode                LastWriteTime     Length Name
----                -------------     ------ ----
-a---          2/10/2008   9:12 PM          0 abc

PS >
```

Removing a File

The syntax for removing a file is exactly the same as removing a file because there isn't a parameter for specifying whether we are attempting to remove a file or a folder.

```
PS > remove-item def
PS >
```

> **NOTE**
>
> You can use the `confirm` parameter to get a confirmation prompt on the screen before PowerShell actually carries out the request command, or you can use the `whatIf` parameter to have PowerShell display the commands that would actually be executed if the parameter wasn't passed.

Moving a File

Moving an item and renaming an item are two different things.

```
PS > move-item abc new_directory
PS >
```

> **NOTE**
>
> You typically use `Move-Item` when you want to move an item to a new directory. When you want to change the name of an item, you should be renaming it and not moving it.

Renaming a File

If we want to rename an item, we should not attempt to move it, but use `Rename-Item`.

```
PS > rename-item xyz lmn
PS >
```

Getting the Content of a File

Let's examine the content in a file. To read the data inside of a file, we use the cmdlet `Get-Content`.

```
PS > get-content string.txt
testing
PS >
```

Setting the Content of a File

To write to a file, we have two cmdlets: `Set-Content` writes data to the file, `Add-Content` appends data to the file. It is important to remember the difference between these two or risk losing data. Writing data to a file can do two things: create the file with the appropriate data or overwrite any existing data in the file. We show how we can use the `Set-Content` cmdlet to demonstrate both scenarios. We also use the file `string.txt` we saw in the previous section.

```
PS > set-content string.txt "foo"
PS > get-content string.txt
foo
PS > set-content new_file.txt "foo"
PS > get-content new_file.txt
Foo
```

Appending Content to a File

Add-Content can do two things: It can add data to an existing file, but it can also create a new file and add the data to it.

```
PS > get-content string.txt
foo
2nd line
PS > add-content string2.txt "2nd line"
PS > get-content string2.txt
2nd line
```

Searching for Content in a File

Fortunately, there is a cmdlet to search for data within items. Select-String enables you to search for the contents of a file passed as an argument.

```
PS > get-content string.txt
foo
2nd line
PS > select-string -path string.txt -patt "2nd"

string.txt:2:2nd line

PS >
```

You will normally use this cmdlet for searching through files that you are passing via the pipeline.

```
PS > get-content string.txt|select-string -patt "2nd"

2nd line

PS >
```

> **NOTE**
>
> Searching for strings in multiple files: As we mentioned, we can look through data passed via the pipeline by passing the files to search to the Select-String cmdlet. This is useful when attempting to search recursively through a file system. If we wanted to search through a file system recursively, we would use Get-ChildItem to get the objects we were interested in, and then pass those objects along to Select-String.
>
> ```
> PS > get-childitem . -rec *.txt|foreach-object{select-string $_ -patt "2nd"}
>
> string.txt:2:2nd line
>
> string2.txt:1:2nd line
>
> foobar\string2.txt:1:2nd line
>
> PS >
> ```

> **NOTE**
>
> The Select-String cmdlets works with the file system provider, but does not work with the registry provider; therefore, you cannot use Select-String within the registry to search.

Testing for a File

If you want to check for the existence of a file, the Test-Path cmdlet can help you. When testing for a file, you should pass the value leaf to the pathType parameter to make sure you are looking for a file; otherwise, you could end up matching the name to a directory.

```
PS > test-path -type leaf testing.txt
True
PS >
```

Working with XML Files

Dealing with XML files is another one of PowerShell's strengths. You can load XML data for handy viewing, and you can also edit them.

In the first part of this section, we walk you through various tasks with PowerShell where we create an XML file, and then edit it by adding to it and removing from it. While doing so, we reference an article that originally appeared in the February 2008 issue of *TechNet Magazine*, which you can find online at http://technet.microsoft.com/en-us/magazine/cc194420.aspx.

The online document used VBScript and the older Microsoft.XMLDOM object to handle XML tasks. We are going to use PowerShell and the .NET Framework's System.Xml.XmlDocument class to provide an updated example.

> **NOTE**
>
> XML files are case-sensitive. A node named "Test" will not be seen by PowerShell as the same as "TEST."

> **NOTE**
>
> The 2.0 CTP2 has a few new feature relating to XML:
>
> ► A new cmdlet named ConvertTo-Xml. As of the release of the 2.0 CTP2, the built-in help was not complete for this new cmdlet.

Creating an XML File

We want to end up with an XML document that looks like this:

```
<?xml version='1.0'?>
<itchecklist>
  <computeraudit>
    <computername>atl-ws-001</computername>
  </computeraudit>
</itchecklist>
```

Here's the code we use to create the previous document.

```
# Create our .NET object.
$xmlDoc = new-object System.Xml.XmlDocument
# Call a $xmlDoc method, passing it the name for the root node.
$objroot=$xmlDoc.createelement("itchecklist")
# Add the root node to our object.
$xmldoc.appendchild($objroot)
# Create a child node.
$objrecord=$xmlDoc.createelement("computeraudit")
# Add the child node to our root node.
$objroot.appendchild($objrecord)
# Create another child node.
$objname=$xmldoc.createelement("computername")
# Set the text for the child node.
$objname.set_innertext("atl-ws-001")
# Add the child node to the previous child node.
$objrecord.appendchild($objname)
# Add <?xml version="1.0" ?> to the beginning of the object.
$objintro=$xmldoc.createprocessinginstruction("xml","version='1.0'")
$xmldoc.insertbefore($objintro,$xmldoc.childnodes.item(0))
# Save the document.
$xmldoc.save("test.xml")
```

8

If we use `Get-Content` to load our newly created XML document, we see that we achieved the desired result shown in the previous example.

```
PS > get-content test.xml
<?xml version='1.0'?>
<itchecklist>
  <computeraudit>
    <computername>atl-ws-001</computername>
  </computeraudit>
</itchecklist>
```

Appending an XML File

We have our XML document, but now we want to modify it by adding to the original XML file.

```
# Load the previously created document.
$xmldoc.load("test.xml")
# Get our root node.
$objroot=$xmldoc.documentElement
# Create a child node.
$objrecord=$xmldoc.createElement("computeraudit")
# Add the child node to the root node.
$objroot.appendChild($objrecord)
# Create another child node.
$objname=$xmldoc.createelement("computername")
# Set the text for the child node.
$objname.set_innertext("atl-ws-100")
# Add the child node to the previous child node.
$objrecord.appendchild($objname)
# Create another child node.
$objname=$xmldoc.createelement("auditdate")
# Set the text for the child node.
$objname.set_innertext($(get-date))
# Add the child node to the previous child node.
$objrecord.appendchild($objname)
# Save the document.
$xmldoc.save("test1.xml")
```

Now, our document looks like this:

```
PS> get-content test1.xml
<?xml version="1.0"?>
<itchecklist>
  <computeraudit>
    <computername>atl-ws-001</computername>
  </computeraudit>
  <computeraudit>
    <computername>atl-ws-100</computername>
    <auditdate>03/18/2008 23:11:19</auditdate>
  </computeraudit>
</itchecklist>
```

Modifying an XML File

We have added to our XML document; now, let's show how to modify existing data in our XML file.

```
# Load the XML document.
$xmldoc.load("test1.xml")
# Get our root node.
$objroot=$xmldoc.documentElement
# Use XPath (XML Path Language) to select the nodes we want to modify.
$nodes=$xmldoc.selectnodes("/itchecklist/computeraudit[computername=
'atl-ws-100']/auditdate")
# Use a foreach loop to loop through the results.
foreach($node in $nodes){
  $node.set_innertext($(get-date))
}
# Save the document.
$xmldoc.save("test2.xml")
```

We have just modified an existing node, and our XML document looks like the following:

```
PS> get-content test2.xml
<?xml version="1.0"?>
<itchecklist>
  <computeraudit>
    <computername>atl-ws-001</computername>
  </computeraudit>
  <computeraudit>
```

8

```
    <computername>atl-ws-100</computername>
    <auditdate>03/18/2008 23:11:57</auditdate>
  </computeraudit>
</itchecklist>
```

Deleting from an XML File

Let's look at how we can delete an existing node from our XML file.

```
# Load the XML document.
$xmldoc.load("test2.xml")
# Get our root node.
$objroot=$xmldoc.documentElement
# Use XPath (XML Path Language) to select the nodes we want to delete.
$nodes=$xmldoc.selectnodes("/itchecklist/computeraudit[computername='atl-ws-100']")
# Use a foreach loop to loop through the results.
foreach($node in $nodes){
  $xmldoc.documentelement.removechild($node)
}
# Save the document.
$xmldoc.save("test3.xml")
```

Our document looks like this with a child node removed, which is what our document looked like when we first created it:

```
PS> get-content test3.xml
<?xml version="1.0"?>
<itchecklist>
  <computeraudit>
    <computername>atl-ws-001</computername>
  </computeraudit>
</itchecklist>
```

Loading an XML File

Before we show how to load an XML file, let's note what we did in the previous sections: We used the Get-Content cmdlet to read the contents of an XML-formatted file. Using this method provides us with contents of the XML-formatted file, but this isn't useful except for reading the file.

The proper way to use the XML features included with PowerShell is to use the [XML] type shortcut (also known as type accelerator).

```
PS > [xml]$xml=get-content test2.xml
```

Processing an XML File

In the previous section, we loaded an XML file into the $xml variable. Let's look at what we can do with our new variable.

```
PSH > $xml
xml                                                            itchecklist
---                                                            -----------
version="1.0"                                                  itchecklist
PSH>$xml.itchecklist
computeraudit
-------------
{computeraudit, computeraudit}
PSH>$xml.itchecklist.computeraudit
computername
------------
atl-ws-001
atl-ws-100
```

We can walk through all the XML nodes in the document. An example that could be handy is looking through the XML output of the new Server Manager included with Windows 2008 for the roles and features on a system.

Using Import-CliXml and Export-CliXml

We cannot split the Import-CliXml and Export-CliXml cmdlets into their own section, so we cover them together here.

Import-CliXml and Export-CliXml cmdlets are provided to handle structured data helping to move data in and out of files. This can help, for example, when one might need to store data. When it comes time to reconstruct the original object, the original properties and values can be accessed, but some of the methods might no longer be available.

Let's create a simple string and datetime object, and then use Export-CliXml to write this object to a XML-formatted file.

```
PS > "test"|export-clixml string.xml
PS > get-date|export-clixml date.xml
```

We've created two XML-formatted files, so let's take a look at the contents of each.

```
PS > get-content string.xml
<Objs Version="1.1"
xmlns="http://schemas.microsoft.com/powershell/2004/04"><S>test</S></Objs>
PS > get-content date.xml
<Objs Version="1.1" xmlns="http://schemas.microsoft.com/powershell/2004/04">
<Obj RefId="RefId-0"><DT>2008-03-11T23:47:4
6.4163463-03:00</DT><MS><Obj N="DisplayHint" RefId="RefId-1">
<TN RefId="RefId-0"><T>Microsoft.PowerShell.Commands.Displ
ayHintType</T><T>System.Enum</T><T>System.ValueType</T><T>System.Object</T>
</TN><ToString>DateTime</ToString><I32>2</I3
2></Obj></MS></Obj></Objs>
```

Some of the key things to take out of the previous contents follow:

▶ From string.xml: The pair <S> and </S> indicate that this is a string object.

▶ From date.xml: The pair <DT> and </DT> indicate that this is a datetime object.

From there, we can take these XML files and move them around from one system to another.

If we use the Import-CliXml cmdlet, we can reconstruct the original objects again.

```
PS > (import-clixml string.xml).gettype().fullname
System.String
PS > (import-clixml date.xml).gettype().fullname
System.DateTime
```

In the previous example, we see we now have our original objects back again. If the XML is imported into another system, the specific .NET class used would also need to exist on the destination system.

Working with CSV Files

PowerShell also has some built-in functionality for dealing with comma-separated value (CSV) files. Import-Csv reads in the file and creates objects based on the contents of the file.

NOTE

The 2.0 CTP2 has a few new features relating to CSV:

▶ A new cmdlet named `ConvertTo-Csv`. As of the release of the 2.0 CTP2, the built-in help was not complete for this new cmdlet.

▶ The existing `Import-Csv` and `Export-Csv` cmdlets now have a new `Delimeter` parameter, which provides support for delimeters other than ",". See the built-in help for the cmdlet for more details.

We look at `Import-Csv` and show an example of reading in a file.

```
PS > get-content server.csv
server,ip
server1,10.10.10.10
server2,10.10.10.11
PS > import-csv server.csv
server                                                          ip
------                                                          --
server1                                                         10.10.10.10
server2                                                         10.10.10.11
PS >
```

Because these are objects, we can use cmdlets like `Select-Object` to get just specific properties. For example, my `server.csv` file might contain all kinds of information regarding each server, but we might need only a printout of the server column.

```
PS >  import-csv server.csv|select server
server
------
server1
server2
PS >
```

We also said something about objects being created when using `Import-Csv`. Using `Get-Member`, we can see these are added as properties to a custom object that PowerShell creates.

```
PS > import-csv server.csv|get-member server,ip
   TypeName: System.Management.Automation.PSCustomObject
Name    MemberType    Definition
----    ----------    ----------
server  NoteProperty  System.String server=server1
ip      NoteProperty  System.String ip=10.10.10.10
```

8

Writing to a CSV File

You can also use PowerShell to create a CSV file from objects passed along the pipeline. For example, you can get a listing of all the processes on the machine and write out particular objects to a CSV file.

```
PS > get-process|export-csv process.csv
```

The previous example dumps a lot of information into the CSV file, so we might want to filter out some of the information by using select-object.

```
PS > get-process|select name,company|export-csv process.csv
```

> **NOTE**
>
> Export-Csv also accepts a noTypeInformation parameter that removes information on the particular object that has just been exported. For example, in the last example, this was printed to the beginning of the resulting file:
>
> #TYPE System.Management.Automation.PSCustomObject

Scenario: Automating File System Management

ProvisionWebFolders.ps1 is a script provided as a complete working example of PowerShell being put to use for task automation. A working copy of this script can be found at www.informit.com/title/9780672329883. You need to provide two parameters to run this script. First, TemplatePath should have its argument set to the source path of the template folder structure copied to new users' Web folders. Second, ImportFile should have its argument set to the name of the CSV import file used to define new users and their Web folder locations. The command to run the ProvisionWebFolders.ps1 script, with sample output shown in Figure 8.1, follows:

```
PS D:\Work> .\ProvisionWebFolders.ps1 .\template .\users.csv
```

The ProvisionWebFolders.ps1 script performs the following sequence of actions:

1. The script verifies that the template folder path exists.

2. The script verifies that the import folder path exists.

3. The script imports the CSV file into the $Targets variable.

4. For each user in $Targets, the script copies the template folder structure to the new user's Web folder.

5. The script sets permissions on each folder, such as the following:

  ▸ Administrators: Owner

  ▸ Administrators: FullControl

  ▸ System: FullControl

  ▸ NewUser: FullControl

FIGURE 8.1   The ProvisionWebFolders.ps1 script being executed

The first code sample contains the header for the ProvisionWebFolders.ps1 script. This header includes information about what the script does, when it was updated, and the script's author. Just after the header are the script's parameters:

```
################################################
# ProvisionWebFolders.ps1
# Used to provision new user Web folders.
#
# Created: 9/12/2006
# Author: Tyson Kopczynski
################################################
param([string] $TemplatePath = $(throw write-host `
    "Please specify the source template path of the folder structure to" `
```

```
"be copied." -Foregroundcolor Red), [string] $ImportFile = $(throw `
write-host "Please specify the import CSV filename." `
-Foregroundcolor Red))
```

Notice how the throw keyword is being used in the param declaration to generate an error when a parameter does not have a defined argument. This technique is used to force a parameter to be defined by stopping execution of the script and providing the script operator with information about the required parameter using the Write-Host cmdlet. When using the Write-Host cmdlet, you can use the Foregroundcolor parameter, as shown in the previous code sample, to control the color of output text. This feature is handy for focusing attention on details of the script status, as shown in Figure 8.2:

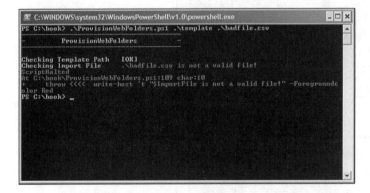

FIGURE 8.2   Colored console output text being used to convey script status

Next, as seen in the following code sample, the script loads the needed file system management functions into its scope:

```
###################################################
# Functions
###################################################
#---------------------------------------------------
# Clear-Inherit
#---------------------------------------------------
# Usage:        Used to protect against inherited access rules
#               and remove all inherited explicitly defined rules.
# $Object:      The directory or file path.  ("c:\myfolder" or
#               "c:\myfile.txt")

function Clear-Inherit{
    param ($Object)
```

```
    $SD = get-acl $Object
    $SD.SetAccessRuleProtection($True, $False)
    set-acl $Object $SD
    }


#----------------------------------------------------
# Set-Owner
#---------------------------------------------------
# Usage:        Used to set the owner on a folder or file.
# $Object:      The directory or file path.  ("c:\myfolder" or
#               "c:\myfile.txt")
# $Identity:    User or Group name. ("Administrators" or
#               "mydomain\user1"

function Set-Owner{
    param ($Object,
        [System.Security.Principal.NTAccount]$Identity)

    # Get the item that will be changed
    $Item = get-item $Object

    # Set the owner
    $SD = $Item.GetAccessControl()
    $SD.SetOwner($Identity)
    $Item.SetAccessControl($SD)
    }


#----------------------------------------------------
# Add-ACE
#---------------------------------------------------
# Usage:        Grants rights to a folder or file.
# $Object:      The directory or file path.  ("c:\myfolder" or
#               "c:\myfile.txt")
# $Identity:    User or group name. ("Administrators" or
#               "mydomain\user1"
# $AccessMask:  The access rights to use when creating the access rule.
#               ("FullControl", "ReadAndExecute, Write", etc.)
# $Type:        Allow or deny access. ("Allow" or "Deny")

function Add-ACE{
    param ($Object,
    [System.Security.Principal.NTAccount]$Identity,
    [System.Security.AccessControl.FileSystemRights]$AccessMask,
    [System.Security.AccessControl.AccessControlType]$Type)
```

```
    $InheritanceFlags = `
        [System.Security.AccessControl.InheritanceFlags]`
        "ContainerInherit, ObjectInherit"
    $PropagationFlags = `
        [System.Security.AccessControl.PropagationFlags]"None"

    # Get the security descriptor for the object
    $SD = get-acl $Object

    # Add the AccessRule
    $Rule = new-object `
        System.Security.AccessControl.FileSystemAccessRule($Identity, `
        $AccessMask, $InheritanceFlags, $PropagationFlags, $Type)

    $SD.AddAccessRule($Rule)
    set-acl $Object $SD
    }
```

NOTE

The preceding functions are used to make file system permission changes. These functions are explained in Chapter 9, "PowerShell and Permissions."

The next code sample contains the beginning of the script's automation portion. First, the script checks to see if the string contained in the $TemplatePath variable is a valid folder path. Then, the script checks to see if the string contained in the $ImportFile variable is a valid file path. To perform these tests, the if...then statements make use of Test-Path cmdlet. This is a handy cmdlet that can be used for verifying whether a folder or file (-pathType container or leaf) is valid. If any of these paths are invalid, the script execution is halted, and information about the invalid paths is returned to script operator:

```
#################################################
# Main
#################################################
write-host "------------------------------------------"
write-host "-          ProvisionWebFolders          -"
write-host "------------------------------------------"
write-host
write-host "Checking Template Path" -NoNewLine

if (!(test-path $TemplatePath -pathType container)){
    throw write-host `t "$TemplatePath is not a valid directory!" `
```

```
        -Foregroundcolor Red
    }
else {
    write-host `t "[OK]" -Foregroundcolor Green
    }

write-host "Checking Import File" -NoNewLine

if (!(test-path $ImportFile -pathType leaf)){
    throw write-host `t "$ImportFile is not a valid file!" -Foregroundcolor Red
    }
else {
    write-host `t "[OK]" -Foregroundcolor Green
    }
```

In the next code sample the rest of the variables that are used in the script are defined.
The first variable $Owner is used by the script to define the owner for each user's Web
folder structure, which in this case is the local Administrators group. Then, the variable
$Targets is defined using the Import-Csv cmdlet. This cmdlet is used to read values from
the import CSV file ($ImportFile) into the $Targets variable, which is used to provision
new users' Web folders:

```
#-------------------
# Set Vars
#-------------------
$Owner = "Administrators"
$Targets = import-csv $ImportFile
```

In the following code sample, the script uses the path and username information from
the information contained in the $Target variable to construct the final destination path
using the Join-Path cmdlet. Then, the script uses the Copy-Item cmdlet to copy the
template folders to the destination path:

```
#-------------------
# Provision Web Folders
#-------------------
write-host
write-host "Provision Web Folders:"

foreach ($Target in $Targets){
    $Path = join-path $Target.DestPath $Target.UserName
    $UserName = $Target.UserName
```

```
write-host $Path

if (!(test-path $Path)){
    copy-item $TemplatePath -Destination $Path -Recurse `
    -ErrorVariable Err -ErrorAction SilentlyContinue


    if (!$Err){
        write-host " Folder " -NoNewLine
        write-host "[COPIED]" -Foregroundcolor Green

        # Used to stop loops
        $Err = $False
```

Next, the script uses the Set-Owner function to change ownership of the user's Web folder structure to the local Administrators group:

```
.{
    trap{write-host "[ERROR] Failed to take ownership!" `
        -Foregroundcolor Red;
        $Script:Err = $True;
        Continue}


    # Set Owner
    write-host " SetOwner for $Owner " -NoNewLine

    Set-Owner $Path $Owner

    if ($Err -eq $False){
        $Items = get-childitem $Path -Recurse
        [void]($Items | foreach-object `
                {Set-Owner $_.FullName $Owner})
        }
    else{
        # Stop the loop
        Continue
        }

    write-host "[OK]" -Foregroundcolor Green
    }
```

You might be wondering why the code for Set-Owner is enclosed in a script block. The dot (.) call operator preceding the script block tells PowerShell to run the script block within the current scope. If the call operator isn't used, PowerShell doesn't run the script block. The reason for creating an independent script block to handle the code for Set-Owner is to ensure that the trap statement is scoped only to this block of code.

In the following code sample, notice that the Administrators group is added to the root folder's security descriptor before inherited permissions are cleared:

```
.{
    trap{write-host "[ERROR] Failed to add rights!" `
        -Foregroundcolor Red;
        $Script:Err = $True;
        Continue}

    # Add Administrators
    write-host " AddACE for Administrators " -NoNewLine

    Add-ACE $Path "Administrators" "FullControl" "Allow"

    if ($Err -eq $False){
        write-host "[OK]" -Foregroundcolor Green
        }
    else{
        # Stop the loop
        Continue
        }
}


.{
    trap{write-host "[ERROR] Failed to clear inherited"`
        "permissions!" -Foregroundcolor Red;
        $Script:Err = $True;
        Continue}

    # Clear inherited permissions
    write-host " ClearInherit " -NoNewLine

    Clear-Inherit $Path

    if ($Err -eq $False){
        write-host "[OK]" -Foregroundcolor Green
        }
    else{
        # Stop the loop
        Continue
        }
}
```

8

The `Clear-Inherit` function clears inherited permissions from the root folder, subfolders, and files, in addition to explicitly defined permissions on all subfolders and files. If the Administrators group didn't have explicitly defined rights on the root folder, the rest of the script wouldn't run because of a lack of rights.

NOTE

Explicitly defined permissions are permissions that are directly defined for a user on an object. Implicitly defined permissions are permissions that are either inherited or defined through membership of a group.

In the last code sample, the SYSTEM account and the user are then granted `FullControl` to the user's web folder, and the script notifies the script operator of its completion:

```
                # Add SYSTEM
                write-host " AddACE for SYSTEM " -NoNewLine

                if ((Add-ACE $Path "SYSTEM" "FullControl" "Allow") -eq $True){
                    write-host "[OK]" -Foregroundcolor Green
                    }

                # Add User
                write-host " AddACE for $UserName " -NoNewLine

                if ((Add-ACE $Path $UserName "FullControl" "Allow") -eq $True){
                    write-host "[OK]" -Foregroundcolor Green
                    }
                }
        else {
            write-host " Folder " -NoNewLine
            write-host "Error:" $Err -Foregroundcolor Red
            }
        }
    else {
        write-host " Folder " -NoNewLine
        write-host "[EXISTS]" -Foregroundcolor Yellow
        }

    write-host
    }

write-host "Done Provisioning Web Folders:"
```

Summary

We first looked at the core cmdlets used when dealing with file systems. We discussed how these core cmdlets provide a common experience among different providers, not only when dealing with file systems.

Then, we focused on how to manage the Windows file system using PowerShell, where we showed how to complete some of the most common administrative tasks done with drives, folders, and files.

This chapter provided an overview of how to manage CSV and XML files using cmdlets created specifically to deal with these specially formatted files.

Finally, the chapter presented a complete file system management script gathering several key concepts already reviewed in the book. Modularizing scripts can provide various advantages, such as reusing code and helping to make scripts more readable.

8

PowerShell and Permissions

W indows permissions can be complex and simple depending on what is needed because, at its core, the security model around Windows permissions was created to be as flexible as possible. For example, you can set permissions for files, directories, registry keys, processes and threads, services, printers, network shares, directory objects, named and anonymous pipes, and kernel objects. However, when combined with its flexibility and core concepts such as ACLs, ACEs, DACLs, SACLs, SIDs, and inheritance, trying to manage Windows permissions using scripting can be a daunting challenge.

In this chapter, the primary goal is to gain a better understanding around how PowerShell handles the management of Windows permissions. To reach that goal, you first review how permissions were managed using Windows Script Host (WSH). Next, you review how PowerShell is used to manage Windows permissions and the slight improvement it provides over past scripting methods. Finally, while reviewing both the WSH and PowerShell methods, you are introduced to set of custom script functions that can be used to manage permissions. These functions serve as examples to show how difficult automating permission changes can be while giving you insight as to how to tackle Windows permission management.

WSH and Permissions

Working with permissions in WSH has limitations. For example, there's no straightforward method for changing permissions on an object. Instead, scripters must choose between using an external utility, such as `cacls`, `xcacls`, `dsacls.exe`, `xcalcs.vbs`, `SubInACL`, or using automation interfaces such `ADsSecurity.dll` or the WMI `Win32_LogicalFileSecuritySetting` class. In either case, none of the listed methods offers a complete or standard solution for working with permissions.

Given these limitations, the `SubInACL` utility is one of the many tools that is often used for managing permissions on an object or group of objects. This tool isn't perfect, but if you script around its shortcomings, it's usually more than satisfactory for making permission changes when compared to what is available via WSH. In addition, `SubInACL` supports files, directories, file shares, printer shares, the registry, system services, and the Internet Information Services (IIS) metabase.

> **NOTE**
>
> You can download `SubInACL` from
> www.microsoft.com/downloads/details.aspx?FamilyId=E8BA3E56-D8FE-4A91-93CF-ED6985E3927B&displaylang=en.

The syntax for `SubInACL` consists of `[/Option] /object_type object_name [[/Action[=Parameter]..]`. This syntax seems simple enough, however, `SubInACL` is a complex permission Swiss army knife that can handle a variety of situations. But, in most cases, you will use `SubInACL` to only complete the following permission changes:

- ▶ Take ownership
- ▶ Dump permissions
- ▶ Add permissions
- ▶ Remove permissions

This list isn't exhaustive, but it does give you a foundation for developing functions that can be frequently reused. Developing reusable functions is a recommended best practice. They can be used in many scripts and reduce the time needed to develop a script. For permission changes, developing reusable functions makes even more sense because working with the supported interfaces in WSH or existing tools can be time consuming. To better illustrate this practice, the next section contains several `SubInACL` functions that have been created to manage folder and file permissions.

SubInACL **Functions**

In this section, four `SubInACL` functions are discussed: `SetOwner`, `DumpPerm`, `AddPerm`, and `RemovePerm`. Each function takes arguments and builds a command string for the `SubInACL` utility. Then, using a `WshShell` object, the `SubInACL` utility is executed using the constructed command string. Next, output in the `log.temp` file from `SubInACL` is read for errors by using the `ParseTempFile` function. Based on the error information derived from `log.temp`, a success or failure status is then written to the console.

SetOwner

This function is used to set the owner for a folder and its subfolders. To use this function, provide the path for the folder you want to define ownership for and the name of the account or group that is to be the owner. The source code for this function is as follows:

```
Function SetOwner(path, account)
    'Used to set the owner on a folder or subfolders.
    On Error Resume Next
    strCommand = "subinacl /verbose /output=log.temp " _
        & "/subdirectories """ & path & """ /setowner=""" & account & """"

    ErrorCode = objWS.Run(strCommand, 0, TRUE)

    If ErrorCode <> 0 Then
        StdOut.Write("   " & account & ":" _
            & " [SetOwner Failed] on " & path)
    Else
        return = inStr(1, ParseTempFile("log.temp"), "will not be processed")

        If Not return = 0 Then
        StdOut.Write("   " & account & ":" _
            & " [SetOwner Failed] on " & path)
        Else
        StdOut.Write("   " & account & ":" _
            & " [SetOwner OK] on " & path)
        End If
    End If

    ErrorCode = vbNullString
End Function
```

DumpPerm

This function is used to clear permission from a folder and its subfolders. To use this function, provide the path for the folder you want to clear permissions from. The source code for this function is as follows:

```
Function DumpPerm(path)
    ' Used to clear permissions from a folder or subfolders.
    On Error Resume Next
    strCommand = "subinacl /verbose /output=log.temp " _
        & "/subdirectories """ & path & """ /perm"
```

```
    ErrorCode = objWS.Run(strCommand, 0, TRUE)

    If ErrorCode <> 0 Then
        StdOut.Write("  Dropped perm on " & path)
    Else
        StdOut.Write("  Dropped perm on " & path)
    End If


    ErrorCode = vbNullString
End Function
```

AddPerm

This function is used to grant a user or group permission to a folder and its subfolders. To use this function, provide the path for the folder you want to add rights to, the name of the account or group to grant rights to, and the type of access being granted. The source code for this function is as follows:

```
Function AddPerm(path, account, access)
    ' Used to grant a user's rights to a folder or subfolders.
    On Error Resume Next
    strCommand = "subinacl /verbose /output=log.temp" _
        & " /subdirectories """ & path & """ /grant=""" _
        & account & """ =" & access

    ErrorCode = objWS.Run(strCommand, 0, TRUE)

    If ErrorCode <> 0 Then
        StdOut.Write("  " & account & ": " & access _
            & " [AddPerm Failed] on " & path)
    Else
        return = inStr(1, ParseTempFile("log.temp"), "will not be processed")

        If Not return = 0 Then
            StdOut.Write("  " & account & ": " & access _
                & " [AddPerm Failed] on " & path)
        Else
            StdOut.Write("  " & account & ": " & access _
                & " [AddPerm OK] on " & path)
        End If
    End If


    ErrorCode = vbNullString
End Function
```

Please review SubInACL documentation to understand the values that can be defined
for the access parameter.

RemovePerm

This function is used to remove rights from a user or group to a folder and its subfolders.
To use this function, provide the path for the folder you want to add rights to, the name
of the account or group to grant rights to, and the type of access being revoked. The
source code for this function is as follows:

```
Function RemovePerm(path, account, access)
    ' Used to remove a user's rights to a folder or subfolders.
    On Error Resume Next
    strCommand = "subinacl /verbose /output=log.temp" _
        & " /subdirectories """ & path & """ /revoke=""" _
        & account & """ =" & access

    ErrorCode = objWS.Run(strCommand, 0, TRUE)

    If ErrorCode <> 0 Then
        StdOut.Write("  " & account & ": " & access _
            & " [AddPerm Failed] on " & path)
    Else
        return = inStr(1, ParseTempFile("log.temp"), "will not be processed")

        If Not return = 0 Then
            StdOut.Write("  " & account & ": " & access _
                & " [AddPerm Failed] on " & path)
        Else
            StdOut.Write("  " & account & ": " & access _
                & " [AddPerm OK] on " & path)
        End IF
    End If

    ErrorCode = vbNullString
End Function
```

PowerShell and Permissions

One of the greater hopes for PowerShell was that it would have soothed the rough edges
associated with attempting to manage Windows permissions (via the command line or
through a script). After all, as shown and explained in this chapter's previous sections, the

lack of interfaces in WSH and the required use of external utilities left a lot to be desired. In fact, one might say that the lack of a standardized management interface within the realm of "Windows Scripting" is frustrating.

In reality, however, working with Windows permissions is a difficult task even when you are full-fledge developer. So, unless there is an interface that acts as an adapter and provides you with a simple set of methods for reading and modifying permissions, your ability as scripter to manage permissions will also be severely handicapped. Unfortunately, although the PowerShell team attempted to improve things, PowerShell's "permissions adapter" has positives and negatives.

Because PowerShell is based on the .NET Framework, it is resigned to using a set of core classes for both representing and working with Windows permissions. Although the classes themselves are powerful and can provide a "developer" with the needed tools to correctly manage or report on permissions, directly working with these classes can be a challenging endeavor, even for a developer.

To remove some of the challenges associated with these classes, the PowerShell team included two cmdlets named Get-ACL and Set-ACL. As you might expect, Get-ACL cmdlet is used to retrieve the security descriptor for a resource, such as a file or registry key, while the Set-ACL cmdlet is used to modify the security descriptor of a resource.

Thanks to the Get-ACL and Set-ACL cmdlets, you might think managing Windows permissions is easier in PowerShell. However, the Set-ACL cmdlet still requires a security descriptor object defined by the System.Security.AccessControl.ObjectSecurity class. Constructing a security descriptor isn't difficult, but managing permissions isn't as straightforward to script as you might have hoped. When faced with terms such as security descriptors and access control rules (ACL), you might be tempted to stick with more familiar tools, such as SubInACL. If you sit down and go through the process step by step, however, it's not as complex as it seems at first glance. It consists of these basic steps:

1. Get the security descriptor (ACL) for an object by using Get-ACL.

2. Build the ACL with access control entries (ACE).

3. Add the ACL to the security descriptor.

4. Bind the new security descriptor to the object by using Set-ACL.

The following code is an example of using these steps:

```
PS > $SD = get-acl "Helena's Programs.csv"
PS > $Rule = new-object
System.Security.AccessControl.FileSystemAccessRule("maiko",
"FullControl","Allow")
PS > $SD.AddAccessRule($Rule)
PS > set-acl "Helena's Programs.csv" $SD
```

The hardest step to understand in this example is building the access rule. An access rule consists of three parameters to define user or group, access right, and access control type. The first parameter, `Identity`, is easy to define because you know the user or group to be added to an access rule. The second parameter, `FileSystemRights`, is more difficult because it requires understanding file system rights to define the access. However, you can use the following command to produce a list of supported rights:

```
PS >
[enum]::GetNames([System.Security.AccessControl.FileSystemRights])
ListDirectory
ReadData
WriteData
CreateFiles
CreateDirectories
AppendData
ReadExtendedAttributes
WriteExtendedAttributes
Traverse
ExecuteFile
DeleteSubdirectoriesAndFiles
ReadAttributes
WriteAttributes
Write
Delete
ReadPermissions
Read
ReadAndExecute
Modify
ChangePermissions
TakeOwnership
Synchronize
FullControl
```

From this list, you can define a single right, such as Modify, or string rights together into a list, such as Read, Write, and Delete. The third parameter, `AccessControlType`, is easy to define because it can be only Allow or Deny.

PowerShell Functions

As with the `SubInACL` utility, a set of reusable permission management functions can be developed for use in your scripts. Examples of such functions follow.

Clear-Inherit

The `Clear-Inherit` function is used to clear inherited permissions from a folder. However, `Clear-Inherit` is probably the wrong name for this function because in addition to preventing inherited permissions from being applied from the parent object and clearing inherited permissions from the root object and sub-objects, it clears explicitly defined permissions on sub-objects. Therefore, before using the `Clear-Inherit` function, it's a good practice to take ownership of the object or make sure you have explicitly defined rights for yourself on the root file system object. If you don't ensure that you have access to file system objects, you might see "access denied" messages after clearing inherited rights. The source code for this function is as follows:

```
#- - - - - - - - - - - - - - - - - - - - - - - - - - - - - - - - - - - - - - - - -
# Clear-Inherit
#- - - - - - - - - - - - - - - - - - - - - - - - - - - - - - - - - - - - - - - - -
# Usage:        Used to protect against inherited access rules
#               and remove all inherited explicitly defined rules.
# $Object:      The directory or file path. ("c:\myfolder" or
#               "c:\myfile.txt")

function Clear-Inherit{
    param ($Object)

    $SD = get-acl $Object
    $SD.SetAccessRuleProtection($True, $False)
    set-acl $Object $SD
    }
```

Set-Owner
The next function, `Set-Owner`, is used to set the owner on a file system object:

```
#- - - - - - - - - - - - - - - - - - - - - - - - - - - - - - - - - - - - - - - - -
# Set-Owner
#- - - - - - - - - - - - - - - - - - - - - - - - - - - - - - - - - - - - - - - - -
# Usage:        Used to set the owner on a folder or file.
# $Object:      The directory or file path. ("c:\myfolder" or
#               "c:\myfile.txt")
# $Identity:    User or Group name. ("Administrators" or
#               "mydomain\user1"

function Set-Owner{
    param ($Object,
        [System.Security.Principal.NTAccount]$Identity)

    # Get the item that will be changed
    $Item = get-item $Object
```

```
# Set the owner
$SD = $Item.GetAccessControl()
$SD.SetOwner($Identity)
$Item.SetAccessControl($SD)
}
```

Clear-SD

The Clear-SD function is used to clear the security descriptor for a file system object. Although the Clear-SD function is used in the file system management script later in this chapter, it's a good illustration of how you can set a security descriptor with **Security Descriptor Definition Language (SDDL)**. SDDL is used to describe a security descriptor as a text string. If the Clear-SD function is used, an object's security descriptor is cleared and then set to FullControl for the Everyone group by using the string "D:PAI(A;OICI;FA;;;WD)".

> **NOTE**
>
> For more information on constructing a security descriptor with the **Security Descriptor String Format**, refer to http://msdn.microsoft.com/library/default.asp?url=/library/en-us/secauthz/security/security_descriptor_string_format.asp.

The following code box contains the source for the Clear-SD function:

```
#---------------------------------------------------
# Clear-SD
#---------------------------------------------------
# Usage:      Used to drop all permissions on a folder or file.
# $Object:    The directory or file path.  ("c:\myfolder" or
#             "c:\myfile.txt")

function Clear-SD{
    param ($Object)

    # Get the security descriptor for the object
    $SD = get-acl $Object

    # Set the SD to Everyone - Full Control
    #
    # Yes, this isn't a best practice; if you don't like it, then
    # set the SD to the current user.
    $SD.SetSecurityDescriptorSddlForm("D:PAI(A;OICI;FA;;;WD)")
    set-acl $Object $SD
    }
```

Add-ACE

Add-ACE is used to grant rights to a file system object for a user or group. This function, although similar to the example at the beginning of this section, also shows how to control inheritance settings for a new access control entry (ACE) with System.Security. AccessControl.PropagationFlags and System.Security.AccessControl. InheritanceFlags enumerations.

```
#--------------------------------------------------
# Add-ACE
#--------------------------------------------------
# Usage:        Grants rights to a folder or file.
# $Object:      The directory or file path.  ("c:\myfolder" or
#               "c:\myfile.txt")
# $Identity:    User or Group name. ("Administrators" or
#               "mydomain\user1"
# $AccessMask:  The access rights to use when creating the access rule.
#               ("FullControl", "ReadAndExecute, Write", etc.)
# $Type:        Allow or deny access. ("Allow" or "Deny")

function Add-ACE{
    param ($Object,
    [System.Security.Principal.NTAccount]$Identity,
    [System.Security.AccessControl.FileSystemRights]$AccessMask,
    [System.Security.AccessControl.AccessControlType]$Type)

    $InheritanceFlags = `
        [System.Security.AccessControl.InheritanceFlags]`
        "ContainerInherit, ObjectInherit"
    $PropagationFlags = `
        [System.Security.AccessControl.PropagationFlags]"None"

    # Get the security descriptor for the object
    $SD = get-acl $Object

    # Add the AccessRule
    $Rule = new-object `
        System.Security.AccessControl.FileSystemAccessRule($Identity, `
        $AccessMask, $InheritanceFlags, $PropagationFlags, $Type)

    $SD.AddAccessRule($Rule)
    set-acl $Object $SD
    }
```

Don't let the name of these flags confuse you, as they control how an ACE is applied to an object and all objects under that object. In the Add-ACE function, the flags are set so that an ACE is applied to file system objects as "This folder, subfolders, and files." This means that the ACE will be applied to the object being modified and propagated to all objects under that object. Propagating the ACE as defined in the Add-ACE function should be sufficient for most file system management tasks. If not, you can modify the function so that it accepts inheritance settings as an argument.

Remove-ACE

The last function is the Remove-ACE function. This function is used to remove an ACE from an ACL:

```
#------------------------------------------------
# Remove-ACE
#------------------------------------------------
# Usage:       Removes rights to a folder or file.
# $Object:     The directory or file path. ("c:\myfolder" or
#              "c:\myfile.txt")
# $Identity:   User or Group name. ("Administrators" or
#              "mydomain\user1"
# $AccessMask: The access rights to use when creating the access rule.
#              ("FullControl", "ReadAndExecute, Write", etc.)
# $Type:       Allow or deny access. ("Allow" or "Deny")

function Remove-ACE{
    param ($Object,
        [System.Security.Principal.NTAccount]$Identity,
        [System.Security.AccessControl.FileSystemRights]$AccessMask,
        [System.Security.AccessControl.AccessControlType]$Type)

    # Get the security descriptor for the object
    $SD = get-acl $Object

    # Remove the AccessRule
    $Rule = new-object `
        System.Security.AccessControl.FileSystemAccessRule($Identity, `
        $AccessMask, $Type)
    $SD.RemoveAccessRule($Rule)
    set-acl $Object $SD
    }
```

Summary

After reading this chapter, you should understand how difficult Windows permissions automation can be. Although the security model is powerful, there isn't a good interface or method to easily manage permissions on objects. As you have seen, WSH provided no built-in interface and solely relied on external utilities or assemblies. PowerShell, on the other hand, provided a set of cmdlets. Even with this minor improvement, managing permissions still tends to be an intimidating task.

As shown in this chapter, if you take the time to figure out a set of reusable script functions, you can attempt to make up for the shortcomings for both WSH and PowerShell.

## CHAPTER 10

PowerShell and the Registry

This chapter explains how PowerShell can be used to manage the Windows Registry. To do this, the chapter explores in-depth examples of managing the Registry using PowerShell.

This chapter also discusses a new feature currently in the 2.0 CTP series called registry transactions and presents a series of working Registry management functions that are based on a real-world situation.

The goal is to give the reader a chance to learn how PowerShell scripting techniques can be applied to meet real-world Registry management and automation needs.

The chapter ends with an example of how to use the new built-in remoting features of the 2.0 CTP to access the registry of remote systems.

Registry Management in PowerShell

In PowerShell, you work with the Registry differently. As discussed in Chapter 4, "Other Key PowerShell Concepts," PowerShell has a built-in Provider, Registry, for accessing and manipulating the Registry on a local machine. By default, the Registry hives available in this provider are HKEY_LOCAL_MACHINE (HKLM) and HKEY_CURRENT_ USER (HKCU). These hives are represented in a PowerShell session as two additional PSDrive objects named HKLM: and HKCU:.

Chapter 4 also stated that accessing data through the Registry provider means PowerShell treats data in the HKLM: and HKCU: PSDrive objects like other hierarchical data stores. Therefore, accessing and manipulating data from these PSDrives requires using the PowerShell core cmdlets, as shown in this example:

```
PS C:\> set-location hkcu:
PS HKCU:\> get-childitem
   Hive: Microsoft.PowerShell.Core\Registry::HKEY_CURRENT_USER
SKC  VC Name                              Property
---  -- ----                              --------
  2   0 AppEvents                         {}
  2  32 Console                           {ColorTable00, ColorTable01,
                                          ColorTab...
 24   1 Control Panel                     {Opened}
  0   2 Environment                       {TEMP, TMP}
  1   6 Identities                        {Identity Ordinal, Migrated5,
                                          Last Us...
  4   0 Keyboard Layout                   {}
  3   1 Printers                          {DeviceOld}
 32   1 Software                          {(default)}
  0   0 UNICODE Program Groups            {}
  2   0 Windows 3.1 Migration Status      {}
  0   1 SessionInformation                {ProgramCount}
  0   8 Volatile Environment              {LOGONSERVER, HOMESHARE,
                                          HOMEPATH, US...
PS HKCU:\> get-itemproperty 'Volatile Environment'
PSPath          :
Microsoft.PowerShell.Core\Registry::HKEY_CURRENT_USER\Volatile
                Environment
PSParentPath  : Microsoft.PowerShell.Core\Registry::HKEY_CURRENT_USER
PSChildName   : Volatile Environment
PSDrive       : HKCU
PSProvider    : Microsoft.PowerShell.Core\Registry
LOGONSERVER   : \\SOL
HOMESHARE     : \\taosage.internal\homes\tyson
HOMEPATH      : \
USERDNSDOMAIN : TAOSAGE.INTERNAL
CLIENTNAME    :
SESSIONNAME   : Console
APPDATA       : C:\Documents and Settings\tyson\Application Data
HOMEDRIVE     : U:


PS HKCU:\>
```

By using the PowerShell core cmdlets, you can manipulate the local Registry as you see fit.

In PowerShell, you access and manipulate the Registry like you do with the file system. For example, to read a Registry value in PowerShell, use the Get-ItemProperty cmdlet, as shown in the following example:

```
PS C:\> $Path = "HKLM:\Software\Microsoft\Windows NT\CurrentVersion"
PS C:\> $Key = Get-ItemProperty $Path
PS C:\> $Key.ProductName
Microsoft Windows XP
PS C:\>
```

To create or modify a Registry value in PowerShell, use the Set-ItemProperty cmdlet:

```
PS C:\> $Path = "HKCU:\Software"
PS C:\> Set-ItemProperty -Path $Path -Name "PSinfo" —Type "String" -
Value "PowerShell_Was_Here"
PS C:\>
PS C:\> $Key = Get-ItemProperty $Path
PS C:\> $Key.info
PowerShell_Was_Here
PS C:\>
```

Remember that the Windows Registry has different types of Registry values. You use the Set-ItemProperty cmdlet to define the Type parameter when creating or modifying Registry values. As a best practice, you should always define Registry values when using the Set-ItemProperty cmdlet. Otherwise, the cmdlet defines the Registry value with the default type, which is String. Other possible types follow:

▶ ExpandString

▶ Binary

▶ DWord

▶ MultiString

▶ Qword

NOTE

Depending on the Registry value you're creating or modifying, the data value you set the named value to needs to be in the correct format. So, if the Registry value is type REG_BINARY, you use a binary value, such as $Bin = 101, 118, 105.

10

To delete a Registry value in PowerShell, you use the `Remove-ItemProperty` cmdlet:

```
PS C:\> $Path = "HKCU:\Software"
PS C:\> Remove-ItemProperty -Path $Path -Name "PSinfo"
PS C:\>
```

These examples give you an idea of how to work with the Registry. It's simple as long as you understand how to use the core cmdlets and remember that working with the Registry is much like working with the Windows file system.

However, there's no built-in cmdlet for accessing the Registry on a remote machine. This omission makes sense because by default, no PowerShell providers are available for accessing remote data stores. Until someone writes a provider you can use to manage the Registry remotely, you can to turn to one existing method, explained later when the `LibraryRegistry.ps1` script is covered.

If you're either using the WS-MANAGEMENT (WSMAN) add-on or the PowerShell 2.0 integration with WSMAN, doing stuff remotely becomes easier. We're going to provide a detailed example later when 2.0 features are discussed.

Adding Other Hives

Only `HKLM:` and `HKCU:` were available by default with PowerShell. You can easily set up the other registry hives and PSDrive objects using the `New-PsDrive` cmdlet. Let's show how one can create a PSDrive for the `HKEY_CURRENT_CONFIG` hive. We're going to name it `HKCC` for short. This procedure can be used to also add the `HKEY_USERS` and `HKEY_CLASSES_ROOT` hives.

```
PS C:\> New-PsDrive -Name HKCC -PsProvider Registry -Root Hkey_Current
_Config

Name         Provider        Root                           CurrentLocation
----         --------        ----                           ---------------
hkcc         Registry        hkey_current_config
PS C:\> Get-PsDrive -PsProvider Registry
Name         Provider        Root                           CurrentLocation
----         --------        ----                           ---------------
HKCC         Registry        Hkey_Current_Config
HKCU         Registry        HKEY_CURRENT_USER
HKLM         Registry        HKEY_LOCAL_MACHINE
PS C:\> cd HKCC:
PS HKCC:\> dir
   Hive: Microsoft.PowerShell.Core\Registry::hkey_current_config

SKC  VC Name                           Property
---  -- ----                           --------
  2   0 Software                       {}
  1   0 System                         {}
PS HKCC:\>
```

As seen in the previous example, a new registry hive has been added to the current PowerShell session.

Registry Transactions

As of the 2.0 CTP2, PowerShell now supports registry transactions. There might be support for transactions in other providers in the future, but only time will tell. This feature relies on new features provided with the base Windows operating system as of Vista and 2008 Server. Unfortunately, by the time CTP2 was released in May 2008, not all of the built-in documentation had been completed.

Transactions provide the ability to perform registry operations as a group of commands that can be similar or different. One way to think about a transaction is when considering a larger number of registry operations that are to be undertaken. Let's say we have a dozen registry changes to make. With transaction support, we can apply or commit all the operations together or roll them all back if there is any kind of failure, for example.

Getting Started

We can check what features our Registry provider supports. If you're running the proper PowerShell version, you will see something similar to what is shown in Figure 10.1:

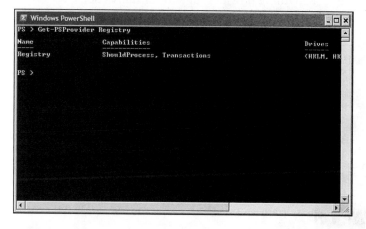

FIGURE 10.1   Using Get-PsProvider to show the provider features

In Figure 10.1, we see that our provider lists transactions as a capability or supported feature.

Several core cmdlets now have also been updated and provide a useTransaction parameter. Let's focus on the New-Item cmdlet, as shown in Figure 10.2.

10

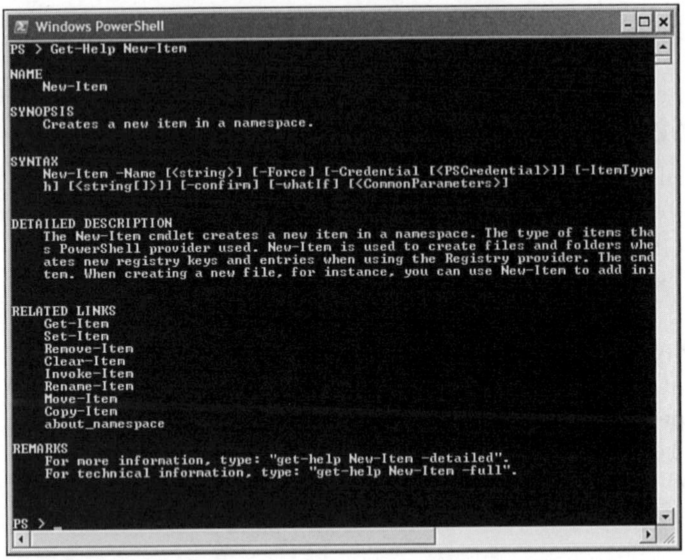

FIGURE 10.2   Using Get-Help to look at the help details for New-Item

In Figure 10.2, you don't notice that anything provides support for transactions. Let's try another method to list the parameters supported by the cmdlet, as shown in Figure 10.3.

FIGURE 10.3   Using Get-Command to view the parameters for New-Item

As previously mentioned, the built-in help provided with PowerShell wasn't fully updated with the information relating to registry transactions by the time the May 2008 2.0 CTP2 was released.

New Cmdlets

The four new cmdlets provided for registry transactions include the following, as also shown in Figure 10.4:

▶ Complete-PSTransaction: Used whenever someone wants to complete or end a particular transaction.

▶ Start-PSTransaction: Used whenever someone wants to start a transaction.

▶ Undo-PSTransaction: Used whenever someone wants to back out of a transaction (restoring everything to its original state before the transaction was actually started).

▶ Use-PSTransaction: Enables a person to use advanced features of the .NET Framework to work with transacted objects (this cmdlet is not covered in this book).

FIGURE 10.4   The four new cmdlets that provide support for transactions

How It Works

The basic procedure to using transactions is to inform PowerShell that we are starting a transaction, and then we run our commands, which potentially might be system changing. At some point, we need to determine whether our transaction is complete so that we can apply whatever changes have been done, or back out of our changes to restore the system to its initial state before we started the transaction.

One thing that must be remembered is that for any particular command to be considered part of the current transaction, the useTransaction parameter must be used, as we show in an example shortly. In other words, it is possible to start a transaction, but actually enter commands outside of the transaction that take effect immediately. Any commands run outside of the transaction cannot be rolled back as part of the current transaction. Also, after a transaction is started, some commands actually behave differently if proper consideration isn't given to the parameters provided to commands that are run. Again, this is shown in an example shortly.

Some additional parameters available when doing transactions include rollbackSeverity and rollbackPreference. These parameters aren't currently well documented, but provide a lot of flexibility on how transactions are rolled back when an error is encountered.

Example: Starting and Committing a Transaction

Let's provide an example of a transaction. To keep things simple, we are going to make only one registry change here.

```
PS C:\> cd HKCU:\
PS HKCU:\> New-Item "testing"
PS HKCU:\> cd testing
PS HKCU:\testing> Start-PSTransaction
PS HKCU:\testing> New-Item "not_using_trans"


   Hive: Microsoft.PowerShell.Core\Registry::HKEY_CURRENT_USER\testing


SKC  VC Name                            Property
---  -- ----                            --------
  0   0 not_using_trans                 {}

PS HKCU:\testing> New-Item "using_trans" -UseTransaction

   Hive: Microsoft.PowerShell.Core\Registry::HKEY_CURRENT_USER\testing


SKC  VC Name                            Property
---  -- ----                            --------
  0   0 using_trans                     {}

PS HKCU:\testing> Get-ChildItem .

   Hive: Microsoft.PowerShell.Core\Registry::HKEY_CURRENT_USER\testing


SKC  VC Name                            Property
---  -- ----                            --------
  0   0 not_using_trans                 {}

PS HKCU:\testing> Get-ChildItem . -UseTransaction

   Hive: Microsoft.PowerShell.Core\Registry::HKEY_CURRENT_USER\testing


SKC  VC Name                            Property
---  -- ----                            --------
  0   0 not_using_trans                 {}
  0   0 using_trans                     {}

PS HKCU:\testing> Complete-PSTransaction
PS HKCU:\testing> Get-ChildItem .

   Hive: Microsoft.PowerShell.Core\Registry::HKEY_CURRENT_USER\testing


SKC  VC Name                            Property
---  -- ----                            --------
  0   0 not_using_trans                 {}
  0   0 using_trans                     {}


PS HKCU:\testing>
```

In the previous example, we used the New-Item cmdlet to create an item in the registry. There are a few things to note:

▶ We used the useTransaction parameter to our second call to New-Item because we had just started a transaction.

▶ Our first call to Get-ChildItem basically showed the current physical state of the registry because we didn't use the useTransaction parameter.

▶ Our second call to Get-ChildItem listed the state of the registry with all previous transacted commands being taken into account.

We've just done our first transaction!

Example: Starting and Undoing a Transaction

Let's provide an example where we actually entered a few commands while in a transaction, and then decided to cancel all the changes we did and restore the system to the state it was in just before we started our transaction.

```
PS HKCU:\testing> Get-ChildItem .


    Hive: Microsoft.PowerShell.Core\Registry::HKEY_CURRENT_USER\testing


SKC  VC Name                          Property
---  -- ----                          --------
  0   0 not_using_trans               {}
  0   0 using_trans                   {}

PS HKCU:\testing> Start-PSTransaction
PS HKCU:\testing> New-Item "rollback_trans" -UseTransaction


    Hive: Microsoft.PowerShell.Core\Registry::HKEY_CURRENT_USER\testing


SKC  VC Name                          Property
---  -- ----                          --------
  0   0 rollback_trans                {}

PS HKCU:\testing> Get-ChildItem .


    Hive: Microsoft.PowerShell.Core\Registry::HKEY_CURRENT_USER\testing


SKC  VC Name                          Property
---  -- ----                          --------
  0   0 not_using_trans               {}
  0   0 using_trans                   {}
```

10

```
PS HKCU:\testing> Get-ChildItem . -UseTransaction

   Hive: Microsoft.PowerShell.Core\Registry::HKEY_CURRENT_USER\testing

SKC  VC Name                            Property
---  -- ----                            --------
  0   0 not_using_trans                 {}
  0   0 using_trans                     {}
  0   0 rollback_trans                  {}

PS HKCU:\testing> Undo-PSTransaction
PS HKCU:\testing> Get-ChildItem .

   Hive: Microsoft.PowerShell.Core\Registry::HKEY_CURRENT_USER\testing

SKC  VC Name                            Property
---  -- ----                            --------
  0   0 not_using_trans                 {}
  0   0 using_trans                     {}

PS HKCU:\testing>
```

In this case, we used Undo-PsTransaction to cancel all the changes we made since we started our transaction.

Example: Performing a Transaction That Has Errors

We've shown two examples of transactions where we actually controlled what occurred. Now, let's say we started a transaction and an error occurred. By default, PowerShell stops the current transaction and restores the system to its original state.

```
PS HKCU:\testing> Get-ChildItem .

   Hive: Microsoft.PowerShell.Core\Registry::HKEY_CURRENT_USER\testing

SKC  VC Name                            Property
---  -- ----                            --------
  0   0 not_using_trans                 {}
  0   0 using_trans                     {}

PS HKCU:\testing> Start-PSTransaction
PS HKCU:\testing> Remove-Item "not_there"
Remove-Item : Cannot find path '\not_there' because it does not exist.
At line:1 char:12
```

```
+ Remove-Item <<<<  "not_there"
PS HKCU:\testing> Complete-PSTransaction
PS HKCU:\testing> Start-PSTransaction
PS HKCU:\testing> Remove-Item "not_there" -UseTransaction
Remove-Item : Cannot find path '\not_there' because it does not exist.
At line:1 char:12
+ Remove-Item <<<<  "not_there" -UseTransaction
PS HKCU:\testing> Complete-PSTransaction
Complete-PSTransaction : Cannot commit transaction. The transaction
has been rolled back.
At line:1 char:23
+ Complete-PSTransaction <<<<
PS HKCU:\testing>
```

The previous example shows two things:

▶ We show that it is not just any kind of error that will stop our transaction. We must use the useTransaction parameter.

▶ We cause an error with the useTranscation parameter, which causes our transaction to stop and be rolled back by the system.

It is important to remember to use the useTranscation parameter when we want to take into account that we are dealing with a transaction.

Simplifying Registry Management

This section focuses on a PowerShell script for reading and manipulating the Registry. The script is being presented as a reusable library file using reusable functions. To use such a library in PowerShell, you include or dot source the library file you want in your script or console session.

The script examples in this section contain a series of functions for reading and modifying the Registry on a local host or remote machine. To use these functions, scripters can copy them into a script or call them from a library file that has been included or dot sourced into the script.

In addition to reducing the time to create scripts, using reusable code stored in a library file makes your code more standardized and interchangeable. In fact, Jeffrey Snover, the PowerShell architect, has often recommended following this best practice for scripting.

The LibraryRegistry.ps1 Script

LibraryRegistry.ps1 is a PowerShell script that we are going to look at in detail. A working copy of this script can be found at www.informit.com/title/9780672329883. Before using this library file in a PowerShell console session, it must be dot sourced.

10

The dot sourcing format is a period followed by a space and then the filename, as in this example: . .\myscript.ps1. To dot source LibraryRegistry.ps1 from a PowerShell console session, use the following command:

```
PS C:\>. "D:\Scripts\LibraryRegistry.ps1"
```

However, dot sourcing a script file every time you want to use its set of functions tends to be more work than it should be. When you dot source a script file, the contents are loaded into your current PowerShell console session's global scope. If you close that session and open a new session, everything that was in the global scope is discarded, forcing you to dot source the script file every time you start a new session.

To avoid this problem, you can use a PowerShell profile to control the configuration of your PowerShell console. By using a PowerShell profile, such as Profile.ps1, and dot sourcing your script files in a profile file, you have everything you need already loaded in the global scope every time you start a new console session. Here's an example of a Profile.ps1 file:

```
. "D:\Scripts\LibraryRegistry.ps1"
set-location C:\
cls
# Welcome Message
"Welcome to back to more reg fun: " + $ENV:UserName
```

NOTE

LibraryRegistry.ps1 can also be dot sourced in a script file. Dot sourcing a .ps1 script file as such tells PowerShell to load the script into the calling script's scope. Remember that a script's parent scope can be a PowerShell session or another script.

After a new PowerShell session is loaded with the customized Profile.ps1, the console prompt looks like this:

```
Welcome to back to more reg fun: script_master_snover
PS C:\>
```

By retrieving information from the Function PSDrive object, as shown in the following example, you can determine whether the Registry functions defined in LibraryRegistry.ps1 have been loaded into the current PowerShell session:

```
PS C:\> Get-ChildItem Function:

CommandType        Name                    Definition
-----------        ----                    ----------
Function           prompt                  'PS ' + $(Get-Location) + $(...
Function           TabExpansion            ...
Function           Clear-Host              $spaceType = [System.Managem...
Function           more                    param([string[]]$paths);  if...
Function           help                    param([string]$Name,[string[...
Function           man                     param([string]$Name,[string[...
Function           mkdir                   param([string[]]$paths); New...
Function           md                      param([string[]]$paths); New...
Function           A:                      Set-Location A:
Function           B:                      Set-Location B:
Function           C:                      Set-Location C:

...

Function           W:                      Set-Location W:
Function           X:                      Set-Location X:
Function           Y:                      Set-Location Y:
Function           Z:                      Set-Location Z:
Function           Get-RegValue            param($Computer, $KeyPath, $...
Function           Set-RegKey              param($Computer, $KeyPath) $...
Function           Set-RegValue            param($Computer, $KeyPath, $...
Function           Remove-RegKey           param($Computer, $KeyPath) $...
Function           Remove-RegValue         param($Computer, $KeyPath, $...


PS C:\>
```

Notice in the preceding example that five different Reg functions can be used in the current PowerShell session to read and manipulate subkeys under the HKEY_LOCAL_MACHINE hive for the local host or remote machines. The remainder of this section gives you more information about these functions because we will look at each one and discuss what is being done by that particular piece of code.

Get-RegValue Function

The Get-RegValue function retrieves a Registry value for under the HKEY_LOCAL_MACHINE hive. This function requires defining the following parameters:

▶ $Computer—The name or IP address of the computer to retrieve Registry information from; "." can be used to denote the local host.

▶ $KeyPath—The key path where the Registry value is located.

▶ $ValueName—The name of the Registry value from which you're trying to retrieve data.

▶ $Type—A defined string representing the type of Registry value from which data is being retrieved, such as BIN (REG_BINARY), DWORD (REG_DWORD), EXP (REG_EXPAND_SZ), MULTI (REG_MULTI_SZ), and STR (REG_SZ).

Here is the code for the function itself:

```
#-----------------------------------------------------
# Get-RegValue
#-----------------------------------------------------
# Usage:        Used to read an HKLM Registry value
#               on a local or remote machine.
# $Computer:    The name of the computer.
# $KeyPath:     The Registry key path.
#               ("SYSTEM\CurrentControlSet\Control")
# $ValueName:   The Registry value name. ("CurrentUser")
# $Type:        The Registry value type. ("BIN", "DWORD",
#               "EXP", "MULTI", or "STR")

function Get-RegValue{
    param ($Computer, $KeyPath, $ValueName, $Type)

    $HKEY_LOCAL_MACHINE = 2147483650

    trap{write-host "[ERROR] $_" -Foregroundcolor Red; Continue}

    $Reg = get-wmiobject -Namespace Root\Default -computerName `
        $Computer -List | where-object `
        {$_.Name -eq "StdRegProv"}

    if ($Type -eq "BIN"){
        return $Reg.GetBinaryValue($HKEY_LOCAL_MACHINE, $KeyPath, `
            $ValueName)
        }
    elseif ($Type -eq "DWORD"){
        return $Reg.GetDWORDValue($HKEY_LOCAL_MACHINE, $KeyPath, `
            $ValueName)
        }
    elseif ($Type -eq "EXP"){
        return $Reg.GetExpandedStringValue($HKEY_LOCAL_MACHINE, `
            $KeyPath, $ValueName)
```

```
    }
elseif ($Type -eq "MULTI"){
    return $Reg.GetMultiStringValue($HKEY_LOCAL_MACHINE, `
        $KeyPath, $ValueName)
    }
elseif ($Type -eq "STR"){
    return $Reg.GetStringValue($HKEY_LOCAL_MACHINE, `
        $KeyPath, $ValueName)
    }
}
```

The following example shows how to use this function:

```
PS C:\> get-regvalue "Arus" "SOFTWARE\Voltron" "BlueLion" "BIN"
```

Set-RegKey Function

The Set-RegKey function creates a Registry key under the HKEY_LOCAL_MACHINE hive. This function requires defining the following parameters:

- ► $Computer—The name or IP address of the computer to create the key on; "." can be used to denote the local host.

- ► $KeyPath—The key path for the new Registry key.

Here is the code for the function itself:

```
#-----------------------------------------------------
# Set-RegKey
#-----------------------------------------------------
# Usage:        Used to create/set an HKLM Registry key
#               on a local or remote machine.
# $Computer:    The name of the computer.
# $KeyPath:     The Registry key path.
#               ("SYSTEM\CurrentControlSet\Control")

function Set-RegKey{
    param ($Computer, $KeyPath)

    $HKEY_LOCAL_MACHINE = 2147483650

    trap{write-host "[ERROR] $_" -Foregroundcolor Red; Continue}
```

10

```
$Reg = get-wmiobject -Namespace Root\Default -computerName `
    $Computer -List | where-object `
    {$_.Name -eq "StdRegProv"}

return $Reg.CreateKey($HKEY_LOCAL_MACHINE, $KeyPath)
}
```

Here's an example of using this function:

```
PS C:\> Set-RegKey "Arus" "SOFTWARE\Voltron"
```

Set-RegValue Function

The Set-RegValue function creates or changes a Registry value under the HKEY_LOCAL_MACHINE hive. This function requires defining the following parameters:

▶ $Computer—The name or IP address of the computer on which to create or change a Registry value; "." can be used to denote the local host.

▶ $KeyPath—The key path where the Registry value is located.

▶ $ValueName—The name of the Registry value you're trying to create or change.

▶ $Value—The data to which to set the Registry value.

▶ $Type—A defined string representing the type of Registry value being created or changed, such as BIN (REG_BINARY), DWORD (REG_DWORD), EXP (REG_EXPAND_SZ), MULTI (REG_MULTI_SZ), and STR (REG_SZ).

Here is the code for the function itself:

```
#----------------------------------------------------
# Set-RegValue
#----------------------------------------------------
# Usage:       Used to create/set an HKLM Registry value
#              on a local or remote machine.
# $Computer:   The name of the computer.
# $KeyPath:    The Registry key path.
#              ("SYSTEM\CurrentControlSet\Control")
# $ValueName:  The Registry value name. ("CurrentUser")
# $Value:      The Registry value. ("value1", Array, Integer)
# $Type:       The Registry value type. ("BIN", "DWORD",
#              "EXP", "MULTI", or "STR")
```

```
function Set-RegValue{
    param ($Computer, $KeyPath, $ValueName, $Value, $Type)

    $HKEY_LOCAL_MACHINE = 2147483650

    trap{write-host "[ERROR] $_" -Foregroundcolor Red; Continue}

    $Reg = get-wmiobject -Namespace Root\Default -computerName `
        $Computer -List | where-object `
        {$_.Name -eq "StdRegProv"}

    if ($Type -eq "BIN"){
        return $Reg.SetBinaryValue($HKEY_LOCAL_MACHINE, $KeyPath, `
            $ValueName, $Value)
    }
    elseif ($Type -eq "DWORD"){
        return $Reg.SetDWORDValue($HKEY_LOCAL_MACHINE, $KeyPath, `
            $ValueName, $Value)
    }
    elseif ($Type -eq "EXP"){
        return $Reg.SetExpandedStringValue($HKEY_LOCAL_MACHINE, `
            $KeyPath, $ValueName, $Value)
    }
    elseif ($Type -eq "MULTI"){
        return $Reg.SetMultiStringValue($HKEY_LOCAL_MACHINE, `
            $KeyPath, $ValueName, $Value)
    }
    elseif ($Type -eq "STR"){
        return $Reg.SetStringValue($HKEY_LOCAL_MACHINE, `
            $KeyPath, $ValueName, $Value)
    }
}
```

The following example shows how to use this function:

```
PS C:\> $Multi = "PowerShell", "is", "fun!"
PS C:\> Set-RegValue "Arus" "SOFTWARE\Voltron" "Lion_Statement"
$Multi "MULTI"
```

Remove-RegKey Function

The Remove-RegKey function deletes a Registry key from the HKEY_LOCAL_MACHINE hive. This function requires defining the following parameters:

▶ $Computer—The name or IP address of the computer where you're deleting the key; "." can be used to denote the local host.

▶ $KeyPath—The key path for the Registry key to delete.

Here is the code for the function itself:

```
#---------------------------------------------------
# Remove-RegKey
#---------------------------------------------------
# Usage:        Used to delete an HKLM Registry key
#               on a local or remote machine.
# $Computer:    The name of the computer.
# $KeyPath:     The Registry key path.
#               ("SYSTEM\CurrentControlSet\Control")

function Remove-RegKey{
    param ($Computer, $KeyPath)

    $HKEY_LOCAL_MACHINE = 2147483650

    trap{write-host "[ERROR] $_" -Foregroundcolor Red; Continue}

    $Reg = get-wmiobject -Namespace Root\Default -computerName `
        $Computer -List | where-object `
        {$_.Name -eq "StdRegProv"}

    return $Reg.DeleteKey($HKEY_LOCAL_MACHINE, $KeyPath)
    }
```

An example of using this function is shown here:

```
PS C:\> Remove-RegKey "Arus" "SOFTWARE\Voltron"
```

Remove-RegValue Function

The Remove-RegValue function deletes a Registry value from the HKEY_LOCAL_MACHINE hive. You must define the following parameters:

▶ $Computer—The name or IP address of the computer where you're creating the key; "." can be used to denote the local host.

▶ $KeyPath—The key path where the Registry value resides.

▶ $ValueName—The name of the Registry value being deleted.

Here is the code for the function itself:

```
#----------------------------------------------------
# Remove-RegValue
#----------------------------------------------------
# Usage:        Used to delete an HKLM Registry value
#               on a local or remote machine.
# $Computer:    The name of the computer.
# $KeyPath:     The Registry key path.
#               ("SYSTEM\CurrentControlSet\Control")
# $ValueName:   The Registry value name. ("CurrentUser")

function Remove-RegValue{
    param ($Computer, $KeyPath, $ValueName)

    $HKEY_LOCAL_MACHINE = 2147483650

    trap{write-host "[ERROR] $_" -Foregroundcolor Red; Continue}

    $Reg = get-wmiobject -Namespace Root\Default -computerName `
        $Computer -List | where-object `
        {$_.Name -eq "StdRegProv"}

    return $Reg.DeleteValue($HKEY_LOCAL_MACHINE, $KeyPath, $ValueName)
    }
```

Here's an example of using this function:

```
PS C:\> Remove-RegValue "Arus" "SOFTWARE\Voltron" "Lion_Statement"
```

10

Using the Library
Now that you understand the Registry functions in the LibraryRegistry.ps1 script, you can practice using these functions. The first step is to create a Registry key called Turtle_Worm under the HKLM\Software key on an Active Directory domain controller named DC1. To do this, use the following command:

```
PS C:\> Set-RegKey "DC1" "SOFTWARE\Turtle_Worm"


__GENUS            : 2
__CLASS            : __PARAMETERS
__SUPERCLASS       :
__DYNASTY          : __PARAMETERS
__RELPATH          :
__PROPERTY_COUNT   : 1
__DERIVATION       : {}
__SERVER           :
__NAMESPACE        :
__PATH             :
ReturnValue        : 0


PS C:\>
```

The command returns a WMI object that contains no information. If any error occurred, the trap in the function writes the error information to the console, as shown in this example:

```
PS C:\> Set-RegKey "Pinky" "SOFTWARE\Turtle_Worm"
[ERROR] The RPC server is unavailable. (Exception from HRESULT:
0x800706BA)
PS C:\>
```

Next, you create values under the `Turtle_Worm` Registry key with the following set of commands:

```
PS C:\> $Bin = 101, 118, 105, 108, 95, 116, 117, 114, 116, 108, 101
PS C:\> Set-RegValue "DC1" "SOFTWARE\Turtle_Worm" "binValue" $Bin "BIN"


__GENUS            : 2
__CLASS            : __PARAMETERS
__SUPERCLASS       :
__DYNASTY          : __PARAMETERS
__RELPATH          :
__PROPERTY_COUNT   : 1
__DERIVATION       : {}
__SERVER           :
__NAMESPACE        :
```

```
__PATH             :
ReturnValue        : 0



PS C:\> $Null = Set-RegValue "DC1" "SOFTWARE\Turtle_Worm" "dwordValue" "1"
"DWORD"
PS C:\> $Null =Set-RegValue "DC1" "SOFTWARE\Turtle_Worm" "expValue"
"%SystemRoot%\system32\Turtle_Hacker.dll" "EXP"
PS C:\> $Multi = "PowerShell", "is", "fun!"
PS C:\> $Null = Set-RegValue "DC1" "SOFTWARE\Turtle_Worm" "multiValue"
$Multi "MULTI"
PS C:\> $Null = Set-RegValue "DC1" "SOFTWARE\Turtle_Worm" "strValue" "Reg
work done!" "STR"
PS C:\>
```

These steps simulate creating a Registry key and its values. Next, you use the Registry library functions to determine whether a set of values exists. To do this, use the Get-RegValue function:

```
PS C:\> Get-RegValue "DC1" "SOFTWARE\Turtle_Worm" "binValue" "BIN"


__GENUS            : 2
__CLASS            : __PARAMETERS
__SUPERCLASS       :
__DYNASTY          : __PARAMETERS
__RELPATH          :
__PROPERTY_COUNT   : 2
__DERIVATION       : {}
__SERVER           :
__NAMESPACE        :
__PATH             :
ReturnValue        : 0
uValue             : {101, 118, 105, 108...}



PS C:\> Get-RegValue "DC1" "SOFTWARE\Turtle_Worm" "dwordValue" "DWORD"


__GENUS            : 2
__CLASS            : __PARAMETERS
```

10

```
__SUPERCLASS      :
__DYNASTY         : __PARAMETERS
__RELPATH         :
__PROPERTY_COUNT  : 2
__DERIVATION      : {}
__SERVER          :
__NAMESPACE       :
__PATH            :
ReturnValue       : 0
uValue            : 1


PS C:\> Get-RegValue "DC1" "SOFTWARE\Turtle_Worm" "expValue" "EXP"


__GENUS           : 2
__CLASS           : __PARAMETERS
__SUPERCLASS      :
__DYNASTY         : __PARAMETERS
__RELPATH         :
__PROPERTY_COUNT  : 2
__DERIVATION      : {}
__SERVER          :
__NAMESPACE       :
__PATH            :
ReturnValue       : 0
sValue            : C:\WINDOWS\system32\Turtle_Hacker.dll


PS C:\> Get-RegValue "DC1" "SOFTWARE\Turtle_Worm" "multiValue" "MULTI"


__GENUS           : 2
__CLASS           : __PARAMETERS
__SUPERCLASS      :
__DYNASTY         : __PARAMETERS
__RELPATH         :
__PROPERTY_COUNT  : 2
__DERIVATION      : {}
__SERVER          :
__NAMESPACE       :
__PATH            :
```

```
ReturnValue         : 0
sValue              : {PowerShell, is, fun!}



PS C:\> Get-RegValue "DC1" "SOFTWARE\Turtle_Worm" "strValue" "STR"



__GENUS             : 2
__CLASS             : __PARAMETERS
__SUPERCLASS        :
__DYNASTY           : __PARAMETERS
__RELPATH           :
__PROPERTY_COUNT    : 2
__DERIVATION        : {}
__SERVER            :
__NAMESPACE         :
__PATH              :
ReturnValue         : 0
sValue              : Reg work done!

PS C:\>
```

As you can see from the WMI objects returned, if a value exists, its information is returned as a sValue or uValue property. If the value or key doesn't exist, the ReturnValue property is the integer 2. If the ReturnValue property is set to the integer 0, it indicates that the WMI method was completed successfully.

Now that you have verified that values under the Turtle_Worm Registry key exist on DC1, it's time to delete the Turtle_Worm Registry key and its values. There are two methods to perform this task. First, you can delete each value by using the Remove-RegValue function, as shown in the following example:

```
PS C:\> Remove-RegValue "DC1" "SOFTWARE\Turtle_Worm" "binValue"



__GENUS             : 2
__CLASS             : __PARAMETERS
__SUPERCLASS        :
__DYNASTY           : __PARAMETERS
__RELPATH           :
__PROPERTY_COUNT    : 1
__DERIVATION        : {}
__SERVER            :
```

```
__NAMESPACE         :
__PATH              :
ReturnValue         : 0


PS C:\>
```

The other method is using the Remove-RegKey function to delete the Turtle_Worm Registry key, which deletes all its subkeys and their values, as shown here:

```
PS C:\> Remove-RegKey "sol" "SOFTWARE\Turtle_Worm"


__GENUS             : 2
__CLASS             : __PARAMETERS
__SUPERCLASS        :
__DYNASTY           : __PARAMETERS
__RELPATH           :
__PROPERTY_COUNT    : 1
__DERIVATION        : {}
__SERVER            :
__NAMESPACE         :
__PATH              :
ReturnValue         : 0


PS C:\>
```

Using 2.0 CTP Features

Our previous example was basically focused on using what features PowerShell 1.0 provided us for remoting: WMI. We also wrote a bunch of functions to help us out. Let's fast-forward now to the 2.0 CTP. 2.0 CTP provides us with built-in features for helping make things easier when dealing with remote systems.

We aren't going to go over all of the core ideas from the previous example, but we will show a simple example using 2.0 features to show how things have improved. We also differentiate how things differ if we are dealing with a domain versus a workgroup or workgroups.

Scenario Details

In this scenario, we work with two systems: one Windows Vista SP1 system and one Windows Server 2008 system. Let's get right into how things can differ if we are in a domain versus a workgroup.

If we're dealing with systems in a domain, we can create one single credential object and use it against all our systems. Even easier, if we're actually running the script as a user with domain administrator privileges, we don't need to worry about creating a credential object.

We are now going to look at an example where we are dealing with two different Administrator accounts. (Actually, they just have different passwords.) On Vista, we aren't using the built-in Administrator account, but a user with Administrator privileges. On Server 2008, we are using the local Administrator account.

We are going to run our commands locally on the Vista box, so a credential object doesn't need to be created locally, but we are going to also query the remote Server 2008 box. For that system, we need to create a credential object.

We list the version of PowerShell running on the local machine and the remote machine. We query the properties of this particular registry key: HKEY_LOCAL_MACHINE\Software\ Microsoft\PowerShell\1\PowerShellEngineVersion.

Running the Commands

We are going to try to use the Get-ItemProperty cmdlet to get our information. Let's try to accomplish this with one command.

```
PS C:\> Invoke-Command -ComputerName server08,localhost '
>> -ScriptBlock {Get-ItemProperty
HKLM:\software\Microsoft\PowerShell\1\PowerShellEngine| '
>> Select-Object PowershellVersion}|Select-Object
ComputerName,PowershellVersion
>>
Invoke-Command : [server08] Access is denied.
At line:1 char:15
+ Invoke-Command <<<<  -ComputerName server08,localhost '

ComputerName                                        PowerShellVersion
------------                                        -----------------
localhost                                           2.0
PS C:\>
```

That one single command didn't go well because our current credentials on the local machine don't match what the remote system required. Because we can specify only one credential object on the command line as an argument to Invoke-Command, we use pre-created runspaces to run our command.

```
PS C:\> $creds_server08=Get-Credential
cmdlet Get-Credential at command pipeline position 1
Supply values for the following parameters:
```

```
Credential
PS C:\> $rs_server08=New-Runspace -ComputerName server08 -Credential
$creds_server08
PS C:\> $rs_vista=New-Runspace
PS C:\> Invoke-Command -Runspace $rs_server08,$rs_vista `
>> -ScriptBlock {Get-ItemProperty
HKLM:\software\Microsoft\PowerShell\1\PowerShellEngine| `
>> Select-Object PowershellVersion}|Select-Object
ComputerName,PowershellVersion
>>
ComputerName                                          PowerShellVersion
------------                                          -----------------
localhost                                             2.0
server08                                              2.0
PS C:\>
```

In the previous example, we created a credential object for the remote server. Then, we used that credential object to create a runspace on the remote system. Because we could use this runspace later, we pass the runspace object to a variable we could easily remember.

Our local runspace is simple to create and doesn't actually require that we create a credential object, because our current logged on credentials are automatically used.

We then call the Invoke-Command cmdlet and pass it two runspaces that we just created. From there, the output is exactly what we wanted: a listing of the servers and the PowerShell version installed.

Underneath the covers, all the remote communications was done via WSMAN to the remote 2008 system.

Cleaning Up

Just to provide a good example of cleaning up after ourselves, we are going to remove the runspaces we just created. If we issue a Get-Runspace, we see all of the runspaces we created in our current session.

```
PS C:\> Get-Runspace
SessionId Name                ComputerName    State     Shell
--------- ----                ------------    -----     -----
        1 Runspace1           server08        Opened    Microsoft.PowerShell
        2 Runspace2           localhost       Opened    Microsoft.PowerShell
PS C:\> Get-Runspace|Remove-Runspace
PS C:\> Get-Runspace
PS C:\>
```

Closing these off is as easy as piping our `Get-Runspace` to `Remove-Runspace`, and all the runspaces will be gone.

NOTE

If you run into any kind of problems with runspaces, make sure to check out the local FAQ on remoting:

```
PS > Get-Help about_remote_FAQ
```

Summary

This chapter focused on how to manage the Windows Registry using PowerShell.

We first looked at some of the basics of the Registry provider, and then showed how you can add additional registry hives beyond what is provided by default with PowerShell.

Next, we looked at 2.0 feature: registry transactions. We examined how transactions work and provided a few examples demonstrating the new functionality.

We looked at how PowerShell, in conjunction with WMI, can be used to remotely manage the Registry on a machine. Using both WMI and PowerShell, you should be able to accomplish any future Registry automation tasks required.

How to use reusable code and library files were also introduced in this chapter. As explained in Chapter 12, "PowerShell Scripting Best Practices," reusing code is an important practice that can reduce the amount of time it takes to develop a script. This chapter further expanded the concept of reusable code by showing you how to implement it in the form of a library file based on a real-world example.

We finished off the chapter with a 2.0 CTP example of accessing a remote registry. With the remoting capabilities built-in 2.0, managing remote registries is much easier to accomplish.

CHAPTER 11

PowerShell and WMI

Windows Management Instrumentation (WMI) is a common interface and object model to access information from and to manage operating systems, services, applications, devices, and so on. The basis for WMI is the Web-Based Enterprise Management (WBEM) standard, which is a derivation of the Common Information Model (CIM) standard. Both the WBEM and CIM standards are published by the Distributed Management Task Force (DMTF) and are used to define how managed IT elements are represented as a common set of objects.

Being Windows-based, DCOM is used to implement WMI. Using DCOM, WMI connections can easily be made to remote systems. This ability to manage systems remotely is one of the many reasons WMI is a useful automation interface. Other reasons include:

▶ WMI has the capability to be employed through a variety of different languages, allowing for flexibility when scripters use it to complete automation tasks.

▶ Many of Microsoft's products provide WMI providers that can be used for management of that product. WMI providers implement functionality that is described in a WMI class. These classes, like a .NET class, define a set of members that can be used.

The last bullet underscores why WMI is important to all PowerShell users. At the time that this book was being written, a number of Microsoft products started to either include PowerShell as their management interface or had PowerShell support in their roadmaps. This meant that a number of Microsoft products still were not directly manageable through PowerShell or the .NET Framework. Coupled with the fact that PowerShell 1.0 did not have a built-in remoting capability, WMI was in many cases still the best interface for both managing a number of Microsoft products and remote machines.

Needless to say, this does not mean the PowerShell product team was not aware of these challenges. To address these issues the team worked tirelessly to expand PowerShell's adoption within Microsoft and with third-party developers. The culmination of this work was an announcement in November of 2007 that Microsoft would make PowerShell part of its Common Engineering Criteria (CEC) for 2009. Microsoft's CEC is a framework that Windows Server System products must meet to ensure they are developed around a common set of guidelines and requirements. By PowerShell's inclusion in this framework, every server product released by Microsoft must ship with some form of PowerShell support during Microsoft's financial year 2009 (July 1, 2008).

In addition to evangelizing PowerShell's adoption in Microsoft's product groups, the team is also working on addressing its lack of remoting support. In the PowerShell 2.0 CTP release, a new feature called PowerShell remoting was unveiled. Using this feature a PowerShell user can now run commands and cmdlets against remote machines. Details about this feature and how it can be used are reviewed in Chapter 17, "PowerShell 2.0 Features." Please note that this feature is still under development, so it might undergo additional changes.

> **NOTE**
>
> Using WMI to manage remote machines is useful. However, making DCOM connections to a remote machine is not always possible (for example through a firewall). PowerShell 2.0's remoting feature solves this problem by using Windows Remote Management (WSMAN), which interacts with remote machines using the WS-Management Simple Object Access Protocol (SOAP)-based protocol.

Although these developments are positive, WMI is still a useful interface for managing a number of different Microsoft products and remote machines. In fact, it can't be under-scored enough the importance of understanding how to use WMI from within PowerShell. For example, if you wanted to manage IIS 7.0 and Terminal Services on a Windows Server 2008 machine, both server roles provide a WMI provider that can be used. Considering that these interfaces are available, it is easy to use PowerShell's capability to interface with WMI to complete any number of automation tasks.

The goal of this chapter is to instill upon you an understanding for how WMI is used within PowerShell. To accomplish this task, the chapter provides details for how PowerShell interacts with WMI and some of the differences between this interaction and Windows Script Host (WSH). After exploring these details, the chapter then examines the new features that are currently included in the PowerShell 2.0 CTP. Finally, a real-world scripting scenario is presented; it uses WMI and PowerShell to complete a management task.

Comparing WMI Usage Between WSH and PowerShell

To use WMI via WSH, you use a set of objects in the Scripting API for WMI with the WSH methods CreateObject and GetObject (or another scripting language's methods for creating or connecting to COM objects). In this way, you can connect to a WMI object that might be a WMI class or an instance of a WMI class.

There are two methods to connect to a WMI object. The first is to create a SWbemServices object with the corresponding CreateObject method, and then connect to a WMI object by specifying that object's path. For the purpose of this discussion, however, you should focus on the second method. This method uses a "winmgmts:" **moniker string** (a standard COM mechanism for encapsulating the location and binding of another COM object). These methods are similar, but the SWbemServices object method is often chosen for error handling and authentication reasons, and the moniker string is usually chosen for convenience because a connection can be made with a single statement.

Using WMI in WSH

The following VBScript example uses a moniker string, which connects to a remote machine and then returns the amount of installed RAM:

```
On Error Resume Next
Dim objWMIService, objComputer, colItems
Dim strComputerName

strComputerName = "Jupiter"

Set objWMIService = GetObject("winmgmts:\\" & strComputerName _
        & "\root\cimv2")

Set colItems = objWMIService.ExecQuery _
    ("Select * from Win32_ComputerSystem")

For Each objItem in colItems
    WScript.Echo "Total RAM is: " _
        & FormatNumber((objItem.TotalPhysicalMemory \ 1024) _
        \ 1000, 0, 0, 0, -1) & " MB"
Next
```

Saving the script as getmemory.vbs, and then running it by using cscript, produces the following results:

```
C:\>cscript getmemory.vbs
Microsoft (R) Windows Script Host Version 5.6
Copyright (C) Microsoft Corporation 1996-2001. All rights reserved.

Total RAM is: 774 MB
C:\>
```

The following sections walk through this script to show you how it gets the installed memory information from the remote machine Jupiter.

Step One

First, you connect to the WMI service object under the root\cimv2 namespace on Jupiter, as shown here:

```
Set objWMIService = GetObject("winmgmts:\\" & strComputerName _
        & "\root\cimv2")
```

Step Two

Next, you use the ExecQuery method of the WMI service object with the WMI Query Language (WQL) to create an object bound to an instance of the Win32_ComputerSytem class, as shown in this example:

```
Set colItems = objWMIService.ExecQuery _
    ("Select * from Win32_ComputerSystem")
```

Step Three

Finally, using the colItems variable and a for loop, you step through the newly created object collection and retrieve memory information from the TotalPhysicalMemory property. After formatting the numeric value with the FormatNumber function, you write the amount of memory (in megabytes) installed on the remote machine to the cmd command prompt, as shown in the following code:

```
For Each objItem in colItems
    WScript.Echo "Total RAM is: " _
        & FormatNumber((objItem.TotalPhysicalMemory / 1024) _
        / 1000, 0, 0, 0, -1) & " MB"
Next
```

Using WMI in PowerShell

Using WMI in PowerShell has similar conceptual logic as in WSH. The main difference is that the PowerShell methods are based on WMI .NET instead of the WMI Scripting API. You have three methods for using WMI in PowerShell:

▶ WMI .NET (which is the .NET System.Management and System.Management.Instrumentation namespaces)

▶ The Get-WmiObject cmdlet

▶ The PowerShell WMI type accelerators: [WMI], [WMIClass], and [WMISearcher]. The first method, using the System.Management and System.Management. Instrumentation namespaces, isn't discussed in this chapter because it's not as practical as the other methods. It should be only a fallback method in case PowerShell isn't correctly encapsulating an object within a PSObject object when using the other two methods.

Understanding the Get-WmiObject Cmdlet

The second method, the Get-WmiObject cmdlet, can be use to retrieve WMI objects and gather information about WMI namespaces and classes. This cmdlet is simple to use, because it usually involves specifying the name of WMI class or namespace you want interact with. For example, getting an instance of the local Win32_ComputerSystem class requires the name of the class, as shown here:

```
PS > get-wmiobject "Win32_ComputerSystem"

Domain              : companyabc.com
Manufacturer        : Hewlett-Packard
Model               : Pavilion dv8000 (ES184AV)
Name                : Wii
PrimaryOwnerName    : Damon Cortesi
TotalPhysicalMemory : 2145566720

PS >
```

The next example, which is more robust, connects to the remote machine named Jupiter and gets an instance of the Win32_Service class in which the instance's name equals Virtual Server. The result is an object containing information about the Virtual Server service on Jupiter:

```
PS > get-wmiobject -class "Win32_Service" -computerName "Jupiter"
-filter "Name='Virtual Server'"
```

```
ExitCode  : 0
Name      : Virtual Server
ProcessId : 656
StartMode : Auto
State     : Running
Status    : OK

PS >
```

The following command returns the same information as the previous one but makes use
of a WQL query:

```
PS > get-wmiobject -computerName "Jupiter" -query "Select * From
Win32_Service Where Name='Virtual Server'"

ExitCode  : 0
Name      : Virtual Server
ProcessId : 656
StartMode : Auto
State     : Running
Status    : OK

PS >
```

Finally, here's an example of using Get-WmiObject to gather information about a
WMI class:

```
PS > get-wmiobject -namespace "root/cimv2" -list | where {$_.Name -eq
"Win32_Product"} | format-list *

Name              : Win32_Product
__GENUS           : 1
__CLASS           : Win32_Product
__SUPERCLASS      : CIM_Product
__DYNASTY         : CIM_Product
__RELPATH         : Win32_Product
__PROPERTY_COUNT  : 12
__DERIVATION      : {CIM_Product}
__SERVER          : PLANX
__NAMESPACE       : ROOT\cimv2
__PATH            : \\PLANX\ROOT\cimv2:Win32_Product

PS >
```

Although using Get-WmiObject is simple, using it almost always requires typing a long command string. This drawback brings you to the third method for using WMI in PowerShell: the WMI type accelerators.

[WMI] **Type Accelerator**

The [WMI] type accelerator for the ManagementObject class takes a WMI object path as a string and gets a WMI object bound to an instance of the specified WMI class, as shown in this example:

```
PS > $CompInfo =
[WMI]'\\.\root\cimv2:Win32_ComputerSystem.Name="PLANX"'
PS > $CompInfo


Domain                : companyabc.com
Manufacturer          : Hewlett-Packard
Model                 : Pavilion dv8000 (ES184AV)
Name                  : PLANX
PrimaryOwnerName      : Frank Miller
TotalPhysicalMemory   : 2145566720


PS >
```

NOTE

To bind to an instance of a WMI object directly, you must include the key property in the WMI object path. For the preceding example, the key property is Name.

[WMIClass] **Type Accelerator**

The [WMIClass] type accelerator for the ManagementClass class takes a WMI object path as a string and gets a WMI object bound to the specified WMI class, as shown in the following example:

```
PS > $CompClass = [WMICLASS]"\\.\root\cimv2:Win32_ComputerSystem"
PS > $CompClass

Win32_ComputerSystem

PS > $CompClass | format-list *

Name              : Win32_ComputerSystem
__GENUS           : 1
__CLASS           : Win32_ComputerSystem
```

```
__SUPERCLASS      : CIM_UnitaryComputerSystem
__DYNASTY         : CIM_ManagedSystemElement
__RELPATH         : Win32_ComputerSystem
__PROPERTY_COUNT  : 54
__DERIVATION      : {CIM_UnitaryComputerSystem, CIM_ComputerSystem,
CIM_System,

                    CIM_LogicalElement...}
__SERVER          : PLANX
__NAMESPACE       : ROOT\cimv2
__PATH            : \\PLANX\ROOT\cimv2:Win32_ComputerSystem

PS >
```

[WMISearcher] **Type Accelerator**

The [WMISearcher] type accelerator for the ManagementObjectSearcher class takes a WQL string and creates a WMI searcher object. After the searcher object is created, you use the Get method to get a WMI object bound to an instance of the specified WMI class, as shown here:

```
PS > $CompInfo = [WMISearcher]"Select * From Win32_ComputerSystem"
PS > $CompInfo.Get()

Domain               : companyabc.com
Manufacturer         : Hewlett-Packard
Model                : Pavilion dv8000 (ES184AV)
Name                 : PLANX
PrimaryOwnerName     : Miro
TotalPhysicalMemory  : 2145566720

PS >
```

Working with WMI

In the first part of this chapter, you where presented with background information about WMI and a comparison between how WMI is used in WSH and PowerShell. In the next couple of sections, you learn how to work with WMI classes and class instances in relation to different examples. The end goal of these sections is to help you better understand how WMI can be employed to complete automation tasks from inside a PowerShell console session. The first step to gaining a working understanding of WMI is to examine how it is structured.

Like a .NET Framework namespace, a WMI namespace is a logical grouping of WMI classes and instances. To create this mapping, a WMI provider typically registers its own WMI namespace (and associated classes or instances) into the WMI repository. Table 11.1 shows a mapping between several providers and their associated namespaces:

TABLE 11.1   WMI Providers and Namespaces

Provider	Namespaces
Internet Information Services (IIS)	`root\microsoftiisv2`
Active Directory	`root\directory\ldap`
Terminal Services	`root\cimv2\TerminalServices`
Win32	`root\cimv2`

Although the list shown in the table is not all inclusive, it does provide you with a sense of how WMI is structured into a hierarchical framework (WMI repository). In the past, you might use any number of different tools to learn what namespaces, classes, and instances are available to you in the WMI repository. For example:

▶ **Scriptomatic**—A HTA utility that can be used to write WMI scripts.

▶ **MSDN's WMI documentation**—This is always a good source of information.

▶ **wbemtest.exe**—A GUI-based utility that enables you to access and manipulate the WMI repository.

▶ **Third-party applications**—There are a lot of utilities that have been developed to assist people with understanding the WMI repository and using it.

▶ **PowerShell**—By using the `Get-WmiObject` cmdlet directly from within a PowerShell console session.

Of the five options listed, you might as well just use PowerShell, because it has the capability to explore the WMI repository. Therefore, you have no reason to leave the console to complete this task. However, before starting down this exploration track, you must first understand that the top level namespace is called Root. Children of the Root namespace can be namespaces or WMI classes. Each namespace contains a class called __namespace. Creating an instance of this class gives you list of all the child namespaces under the parent namespace. For example:

```
PS > get-wmiobject -Namespace:"root" __NameSpace | ft name
name
----
ServiceModel
...
aspnet
MSCluster
WMI
```

```
CIMV2
MicrosoftActiveDirectory
MicrosoftIISv2
...
MicrosoftDfs

PS >
```

The previous command example shows the Get-WmiObject cmdlet being used in conjunction with the Namespace parameter to create an instance of the __Namespace class. The table that is returned contains the namespaces that are under the Root namespace. To examine the child namespaces under one of the listed namespaces, modify the WMI path, as shown in the next command example:

```
PS > get-wmiobject -Namespace:"root\MicrosoftIISv2" __NameSpace | ft namename
```

Unfortunately, executing the previous command does not return anything. This indicates that there are no child namespaces under the MicrosoftIISv2 namespace. Instead, to return a list of classes under this namespace, execute the following command:

```
PS > get-wmiobject -List -Namespace:"root\MicrosoftIISv2"
```

By using the List switch parameter, the resulting two column list contains all the classes that fall under the MicrosoftIISv2 namespace. The list is daunting, but after you find the right class, you can then employ that class to either gather information or complete a task. For example:

```
PS > get-wmiobject IIsWebService -Namespace:"root\MicrosoftIISv2" | ft
name, caption, state -AutoSize

name  caption                               state
----  -------                               -----
W3SVC World Wide Web Publishing Service Running

PS >
```

The prior command example uses the Get-WmiObject cmdlet in conjunction with the IIsWebService class to return information about the W3SVC service status on the local machine. Additionally, you can also use the IIsWebService class to interact with the W3SVC service, as shown in the following command:

```
PS > (get-wmiobject IIsWebService
-Namespace:"root\MicrosoftIISv2").StopService()


__GENUS             : 2
__CLASS             : __PARAMETERS
__SUPERCLASS        :
__DYNASTY           : __PARAMETERS
__RELPATH           :
__PROPERTY_COUNT    : 1
__DERIVATION        : {}
__SERVER            :
__NAMESPACE         :
__PATH              :
ReturnValue         : 0


PS >
```

The output doesn't look good; however, in the previous example, the Get-WmiObject cmdlet in conjunction with the IIsWebService class is again used. This time around, the StopService method is used to stop the W3SVC service. To restart the service, you can again use a method from the IIsWebService class. If you are not familiar with the members of this class, like all other PSObject objects, you can use the Get-Member cmdlet to interrogate an object generated from this class. For example:

```
PS > get-wmiobject IIsWebService -Namespace:"root\MicrosoftIISv2" | gm
-MemberType method

   TypeName:
System.Management.ManagementObject#root\MicrosoftIISv2\IIsWebService
...
```

With the list of methods that is returned from the previous command example, you should be able to determine which method can be used to restart the W3SVC service.

If at this point in the section, do you feel that exploring or working with WMI in PowerShell can be cumbersome? If you do, you are not alone. However, the root cause for the clumsiness is WMI itself. Unfortunately, PowerShell 1.0, being a first generation product, just doesn't do an end-all job at masking WMI's strange structure and formatting from those that would prefer a more normalized form. Instead, it makes WMI, for the first time, easily accessible from the command line and scripts.

The PowerShell WMI Explorer

If you find using the PowerShell console too awkward to explore the WMI repository, there is a great utility that was created by Marc van Orsouw that can be used instead. This utility is called the "PowerShell WMI Explorer" and can be downloaded from his web site at http://thepowershellguy.com. As its name suggests, the utility enables you to explore WMI from PowerShell within a graphical interface. Amazingly, van Orsouw was able to build this entire utility using only one PowerShell script (WmiBrowser.ps1), and no additional DLLs, cmdlets, or files are needed. Figure 11.1 shows an example of the PowerShell WMI Explorer being executed.

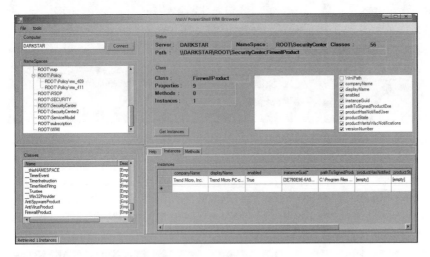

FIGURE 11.1   The PowerShell WMI Explorer

Understanding Providers

WMI providers are just COM objects that monitor one or more managed objects. These managed objects can include a physical or logical component, such as the file system, a network adapter, the operating system itself, a process, a service, or even a hard disk drive. Like a Windows driver, a WMI provider acts as a gateway for data being returned from a managed object and messages that are sent from WMI to that object.

The physical structure of a WMI provider consists of a DLL and a Managed Object Format (MOF) file. MOF files are derived from DMTF's CIM standard and contain definitions of classes and instances that are implemented by a provider. Both the DLL and MOF files for each provider can be found under the %WINDIR%\System32\Wbem directory. An example of default Windows provider is the Win32 provider. This provider defines the classes used to describe hardware or software available on Windows systems and the relationships among them.

Understanding WQL

WMI can be queried using a subset of the American National Standards Institute Structured Query Language (ANSI SQL). This subset is called the Windows Management

Instrumentation Query Language (WQL). Although WQL is based on the standard SQL syntax, you cannot use it to perform updates, inserts, or deletes. Instead, you can query for classes, their instances, associations, and so on.

Because of its SQL inheritance, working with WQL is fairly easy, as shown in previous Get-WmiObject and [WMISearcher] examples. As a refresher, here is another example:

```
PS > $Procs = [WMISearcher]"Select * From Win32_Process Where Name =
'powershell.exe'"
PS > $Procs.Get()| fl name, processid

name       : powershell.exe
processid : 4440

PS >
```

In the previous command, a WQL query statement is unused in conjunction with the [WMISearcher] type accelerator to retrieve all instances of the Win32_Process class that have a name equal to powershell.exe. The resulting object collection is then dumped into the $Procs variable. Next, the WMI Get method is used to initialize the resulting objects and return information about them. In this case, there is only one object in the collection, and the information about the object is displayed in a formatted list.

Interestingly, you can also use the Get-WmiObject cmdlet's filter parameter to achieve the same information that is returned using a WQL query. An example of this is shown here:

```
PS > $Procs = get-wmiobject Win32_Process -filter "Name = 'powershell.exe'"
PS > $Procs | fl name, processid

name       : powershell.exe
processid : 4440

PS >
```

In the previous command example, the filter parameter is used to retrieve all instances of the Win32_Process class that have a name equal to powershell.exe. The resulting object collection is then dumped into the $Procs variable. Next, the object collection is piped to the Format-List cmdlet, and name and processid are returned to the console. The major difference between this example and the [WMISearcher] type accelerator example is with the objects that are returned. With the [WMISearcher] example, the objects returned are instances of the ManagementObjectSearcher class. Therefore, the Get method is used to initialize the related Win32_Process objects. With the second example, the Get-WmiObject cmdlet returned objects that were instances of the ManagementObject class.

PowerShell 2.0 Changes

Throughout this chapter, you are shown how PowerShell interacts with WMI. In most cases, this interaction enables an administrator to rapidly use WMI to complete a task directly from the PowerShell console or a script. Nonetheless, there is room for improvement. Examples of this can be found within the unwieldy commands, structures, and data that can prove confusing to an administrator who isn't as familiar with WMI's internals as a developer.

AuthenticationLevel **and** ImpersonationLevel

Like other noted shortcomings, the PowerShell team is aware of the problems with the WMI implemtation in PowerShell and is actively working on solutions. Examples of this work can be found within some of the new WMI-related changes that are found in the PowerShell 2.0 CTP. The first of these changes is the fix for what proved a major shortcoming with the Get-WmiObject cmdlet in PowerShell 1.0. For example, if you attempted to use this cmdlet in conjunction with the IIsWebService class to manage the W3SVC service on a remote machine, you would encounter the following problem:

```
PS > get-wmiobject -class IIsWebService -namespace
"root\microsoftiisv2" -Computer sc1-app01
Get-WmiObject : Access denied
At line:1 char:14
+ Get-WMIObject <<<<  -class IIsWebService -namespace
"root\microsoftiisv2" -computer sc1-app01
```

This is normal behavior for any of the IIS WMI classes because they require the AuthenticationLevel property defined as PacketPrivacy. The AuthenticationLevel property is an integer that defines the COM Authentication level that is assigned to an object. In the end, it determines how DCOM will protect information sent from WMI.

Although defining the AuthenticationLevel property in WSH was a simple line of code, in PowerShell 1.0's version of the Get-WmiObject cmdlet, there was no method to define this property. Additionally, there wasn't a way to change either the ImpersonationLevel property or enable all privileges, both of which are often requirements when working with WMI. To correct this problem, the product team has updated the Get-WmiObject cmdlet in the PowerShell 2.0 CTP to include new parameters to define the AuthenticationLevel and ImpersonationLevel properties and enable all privileges. Additionally, these parameters work with the new WMI cmdlets (Invoke-WMIMethod; Remove-WMIObject; and Set-WMIInstance) that were also introduced in the CTP. For example:

```
PS > get-wmiobject -class IIsWebService -namespace "root\microsoftiisv2"
-Computer sc1-app01 —Authentication 6
```

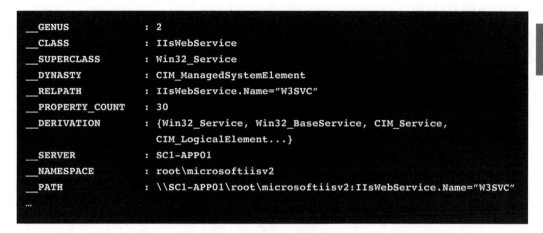

```
__GENUS            : 2
__CLASS            : IIsWebService
__SUPERCLASS       : Win32_Service
__DYNASTY          : CIM_ManagedSystemElement
__RELPATH          : IIsWebService.Name="W3SVC"
__PROPERTY_COUNT   : 30
__DERIVATION       : {Win32_Service, Win32_BaseService, CIM_Service,
                     CIM_LogicalElement...}
__SERVER           : SC1-APP01
__NAMESPACE        : root\microsoftiisv2
__PATH             : \\SC1-APP01\root\microsoftiisv2:IIsWebService.Name="W3SVC"
...
```

In the previous example, the `Authentication` parameter is used to define the `AuthenticationLevel` property. In this case, the value is defined as 6 (`PacketPrivacy`). The definitions for the rest of the allowed values for the `Authentication` property are shown in Table 11.2:

TABLE 11.2   AuthenticationLevel Property Values

Value	Authentication Level	Notes
-1	Unchanged	
0	Default	
1	None	No authentication is performed.
2	Connect	Authentication is performed only when the client establishes a relationship with the application.
3	Call	Authentication is performed only at the beginning of each call when the application receives the request.
4	Packet	Authentication is performed on all data received from the client.
5	PacketIntegrity	All the data transferred between client and application is authenticated and verified.
6	PacketPrivacy	The properties of the other authentication levels are used, and all data is encrypted.

The `AuthenticationLevel` property is used to govern the degree to which a remote WMI service is allowed complete tasks on your behalf. The values that are supported by this property are defined in Table 11.3:

TABLE 11.3   ImpersonationLevel Property Values

Value	Impersonation Level	Notes
0	Default	
1	Anonymous	Anonymous COM impersonation level that hides the identity of the caller. Calls to WMI can fail with this impersonation level.
2	Identify	Identify-level COM impersonation level that allows objects to query the credentials of the caller. Calls to WMI can fail with this impersonation level.
3	Impersonate	Impersonate-level COM impersonation level that allows objects to use the credentials of the caller. This is the recommended impersonation level for WMI calls.
4	Delegate	Delegate-level COM impersonation level that allows objects to permit other objects to use the credentials of the caller. This level, which works with WMI calls but can constitute an unnecessary security risk, is supported only under Windows 2000.

NOTE

Using the Delegate impersonation level is generally considered a security risk because it permits the remote WMI service to pass credentials on to other objects.

Set-WMIInstance **Cmdlet**

The Set-WMIInstance cmdlet was developed to reduce the number of steps needed to change a read-write WMI property (or property that allowed direct modification). For example, in PowerShell 1.0, the following set of commands might be used to change Windows Terminal Service's ActiveSessionLimit:

```
PS > $TSSessionSetting = get-wmiobject "Win32_TSSessionSetting"
PS > $TSSessionSetting.ActiveSessionLimit = 1
PS > $TSSessionSetting.Put
```

By using the Set-WMIInstance cmdlet, you can complete the same task using a single command:

```
PS > set-wmiinstance —class "Win32_TSSessionSetting" —argument
@{ActiveSessionLimit=1}
```

In the previous example, the `class` parameter is defined as a `Win32_TSSessionSetting`; however, the `argument` parameter is defined as a HashTable that contains the property and the value the property will be set to. Additionally, because this parameter requires an argument that is a HashTable, to define multiple property and value pairs, you need to separate the pairs with a semicolon, as shown here:

```
—argument @{ActiveSessionLimit=1;BrokenConnectionPolicy=0}
```

However, the true power of this cmdlet is to use the `computername` parameter to change read-write WMI properties on multiple machines at once. For example:

```
PS > set-wmiinstance —class "Win32_TSSessionSetting" —argument
@{ActiveSessionLimit=1} —computername sc1-app01,sc1-app02
```

The arguments for the `computername` parameter can be a NetBIOS name, a fully-qualified domain name (FQDN), or an IP address. Additionally, each argument must be separated by a comma.

Invoke-WMIMethod **Cmdlet**

Two different types of methods exist with WMI: instance or static. With static methods, you must invoke the method from the class itself, whereas instance methods are invoked on specific instances of a class. In PowerShell 1.0, working with instance methods was fairly straightforward as you only needed to create an object of a particular instance of a WMI class. However, to work with a static method requires a fairly complex and unintuitive WQL statement, as shown in the following example:

```
PS > $ProcFac = get-wmiobject -query "SELECT * FROM Meta_Class WHERE
__Class = 'Win32_Process'" -namespace "root\cimv2"
PS > $ProcFac.Create("notepad.exe ")
```

You can also use the [WMIClass] type accelerator, as shown here:

```
PS > $ProcFac = $ProcFac = [wmiclass]"Win32_Process"
PS > $ProcFac.Create("notepad.exe ")
```

If you wanted to use the `Get-WMIObject` cmdlet or were having problems with the [WMIClass] type accelerator, employing the use of the noted WQL statement wasn't command line friendly. To fill this noted gap, the PowerShell product team introduced the `Invoke-WMIMethod` cmdlet in PowerShell 2.0.

As its name suggests, the purpose of the `Invoke-WMIMethod` cmdlet is to make it easier to directly invoke WMI methods. To use this cmdlet to invoke a static method, use the following command:

```
PS > invoke-wmimethod -path "Win32_Process" -name "create"
-argumentList "notepad.exe "
```

In the previous command example, the `path` parameter requires the name of the WMI class from which the method is to be invoked from. In this case, the method being invoked is the `Create` method as defined for the `name` parameter. If you were invoking an instance method, the argument for the path parameter would need to be the complete path to an existing WMI instance. For example:

```
PS > invoke-wmimethod -path "Win32_Process.Handle='42144'" -name
terminate
```

The `argumentList` parameter is used to define any arguments that a method requires when it is invoked. In cases where the method requires multiple values or you want to pass multiple values, you must assign those values into an array. Then, the array must be defined as the argument for the `argumentList` parameter.

NOTE

Values for methods are not in the same order as used with the WMI's scripting API. Instead, values are ordered such as they appear in Wbemtest.exe.

Remove-WMIObject **Cmdlet**

The last new cmdlet to be introduced in PowerShell 2.0 is the `Remove-WMIObject` cmdlet. This cmdlet is used to remove instances of a WMI objects. For example, to terminate a process in using WMI in PowerShell 1.0, you might use the following set of commands:

```
PS > $Proc = get-wmiobject -class "Win32_Process" -filter
"Name='wordpad.exe'"
PS > $Proc.Terminate()
```

However, depending on the type of WMI object that you are trying to remove, several methods would need to be used. For instance, to delete a folder using WMI in PowerShell 1.0, use the following command:

```
PS > $Folder = get-wmiobject -query "Select * From Win32_Directory
Where Name ='C:\\Scripts'"
PS > $Folder.Delete()
```

Conversely, using the Remove-WMIObject cmdlet, you can remove instances of any type of WMI object. For example, to remove an instance of the Win32_Process class, use the following commands:

```
PS > $Proc = get-wmiobject -class "Win32_Process" -filter
"Name='wordpad.exe'"
PS > $Proc | remove-wmiobject
```

The following commands are used to remove a directory:

```
PS > $Folder = get-wmiobject -query "Select * From Win32_Directory
Where Name ='C:\\Scripts'"
PS > $Folder | remove-wmiobject
```

Scripting Scenario: MonitorMSVS.ps1

Before this script was developed, companyabc.com was in the process of switching most of its physical hardware-based application servers to virtual machines that were located on a Microsoft Virtual Server 2005 host. As part of this switch, the company wanted a simple yet effective method for monitoring the virtual machines on the virtual server host. However, an effective monitoring platform, such as Microsoft Operations Manager (MOM), wasn't in place. The IT department suggested an automation script to meet the company's short-term monitoring needs. In turn, the company developed one that administrators could use to perform the virtual machine monitoring.

The MonitorMSVS.ps1 is a PowerShell conversion of an existing VBScript based script named MonitorMSVS.wsf. A working copy of both these scripts can be found at www.informit.com/title/9780672329883. To execute this script, define the ServerName parameter, which should have its argument set to the name of the Virtual Server 2005 system hosting the virtual machines to be monitored. Here's the command to run MonitorMSVS.ps1, with an example of the output shown in Figure 11.2:

```
PS D:\Scripts> .\MonitorMSVS.ps1 -ServerName Jupiter
```

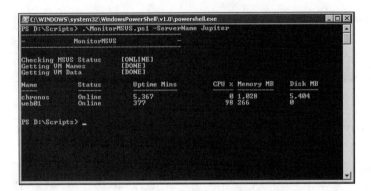

FIGURE 11.2   The MonitorMSVS.ps1 script being executed

NOTE

In the command to run the MonitorMSVS.ps1 script, the ServerName parameter is named in the command string, whereas in the example from Chapter 6, "The PowerShell Language," the script's parameters aren't named in the command string. In PowerShell, you can name or partially name parameters when running a script, as shown here:

```
.\MonitorMSVS.ps1  -S Jupiter
```

If you define the arguments in an order matching how parameters are defined in the script, the parameters don't need to be named at all when running a script, as shown here:

```
.\MonitorMSVS.ps1 Jupiter
```

The MonitorMSVS.ps1 script performs the following sequence of actions:

1. The script pings the specified Microsoft Virtual Server (MSVS) to verify that the server is operational.

2. The script connects to the Microsoft Virtual Server Administration Web site and retrieves a list of virtual machines on that MSVS host. The list of virtual machines is defined as the $Servers variable.

3. The script uses the Get-WmiObject cmdlet to retrieve a collection of instances of the VirtualMachine class, which is defined as the $VirtualMachines variable.

4. For each virtual machine object in the $Servers variable, the script adds the virtual machine's current status as another member of that object. If the virtual machine is online (present in the $VirtualMachines collection), the script also adds current values for the Uptime, CpuUtilization, PhysicalMemoryAllocated, and DiskSpaceUsed properties as members of the virtual machine object.

5. The script returns the information to the PowerShell console by using the Format-Table cmdlet.

The first code snippet contains the header for the MonitorMSVS.ps1 script. This header includes information about what the script does, when it was updated, and the script's author. Just after the header is the script's only parameter ($ServerName):

```
#################################################
# MonitorMSVS.ps1
# Used to monitor Microsoft Virtual Server 2005.
#
# Created: 12/01/2006
# Author: Tyson Kopczynski
#################################################
param([string] $ServerName = $(throw write-host '
    "Please specify the name of the MSVS host to monitor!" '
    -Foregroundcolor Red))
```

The next code snippet contains the beginning of the script's automation portion. First, the variable $URL is defined as the URL for the MSVS host's Virtual Server Administration Web site. Then, like the MonitorMSVS.wsf script, MonitorMSVS.ps1 uses an ICMP ping to verify that the specified MSVS host is operational before continuing. However, the MonitorMSVS.ps1 script uses the Net.NetworkInformation.Ping class instead of WMI to conduct the ping. Either method, including ping.exe, could have been used, but Net.NetworkInformation.Ping requires less work and less code. The choice of a method doesn't matter, however, as long as you try to predict where the script will fail and handle that failure accordingly.

```
#################################################
# Main
#################################################
$URL = "http://$($ServerName):1024/VirtualServer/VSWebApp.exe?view=1"


#--------------------
# Begin Script
#--------------------
write-host "----------------------------------------"
write-host "-            MonitorMSVS              -"
write-host "----------------------------------------"
write-host
write-host "Checking MSVS Status" -NoNewLine


.{
```

```
    trap{write-host 't "[ERROR]" -Foregroundcolor Red;
        throw write-host $_ -Foregroundcolor Red;
        Break}

    $Ping = new-object Net.NetworkInformation.Ping
    $Result = $Ping.Send($ServerName)

    if ($Result.Status -eq "Success"){
        write-host 't "[ONLINE]" -Foregroundcolor Green
        }
    else{
        write-host 't "[OFFLINE]" -Foregroundcolor Red
        write-host
        Break
        }
}
```

If the MSVS host is operational, script writes to the console that the host is "ONLINE" and continues execution of the script. Conversely, if the MSVS host is not operations, the script writes to the console that the host is "OFFLINE" and halts execution of the script.

After the operational status of the MSVS host has been verified, the next step is to connect to the host and retrieve a list of virtual machines that are hosted. The following code snippet completes this task by improving the logic from the original MonitorMSVS.wsf script and showcasing one of PowerShell's more impressive capabilities:

```
#-------------------
# Get list of VMs
#-------------------
$Webclient = new-object Net.WebClient
$Webclient.UseDefaultCredentials = $True

write-host "Getting VM Names" -NoNewLine

.{
    trap{write-host 't "[ERROR]" -Foregroundcolor Red;
        throw write-host $_ -Foregroundcolor Red;
        Break}

    $Data = $Webclient.DownloadString("$URL")

    write-host 't "[DONE]" -Foregroundcolor Green
}
```

```
# This Regex gets a list of server entries from the data returned
$Servers = [Regex]::Matches($Data, '(?<=&amp;vm=)[^"\r\n]*(?=" )')

# There are many duplicates so you need to group them
# Plus, this gives you a better name for your property
$Servers = $Servers | group Value | select Name
```

The MonitorMSVS.wsf script had a major flaw: The WMI query returned information only about virtual machines that were online at the time of the query. If a virtual machine happens to be off when the MonitorMSVS.wsf script runs, there's no way to display that fact to users. A list of all virtual machines and their current status is helpful information for a script used as a monitoring tool.

To gain access to this information, the script must create a list of all virtual machines on the MSVS host. Such a list exists on the Microsoft Virtual Server Administration Web site. To access it, the script uses the Net.WebClient class to connect to the Microsoft Virtual Server Administration Web site remotely and download the HTML content from the Master Status Page.

> **NOTE**
>
> Because PowerShell can use the .NET Framework, it can access Web services as sources for external data or as applications. For example, you can use PowerShell to post and read blogs, check the availability of the Wii on bestbuy.com, or perform an automation task based on data or applications provided by your enterprise's Web services. The possibilities are endless.

In the HTML content that is downloaded, the names of each virtual machine are embedded and repeated several times. To build the list, the script uses the regular expression type accelerator, [Regex], to strip each virtual machine name out of the HTML content and into $Servers variable. The resulting list in the $Servers variable then contains each virtual machine's name, which is repeated several times. To shorten the list so that each virtual machine is listed only once, the script uses the Group-Object cmdlet. The final list, which contains the names of all virtual machines on the specified MSVS host, is then redefined in the $Servers variable.

Next, the script retrieves the virtual machines' performance information from instances of the WMI VirtualMachine class by using the Get-WmiObject cmdlet. The next step is to merge the two resulting data sets: the virtual machine information ($VirtualMachines) and the list of virtual machines ($Servers). To do this, the script steps through each virtual machine object in the $Servers variable. If the virtual machine name is in both object collections, the Add-Member cmdlet is used to extend the virtual machine object in the $Servers variable so that it includes the performance information in the $VirtualMachines variable.

This object extension add an Online status indicator and related property information from $VirtualMachines. If the virtual machine is offline (not in both collections), the script extends the object to include an Offline status indicator. The concept of changing an object dynamically was introduced in Chapter 3, "Advanced PowerShell Concepts," but this example illustrates the power of this feature used in an automation script. The following example shows the code for this process:

```
#--------------------
# Get VM data
#--------------------
write-host "Getting VM Data" -NoNewLine

.{
    trap{write-host 't't "[ERROR]" -Foregroundcolor Red;
        throw write-host $_ -Foregroundcolor Red;
        Break}

    $VSMachines = get-wmiobject -namespace "root/vm/virtualserver" '
        -class VirtualMachine -computername $ServerName
        -ErrorAction Stop

    write-host 't't "[DONE]" -Foregroundcolor Green
}

foreach ($Server in $Servers){
    &{
        $VSMachine = $VSMachines | where {$_.Name -eq $Server.Name}

        if($VSMachine){
            $Uptime = $VSMachine.Uptime / 60
            $Memory =  ($VSMachine.PhysicalMemoryAllocated / 1024) / 1000
            $Disk = ($VSMachine.DiskSpaceUsed / 1024) /1000

            add-member -inputObject $Server -membertype noteProperty '
                -name "Status" -value "Online"
            add-member -inputObject $Server -membertype noteProperty '
                -name "Uptime" -value $Uptime
            add-member -inputObject $Server -membertype noteProperty '
                -name "CPU" -value $VSMachine.CpuUtilization
            add-member -inputObject $Server -membertype noteProperty '
                -name "Memory" -value $Memory
            add-member -inputObject $Server -membertype noteProperty '
                -name "Disk" -value $Disk
        }
        else{
```

```
        add-member -inputObject $Server -membertype noteProperty '
            -name "Status" -value "Offline"
    }
  }
}
```

The last step is writing information in the $Servers variable to the PowerShell console with the Format-Table cmdlet. This cmdlet can add calculated properties; in this case, it's used to change the labels of properties coming from $Servers. The format operator (-f) controls the formatting of these properties, as show in the next code snippet:

```
$Servers | format-table Name, Status '
    ,@{label="Uptime Mins"; expression={"{0:N0}" -f $_.Uptime}} '
    ,@{label="CPU %"; expression={$_.CPU}} '
    ,@{label="Memory MB"; expression={"{0:N0}" -f $_.Memory}} '
    ,@{label="Disk MB"; expression={"{0:N0}" -f $_.Disk}} '
    -wrap
```

NOTE

For more information on the -f operator, refer to the Format method of the System. String class at http://msdn2.microsoft.com/en-us/library/system.string.format.aspx.

Summary

In this chapter, you gained a better understanding for WMI and how it is used in WSH and PowerShell. Additionally, you also saw how PowerShell attempts to make employing WMI easier when compared to WSH. This ease of use can be seen while either using the Get-WMIObject cmdlet, and the noted WMI type accelerators, which both reduce the amount of code needed to complete a WMI-based task. Less code is a wonderful thing considering that WMI is a useful and still relevant interface for completing automation tasks. After all, before PowerShell Remoting was introduced in PowerShell 2.0, WMI was the only interface for completing managing remote systems.

Continuing with the precedent set in PowerShell 1.0, to make WMI easy to use, you also learned that the PowerShell product team introduced several new features. Although the authentication and impersonation additions were aimed at correcting problems, the three new cmdlets (Set-WMIInstance, Invoke-WMIMethod, and Remove-WMIObject) were geared toward further improving the experience administrators had accessing and using WMI directly from the PowerShell command line.

PowerShell Scripting Best Practices

Previous chapters in this book covered a broad range of topics related to scripting in general and PowerShell in specific. Although the authors of this book expect that all this information will be helpful to you as your knowledge of PowerShell progresses, it might be a little overwhelming at first. As you are getting started, it is sometimes most useful to focus on the salient ideas in a given topic and expand your knowledge from there. The goal of this chapter is to bring the key points of this book together in a format that provides you with a framework for understanding and using PowerShell, and it discusses a structured approach to scripting that can be applied to a wide variety of coding and development projects. Although not every scripting project requires this level of detail, any scripts that are used in a production environment will benefit tremendously from applying a clear, well documented, and supportable scripting methodology. Although we don't expect every scripter to be a budding software developer, extending software development guidelines to scripting best practices can give you a good foundation for improving your script writing.

PowerShell Configuration and Usage Recommendations

Several best practice recommendations apply specifically to configuring the PowerShell 2.0 CTP environment. These practices relate primarily to using PowerShell in a secure manner and are also discussed in Chapter 5, "Understanding PowerShell Security."

Digitally Sign PowerShell Scripts and Configuration Files

As a rule, you should always digitally sign your PowerShell scripts and configuration files so that users and machines running your scripts can trust that the code is actually from you and hasn't been tampered with or corrupted. Adhering to this practice also means you can keep the PowerShell execution policy on your machine, in addition to others in your organization, set to AllSigned.

> **NOTE**
>
> Code signing doesn't apply just to PowerShell scripts and configuration files. You can apply the principles of code signing to other items, such as executables, macros, DLLs, other scripts, device drivers, firmware images, and so forth. Other code can benefit from the security of digital signatures, and you can further limit the possibility of untrusted code running in your environment.

Never Set Execution Policies to Unrestricted

Setting your execution policy to Unrestricted is like leaving an open door for malicious code to run on your systems. Because of this risk, you should set your execution policy to RemoteSigned at a minimum. This setting still enables you to run scripts and load configuration files created locally on your machine, but it prevents remote code that hasn't been signed and trusted from running. Note: The RemoteSigned setting isn't foolproof and can allow some remote code to run through PowerShell.

Following these guidelines and becoming proficient in code signing are crucial to guaranteeing that your PowerShell environment doesn't become a target for malicious code. Setting your execution policy to AllSigned increases security even more because it requires that all scripts and configuration files be signed by a trusted source before running or loading them.

Try to Run Scripts with the Minimum Required Rights

IT security practices include following the principle of least privileges, which ensures that entities such as users, processes, and software are granted only the minimum rights needed to perform a legitimate action. For example, if a user doesn't need administrative rights to run a word processing program, there's no reason to grant that user the administrative level of privileges. This principle of least privileges also applies to scripting. When you're developing a script, make an effort to code in a manner that requires the minimum rights to run the script. If users don't know the required rights to run a script, they might try running it with administrative rights, which increases the possibility of causing unwanted and possibly damaging changes to your environment.

> **NOTE**
>
> When you are designing scripts that will be used in a production environment, it is important to provide a clear understanding of what the script does, as well as the rights which are required for the script to run successfully. A great way to accomplish

this is to make the script self-documenting by including key details in the usage state-ment for the script. For example, when a user runs a script with no arguments or a question mark (?), it is possible for the script to display details on the parameters that the script uses. This usage information can easily include details on the rights required to run the script, as well as the specific properties that the script is reading or writing. (This can also be done in the comments for the script.) Although document-ing scripts to this level of detail can be tedious and does add some time to the script development cycle, this kind of information is invaluable for troubleshooting and is well worth the additional time required.

## 12

Centrally Manage PowerShell Remoting Security Settings in Your Enterprise

One of the most powerful new features in PowerShell 2.0 CTP is the introduction of PowerShell Remoting, which allows PowerShell commands to be run on a remote machine. This remoting functionality depends on two components: Windows Remote Management (WSMAN) and Windows Remote Shell (WinRS). Both WSMAN and WinRS support a variety of different authentication options, which if improperly configured can reduce the effective security of your environment and leave machines vulnerable to attack. Although WSMAN and WinRS are generally secure when the installation defaults are left in place, it is easy for a locally privileged user to change these settings. To ensure that WSMAN and WinRS configuration settings are consistently applied to machines that belong to an Active Directory domain, WSMAN and WinRS configuration can be performed through Active Directory Group Policy. A step-by-step procedure for establish-ing a domain-wide Group Policy to administer WSMAN and WinRS settings is described in Chapter 5.

Script Development

The following sections offer best practices for script development that applies to scripting in general. It is highly recommended that when you are developing your own scripts, follow the practices discussed in these sections to some extent or another. By doing this, you should find that your scripts will start to meet stated project requirements, take less time to develop, and have fewer issues when deployed into production.

Treat Scripting Projects as Actual Projects

Developing a script can take as much effort as any software development project. For example, you should make sure to incorporate some prototyping and testing to prevent the script from having any negative impact on an environment. So, whenever you write a script, check the scope of the effect it might have. If the script is complex, takes more than a few minutes to complete its tasks, requires more resources than yourself (such as other people), or carries a high level of risk when its runs, turning the script job into a project might be appropriate.

Use a Development Life Cycle Model

As with all software development projects, you should choose a development life cycle model that fits the needs of your scripting project. These models range from the traditional waterfall model to newer models, such as Agile, Extreme Programming (XP), Spiral, Iterative, and so forth. The choice of a model isn't as important as having a formal process for managing your scripting projects, however.

If the models mentioned here seem overly complex for a scripting project, Figure 12.1 shows a simple series of steps developed for scripting projects.

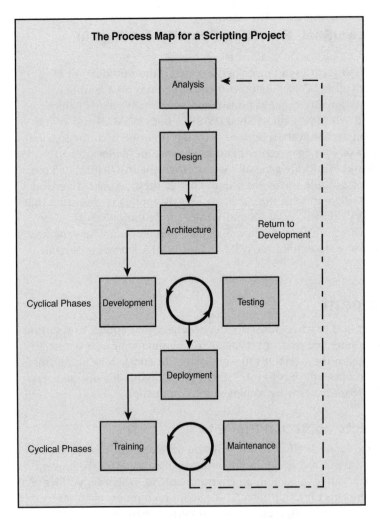

FIGURE 12.1   The process map for a scripting project

Although similar to a full development life cycle model, the steps are simply pointers to tasks that need to be completed for a typical scripting project. You can follow this scripting model or develop your own, but the point of this practice is to choose a method for managing your scripting projects.

Design and Prototype Your Scripts by Using Pseudocode

The idea behind designing and prototyping a script by using pseudocode is that it enables you to develop a script's structure and logic before writing any code. Working out the structure and logic beforehand helps you ensure that your script meets its requirements, and it helps you detect possible logic flaws early in the process. Furthermore, pseudocode is language independent and can be written so that other people, especially those who need to give input on the script design, can read and understand it easily. The following is an example of pseudocode:

```
Param domain
Param resource account CSV file

Bind to domain
Open and read CSV file

For each resource account in CSV file:
    -Create a new account in the specified OU.
    -Set the password (randomly generated complex 14-character password).
    -Log password to admin password archive.
    -Set the user account attributes based on CSV file information.
    -Mail-enable the account.
    -Add the user to the appropriate groups based on CSV file information.
Next
```

Gather Script Requirements Effectively

As with any project, you need to define the problem your script will be solving to determine what's required of it. Sometimes, a script just solves a simple automation need, so its requirements are easy to determine. When a script needs to solve more complex business automation needs, however, you might need to learn more about the business processes being automated to determine its requirements. In either case, to ensure success, you must identify the requirements for a script and have all parties sign off on those requirements. Overlooking these steps in the development process might mean that your final script fails to meet its requirements and is then rejected as a solution for the original business need.

Don't Develop Scripts in a Production Environment

Most scripts are designed to make changes to a system, so there's always the chance that running a script in a production environment could have unwanted or possibly damaging results. Even if a script makes no changes, it could have an undesirable effect, or you might not fully understand the impact. Even worse, when you run the script to test its functionality, you might accidentally run the script outside your designated testing scope and affect production systems. Therefore, developing your scripts in a production environment isn't a good idea.

NOTE

One of the cardinal rules of script development is to avoid making unintended changes to your production environment. Scripts are very powerful and fast-acting tools that can be exceptionally helpful and great time-savers, but with this power must come knowledge and responsibility. Until you fully understand exactly what a script will do, it should **only** be executed in an isolated lab environment. Because of the recent advances in virtualization technology, it is possible to set up a very capable isolated virtual lab environment on a single physical machine. While it does require some additional time to set up this type of isolated lab environment, it provides the flexibility to learn from mistakes in your scripts without accidentally putting your business out of business.

Test, Test, Test

Scripts are usually written to perform some automation task, such as modifying an attribute on every user in an Active Directory domain. The automation task might carry a high or low level of impact, but some form of quality assurance testing should be conducted on the code before running it in a production environment. Scripts in particular should be tested thoroughly because of their potential effect on an environment.

NOTE

A key point to keep in mind when developing your own scripts is that scripts which are only reading information are generally quite safe to run. For example, a script that creates a list of Active Directory user attributes but does not write any information to Active Directory has a very low probability of causing any problems. Whenever your scripts make modifications to objects, it is important to understand what changes are being made, and provide a rollback strategy wherever possible. For example, if you were writing a script to modify the **description** field of every user object in Active Directory, you could use the CSVDE utility to export the existing user description fields to a file prior to running your script. This way, if the script produced some unexpected results, you could review the export file and even reimport the description fields if necessary.

Keep Your Scripts Professional

Many scripters tend to view scripting as a quick and easy way to complete tasks and don't see the need for professional considerations, such as planning, documentation, and standards. This mindset is likely a holdover from the days when scripting was considered a clandestine task reserved for UNIX and Linux coders. Clearly, this view is changing with Microsoft's release of PowerShell. CLI use, scripting, and automation are becoming the foundation for how Windows systems administrators manage their environments. With this change, scripting, with its flexibility and raw power, will be increasingly viewed as a solution to business automation needs and, therefore, a task that should be done with professionalism.

To be professional when creating scripts, you should make sure your work meets a certain level of quality by developing standards for all your scripts to meet: writing clear and concise documentation, following best practices in planning and layout, testing thoroughly, and so forth. Adhering to professional standards can also ensure that others accept your work more readily and consider it more valuable.

Script Design

The following sections offer some ideas on best practices for PowerShell script design. The term "design" is used lightly here, because the goal is to provide insight into design practices that should and should not be followed when writing a PowerShell script. For example, when writing a script, you should validate information that is provided to the script. Again, it is highly recommended that you apply the practices reviewed in these sections to scripts that you develop. Following these practices will help make your scripts more readable, usable, robust, and less buggy.

Put Configuration Information at the Beginning of Scripts

When setting variables, parameters, and so on that control script configuration, you should always place them near the beginning of a script to make locating these items easy for anyone using, reading, or editing the script, as shown in this example:

```
#-------------------
# Set Vars
#-------------------
$Owner = "Administrators"
$Targets = import-csv $ImportFile


#-------------------
# Script Body
#-------------------
...
```

Another reason for this practice is to reduce the number of errors introduced when editing the script configuration. If configuration information is spread throughout a script, it's more likely to be misconfigured, declared multiple times, or forgotten.

Use Comments

You can't assume users or other team members who work with your scripts will understand the logic you've used in a script or be familiar with the methods you used to
perform tasks. Therefore, using comments to assist users in understanding your script is a
good practice. Comments don't always have to be extensive, but should provide enough
information to help users see how the script logic flows. In addition, if your script
includes a complex method, class, or function, adding a comment to explain what it does
is helpful. Another benefit of comments is that the information makes it easier for you to
review or update a script. The following example shows the use of comments to provide
helpful information:

```
#--------------------------------------------------
# Add-DACL
#--------------------------------------------------
# Usage:       Grants rights to a folder or file.
# $Object:     The directory or file path.  ("c:\myfolder" or
#              "c:\myfile.txt")
# $Identity:   User or Group name. ("Administrators" or
#              "mydomain\user1"
# $AccessMask: The access rights to use when creating the access rule.
#              ("FullControl", "ReadAndExecute, Write", etc.)
# $Type:       Allow or deny access. ("Allow" or "Deny")
```

NOTE

Taking the time to add comments to your script can make the difference between a
simple one-off script and a clearly understood production process. You may be able to
understand what your script does, but your team members who support the script may
not have the same level of familiarity with coding. In addition, you may need to revisit
or modify a script years after writing it, and having to review and re-learn your old
undocumented code is a recipe for making mistakes. As the proverb goes, the palest
ink is better than the sharpest memory!

Avoid Hard-Coding Configuration Information

Hard-coding configuration information is a common mistake. Instead of asking users to
supply the required information, the configuration information is hard-coded in variables
or randomly scattered throughout the script. Hard-coding requires users to manually edit
scripts to set the configuration information, which increases the risk of mistakes that
result in errors when running the script. Remember that part of your goal as a scripter is
to provide usable scripts; hard-coding information makes using a script in different environments difficult. Instead, use parameters or configuration files, as shown in the following example, so that users can set configuration information more easily.

```
param([string] $ADSISearchPath=$(throw "Please specify the ADSI Path!"))
```

When Necessary, Use Variables in One Place

If configuration information does need to be hard-coded in a script, use variables to represent the information. Defining configuration information in a variable in one place, instead of several places throughout a script, decreases the chance of introducing errors when the information needs to be changed. Furthermore, having configuration information in a single place, particularly at the beginning of a script, helps reduce the time to reconfigure a script for different environments.

Provide Instructions

Most scripts you develop are written for use by others, such as customers. Therefore, your users are often administrators who aren't comfortable with code and command-line interfaces. Remember that your scripts have to be usable and useful. If you don't include instructions to make sure a novice can run the script and understand what it does, you haven't succeeded as a scripter.

It's common to see scripts without any instructions, with incorrect instructions, or with little explanation of what the script does. For users, these scripts are usually frustrating. Even worse, the users might have no clue about the impact a script might have on their environment, and running it could result in a disaster.

The following example includes instructions that might be in a readme file to explain the script's purpose and how it works:

```
==================================================================
Script Info
==================================================================
Name: AddProxyAddress.ps1
Author: Instructive Scripter
Date: 6/02/2008

Description:
Use this script to add secondary proxy addresses to users based on a CSV import
file. When trying to add the additional proxy addresses, this script checks the
following conditions:

    Does the user exist?
    Is the user mail-enabled?
    Does the proxy address currently exist?

This script will create a log file each time it is run.
```

```
CSV file format:
[sAMAccountName],[ProxyAddresses]
tyson,tyson@companyabc.com;support@companyabc.com
marco,marco@companyabc.com
pete,pete@companyabc.com
syed,syed@companyabc.com

The ProxyAddresses column is ; delimited for more than one proxy address.
```

Perform Validity Checking on Required Parameters

Failing to perform basic validity checks on required parameters is a common mistake. If your script requires input from users, neglecting these validity checks might mean that users enter the wrong input, and the script halts with an error. This oversight might not be a major issue with small scripts, but, with large, complex scripts, it can seriously affect their usability.

Let's say you wrote a script that performs a software inventory. In your development environment consisting of a few machines, you run the script, but fail to provide the correct information for a required parameter. The script runs, and a couple of seconds later, it fails. You realize that you mistyped a parameter, so you correct your mistake and rerun the script.

Then, the systems administrator runs your script against thousands of machines; it runs for six hours and then fails. Reviewing the error information, the administrator discovers the script failed because of a mistyped parameter. At that point, the administrator has already invested six hours only to encounter an error and might conclude your script isn't usable. In other words, you wrote a script that works for your environment, but not the administrator's environment. To prevent this problem, make sure you perform validity checking on required parameters, as shown in the following example:

```
param([string] $TemplatePath = $(throw write-host `
    "Please specify the source template path of the folder structure to" `
    "be copied." -Foregroundcolor Red), [string] $ImportFile = $(throw `
    write-host "Please specify the import CSV filename." `
    -Foregroundcolor Red))

write-host "Checking Template Path" -NoNewLine

if (!(test-path $TemplatePath)){
    throw write-host `t "$TemplatePath is not a valid directory!" `
        -Foregroundcolor Red
    }
else {
```

```
    write-host `t "[OK]" -Foregroundcolor Green
    }

write-host "Checking Import File" -NoNewLine

if (!(test-path $ImportFile)){
    throw write-host `t "$ImportFile is not a valid file!" -Foregroundcolor Red
    }
else {
    write-host `t "[OK]" -Foregroundcolor Green
    }
```

Make Scripts and Functions Reusable

If you have spent time developing sophisticated script functionality, you should take the time to make that functionality reusable. With a common set of scripts or functions, you can also save time when you need to create new scripts. For example, in one script, you created logic for parsing data from a comma-separated value (CSV) file to create an HTML table. Instead of copying and modifying that logic for new scripts, you can create a script or library file that includes this logic so that it can be reused in any script.

Reusability is an important best practice. In PowerShell, the concept of reusability makes even more sense because scripts and library files can be ported easily by calling reusable code from a PowerShell console session or loading the script or library file with a dot-sourced statement. The following example shows a series of script files being called from the PowerShell console as part of the pipeline.

```
PS C:\> .\get-invalidusers.ps1 mydomain.com | .\out-html.ps1 | .\out-ie.ps1
```

Use Descriptive Names Rather Than Aliases

Using aliases in PowerShell can save time, but they make your scripts difficult for users to read. The PowerShell language is designed to be easy to write and read, but your naming standards and use of aliases have an effect on readability. To ensure readability, follow consistent naming standards and use descriptive names rather than aliases whenever possible.

Making your code more readable benefits users trying to understand it and means that future updates and changes will be easier for you, too. If you take the time to follow consistent naming standards and avoid the overuse of aliases, making modifications to the script should be easy.

Provide Status Information for Script Users

Providing status information in an automation script is essential so that users understand how the script is progressing during execution and can confirm whether script tasks have been completed successfully. Status information also lets users know whether any errors have occurred, and it can even indicate how much longer until the script has finished running.

You can provide status information to users in the form of console displays by using the Write-Host and Write-Progress cmdlets, write status information to a log file, or leverage Windows Forms to report on the status of your script. Figure 12.2 shows PowerShell being used to provide status information on a scripted operation which provisions web folders for a group of users.

FIGURE 12.2   Example of how a script can provide status information

---

NOTE

Regardless of the method, the idea is to provide enough status information without overloading users with useless details. If you need different levels of detail when displaying information to users, you can use the Write-Verbose and Write-Debug cmdlets, the Verbose and Debug parameters, or create custom output.

Use the WhatIf and Confirm **Parameters**

PowerShell includes two cmdlet parameters that are designed to help prevent scripters and systems administrators from making unintended changes. The WhatIf parameter is designed to return information about changes that would occur if the cmdlet runs don't actually make those changes, as shown in this example:

```
PS C:\> get-process expl* | stop-process —WhatIf
What if: Performing operation "Stop-Process" on Target "explorer
(2172)".
```

In this example, the process object returned from the Get-Process cmdlet is explorer.exe. Normally, if a process object is then piped to the Stop-Process cmdlet, the received process stops. However, when using the WhatIf parameter with the Stop-Process cmdlet, the command returns information about the changes that would have happened instead of carrying out the command. For example, say you entered this command:

> **WARNING**
>
> Do not run the following command, because it is meant only as an example of what not to do.

```
PS C:\> get-process | stop-process
```

Without the WhatIf parameter, this command would stop your PowerShell console session and your system. Adding the WhatIf parameter gives you information warning that the command would likely result in a system crash, as shown here:

```
PS C:\> get-process | stop-process —WhatIf
What if: Performing operation "Stop-Process" on Target "alg (1048)".
What if: Performing operation "Stop-Process" on Target "ati2evxx (1400)".
What if: Performing operation "Stop-Process" on Target "ati2evxx (1696)".
What if: Performing operation "Stop-Process" on Target "atiptaxx (3644)".
What if: Performing operation "Stop-Process" on Target "BTSTAC~1 (2812)".
What if: Performing operation "Stop-Process" on Target "BTTray (3556)".
What if: Performing operation "Stop-Process" on Target "btwdins (1652)".
What if: Performing operation "Stop-Process" on Target "csrss (1116)".
What if: Performing operation "Stop-Process" on Target "ctfmon (1992)".
What if: Performing operation "Stop-Process" on Target "eabservr (3740)".
What if: Performing operation "Stop-Process" on Target "explorer (2172)".
What if: Performing operation "Stop-Process" on Target "googletalk (1888)".
What if: Performing operation "Stop-Process" on Target
"GoogleToolbarNotifier (2236)".
...
```

The Confirm parameter prevents unwanted modifications by forcing PowerShell to prompt users before making any changes, as shown in this example:

```
PS C:\> get-process expl* | stop-process -confirm

Confirm
Are you sure you want to perform this action?
Performing operation "Stop-Process" on Target "explorer (2172)".
[Y] Yes  [A] Yes to All  [N] No  [L] No to All  [S] Suspend  [?] Help
(default is "Y"):
```

As a best practice, you should use the WhatIf and Confirm parameters whenever possible to identify potentially harmful changes and give users a choice before making these changes.

> **NOTE**
>
> The WhatIf and Confirm parameters are a programmatic way to provide a safety net for the users of your scripts. These parameters are unique to PowerShell and are often not leveraged by scripters. Although you need to include the support for the WhatIf and Confirm parameters in your script, doing so makes it far less likely that your script will accidentally perform an unintentional damaging action. The WhatIf parameter specifically allows you to see the results of a script without actually executing it, making it easy to fine-tune your script before actually running it live. Please note that the WhatIf and Confirm parameters are valid only with cmdlets that actually make modifications, and will not be effective for cmdlets that are merely reading data.

Standards for Scripting

As in software development, your scripting practices should incorporate some form of standardization. The term "standardization" as used here doesn't mean a formal standard, such as one from the International Organization for Standardization (ISO) or Institute of Electrical and Electronics Engineers (IEEE). Instead, it refers to using consistent methods for how your scripts are named, organized, and structured; how they function; and how they handle errors. Standardizing these aspects of your scripts ensures consistency in how others interact with, troubleshoot, and use your scripts.

Using a consistent naming standard across scripts or even within a single script can improve a script's readability. Using a standard script layout benefits those trying to read, troubleshoot, or modify your script. Standardization can also reduce the time you need to develop new scripts. For example, you can create standard forms for common tasks, such as error handling, log file creation, and output formatting. Once these standard forms have been created and tested, it is easy to include these standard forms in future scripts since they have already been proven to function in a consistent manner. This technique allows you to maximize the investment of time that you make in your scripts by reusing script functionality that you have previously developed.

This Book's Scripting Standards

Subsequent chapters in this book focus on real-world examples for PowerShell scripts. Working scripts were pulled from actual projects developed to meet business requirements and are used throughout the remainder of this book. Although the full source code for these scripts is presented in the remaining chapters, the source code has also been provided on the PowerShell Unleashed Reference Web site, which enables you to examine the scripts in usable format. The URL for this Web site is www.informit.com/title/ 9780672329883.

To address a few potential problems of standardization, some choices were made for how to present scripts in this book:

▶ Scripts are limited to the PowerShell and VBScript languages to reduce the complexity of dealing with many different scripting languages.

▶ VBScript scripts reside in a Windows Scripting File (WSF).

▶ Each PowerShell and VBScript is structured with a common layout that's easy to comprehend.

Figures 12.3 and 12.4 are examples of the layouts used in this book.

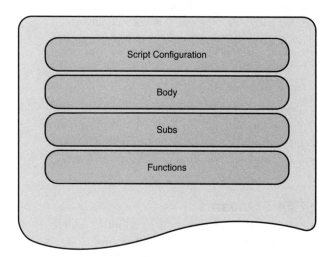

Script Configuration

Body

Subs

Functions

FIGURE 12.3   WSF script layout

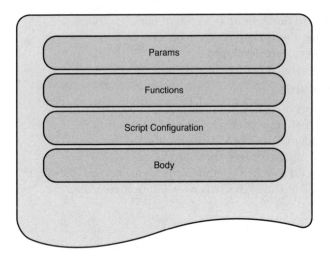

FIGURE 12.4   PowerShell script layout

▶ A digital code-signing certificate from Thawte was purchased, and all PowerShell scripts have been signed by the entity companyabc.com. If you have followed best practices for your execution policy setting, you need to configure companyabc.com as a trusted publisher to run the PowerShell scripts.

NOTE

The scripts provided with this book are functioning scripts. They have been tested and should perform according to their intended purposes. However, this doesn't automatically mean the scripts can be used in a production environment. If you plan to run one of these scripts in a production environment, you should conduct testing on that script first.

▶ PowerShell and VBScript scripts tend to provide the same type of interaction for input and output, although differences can emerge when new concepts are introduced. Overall, however, methods for providing input and output are clear and concise through use of the PowerShell console, log files, and Windows Forms.

PowerShell Community Scripting Standards

One of the defining characteristics of PowerShell as a language is its adoption and advancement by a diverse, worldwide group of scripters and technology professionals. One example of this type of adoption is the PowerShellCommunity.org Web site at http://powershellcommunity.org. The members of PowerShellCommunity.org collaborate on a wide variety of PowerShell topics, including scripts, blog entries, and the latest PowerShell developments from technology vendors. In addition to these types of individual contributions, the community maintains a library of generally agreed-upon best practices for scripting and related topics. Several examples of the PowerShellCommunity.org scripting standards are summarized in this chapter for reference, covering best practices for naming and best practices for script reliability.

Summary of PowerShell Community Naming Best Practices

▶ **Name your scripts and functions using the Verb(-)Noun syntax.** Although you are free to name your scripts and functions in any way you choose, using a Verb-Noun syntax (as in `Get-Process`) makes it easier for others to understand the purpose of your script, and it also provides consistency with the native PowerShell cmdlets. The Verb-Noun syntax is also used by several other programming languages, such as VAX VMS/DCL and AS/400 CL, so following this syntax will also help ensure that your script names are understandable to users with experience in these languages.

▶ **Wherever possible, use verbs from the standard PowerShell verb list.** One of the goals of the PowerShell team was to enable systems administrators to accomplish most of their tasks using just the standard set of PowerShell verbs. This makes it easier for administrators to learn about the properties of new PowerShell nouns, because they will already be familiar with the common verbs that are used to work with new nouns. Running the following commands in a PowerShell session returns a list of all the standard PowerShell verb names:

```
$assembly =
[System.Reflection.Assembly]::LoadWithPartialName("System.Management.Automation")
$types = $assembly.GetTypes() | ? { $_.Name -like "Verbs*" }
$types | % { $_.GetFields() | % { $_.Name } } | Sort
```

▶ **Use unique noun names.** Many times, using generic nouns, such as **Computer** or **User** in a script or function, causes a name collision with an existing noun of the same name. If a name collision does occur, users need to explicitly reference the full path and filename of your script to run it successfully. PowerShell addresses this issue by applying a **PS** prefix to make its nouns unique (as in **PSDrive** or **PSBreakpoint**), and it is recommended that you use a similar method for any nouns that you reference in your scripts (as in **MyTable** or **MyPrinter**).

▶ **Make noun names singular.** Because the English language handles pluralization for different nouns in different ways (as in a single **potato** or several **potatoes**, a single **mouse** or several **mice**), using pluralization in PowerShell noun names can be confusing, especially for those PowerShell users whose first language might not be English. This issue is made more complicated by the fact that not all cmdlets provide support for multiple return values. For example, the `Get-Date` cmdlet can return only a single value, but the `Get-Process` cmdlet can return multiple values. If users of PowerShell had to guess at the capabilities of a cmdlet based on whether the noun portion of the cmdlet name was singular or plural, ease of use would quickly grind to a halt. By using only singular noun names, the issues of pluralization are removed, and PowerShell users can focus on getting the results they need instead of worrying about the peculiarities of English grammar.

▶ **Use pascal casing for script and function names and use camel casing for variable names.** Pascal casing capitalizes the first letter of each word, such as `Get-Process` and `ConvertFrom-StringData`. Camel casing has the first letter of a word in lower case and capitalizes subsequent first letters, such as `remoteComputerName`. Using pascal casing for script names follows the standard used by other PowerShell cmdlets, whereas using camel casing for variable names follows the standards established in the .NET style guidelines. Because of PowerShell's frequent interaction with .NET objects, methods, and properties, it makes sense to adhere to the .NET naming standards for variable names. Both pascal casing and camel casing are discussed in the guide for the NET Framework Design Guidelines. This guide can be found by navigating to http://msdn.microsoft.com and searching on the phrase "NET Framework Design Guidelines for Class Library Developers".

▶ **Provide descriptive variable names.** When you are writing a script, the variable names that you choose can go a long way toward clarifying the actions that a script performs. Applying some thought to your choice of variable names can make your scripts almost self-documenting. Although the variables `$comp` and `$remoteComputerDNSName` function the same way when used in a script, the `$remoteComputerDNSName` variable clearly illustrates the data that the variable contains, and any code statements that contain this variable are much easier to understand as a result. This is especially important in environments where your scripts might be used and modified by multiple administrators with different levels of scripting knowledge. By consistently using descriptive variable names and applying a comparable level of detail in your use of other scripting commands, you can do a great deal to ensure that your scripts will be easier to support and maintain in a production environment.

Summary of PowerShell Community Scripting Reliability Best Practices

▶ **For global variables, add a unique namespace as a prefix.** As with PowerShell verbs and nouns, it is possible to create naming collisions with existing environment variables and produce unpredictable results. One way to reduce the possibility of variable name collisions is to prefix any global variables that you define with a unique identifier for the namespace. This identifier could be your company name, the name of your software application, or similarly unique data. The following example shows the syntax for defining a global variable including the string CompanyABC prefixed to the variable name:

```
${GLOBAL:CompanyABC.PowerShell.SqlCommands.DatabaseCache} =
```

▶ **Ensure that your scripts run successfully in strict mode.** Using strict mode in PowerShell is an optional setting that causes PowerShell to raise a terminating error when a script or expression does not follow best practice coding standards (such as referencing a variable that does not exist). In this respect, it is similar to using the `Option Explicit` statement in VBScript. Strict mode in PowerShell can be turned on or off by using the `Set-StrictMode` cmdlet, and it is enforced only in the scope where you set it. Because some users always run PowerShell with strict mode turned on, it is to your advantage to verify that your scripts will run in strict mode without errors. Otherwise, users have to disable strict mode to run the script, and it is possible that a script that raises an error in strict mode might be written in a way that causes the script to produce unreliable results. A script that can be run successfully in strict mode meets at least a baseline set of programming standards, which helps to validate that the script is suitable for use in a production environment.

▶ **Whenever possible, avoid using aliases in scripts.** Although there is no technical obstacle to including aliases in a script, aliases make the script harder to read and understand for those scripters who are not familiar with all of the PowerShell command aliases. Because the reason behind the PowerShell command aliases is to reduce the number of keystrokes needed when working interactively at the PowerShell command line, there is only a minimal time savings achieved when aliasing commands in a script, which is quickly erased the next time that you need to review the script and have to spend time recalling the commands that you aliased to understand the script. In general, readability and ease of understanding should override speed of data entry when creating a script that will be reused.

Summary

In this chapter, you were presented with several PowerShell scripting best practices. These practices focused on how you develop, design, and secure your scripts so that your overall ability as a scripter improves. The sources for these practices are based both from software development best practices and real-world scripting experience. They are not all inclusive or set in stone to how they apply to your own scripting practices. The goal of this chapter was to prompt your own thought processes around what is considered a good scripting practice. In the end, you might choose to expand on or add to these practices as long as you consider them when sitting down to write your next PowerShell script. After all, the PowerShell team went through all the trouble to produce the perfect shell. That favor should be repaid by trying to produce a well thought out, well designed, and secure script.

PART III

Managing Microsoft Technologies with PowerShell

IN THIS PART

CHAPTER 13

PowerShell as a Management Interface

This chapter explains how PowerShell can be used as a management interface for applications. With new releases, such as Exchange 2007, Microsoft has built the management interface upon the foundation of PowerShell. For instance, when an administrator makes a change in the Microsoft Management Console (MMC) for Exchange, a PowerShell cmdlet is executed in the background to process the request. For developers who want to manage their own applications through PowerShell, Microsoft has released the PowerShell Software Development Kit (SDK) that can be leveraged to create custom cmdlets—which can then be called from a custom command shell, Windows application, or MMC snap-in.

This chapter covers creating a custom cmdlet, creating a custom snap-in, adding parameters to a custom cmdlet, and several other advanced features. Additionally, the scenario covers creating an MMC 3.0 snap-in that uses Yahoo! Maps geocoding functionality to pull coordinates for a street address.

> **NOTE**
>
> All the source code referenced in this chapter are available at www.informit.com/title/9780672329883.

Getting Started

The examples in this chapter are written in C# using Microsoft Visual Studio 2008 Express Edition (Visual Basic .NET is also supported). This is a free development tool from Microsoft and is highly recommended (although not required, one could just as easily write a custom cmdlet in Notepad).

Definitions

For those new to .NET development, here are some definitions for commonly used words that will be seen throughout this chapter (several of these definitions are also found in Chapter 3, "Advanced PowerShell Concepts"):

▶ Namespace—A hierarchical grouping of objects. For example: The `System.Net.Mail` is the namespace where the mail-related objects are located.

▶ Class—An object template that contains methods and properties. For example: The `SmtpClient` class within the `System.Net.Mail` namespace can be used to send an email message.

▶ Method—A function that can be executed by a class object. For example: The `SmtpClient` class exposes a method named `Send`.

▶ Property—A variable that can be set or obtained from a class object. For example: The `Body` property in the `MailMessage` class contains the text in the body of an email message.

▶ Library—A .dll file that contains compiled .NET code. For example: The System.Net.dll library contains compiled code pertaining to the `System.Net` namespace.

▶ Global Assembly Cache—A collection of .NET libraries that are built into the .NET framework.

The PowerShell SDK

The PowerShell SDK is included in the Microsoft Windows Software Development Kit for Vista and .NET 3.0 Runtime Components. Although the SDK was released for Windows Vista, it is also supported on Windows XP SP2 and Windows 2003 SP1 or later.

Installation Instructions

Installing the Microsoft Windows Software Development Kit is a straightforward process.

1. Click **Next** at the Welcome Screen (see Figure 13.1).

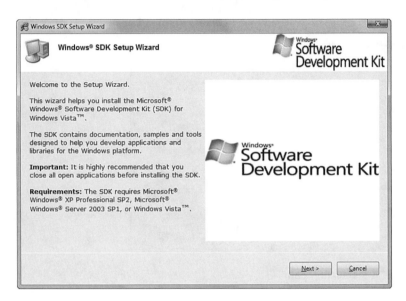

FIGURE 13.1   Vista SDK Welcome Screen

2. Accept the license agreement and click **Next** (see Figure 13.2).

FIGURE 13.2   Vista SDK License Agreement

3. Leave the default install location and click **Next** (see Figure 13.3).

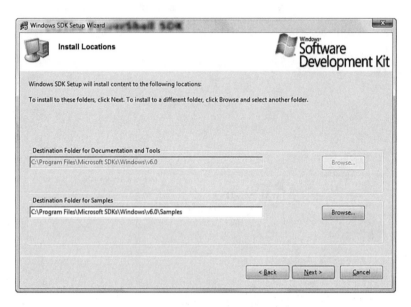

FIGURE 13.3   Vista SDK installation path

4. Select the **.NET Development Tools** under **Developer Tools / Windows Development Tools** (see Figure 13.4).

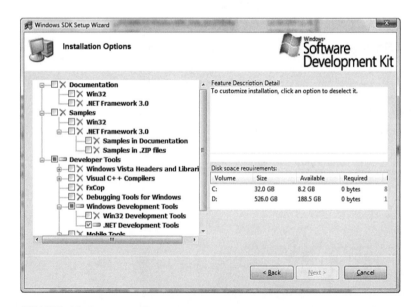

FIGURE 13.4   Vista SDK component selection

5. Click **Next** to begin the installation (see Figure 13.5).

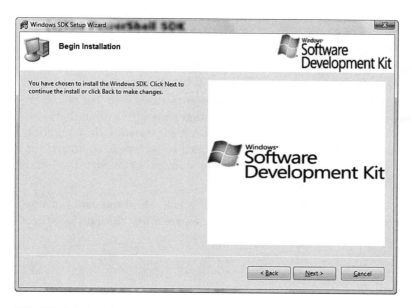

FIGURE 13.5   Vista SDK license install

6. Click **Finish** (see Figure 13.6).

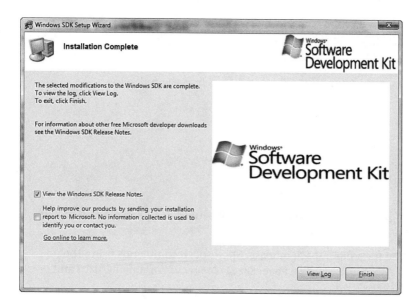

FIGURE 13.6   Vista SDK finished

Creating a Custom Cmdlet

Creating a custom cmdlet is a snap. The following example demonstrates how to create a simple cmdlet that returns "Hello World!"

Naming Conventions

The first step in creating a cmdlet is to determine a name. PowerShell cmdlet names are standardized using the verb-noun format. Each cmdlet begins with a verb that describes what type of command the cmdlet is going to execute—and ends with a noun that describes what object the cmdlet is going to execute against. For instance, the commonly used Get-Command cmdlet begins with the verb "Get," which is the type of command the cmdlet is going to execute. It ends with the noun "Command," which is what the cmdlet is going to execute against.

When naming a custom cmdlet, Microsoft has provided several sets of standard verbs to choose from in the System.Management.Automation namespace. The classes include the following:

- VerbsCommon
- VerbsCommunications
- VerbsData
- VerbsDiagnostic
- VerbsLifecycle
- VerbsOther
- VerbsSecurity

Each of these classes contains commonly used verbs, such as the following:

- Get
- Set
- Start
- Stop

The noun should also be singular, not plural. So, for example, Get-Command is acceptable, but Get-Commands is not.

When selecting a name for a namespace or class, Microsoft recommends using the naming convention of ApplicationName.PowerShell.Commands for a namespace and VerbNounCommand for a class.

The following is an example of the correct naming convention from one of the SDK libraries, as displayed in the Visual Studio Object Browser (see Figure 13.7).

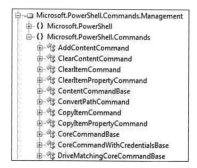

FIGURE 13.7   Visual Studio Object Browser

Setting Up a Project

After the appropriate names are chosen, a new class for a custom cmdlet can be created. If Visual Studio is being used, create a new Class Library project named HelloWorld (see Figure 13.8).

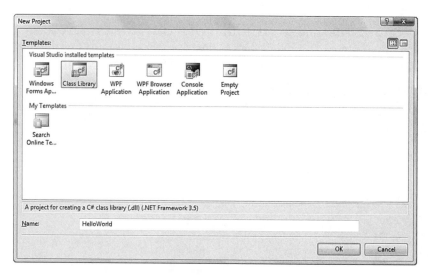

FIGURE 13.8   New Visual Studio project

Next, add a reference to the System.Management.Automation.dll by completing the following steps (see Figure 13.9).

1. From the toolbar, select Project >> Add Reference.

2. Click the browse tab. (The libraries from the PowerShell SDK are not loaded in the Global Assembly Cache so they won't show up on the default list.)

3. Navigate to C:\Program Files\Reference Assemblies\Microsoft\ WindowsPowerShell\v1.0 and select System.Management.Automation.dll.

4. Click OK.

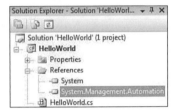

FIGURE 13.9   Add a Visual Studio reference.

Writing the Code

The required attributes for a new cmdlet class include a verb and a noun, as described previously. The class must also be a public class to be executed as a cmdlet from within PowerShell.

The two cmdlet classes are Cmdlet and PSCmdlet. The Cmdlet class is more flexible and can be called directly from other .NET code, whereas the PSCmdlet class must execute in a PowerShell runspace (but has the primary benefit of being able to call PowerShell scripts).

In the following example, the Cmdlet class has been inherited in the HelloWorld. PowerShell.Commands namespace. For the verb attribute, the VerbsCommon.Get property is used; for the noun attribute, "HelloWorld" is used. When executed from within PowerShell, the cmdlet name will be Get-HelloWorld.

```
using System.Management.Automation;

namespace HelloWorld.PowerShell.Commands
{
    [Cmdlet(VerbsCommon.Get, "HelloWorld")]
    public class GetHelloWorld : Cmdlet
    {

    }
}
```

A custom cmdlet must override one of the following methods that are contained in the Cmdlet and PSCmdlet classes: BeginProcessing, ProcessRecord, or EndProcessing. Each method is executed in sequence at a different phase of the cmdlet lifecycle, so the particular method that should be selected depends on whether one intends to process input from the pipeline.

If a custom cmdlet needs to perform any pre-processing before receiving pipeline input, you should use the `BeginProcesses` method. If the cmdlet must receive pipeline input, you should use the `ProcessRecord` method. If the cmdlet will not receive pipeline input, you should use the `EndProcessing` method.

To return data to the pipeline, you must use the `WriteObject` method and pass the output data.

In the following example, the `ProcessRecord` method has been overridden (details on handling input come later in the section "Creating Custom Parameters"), and the simple string "Hello World!" is sent to the pipeline.

```
using System.Management.Automation;

namespace HelloWorld.PowerShell.Commands
{
    [Cmdlet(VerbsCommon.Get, "HelloWorld")]
    public class GetHelloWorld : Cmdlet
    {
        protected override void ProcessRecord()
        {
            WriteObject("Hello World!");
        }
    }
}
```

Creating a Custom Snap-In

A PowerShell snap-in contains cmdlets that can be executed from within PowerShell. To execute a custom cmdlet, you must create a custom snap-in that is registered from within PowerShell.

The first step is to add a reference to the `System.Configuration.Install` library that is part of the Global Assembly Cache. This library is required to write a custom installer for our snap-in.

Next, create another public class and inherit `PSSnapIn`, which resides in the `System.ComponentModel` namespace. Microsoft recommends using the `VerbNounPSSnapIn` naming convention for these classes.

Finally, add the `RunInstaller` attribute so that installutil.exe can be invoked to register the snap-in after it is compiled.

In the following example, the custom `PSSnapIn` class has been named `GetHelloWorldPSSnapIn`.

```
using System.Management.Automation;
using System.ComponentModel;

namespace HelloWorld.PowerShell.Commands
{
    [Cmdlet(VerbsCommon.Get, "HelloWorld")]
    public class GetHelloWorld : Cmdlet
    {
        protected override void ProcessRecord()
        {
            WriteObject("Hello World!");
        }
    }
}


[RunInstaller(true)]
public class GetHelloWorldPSSnapIn : PSSnapIn
{

}
```

Three required properties must be overridden for a custom snap-in: Name, Vendor, and Description.

```
[RunInstaller(true)]
public class GetHelloWorldPSSnapIn : PSSnapIn
{
        public override string Name
        {
            get
            {
                return "GetHelloWorldPSSnapIn";
            }
        }
        public override string Vendor
        {
            get
            {
                return "Companyabc";
            }
        }
        public override string Description
        {
```

```
            get
            {
                return "Returns Hello World!";
            }
        }
    }
}
```

The complete code for a custom cmdlet and snap-in displays as follows:

```
using System.Management.Automation;
using System.ComponentModel;

namespace HelloWorld.PowerShell.Commands
{
    [Cmdlet(VerbsCommon.Get, "HelloWorld")]
    public class GetHelloWorld : Cmdlet
    {
        protected override void ProcessRecord()
        {
            WriteObject("Hello World!");
        }
    }


    [RunInstaller(true)]
    public class GetHelloWorldPSSnapIn : PSSnapIn
    {
        public override string Name
        {
            get
            {
                return "GetHelloWorldPSSnapIn";
            }
        }
        public override string Vendor
        {
            get
            {
                return "Companyabc";
            }
        }
        public override string Description
        {
```

```
        get
        {
            return "Returns Hello World!";
        }
    }
  }
}
```

With the code completed, it can now be compiled into a .dll library. If Visual Studio is being used, select Build >> Build Solutions from the toolbar. To compile the code using the command line, use the following commands:

```
PS> $r = "$Env:ProgramFiles\Reference
Assemblies\Microsoft\WindowsPowerShell\v1.0\System.Management.
Automation.dll"
PS> set-alias csc "$env:windir/Microsoft.NET/Framework/v2.0.50727/csc"
PS> csc /target:library /r:$r HelloWorld.cs
```

After the code has been compiled, the snap-in must be registered with PowerShell. Be aware that this requires administrator privileges, so do a RunAs if a low-privilege account is being used.

The following commands are used to register the snap-in:

```
PS> $HelloWorld =  HelloWorld.dll
PS> set-alias installutil
"$env:windir\Microsoft.NET\Framework\v2.0.50727\installutil"
PS> installutil $HelloWorld
```

To confirm that the snap-in has been registered, run the Get-PSSnapIn cmdlet with the -registered parameter:

```
PS> Get-PSSnapIn –Registered

Name         : GetHelloWorldPSSnapIn
PSVersion    : 1.0
Description  : Returns Hello World!

PS>
```

Add the snap-in to PowerShell with `Add-PSSnapIn` cmdlet:

```
PS> Add-PSSnapIn GetHelloWorldPSSnapIn
```

To confirm that our cmdlet is now available, run `Get-Command Get-HelloWorld`:

```
PS> Get-Command Get-HelloWorld

CommandType     Name
-----------     ----
Cmdlet          Get-HelloWorld

PS>
```

Finally, the custom cmdlet `Get-HelloWorld` can now be executed in PowerShell!

```
PS> Get-HelloWorld
Hello World!
```

Creating Custom Parameters

Cmdlets can accept two types of parameters: command-line parameters and pipeline parameters.

Command-line parameters come after the command and modify how the command operates. For instance, the `Get-Command` cmdlet returns a list of all available PowerShell commands. However, if the `–name` parameter is used, information on a specific command is returned.

Likewise, many cmdlets also accept parameters from the pipeline. For example, the `Format-List` cmdlet accepts objects from an upstream cmdlet and outputs it in a list format, as opposed to the more common table format.

Again, to create a custom parameter, the first step is to come up with a name. PascalCase, or capitalizing the first letter of each word, is the recommended format.

It is also recommended to use common parameter names that are already established, such as Name, ID, Property, and Location. This is particularly important when receiving input from the pipeline, because PowerShell has the functionality to match like-types.

NOTE

Microsoft maintains a list of recommended parameter names here:
http://msdn2.microsoft.com/en-us/library/ms714468(VS.85).aspx

In the following example, a public string property named Location has been created that inherits the Parameter class. Get and Set functionality has also been added:

```
private string myLocation;

[Parameter()]
public string Location
{
    get
    {
        return myLocation;
    }
    set
    {
        myLocation = value;
    }
}
```

To enable a cmdlet to accept pipeline parameters, set the ValueFromPipeline attribute to true.

```
private string myLocation;

[Parameter(ValueFromPipeline = true)]
public string Location
{
    get
    {
        return myLocation;
    }
    set
    {
        myLocation = value;
    }
}
```

Now that the parameter class is complete, the cmdlet must be modified to properly process any object that is received. In the following example, this has been accomplished by checking to determine whether the private myLocation string is null. If it is not null, an alternate message is output to the pipeline.

```
protected override void ProcessRecord()
{
    if (myLocation == null)
    {
        WriteObject("Hello World!");
    }
    else
    {
        WriteObject("Hello " + myLocation + "!");
    }
}
```

In the following example, the cmdlet is executed using no input, a command-line parameter, and a pipeline parameter, respectively:

```
PS> Get-HelloWorld
Hello World!
PS> Get-HelloWorld —Location "San Francisco"
Hello San Francisco!
PS> echo "Los Angeles" | Get-HelloWorld
Hello Los Angeles!
```

Advanced Parameter Functionality

In addition to the basic functionality of parameters outlined in this chapter, some advanced options are also useful.

Arrays

Arrays can be used to accept multiple instances of an object. In the following example, the single Location string has been changed to accept an array of strings:

```
private string[] myLocation;

[Parameter(ValueFromPipeline = true)]
public string[] Location
{
```

```
    get
    {
        return myLocation;
    }
    set
    {
        myLocation = value;
    }
}
```

The `ProcessRecord` override is then modified to output each string in the array:

```
protected override void ProcessRecord()
{
    if (myLocation == null)
    {
        WriteObject("Hello World!");
    }
    else
    {
        foreach (string location in myLocation)
        {
            WriteObject("Hello " + location + "!");
        }
    }
}
```

Now the user can input multiple locations with a single command:

```
PS> Get-HelloWorld –Location "Portland","Sacramento"
Hello Portland!
Hello Sacramento!
```

Position

The `Position = X` property can be used to identify the order in which a parameter will appear after a command so that the user does not need to use the –Parameter command-line switch. In the following example, the `Position` property is set to zero, so the first object that follows the Get-HelloWorld command becomes the Location parameter value:

```
[Parameter(Position = 0)]
public string Location
```

```
PS> Get-HelloWorld "Oakland"
Hello Oakland!
```

Mandatory

The Mandatory = true property can be used to enforce a parameter. If the user does not supply the parameter, PowerShell will prompt for it:

```
[Parameter(Mandatory = true)]
public string Location
```

```
PS> Get-HelloWorld
cmdlet Get —HelloWorld at command pipeline position 1
Supply values for the following parameters:
Location: San Diego
Hello San Diego!
```

HelpMessage

The HelpMessage = string property can be used to add help to a parameter. In the following example, we set a help message with the value "Sample Help Message:"

```
[Parameter(HelpMessage="Sample Help Message", Mandatory= true)]
public string Location
```

```
PS> Get-HelloWorld
cmdlet Get —HelloWorld at command pipeline position 1
Supply values for the following parameters:
(Type !? for Help.)
Location: !?
Sample Help Message
```

13

Alias

The Alias attribute can be used to set an alternative name for a parameter. In the following example, we set an alias for the Location parameter named Loc:

```
[Alias("Loc")]
[Parameter()]
public string Location
```

```
PS> Get-HelloWorld —Loc "Seattle"
Hello Seattle!
```

Input Validation

Parameters also have excellent built-in support for input validation. This enables cmdlet developers to set limits on exactly what type of input is acceptable.

ValidateLength

The ValidateLength attribute can be used to ensure that an input value meets minimum and maximum length requirements. The first value is the minimum length, and the second value is the maximum length. In the following example, the minimum length is set to 5 characters, and the maximum length is set to 10 characters:

```
[ValidateLength(5,10)]
[Parameter()]
public string Location
```

```
PS> Get-HelloWorld —Location "San"
Get-HelloWorld : Cannot validate argument because its length (3) is
too small. Specify a length that is greater than or equal to "5" and
try again.
At line:1 char:25
+ get-helloworld -location  <<<< "San"
PS> Get-HelloWorld —Location "San Francisco"
Get-HelloWorld : Cannot validate argument because its length (13) is
too long. Specify a length that is less than or equal to "10" and try
again.
At line:1 char:25
+ get-helloworld -location  <<<< "San Francisco"
```

ValidateRange

The `ValidateRange` attribute can be used to ensure than an input integer is within a predefined numeric range. The first value is the minimum value, and the second value is the maximum value. In the following example, the `Location` attribute has been changed to an `int`, and the `ValidateRange` attribute is set to accept a number between 5 and 10:

```
[ValidateRange(5,10)]
[Parameter()]
public int Location
```

```
PS> Get-HelloWorld —Location 1
Get-HelloWorld : The argument (1) was smaller than the minimum range (5).
Specify a value greater than or equal to the MinRange value and try again.
At line:1 char:25
+ get-helloworld -location  <<<< 1
PS> Get-HelloWorld —Location 11
Get-HelloWorld : The argument (11) was greater than the maximum range (10).
At line:1 char:25
+ get-helloworld -location  <<<< 11
```

ValidatePattern

The `ValidatePattern` attribute can be used to ensure than an input integer meets a specific series of values. This is particularly useful for values, such as license plate numbers, that do not fall between a specific numeric range but still have a strict format that must be followed. In the following example, the `ValidatePattern` attribute is looking for a value that matches the California license plate format of number-letter-letter-letter-number-number-number:

```
[ValidatePattern("[0-9][a-z][a-z][a-z][0-9][0-9][0-9]")]
[Parameter()]
public string Location
```

```
PS> Get-HelloWorld —Location 0abc1234
Hello 0abc1234!
PS> Get-HelloWorld —Location 0abcd123
Get-HelloWorld : Cannot validate argument "0abcd123" because it does
not match pattern "[0-9][a-z][a-z][a-z][0-9][0-9][0-9]".
At line:1 char:25
+ get-helloworld -location  <<<< 0abcd123
```

ValidateSet

The ValidateSet attribute can be used to accept only a specific value or set of values. There is also an optional parameter IgnoreCase=Boolean to determine whether the parameter is case sensitive (the default is case insensitive). In the following example, San Bruno and San Jose are the only valid input values that will be accepted:

```
[ValidateSet("San Bruno","San Jose", IgnoreCase = false)]
[Parameter()]
public string Location
```

```
PS> Get-HelloWorld —Location "San Bruno"
Hello San Bruno!
PS> Get-HelloWorld —Location "San Jose"
Hello San Jose!
PS> Get-HelloWorld —Location "San Juan"
Get-HelloWorld : Cannot validate argument "San Juan" because it does
not belong to the set "San Bruno, San Jose".
At line:1 char:25
+ get-helloworld -location  <<<< "San Juan"
```

ValidateCount

The ValidateCount attribute can be used to accept a specific number of input values. This is useful if a parameter is an array that should be only of a specific size. In the following example, only two values can be input:

```
[ValidateCount(1,2)]
[Parameter()]
public string[] Location
```

```
PS> Get-HelloWorld —Location "Las Vegas","Reno"
Hello Las Vegas!
Hello Reno!
PS> Get-HelloWorld —Location "Las Vegas","Reno","Lake Tahoe"
Get-HelloWorld : Cannot validate arguments because the number of
supplied arguments (3) exceeds the maximum number of allowed arguments
(2). Specify less than 2 arguments and try again.
At line:1 char:25
+ get-helloworld -location  <<<< "Las Vegas","Reno","Lake Tahoe"
```

Lastly, the following common parameter names are reserved and should not be used: Confirm, Debug, ErrorAction, ErrorVariable, OutBuffer, OutVariable, Verbose, and WhatIf. The following aliases are also reserved: db, ea, ev, ov, ob, and vb.

Supporting `Get-Help`

`Get-Help` is a commonly used cmdlet, and it is expected that any custom cmdlets support it.

Help for a custom cmdlet is written in a formatted XML file. This provides an easy way for a cmdlet developer to fill in the necessary fields so that the help is output in a standardized format.

The XML file must follow the standardized naming scheme, which is <libraryname>. dll-Help.xml. For the `Get-HelloWorld` cmdlet, the XML help file is named HelloWorld. dll-Help.xml.

When `Get-Help` is run against a cmdlet, several predefined sections are populated with data from the XML help file. Before proceeding, take a moment to run `Get-Help` `Get-Command` `-full` to see an example of what a complete help section looks like.

Header

After the XML file is created, the first step is to add the header. This provides the schema information, which sets the rules for how the XML file must be formatted and populated.

```
<?xml version="1.0" encoding="utf-8" ?>
<helpItems xmlns="http://companyabc" schema="maml">
  <command:command
  xmlns:maml="http://schemas.microsoft.com/maml/2004/10"
  xmlns:command="http://schemas.microsoft.com/maml/dev/command/2004/10"
  xmlns:dev="http://schemas.microsoft.com/maml/dev/2004/10">
    <!--Your information here-->
  </command:command>
</helpItems>
```

> **NOTE**
>
> It is important to remember that XML files are case sensitive.

Name and Synopsis

The first section of the XML file is the `<command:details>` node, which populates the Name and Synopsis sections of `Get-Help`.

13

The `<command:name>` node is required and must match the name of the cmdlet; otherwise, `Get-Help` returns an error.

The `<command:verb>` node is the verb portion of the cmdlet name.

The `<command:noun>` node the noun portion of the cmdlet name.

The `<maml:description>` node is actually what appears under the Synopsis section.

```
<command:details>
  <command:name>Get-HelloWorld</command:name>
  <command:verb>Get</command:verb>
  <command:noun>HelloWorld</command:noun>
  <maml:description>
    <maml:para>Returns Hello World!</maml:para>
  </maml:description>
</command:details>
```

> **NOTE**
>
> The `<maml:para>` node appears frequently in the XML code and indicates a separate paragraph.

Syntax

The next section of the XML file is the `<command:syntax>` node, which populates the Syntax sections of `Get-Help`. If a cmdlet has multiple parameter sets, multiple `syntaxItem` nodes can be added for each set. Because the `Get-HelloWorld` cmdlet has only one parameter set, only one `syntaxItem` is supplied.

The `<maml:name>` node is the name of the cmdlet as it will appear in the Syntax section.

The `<command:parameter>` node contains several attributes:

▶ `required=boolean`—Indicates whether the parameter is required

▶ `globbing=boolean`—Indicates whether the parameter supports wildcards

▶ `pipelineInput=boolean`—Indicates whether the parameter supports pipeline input

▶ `position=int`—Indicates if the parameter supports the position attribute and what location it is at

The `<command:parameterValue>` node is the object type the parameter accepts.

Multiple `<command:parameter>` sub-nodes can be added when a cmdlet accepts multiple parameters.

```
<command:syntax>
  <command:syntaxItem>
    <maml:name>Get-HelloWorld</maml:name>
    <command:parameter required="false" globbing="false"
     pipelineInput="true" position="0">
      <maml:name>Location</maml:name>
      <command:parameterValue>string</command:parameterValue>
    </command:parameter>
  </command:syntaxItem>
</command:syntax>
```

13

NOTE

Be careful for typos in the cmdlet name and parameter name nodes, because they are not validated to match the actual values when the help file is registered.

Detailed Description

The next section of the XML file is the `<maml:description>` node, which populates the Detailed Description section of Get-Help.

```
<maml:description>
  <maml:para>Returns Hello World! or allows the user to supply a
   custom location!</maml:para>
</maml:description>
```

Parameters

The next section of the XML file is the `<maml:parameters>` node, which populates the Parameters section of Get-Help. This section is different from the parameters that are displayed under the Syntax section and are intended to be more detailed.

The node structure is also essentially the same, with the exception of the new `<maml:description>` node, which contains a description of the parameter.

This section is visible when using the –Full or –Detailed command-line parameters of Get-Help.

```
<command:parameters>
  <command:parameter required="false" globbing="false"
   pipelineInput="true" position="0">
    <maml:name>Location</maml:name>
```

```
   <maml:description>
     <maml:para>This parameter will be output as part of Hello
        Location!</maml:para>
   </maml:description>
   <command:parameterValue>string</command:parameterValue>
   <dev:defaultValue>World</dev:defaultValue>
  </command:parameter>
 </command:parameters>
```

Input Type

The next section of the XML file is the `<command:inputTypes>` node, which populates the Input Type section of `Get-Help`. The input type should indicate the object type that is accepted as input, such as a string.

Multiple Input Types can be specified using the sub-node `<command:inputType>`. The `<dev:type>` node contains the actual value that is returned.

```
<command:inputTypes>
  <command:inputType>
    <dev:type>
      <maml:name>string</maml:name>
    </dev:type>
  </command:inputType>
</command:inputTypes>
```

Return Type

The next section of the XML file is the `<command:outputTypes>` node, which populates the Return Type section of `Get-Help`. This is similar to the previous Input Type section, and it should also indicate the object type that is returned as output, such as a string.

```
<command:returnValues>
  <command:returnValue>
    <dev:type>
      <maml:name>string</maml:name>
    </dev:type>
  </command:returnValue>
</command:returnValues>
```

Notes

The Notes section consists of both notes and examples.

The notes are populated by the `<maml:alertSet>` node. The `<maml:title>` node is the header that is displayed above the note, and the `<maml:alert>` node is the actual note itself.

```
<maml:alertSet>
  <maml:title>Additional Notes</maml:title>
  <maml:alert>
    <maml:para>This is really just a simple cmdlet, there isn't
    much to say</maml:para>
  </maml:alert>
</maml:alertSet>
```

The examples are populated by the `<command:examples>` node. Multiple examples can be supplied using the sub-node `<command:example>`.

The `<maml:title>` node should indicate the example number.

The `<dev:code>` node should include an example of the syntax to run the command.

The `<dev:remarks>` node should include an example of the output from the command.

```
<command:examples>
  <command:example>
    <maml:title>---------  EXAMPLE 1  ---------</maml:title>
    <dev:code>Get-HelloWorld "San Francisco"</dev:code>
    <dev:remarks>
      <maml:para>This will return Hello San Francisco!</maml:para>
    </dev:remarks>
  </command:example>
</command:examples>
```

Related Links

The `<maml:relatedLinks>` node populates the Related Links section of `Get-Help`. Typically, this section includes cmdlets that are often used in conjunction with the custom cmdlet.

Note that in this case the `<maml:navagationLink>` sub-node is different from the parent node. Multiple instances of `<maml:navagationLink>` can be supplied. The actual data is contained in the `<maml:linkText>` node.

```
<maml:relatedLinks>
  <maml:navigationLink>
    <maml:linkText>Get-Help</maml:linkText>
  </maml:navigationLink>
</maml:relatedLinks>
```

Output

To include the XML help file when the cmdlet is registered, it must be in the same location as the compiled .dll library.

After it has been registered, it can now be accessed normally from Get-Help.

Here is the output from Get-Help Get-HelloWorld –full:

```
PS> Get-Help Get-HelloWorld —full
NAME
    Get-HelloWorld

SYNOPSIS
    Returns Hello World!

SYNTAX
    Get-HelloWorld [[-Location] [<string>]] [<CommonParameters>]

DETAILED DESCRIPTION
    Returns Hello World! or allows the user to supply a
            custom location!

PARAMETERS
    -Location [<string>]
        This parameter will be output as part of Hello
            Location!

        Required?                     false
        Position?                     0
        Default value                 World
        Accept pipeline input?        true
        Accept wildcard characters?   false

    <CommonParameters>
        This cmdlet supports the common parameters: -Verbose, -Debug,
        -ErrorAction, -ErrorVariable, and -OutVariable. For more
information,
        type, "get-help about_commonparameters".

INPUT TYPE
    string

RETURN TYPE
    string
```

```
NOTES
    Additional Notes

        This is really just a simple cmdlet, there isn't
        much to say

    ----------    EXAMPLE 1    ----------

    Get-HelloWorld "San Francisco"

    This will return Hello San Francisco!

RELATED LINKS
    Get-Help

PS>
```

Runspaces

A runspace can be used to execute PowerShell commands from within a .NET-based application. The following example creates a simple .NET executable that calls the Get-HelloWorld cmdlet.

As with the previous example that creates a custom cmdlet, you must first add a Reference to the System.Management.Automation.dll.

At this point, the application looks as follows:

```
using System;
using System.Management.Automation.Runspaces;

namespace HelloWorldConsole
{
    class HelloWorldConsole
    {
        static void Main(string[] args)
        {

        }
    }
}
```

The next step is to create a runspace configuration. This is required to create a runspace and can be used to add a custom snap-in.

The following example adds the `GetHelloWorldPSSnapIn`:

```
RunspaceConfiguration HelloWorldConfig =
  RunspaceConfiguration.Create();
PSSnapInException ex;
HelloWorldConfig.AddPSSnapIn("GetHelloWorldPSSnapIn", out ex);
```

Next, the runspace itself can be created using the runspace configuration.

The following example creates a runspace and then opens it:

```
Runspace HelloWorldRunspace =
  RunspaceFactory.CreateRunspace(HelloWorldConfig);
HelloWorldRunspace.Open();
```

After the runspace has been initialized, cmdlets can be called.

The following example calls the `Get-HelloWorld` cmdlet and sets the `Location` parameter:

```
Command HelloWorldCmdlet = new Command("Get-HelloWorld");
HelloWorldCmdlet.Parameters.Add("Location", "San Dimas");
```

Next, a pipeline object must be created. The pipeline object in the .NET executable functions just like a pipeline from within PowerShell. Multiple cmdlets can be called, and output can be passed down the chain.

. In the following example, the command that was created previously is added to the pipeline. After the pipeline is invoked, it returns a `PSObject` collection.

> **NOTE**
>
> The `Collection` class is in the `System.Collections.ObjectModel` namespace, and the `PSObject` class is in the `System.Management.Automation` namespace.

```
Pipeline HelloWorldPipeline = HelloWorldRunspace.CreatePipeline();
HelloWorldPipeline.Commands.Add(HelloWorldCmdlet);
Collection<PSObject> HelloWorldOutput = HelloWorldPipeline.Invoke();
```

The output is written to the console:

```
Console.WriteLine(HelloWorldOutput[0]);
```

The complete source code looks like this:

```
using System;
using System.Management.Automation.Runspaces;
using System.Collections.ObjectModel;
using System.Management.Automation;

namespace HelloWorldConsole
{
    class HelloWorldConsole
    {
        static void Main(string[] args)
        {
            RunspaceConfiguration HelloWorldConfig =
                RunspaceConfiguration.Create();
            PSSnapInException ex;
            HelloWorldConfig.AddPSSnapIn("GetHelloWorldPSSnapIn",
                out ex);

            Runspace HelloWorldRunspace =
                RunspaceFactory.CreateRunspace(HelloWorldConfig);
            HelloWorldRunspace.Open();

            Command HelloWorldCmdlet = new Command("Get-HelloWorld");
            HelloWorldCmdlet.Parameters.Add("Location", "San Dimas");

            Pipeline HelloWorldPipeline =
                HelloWorldRunspace.CreatePipeline();
            HelloWorldPipeline.Commands.Add(HelloWorldCmdlet);
            Collection<PSObject> HelloWorldOutput =
                HelloWorldPipeline.Invoke();

            Console.WriteLine(HelloWorldOutput[0]);
        }
    }
}
```

13

After compiling the code into an executable, it can now be run:

```
PS> .\HelloWorldConsole.exe
Hello San Dimas!
```

Scenario: Geocoding in MMC 3.0

As mentioned at the beginning of the chapter, the management interface for new Microsoft products is built upon the foundation of PowerShell. This gives administrators the ability to fully manage their products from the command line.

However, for most administrators, managing a product such as Exchange entirely from the command line is not practical. With MMC 3.0, Microsoft is wrapping the PowerShell cmdlets into a graphical user interface that enables any administrator to easily manage the product with a simple point-and-click.

In this scenario, Company ABC is working on a product to track the location of its customers so that it can determine when it makes sense to open a new shipping depot. Developers at Company ABC must come up with a way to resolve the longitude and latitude of each customer address.

Get-Coordinates **Cmdlet**

Yahoo! offers an excellent Geocoding API as part of its Yahoo! Maps web application. Developers at Company ABC decided to leverage this API for their Get-Coordinates cmdlet.

> **NOTE**
>
> For more information about the Yahoo! Geocoding API, visit this address:
>
> http://developer.yahoo.com/maps/rest/V1/geocode.html

The Get-Coordinates cmdlet must accept parameters for street, city, and state. These parameters will in turn be used to create a full web address from which the cmdlet will then receive a formatted XML file that contains the longitude and latitude.

Here is the complete source code for the cmdlet:

```
using System.Management.Automation;
using System.ComponentModel;
using System.Xml;
using System;

namespace GetCoordinates.PowerShell.Commands
{
```

```
[Cmdlet(VerbsCommon.Get, "Coordinates")]
public class GetCoordinates : Cmdlet
{
    protected override void ProcessRecord()
    {
        XmlDocument geocode = new XmlDocument();
        geocode.Load("http://local.yahooapis.com/MapsService/"
            + "V1/geocode?appid=YahooDemo&street="
            + myStreet + "&city=" + myCity + "&state=" + myState);

        string latitude =
            geocode.GetElementsByTagName("Latitude")[0].InnerText;
        string longitude =
            geocode.GetElementsByTagName("Longitude")[0].InnerText;
        string zip =
            geocode.GetElementsByTagName("Zip")[0].InnerText;

        WriteObject(latitude + "," + longitude + "," + zip);
    }

    private string myStreet;
    private string myCity;
    private string myState;

    [Parameter()]
    public string Street
    {
        get
        {
            return myStreet;
        }
        set
        {
            myStreet = value;
        }
    }
    [Parameter()]
    public string City
    {
        get
        {
            return myCity;
        }
        set
        {
```

13

```
                myCity = value;
            }
        }
        [Parameter()]
        public string State
        {
            get
            {
                return myState;
            }
            set
            {
                myState = value;
            }
        }
    }


[RunInstaller(true)]
public class GetCoordinatesPSSnapIn : PSSnapIn
{
    public override string Name
    {
        get
        {
            return "GetCoordinatesPSSnapIn";
        }
    }
    public override string Vendor
    {
        get
        {
            return "Companyabc";
        }
    }
    public override string Description
    {
        get
        {
            return "Returns Coordinates";
        }
    }
    }
}
```

As with all cmdlets, the `Get-Coordinates` cmdlet must be compiled and registered with installutil.exe before it can be used in PowerShell.

```
PS> $GetCoordinates = GetCoordinates.dll
PS> set-alias installutil
"$env:windir\Microsoft.NET\Framework\v2.0.50727\installutil"
PS> installutil $GetCoordinates
```

Here is the output from the cmdlet after it has been run:

```
PS> Get-Coordinates —street "1600 Pennsylvania Ave" —city Washington
—state DC
38.898590,-77.036473,20006
```

Get-Coordinates **User Control**

MMC 3.0 snap-ins can be created using simple User Controls designed in Visual Studio. The User Control in this scenario creates a runspace and calls the `Get-Coordinates` cmdlet.

To create a User Control in Visual Studio, right-click on the project name inside the Solution Explorer and select Add >> User Control (see Figure 13.10).

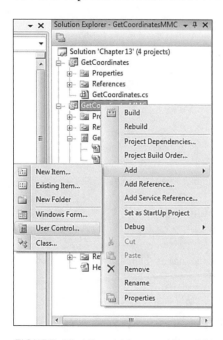

FIGURE 13.10   Add a new Visual Studio User Control

In the design view, a simple interface was created using the textbox and label controls, along with a button to initialize the search (see Figure 13.11).

FIGURE 13.11   The complete Geocode User Control

The code-behind for the User Control is also straightforward. The cmdlet parameters are taken from their respective TextBox controls. A pipeline is created, the cmdlet is added to it, and then the pipeline is invoked. The resultant output is then converted into a string, split, and used to populate the result controls.

Here is the complete source code for the User Control code-behind:

```
using System.Management.Automation.Runspaces;
using System.Windows.Forms;
using System;
using System.Collections.ObjectModel;
using System.Management.Automation;

namespace GetCoordinates.ManagementConsole
{
    public partial class GetCoordinatesControl : UserControl
    {
        public GetCoordinatesControl()
        {
            InitializeComponent();
            this.Dock = DockStyle.Fill;
        }

        private void Button_Search_Click(object sender, EventArgs e)
        {
            RunspaceConfiguration GetCoordinatesConfig =
                RunspaceConfiguration.Create();
            PSSnapInException ex;
            GetCoordinatesConfig.AddPSSnapIn("GetCoordinatesPSSnapIn",
                out ex);

            Runspace GetCoordinatesRunspace =
                RunspaceFactory.CreateRunspace(GetCoordinatesConfig);
            GetCoordinatesRunspace.Open();
```

```
Command GetCoordinatesCmdlet =
    new Command("Get-Coordinates");
GetCoordinatesCmdlet.Parameters.Add("Street",
    TextBox_Street.Text);
GetCoordinatesCmdlet.Parameters.Add("City",
    TextBox_City.Text);
GetCoordinatesCmdlet.Parameters.Add("State",
    TextBox_State.Text);

Pipeline GetCoordinatesPipeline =
    GetCoordinatesRunspace.CreatePipeline();
GetCoordinatesPipeline.Commands.Add(GetCoordinatesCmdlet);
Collection<PSObject> GetCoordinatesOutput =
    GetCoordinatesPipeline.Invoke();
string[] output =
    GetCoordinatesOutput[0].ToString().Split(new char[]
    { ',' });

TextBox_Latitude.Text = output[0];
TextBox_Longitude.Text = output[1];
TextBox_ZipCode.Text = output[2];
        }
    }
}
```

13

Get-Coordinates **MMC**

The first step to create an MMC 3.0 snap-in is to add a reference to the
Microsoft.ManagementConsole.dll library. Fortunately, this is included in the Microsoft
Windows Software Development Kit for Vista, so there is nothing additional that needs to
be installed.

NOTE

The default location for this file is in C:\Program Files\Reference Assemblies\
Microsoft\mmc\v3.0.

Each snap-in must have a unique GUID. Microsoft has created a utility named
guidgen.exe, which is the simplest way to create a new GUID.

After guidgen.exe is executed (see Figure 13.12), select `Registry Format` and click the Copy button.

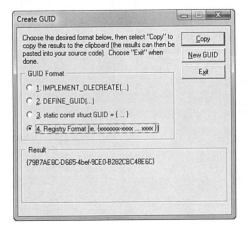

FIGURE 13.12   GuidGen.exe

Next, add a new class definition to the Visual Studio project. The new class inherits the `SnapIn` class. Two attributes are required: a `GUID` (which can be pasted in from the guidgen.exe application) and a `DisplayName`. The `DisplayName` displays under "Available snap-ins" when the snap-in is added to an MMC console.

Additionally, another new class that inherits the `SnapInInstaller` class is required so that installutil.exe can be used to register the snap-in.

```
using System;
using Microsoft.ManagementConsole;
using System.ComponentModel;


namespace GetCoordinates.ManagementConsole
{
    [SnapInSettings("{D234951B-FCCC-4149-9182-E34F431D0A8C}",
        DisplayName = "GetCoordinates")]
    public class GetCoordinatesMMC : SnapIn
    {
    }
```

```
    [RunInstaller(true)]
    public class GetCoordinatesMMCInstaller : SnapInInstaller
    {
    }
}
```

MMC is designed to support multiple snap-ins, so each snap-in must have its own node. The `DisplayName` property of the node appears under "Console Root" after the snap-in is added to an MMC console.

The final code required is to create a `FormViewDescription`. Multiple types of FormViews can be used—the `FormViewDescription` is the class that is required to create a WinForm with a User Control.

In the following code, a new `FormViewDescription` is added, and the `ControlType` property is set to the `GetCoordinatesControl` that was created previously. The `FormViewDescription` is then added to the node.

```
public GetCoordinatesMMC()
{
    this.RootNode = new ScopeNode();
    this.RootNode.DisplayName = "GetCoordinates";

    FormViewDescription GetCoordinatesFormViewDescription =
        new FormViewDescription();
    GetCoordinatesFormViewDescription.DisplayName =
        "GetCoordinates";
    GetCoordinatesFormViewDescription.ControlType =
        (typeof(GetCoordinatesControl));

    this.RootNode.ViewDescriptions.Add(
        GetCoordinatesFormViewDescription);
    this.RootNode.ViewDescriptions.DefaultIndex = 0;
}
```

Finally, the code must be compiled and registered with installutil.exe.

```
PS> $GetCoordinatesMMC =  GetCoordinatesMMC.dll
PS> set-alias installutil
"$env:windir\Microsoft.NET\Framework\v2.0.50727\installutil"
PS> installutil $GetCoordinatesMMC
```

It can then be added to MMC and used as a snap-in (see Figure 13.13)!

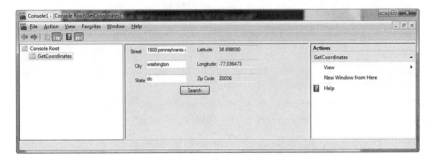

FIGURE 13.13   Finished Geocode MMC snap-in

Summary

In this chapter, you learned how to create a PowerShell cmdlet and how to execute that cmdlet from within an MMC 3.0 snap-in. Advanced functionality, such as creating parameters, supporting Get-Help, input validation, and creating runspaces in .NET were explained in detail.

PowerShell offers a new standard for command-line interfaces, and MMC 3.0 offers a new standard for GUIs. Now that Microsoft has established a precedent that its applications can be managed by both interfaces, users will begin to expect similar functionality in any third-party applications that they administer.

As a developer, this is both an exciting and challenging turn of events. Although new technologies and coding techniques must be learned, the user experience will be significantly improved as a result.

## CHAPTER 14

PowerShell and Active Directory

Administrators have always desired a unified method for managing Active Directory from both the command line or through automation scripts. To some extent, tools (executables) have been developed by either Microsoft or third parties to manage Active Directory via the command line. When used in conjunction with automation interfaces, such as Active Directory Services Interfaces (ADSI) and Window Script Host (WSH), these administrators have always been able to jury-rig the management task at hand. With the introduction of PowerShell, the paradigm is changing. For the first time, there is now a single interface, both command line and scripting, for managing Active Directory.

In this chapter, you explore how PowerShell can be used to manage Active Directory. In doing so, you first discover the different approaches Windows Script Host (WSH) and PowerShell take for completing Active Directory management tasks. Next, after gaining insight into how PowerShell interacts with Active Directory, you then review the two cornerstones of Active Directory management: managing objects and searching for objects. To complete this task, both topics are reviewed in detail while stepping through a series of examples. Finally, you review a script scenario that uses the information presented in this chapter.

Understanding the Interfaces

Before learning how to use PowerShell to manage Active Directory, you need to first gain a better understanding for the existing automation interfaces that are used to manage Active Directory. The first interface that you need to understand is called **Active Directory Services Interfaces**. ADSI is the primary programming interface for managing Active Directory. Any Active Directory management tool typically uses ADSI to interact with Active Directory. Similarly, when managing Active Directory through a script, you usually use ADSI.

To use ADSI as a component in your scripts, you need to understand several key concepts. First, ADSI consists of a series of providers: Lightweight Directory Access Protocol (LDAP), Novell Directory Services (NDS), Novell NetWare 3.x (NWCOMPAT), and Windows NT (WinNT). These providers enable external programs and scripts to manage a variety of network-based directories and data repositories, such as Active Directory, Novell NetWare 4.x NDS, and NetWare 3.x Bindery, in addition to any LDAP-compliant directory service infrastructure (LDAP V2 and up). However, additional ADSI providers can be developed to support other types of data repositories. For example, Microsoft has an Internet Information Services (IIS) ADSI provider for managing IIS.

Second, an ADSI provider implements a group of COM objects to manage network directories and data repositories. For example, an administrator can use the ADSI WinNT provider to bind to and manage Windows domain resources because it includes objects for users, computers, groups, and domains, among others. Objects made available by an ADSI provider typically reside in the target resource you want to manage. By accessing the applicable ADSI provider, a program or script can bind to an object and manage it with a set of methods and properties defined for that object.

Third, ADSI provides an abstraction layer so that you can manage objects across different directory services and data repositories. This abstraction layer, called the IADs interface, defines a set of properties and methods as the foundation for all ADSI objects. For example, an ADSI object accessed through the IADs interface has the following features:

- ▶ An object can be identified by name, class, or ADsPath.

- ▶ An object's container can manage that object's creation and deletion.

- ▶ An object's schema definition can be retrieved.

- ▶ An object's attributes can be loaded into the ADSI property cache, and changes to those attributes can be committed to the original data source.

- ▶ Object attributes loaded into the ADSI property cache can be modified.

Fourth, ADSI provides an additional interface (IADsContainer) for objects that are considered containers (such as organizational units [OUs]). When bound to a container object, this interface provides a set of common methods for creating, deleting, moving, enumerating, and managing child objects.

Fifth, ADSI maintains a client-side property cache for each ADSI object you bind to or create. Maintaining this local cache of object information improves the performance of reading from and writing to a data source because a program or script needs to access the data source less often. What's important to understand about the property cache is that object information it contains must be committed to the original data source. If new objects or object changes aren't committed to the original data source, those changes will not be reflected.The second interface that needs to be understood is called **ActiveX Data Objects (ADO)**. ADO allows applications or scripts to access data from different data sources by using a series of underlying Object Linking and Embedding Database (OLE DB) providers. One of these providers is an **ADSI OLE DB (ADODB)** provider that enables you to use ADO and its support for Structured Query Language (SQL) or LDAP to perform rapid searches in Active Directory.

Using the ADODB provider is an efficient method for conducting searches of Active Directory. When using this provider, searches can be performed through a single operation and without any need to bind to an existing object. However, the ADODB provider allows searches to be performed only in the LDAP namespace, and the record set that is returned from the provider is read-only.

Managing Active Directory Using WSH

In **Window Script Host (WSH)**, two interfaces manage Active Directory. The first interface consists of employing WScript Object's `GetObject` method to bind to Active Directory or an object in Active Directory. Then, once bound, you can perform additional actions to either the object or its child objects. An example of this is shown in the following script snippet, which uses ADSI's LDAP provider and an object's `LDAP ADsPath`:

```
Set objUser = GetObject("LDAP://CN=Garett Kopczynski,OU=Accounts,OU=Managed
Objects,DC=companyabc,DC=com")
```

As shown in the previous example, the `objUser` variable contains the resulting object that is returned from the `GetObject` method. In this case, that object happens to be the user object that has the `CN=Garett Kopczynski`. You can also perform the same task using ADSI's WinNT provider. An example of this is shown in the following code snippet:

```
Set objUser = GetObject("WinNT://companyabc.com/garett")
```

The only difference from the first example is that the WinNT provider and a `WinNT ADsPath` are used. In either case, an object is returned that relates to the user object named `CN=Garett Kopczynski`. However, the resulting object from the WinNT provider is different from an object created using the LDAP provider. The cause for this difference is based on the fact that the WinNT provider supports features that are available only within Windows NT domains. Because of this limitation, the WinNT provider exposes fewer attributes than the LDAP provider, which unfortunately restricts the number of management tasks that can be completed using this provider.

Another limitation with the WinNT provider is that it supports only a flat namespace that is contrastingly different from the object hierarchy found in Active Directory. Because of this difference, the WinNT provider is unaware of objects, such as Organization Units, or

14

certain object relationships, such as nested Global and Universal security groups. With this limitations in mind, it is generally recommend that the WinNT provider be used only for managing Windows NT 4.0 Domains or local account/group objects on Windows machines. However, the LDAP provider should be used for managing Active Directory.

> **NOTE**
>
> The Windows NT SAM database is not LDAP compliant. Because of this limitation, you cannot use the LDAP provider to manage Windows NT 4.0 Domains or account/group objects on Windows machines.

The second interface is to use WScript Object's `CreateObject` method to create an ADODB object and conduct Active Directory searches. An example of performing an LDAP-based ADODB search is shown in the following example:

```
Set objConnection = CreateObject("ADODB.Connection")
Set objCommand = CreateObject("ADODB.Command")
objConnection.Provider = "ADsDSOObject"
objConnection.Open("Active Directory Provider")
objCommand.ActiveConnection = objConnection
objCommand.Properties("Page Size") = 1000
objCommand.CommandText = _
        "<LDAP://companyabc.com>;(&(objectCategory=user)" _
      & "(sAMAccountName=tyson));sAMAccountName,distinguishedName;subtree"
Set objRecordSet = objCommand.Execute
```

As shown in the previous example, the `objConnection` variable contains the resulting object that is returned from the `CreateObject` method. Next, an ADODB command object is created and set to the `objCommand` variable. Then, in the next few steps, any needed ADODB parameters about the search to be performed are defined. The most important of these parameters is the `CommandText` parameter, which contains the filter string that is used to perform the search. In this case, a search is being performed for a user within the companyabc.com domain who has a `sAMAccountName=Tyson`. Finally, the LDAP search is executed using the ADODB `Execute` method. If the user exists, the resulting ADO record set consists of the user's `sAMAccountName` and `distinguishedName`.

Managing Active Directory Using PowerShell

In PowerShell, you can use two component classes within the .NET Framework's `System.DirectoryServices` namespace to access, manage, and search for Active Directory objects: the `DirectoryEntry` class and the `DirectorySearcher` class. Both of these classes are explained in the next few sections.

DirectoryEntry [ADSI]

The DirectoryEntry class is used as an interface for completing several tasks around the management of directory objects. Some of these tasks include binding to objects, reading their properties, updating their attributes, creating new objects, moving objects, renaming objects, and even deleting objects. Although this class is primarily intended for managing Active Directory objects through either ADSI's LDAP or WinNT providers, you can also use the class to manage all the other data repositories that are supported by ADSI.

To use this interface, use the New-Object cmdlet to create an instance of the DirectoryEntry class, as shown in the next example:

```
PS > $User = new-object
DirectoryServices.DirectoryEntry("LDAP://CN=Garett
Kopczynski,OU=Accounts,OU=Managed Objects,DC=companyabc,DC=com")
```

Additionally, the DirectoryEntry class is represented in PowerShell by the built-in [ADSI] type accelerator. This type accelerator is similar to the [WMI] type accelerator because you specify the object path to which you're connecting to. However, instead of a WMI object path, the [ADSI] type accelerator's object path must be in the form of an AdsPath path, as shown in this example:

```
PS > $User = [ADSI]"LDAP://CN=Garett Kopczynski,OU=Accounts,OU=Managed
Objects,DC=companyabc,DC=com"
```

Although the preceding example uses ADSI's LDAP provider, you can additionally choose to use of all the other providers that are available. For example, if you want to access the same user account but with ADSI's WinNT provider, you might use the following command:

```
PS > $User = [ADSI]"WinNT://companyabc.com/garett"
```

DirectorySearcher [ADSISearcher]

Much like ADODB, the DirectorySearcher class is similarly used for performing read-only LDAP searches against an LDAP-based directory. However, instead of using ADODB, the DirectorySearcher class makes use of a component library called ADO.NET. This library is a base class library that is included with the .NET Framework and can be used to access and modify data stored in relational database systems. Although similar in nature to ADODB, ADO.NET tends to be considered the next evolution of the older interface by making many needed improvements in the areas of performance and standardization (via XML).

14

> **NOTE**
>
> **Read-only LDAP** searches against an **LDAP-based directory** are two important
> concepts that should be noted about the `DirectorySearcher` class.

Like the `DirectoryEntry` class, you must use the `New-Object` cmdlet to create an instance
of the `DirectorySearcher` class. Then, after the instance is created, you can execute a
search using that instance, as shown in the following example:

```
PS > $Searcher = new-object DirectoryServices.DirectorySearcher
PS > $Searcher.Filter = "(samAccountName=garett)"
PS > $User = $Searcher.FindOne().GetDirectoryEntry()
```

In the preceding example, a `$Searcher` object is first created using the `New-Object` cmdlet.
Next, an LDAP filter statement is constructed to find the user account with a
samAccountName=garett. Finally, the search is executed using the `FindOne` method, and
the results are dumped into the `$User` variable.

Additionally, the CTP build of PowerShell 2.0 introduces the `[ADSISearcher]` type accelerator that is a representation of the `DirectorySearcher` class. The following example
shows how this type accelerator is used:

```
PS > $Searcher = [ADSISearcher] [ADSI]""
PS > $Searcher.Filter = "(samAccountName=garett)"
PS > $User = $Searcher.FindOne()
```

For the most part, the steps shown are similar to the steps reviewed in the
`DirectorySearcher` example. The only notable difference in the previous example is that
the `[ADSISearcher]` type accelerator is used instead of the `New-Object` cmdlet to create an
instance of the `DirectorySearcher` class.

DirectoryServices.ActiveDirectory

In addition to the `DirectoryEntry` and `DirectorySearcher` classes and their associated
type accelerators, a third .NET Framework interface can be used to access and mange
Active Directory. `DirectoryServices.ActiveDirectory` is a .NET Framework namespace
that is not based on ADSI, and the components in it are purely dedicated for the management of Active Directory's configuration and related infrastructure. The following code
snippet is an example of using this namespace:

```
PS > $Forest =
[System.DirectoryServices.ActiveDirectory.Forest]::GetCurrentForest()
PS > $Forest | select *role* | fl
```

In the previous example, the static method `GetCurrentForest` of the `DirectoryServices.ActiveDirectory.Forest` class is used to create an object that represents the forest, which is then dumped into the `$Forest` variable. Next, using that object, the `Select-Object` and `Format-List` cmdlets are used to create a report that contains the current Schema Master and Domain Naming Master FSMO role owners.

PowerShell's Active Directory Imperfections

Although having access to the .NET Framework to manage Active Directory can be powerful, the way PowerShell interacts with these interfaces can prove frustrating and unintuitive at times. As a result, an administrator has to understand several nuances to effectively use PowerShell to manage Active Directory. An explanation of these issues follows:

- ▶ PowerShell's versions of objects based on the `DirectoryEntry` class tend to lack the actual methods and properties that are useful to manage directory objects. As a result, you often have to use the `PSBase` method to expose the underlying base object.

- ▶ Even when the base object is exposed, not all of the relevant methods are exposed, which means that you will find yourself having to refer to MSDN documentation.

- ▶ The order of properties and methods for creating new objects can at times be different from what is required by ADSI.

The following steps demonstrate how to use PowerShell and the `DirectoryEntry` class to create a user account. When reviewing these steps, you should gain a better understanding about the difficulties that might be encountered when using PowerShell's interpretation of the `DirectoryEntry` class to manage Active Directory objects.

1. First, use the following command to bind an OU:

```
PS > $OU = new-object
DirectoryServices.DirectoryEntry("LDAP://OU=Accounts,DC=companyabc,
DC=com")
```

2. Next, you need to use the `Create` method to create the user and the `SetInfo` method to write the new object into Active Directory. Use the following commands to complete this task:

```
PS > $User = $OU.Create("User", "CN=mkopczynski")
PS > $User.SetInfo()
```

3. Now, use **Active Directory Users and Computers** to review the changes that have been made.

14

4. Notice that the user still needs to be enabled and the account name attributes are not correctly defined. Next, execute the next couple of commands to enable the account and to correct the name attributes:

```
PS > $User.sAMAccountName = "mkopczynski"
PS > $User.sn = "Maiko"
PS > $User.givenName = "Kopczynski"
PS > $User.Description = "Kansai-ben is hard!"
PS > $User.userPrincipalName = "mkopczynski"
PS > $User.SetInfo()
PS > $User.SetPassword('H@rdPassword1')
PS > $User.PSBase.InvokeSet("AccountDisabled", $False)
PS > $User.SetInfo()
```

At any point in the preceding example, if you were to examine the objects in the $OU or $User variables using the Get-Member cmdlet, you would find missing properties and methods. In other words, when PowerShell constructs the PSObject it doesn't correctly expose the underlying object's members. To get at these members and use them in a command or script, you need to look at the base (PSBase) object. The following command is an example that shows how to list all of the properties in the PSBase object:

```
PS > $User.PSBase.Properties
```

Another problem with PowerShell's interaction with the DirectoryEntry class is shown in the command that is issued to enable the account. In this command, the InvokeSet method from the PSBase object is being called to set the AccountDisabled attribute. The InvokeSet method is being used because of a bug in how PowerShell handles certain object properties. Because of this bug, there is inconsistent behavior when attempting to use PowerShell's "." notation or using ADSI's Put and PutEx methods to define object properties. If this type of behavior, or any other type of inconsistency, is encountered, it is recommended that you attempt to use the properties or methods from the based object (PSBase). If you find these problems too cumbersome, you can also turn to other third-party products or community projects to manage Active Directory through PowerShell.

> **NOTE**
>
> An example of a third-party product is Quest's AD cmdlets, which can be used to manage and search for objects in Active Directory. These cmdlets can make a great addition to your toolbox, are free, and can easily be downloaded from Quest's Web site.

PowerShell's CTP2 Improvements

In early May 2008, the PowerShell team released an updated CTP version of PowerShell 2. As part of this release, an improvement was made in how the [ADSI] type adapter handled an object's members. With this improvement, you can now directly access many of the "missing" methods and properties that were previously accessible only by using the PSBase method. For example:

```
PS > $User.PSBase.Properties
--becomes--
PS > $User.Properties
```

Managing Objects

Managing objects using PowerShell consists of binding to an object and then using its members to either read or modify its properties. In concept, this sounds simple. However, because of bugs or shortcomings in how PowerShell interacts with the DirectoryEntry class, managing objects can sometimes be frustrating. Over the next several sections, the goal is to reduce this frustration. To reach this goal, you read through a detailed explanation about how to bind to objects, and then you see examples about how to manage objects using PowerShell.

Binding

The DirectoryEntry class's primary function in life is to facilitate the act of "binding" to objects so that they can then be managed. When you bind to an object, a relationship is created between a programmatic object and the specified object in Active Directory (or other supported data repositories). Then, by using this relationship, the programmatic object can be used to perform any number of tasks against the bound object from Active Directory. These tasks include, but are not limited to, reading properties, modifying properties, and moving or deleting objects. An example of this relationship being established is shown in the following code snippet:

```
PS > $OU = new-object
DirectoryServices.DirectoryEntry("LDAP://OU=Accounts,DC=companyabc,DC=com")
```

In the preceding example, the DirectoryEntry class is used to bind to the Accounts OU. The object that results from this action is then dumped into the $OU variable.

> **NOTE**
>
> Active Directory supports both the LDAP and WinNT ADSI providers for accessing and managing objects.

Binding Strings

Binding to an object in Active Directory requires a binding string. A "binding string" is a text-based string that uniquely identifies an object in Active Directory. More commonly referred to as AdsPath, a binding string typically consists of a unique name or path to an object appended to an ADSI provider moniker. For example:

```
"LDAP://OU=Accounts,DC=companyabc,DC=com"
```

The previous example's binding string is composed of an LDAP provider moniker followed by the Distinguished Name for the Accounts OU. An LDAP provider moniker supports the following format for an AdsPath:

```
"LDAP://<Host>:<Port>/<ObjectName>"
```

- ► **Host**—Specifies the host name, IP address, or domain name to use. [Optional]
- ► **Port**—Specifies the port to use for the connection. If this parameter is not defined, port 389 is used. [Optional]
- ► **ObjectName**—Specifies the Distinguished Name or GUID of an object.

In addition to the LDAP provider moniker, Active Directory objects can also be accessed using both the WinNT and GC provider monikers. The GC provider moniker instructs ADSI to connect to a global catalog server in Active Directory using the LDAP provider. When using the GC provider moniker, the format for the AdsPath is exactly the same as the LDAP provider moniker. For example:

```
"GC://OU=Accounts,DC=companyabc,DC=com"
```

When using the WinNT provider moniker, the format for the AdsPath can be any of the following:

```
"WinNT://<domain name>"
"WinNT://<domain name>/<server>"
"WinNT://<domain name>/<path>"
"WinNT://<domain name>/<object name>"
"WinNT://<domain name>/<object name>,<object class>"
"WinNT://<server>"
"WinNT://<server>/<object name>"
"WinNT://<server>/<object name>,<object class>"
```

Special Characters

In LDAP, several special characters shouldn't be used in an object's name. These characters follow:

```
,\/#+<>;"=
```

For more information about these special characters and their usages in LDAP, please see *RFC 1779 (A String Representation of Distinguished)*. If a special character is used for an object's name, the backslash "\" character needs to be placed in front of the character in an ADsPath. For example:

```
"LDAP://CN=Kopczynski\, Maiko,OU=Accounts,DC=companyabc,DC=com"
```

Failure to escape the "," character results in an error being raised when a connection to the object is attempted.

Authentication

By default, both the [ADSI] type accelerator and the DirectoryEntry class connect to a domain using the user context that created the object instance. If you want to authenticate using a different user or to a different domain that requires authentication, addition authentication information needs to be provided.

Unfortunately, the [ADSI] type accelerator does not provide an authentication interface, which means that the DirectoryEntry class must be used instead. To authenticate to a domain when using the DirectoryEntry class, your command should be structured as follows:

```
PS > $User = new-object
DirectoryServices.DirectoryEntry("LDAP://CN=Garett
Kopczynski,OU=Accounts,OU=Managed Objects,DC=companyabc,DC=com",
"<username>", "<password>")
```

In the previous example, the <username> and <password> strings would be replaced with username and password that would be used to authenticate to the domain.

Working with Objects

When using PowerShell to work with objects in Active Directory, several different interfaces are available for reading and modifying their properties. You can use PowerShell's "." notation to access an objects members. For example:

```
PS > $User.description
```

Alternatively, you can use the methods that are supported by ADSI, as shown in the following example:

```
PS > $User.Get("description")
```

A complete list of these methods is provided in Table 14.1.

TABLE 14.1   ADSI Methods

Method	Usage
Put	Used to write a value to an attribute.
PutEx	Used to write a value or an array of values to an attribute. This method can also be used to clear, append, update, and delete values.
Get	Used to read a value(s) from an object's attribute.
GetEx	Used to read a value(s) from an object's attribute. Always returns an array.
SetPassword	Used to set a user's password.
ChangePassword	Used to change a user's password.
GetInfo	Used to reload the client side property cache for an object.
GetInfoEx	Used to reload the client side property cache for a particular object attribute.
SetInfo	Used to write changes to an object.
Create	Used to create an object.
Delete	Used to delete an object.
MoveHere	Used to move an object into the current container.
Add	Used to add an object to a group.
Remove	Used to remove an object from a group.

Finally, if issues are encountered with the other interfaces, you can also use the methods provided by the underlying base object. For example:

```
PS > $User.psbase.InvokeSet("description", "This will always work!")
```

A list of the more notable base object methods is provided in Table 14.2.

TABLE 14.2   Base Object Methods

Method	Usage
MoveTo	Used to move an object to a container.
CommitChanges	Used to write changes to an object.
Invoke	Used to invoke an ADSI method.
InvokeGet	Used to read a value(s) from an object's attribute.
InvokeSet	Used to write a value to an attribute.
Rename	Used to rename an object.

Examples

The next few examples are designed to better explain how the listed methods in the prior section are used to manage Active Directory objects. The goal of these examples is to illustrate some of the finer points and shortcomings of trying to use PowerShell to manage Active Directory.

Creating Objects

The following example shows how to create a new user account:

```
PS > $OU = new-object DirectoryServices.DirectoryEntry("LDAP://
OU=Managed Objects,DC=companyabc,DC=com")
PS > $User = $OU.Create("User", "CN=mkopczynski")
PS > $User.SetInfo()
PS > $User.sAMAccountName = "mkopczynski"
PS > $User.sn = "Maiko"
PS > $User.givenName = "Kopczynski"
PS > $User.Description = "Kansai-ben is hard!"
PS > $User.userPrincipalName = "mkopczynski"
PS > $User.SetInfo()
PS > $User.SetPassword('H@rdPassword1')
PS > $User.PSBase.InvokeSet("AccountDisabled", $False)
PS > $User.SetInfo()
```

The following example shows the steps involved with creating a new group:

```
PS > $OU = [ADSI]"LDAP://OU=Managed Objects,DC=companyabc,DC=com"
PS > $Group = $OU.Create("Group", "CN=MyFirstGroup")
PS > $Group.SetInfo()
PS > $Group.sAMAccountName = "MyFirstGroup"
PS > $Group.PSBase.InvokeSet("GroupType", "2147483656")
PS > $Group.SetInfo()
```

14

Modifying Objects

The following example shows how to modify a user object:

```
PS > $User = [ADSI]"LDAP://CN=Andrew Abbate,OU=Managed
Objects,DC=companyabc,DC=com"
PS > $User.PSBase.InvokeSet("Info", "Likes to play golf with the Pope.")
PS > $User.PutEx(3, "url", @("www.readmyblog.com"))
PS > $User.psbase.CommitChanges()
```

The following example shows how to add a group member:

```
PS > $Group = [ADSI]"LDAP://CN=MyFirstCEO,OU=Groups,OU=Managed
Objects,DC=companyabc,DC=com"
PS > $Group.Add("LDAP://CN=Irobin Peoples,OU=Accounts,OU=Managed
Objects,DC=companyabc,DC=com")
PS > $Group.psbase.CommitChanges()
```

Moving Objects

The following example shows how to move an object to a different container:

```
PS > $User = [ADSI]"LDAP://CN=Black Knight,OU=Accounts,OU=Managed
Objects,DC=companyabc,DC=com"
PS > $User.psbase.moveto("LDAP://OU=Managed
Objects,DC=companyabc,DC=com")
```

Disabling Accounts

The following example shows how to disable a user account:

```
PS > $User = [ADSI]"LDAP://CN=mkopczynski,OU=Managed
Objects,DC=companyabc,DC=com"
PS > $User.PSBase.InvokeSet("AccountDisabled", $True)
PS > $User.psbase.CommitChanges()
```

Deleting Objects

The following example shows how to delete an object from a container:

```
PS > $OU = [ADSI]"LDAP://OU=Managed Objects,DC=companyabc,DC=com"
PS > $OU.Delete("User", "CN=mkopczynski")
```

Searching for Objects

By default, an object that is based on the `DirectorySearcher` class does not need any of its properties defined to perform a search against Active Directory. If you want, you can use the default object that is created by either the `New-Object` cmdlet or the `[ADSISearcher]` type accelerator. An example of just using the default object is shown in the following sequence of commands:

```
PS > $Searcher = new-object DirectoryServices.DirectorySearcher
PS > $Searcher.FindAll()
```

Although the previous example returns all of the objects in the currently authenticated domain, the results are not useful. Making the search results useful means that you need to narrow the search based on a set of predetermined requirements. However, before you can do that, you need to gain a better understanding about how the `DirectorySearcher` class is used. To complete this task, in the next few sections, you review several important `DirectorySearcher` properties and how they play a role in performing Active Directory searches.

SearchRoot

The `SearchRoot` property is used to define the node where a search is to begin from. This is unlike ADODB, which takes an `AdsPath` as the base where a search is to begin. The value for the `SearchRoot` property must be a `DirectoryEntry` object or Null (which is translated as the currently logged onto domain). An example of using the `SearchRoot` property is shown here:

```
PS > $OU = [ADSI]"LDAP://OU=Managed Objects,DC=companyabc,DC=com"
PS > $Searcher = new-object System.DirectoryServices.DirectorySearcher
PS > $Searcher.SearchRoot = $OU
```

Filter

The `filter` property is used to define the query that is used during a search. The value for this property must be a string that is in an LDAP search filter syntax format as defined in RFC 2254. If the value is not defined, the default value `"(objectClass=*)"` is used, which retrieves all objects.

An LDAP search filter is a collection of conditions that a search is based on. When certain conditions are met within the collection, the related Active Directory objects are then included with the other objects that are returned from the search. Each condition in the collection is in the form of an expression that is enclosed in parentheses. The result from each expression returns a Boolean result and is constructed using relational operators, such as: =, ~=, >=, and <=.

NOTE

RFC 2254 states that the < and > operators are not supported.

Each expression is in the form of an `<attribute>` and `<value>`, which is then separated by any of the noted operators. For example:

```
"(cn=Daisuke)"
```

Logical Operators

To combine several conditions together into a into a single filter statement, you can use three additional logical operators. These operators and their usage follow:

- ▶ **&**—or the `"And"` operator, means that all conditions operated by `"&"` must be met for a record to be included in the returned set of objects.

- ▶ **|**—or the `"Or"` operator, means that any condition operated by `"|"` must be met for a record to be included in the returned set of objects.

- ▶ **!**—or the `"Not"` operator, means that the condition operated by `"!"` must return false for a record to be included in the returned set of objects.

To use these operators with a collection of conditions, nest the conditions within sets of parentheses. For example, to return the object that has both the `objectClass=user` and `cn=Daisuke`, use the following filter statement:

```
"(&(objectClass=user)(cn=Daisuke))"
```

To return objects that have an `objectClass=user` and `cn=Daisuke` or `cn=Sophie`, use the following filter statement:

```
"(&(objectClass=user)(|(cn=Daisuke)(cn=Sophie)))"
```

Finally, to return objects that have an `objectClass=user` and `cn=Daisuke` or `cn=Sophie`, but do not include the object with `cn=Wen-Ai`, use the following filter statement:

```
"(&(objectClass=user)(|(cn=Daisuke)(cn=Sophie))(!cn=Wen-Ai))"
```

Wildcards

By using the "*" character, you can add wildcards to conditions in an LDAP search filter. For example, you can use the following filter statement to retrieve user accounts that have a description:

```
"(&((objectCategory=person)(objectClass=user)(Description=*)))"
```

Alternatively, you can retrieve machine accounts that have DNS host names that start with sc1 but do not start with sc1-dc, as shown in the next example:

```
"(&((objectClass=computer)(dNSHostName=sc1*))(!(dNSHostName=sc1-dc*)))"
```

The only limitation to using the wildcard character is that it can't be used with object attributes that are Distinguished Names (DN). For example, attempting to perform a wildcard search against the distinguishedName or memberOf attributes isn't feasible.

Special Characters

Sometimes, the names of objects might have characters that are used to construct an LDAP search filter. If you encounter this scenario, use any of following escape sequences described in Table 14.3 to include those characters as literals in a filter statement:

TABLE 14.3   LDAP Search Filter Special Characters

ASCII Character	Escape Sequence
*	\2a
(	\28
)	\29
\	\5c
Null	\00
/	\2f

If the search filter contains binary data, that data needs to be represented such that each byte has the backslash "\" escape character before two hexadecimal digits. For example, to retrieve the object with GUID = "659cd735f7fc4182b007b650b621d4de", use the following filter statement:

```
"(objectGUID=\65\9c\d7\35\f7\fc\41\82\b0\07\b6\50\b6\21\d4\de)"
```

14

Other Examples

Instead of using both the objectCategory and objectClass property to search for user accounts, you can just use the sAMAccountType property, as shown here:

```
"(&((sAMAccountType=805306368)(Description=*)))"
```

To retrieve all user accounts that are disabled, use the following filter statement:

```
"(&((sAMAccountType=805306368)(userAccountControl:1.2.840.113556.1.4.8
03:=2)))"
```

Conversely, to see all the accounts that are not disabled, use this filter statement:

```
"(&((sAMAccountType=805306368))(!(userAccountControl:1.2.840.113556.1.
4.803:=2)))"
```

To see what user accounts that are not disabled and have "Password Never Expires" set, use this filter statement:

```
"(&((sAMAccountType=805306368)(userAccountControl:1.2.840.113556.1.4.8
03:=65536))(!(userAccountControl:1.2.840.113556.1.4.803:=2)))"
```

To find users that are members of a particular group, use the following filter statement:

```
"(&((sAMAccountType=805306368)(memberOf=CN=All-Sales,OU=Groups,
OU=Managed Objects,DC=companyabc,DC=com)))"
```

To find universal security groups, use the next filter statement:

```
(&(objectCategory=group)((&(groupType:1.2.840.113556.1.4.803:=8)
(!(groupType:1.2.840.113556.1.4.803:=-2147483648)))))
```

To find users that have a badPwdCount greater than or equal to 1, use the following filter statement:

```
"(&((sAMAccountType=805306368)(badPwdCount >=1)))"
```

SearchScope

The SearchScope property is used to define the scope of the search to be performed. The value for this property can be one of the three following strings:

▶ **Base**—Limits the search to the base object. The result for a scoped search of Base contains a maximum of one object.

▶ **OneLevel**—Limits the search to immediate child objects of the base object. The result for a scoped search of OneLevel excludes the base object.

▶ **Subtree**—Forces the search to be performed against an entire Subtree, which includes the base object and all its child objects. If no value is defined for the SearchScope property, a Subtree scoped search is performed.

The following is an example of using the SearchScope property:

```
PS > $Searcher = new-object System.DirectoryServices.DirectorySearcher
PS > $Searcher.SearchScope= "OneLevel"
```

PageSize

The PageSize property is used to define the maximum number of objects returned in a search. After the number of objects equals the PageSize in a search, the results are returned to the client. Then, if the search is not yet complete, the client restarts the search where it left off until the number of objects again equals the PageSize or the search is complete. If a value for the PageSize property is not defined, the default value of 0 is used.

The following example uses the PageSize property:

```
PS > $Searcher = new-object System.DirectoryServices.DirectorySearcher
PS > $Searcher.PageSize = 500
```

SizeLimit

The SizeLimit property is used to define the maximum number of objects that are to be returned in a search. The default value for the SizeLimit property is 0, or you can use the server-determined size limit. By default, Active Directory's search size limit is 1000 objects, or an administrator can specify the limit by modifying the MaxPageSize attribute. If you want your search to return more records, either the limited specified in the MaxPageSize attribute or the SizeLimit property, you need to page the search by using the PageSize property.

The following is an example of using the `SizeLimit` property:

```
PS > $Searcher = new-object System.DirectoryServices.DirectorySearcher
PS > $Searcher.SizeLimit = 1000
```

PropertiesToLoad

When performing an ADSI-based search that uses the LDAP dialect, you must specify the name of the attributes that are to be retrieved. For example:

```
"<LDAP://DC=companyabc,DC=com>;(objectClass=*);cn,adspath,sn,givenName
;subTree"
```

In the previous example, the LDAP search filter returns all objects in the companyabc.com domain, in addition to the cn, adspath, sn, and givenName attributes and their associated values. However, when using PowerShell and the DirectorySearcher class to conduct searches, the attributes to be retrieved are specified by using the PropertiesToLoad property. The following code box shows an example:

```
PS > $Searcher = new-object System.DirectoryServices.DirectorySearcher
PS > $Searcher.PropertiesToLoad.Add("givenName")
PS > $Searcher.PropertiesToLoad.Add("sn")
```

After the shown commands are issued, the sn and givenName attributes are added into the PropertiesToLoad property. This doesn't mean that you need to specify the properties that are to be retrieved. By default, the value for the PropertiesToLoad property is an empty StringCollection that retrieves all attributes of an object. Instead, the PropertiesToLoad property is used to reduce the amount of data retrieved by a search.

Putting It All Together

Now that you have an understanding about how the different properties of the DirectorySearcher class are used to perform searches, this last section puts all the pieces together and conducts an actual search for objects in Active Directory. To complete this task, execute the following series of commands:

```
PS > $OU = [ADSI]"LDAP://OU=Sales,OU=Managed
Objects,DC=companyabc,DC=com"
PS > $Searcher = new-object System.DirectoryServices.DirectorySearcher
PS > $Searcher.SearchRoot = $OU
```

```
PS > $Searcher.Filter = "(&((sAMAccountType=805306368)
(userAccountControl:1.2.840.113556.1.4.803:=2)))"
PS > $Searcher.SearchScope= "OneLevel"
PS > $Searcher.PageSize = 500
PS > $Searcher.PropertiesToLoad.Add("givenName")
PS > $Searcher.PropertiesToLoad.Add("sn")
PS > $Users = $Searcher.FindAll()
```

In the previous example, a search is completed that returns all disabled user accounts located directly under the Sales OU. To complete this search, a new DirectorySearcher object ($Searcher) is created. Then, the Filter, SearchScope, PageSize, PropertiesToLoad properties are defined for that object. Lastly, a search is executed using the FindAll method, and the returned objects are dumped into the $Users variable.

14

> **NOTE**
>
> When using the FindAll method, all the unmanaged resources from the SearchResultCollection are not released during garbage collection. In certain scenarios, this behavior can cause resource issues (memory leaks) while executing searches. To prevent these problems from occurring, you need to use the Dispose method to remove the SearchResultCollection object when you are done with it.

Scripting Scenario: ChangeLocalAdminPassword.ps1

The ChangeLocalAdminPassword.ps1 script was developed to address a time-consuming task for systems administrators. This task is the routine (as in scheduled) or forced (because the network was attacked) local administrator password change. Changing this password ranks as one of the biggest chores of systems management activities, and administrators often neglect this task because it's so tedious.

For example, companyabc.com operates a Windows Server 2003 server farm of 500 servers. As part of the company's security practices, the IT department tried to change the local administrator password routinely on all 500 servers, usually every 30 days or when a systems administrator left the company. Because of the time and effort to change the administrator password on 500 servers, the IT department tended to fall behind schedule in completing this task. Eventually, the department stopped trying to change local administrator passwords, which soon resulted in a major security incident: An external entity took advantage of the lapse in password management practices to commandeer a number of companyabc.com's servers and demanded a ransom to return control of these systems.

This incident prompted the IT department to seek a way to change local administrator passwords quickly and en masse. The department decided to use an automation script that creates a list of servers in a specified OU, and then connects to each server and changes the local administrator password. To meet this need, the ChangeLocalAdminPassword.ps1 script was developed.

A working copy of this script can be downloaded from the www.informit.com/title/ 9780672329883. Running this script requires defining one parameter: OUDN. This parameter's argument should be set to the distinguishedName of the OU containing the servers that need to have their local administrator passwords changed. Here's the command to run the ChangeLocalAdminPassword.ps1 script:

```
PS D:\Scripts> .\ChangeLocalAdminPassword.ps1 "OU=Servers,OU=Managed
Objects,DC=companyabc,DC=com"
```

Figures 14.1 and 14.2 show the ChangeLocalAdminPassword.ps1 script being executed.

FIGURE 14.1   The ChangeLocalAdminPassword.ps1 during execution

FIGURE 14.2   The ChangeLocalAdminPassword.ps1 script after execution has finished

The ChangeLocalAdminPassword.ps1 script performs the following sequence of actions:

1. The script dot sources the LibraryCrypto.ps1 library file, which contains a function for randomly generating passwords.

2. The script creates a new `DataTable` object (`$ServersTable`) by using the .NET `System.Data.DataSet` class. This `DataTable` object is used later in the script to store status information about machines in the specified OU.

3. In addition, the script creates an error log named `ChangeLocalAdminPassword_Errors.log` by using the `Out-File` cmdlet. This error log displays detailed error information to users.

4. The script connects to the current logon domain by using the `Get-CurrentDomain` function. Using the object returned from this function, the script then writes the domain's name to the PowerShell console. If this connection fails, the script halts.

5. The script verifies that the specified OU exists in the current domain by using the `Get-ADObject` function. If the OU is not valid, the script halts.

6. The script uses the `Set-ChoiceMesssage` and `New-PromptYesNo` functions to ask users whether they want a randomly generated password or one they specify. For randomly generated passwords, the script uses the `New-RandomPassword` function from the `LibraryCrypto.ps1` library file to generate a password of a specified length that's stored as a secure string (`$Password`) and returned to the user for verification. For user-specified passwords, the script uses the `Read-Host` cmdlet with the `AsSecureString` property to collect the password and store it in a secure string (`$Password`).

7. The script uses the `DirectoryEntry` class to bind to the specified OU in Active Directory and then the `DirectorySearcher` class to create a `$Searcher` object. The `SearchRoot` property for the `$Searcher` object is set to the bound OU object, and an LDAP search is performed to populate the `$Computers` variable with all servers in the OU.

8. The script uses the `System.Net.NetworkInformation.Ping` class to ping each server that is in the `$Servers` object collection. If a server replies, a new row is added into the `$ServersTable` `DataTable`, which consists of the server's name and its `"Online"` status. If a server doesn't reply, a new row is still added into the `$ServersTable` `DataTable`; however, that server's status is set to `"Offline"`.

9. The script uses the `System.Net.NetworkInformation.Ping` class to ping each server in the `$Computers` object collection. If a server replies, a new row is created in the `$ServersTable` `DataTable` consisting of the server's name and its `"Online"` status. If a server doesn't reply, a new row is created in the `$ServersTable` `DataTable` with the server's status set to `"Offline"`.

10. The listing of servers and their status is sent to the script's error log for future reference by using the `Out-File` cmdlet.

11. The script uses the `System.Runtime.InteropServices.Marshal` class to convert the secure string stored in the `$Password` variable to a regular string that can be used later in the script.

12. For each server with an "Online" status in $ServersTable, the Get-WmiObject cmdlet is used to connect to the server and return a list of user accounts. The local administrator account has a security ID (SID) ending with "-500". The script binds to this account by using the ADSI WinNT provider and changes its password to the string now stored in the $Password variable.

Here's the LibraryCrypto.ps1 library file:

```
##################################################
# LibraryCrypto.ps1
# Functions within this file can be used to perform
# crypto operations.
#
# Created: 11/3/2006
# Author: Tyson Kopczynski
##################################################
#-------------------------------------------------
# New-RandomPassword
#-------------------------------------------------
# Usage:        Used to generate a random password.
# $Size:        The length of the password to generate.

function New-RandomPassword{
    param ([int] $Size)

    $Bytes = new-object System.Byte[] $Size
    $Chars = "abcdefghijklmnopqrstuvwxyz".ToCharArray()
    $Chars += "ABCDEFGHIJKLMNOPQRSTUVWXYZ".ToCharArray()
    $Chars += "0123456789'~!@#$^*()-_=+[]{}'\|;:'''",./".ToCharArray()

    $Crypto =
        new-object System.Security.Cryptography.RNGCryptoServiceProvider

    # Now you need to fill an array of bytes with a
    # cryptographically strong sequence of random nonzero values.
    $Crypto.GetNonZeroBytes($Bytes)

    foreach ($Byte in $Bytes){

        # For each Byte, perform a modulo operation
        $Password += $Chars[$Byte % ($Chars.Length - 1)]
        }

    # Finally, return the random password as a SecureString
    ConvertTo-SecureString "$Password" -AsPlainText -Force
    }
```

ChangeLocalAdminPassword.ps1 uses the New-RandomPassword function from the LibraryCrypto.ps1 file to generate random passwords of a specified length based on a predetermined set of allowed characters. To do this, the function uses the .NET System.Security.Cryptography.RNGCryptoServiceProvider class as a cryptographically strong random number generator.

A random number generator improves the strength of passwords, even those consisting of both characters and numbers. The New-RandomPassword function uses the random number generator to generate random characters for passwords. To do this, the function first takes the specified length of the random password and creates a System.Byte array ($Bytes) of the same length. It then defines a character array ($Chars) consisting of all possible characters that can make up the random passwords.

Next, New-RandomPassword creates a random number generator ($Crypto) by using the System.Security.Cryptography.RNGCryptoServiceProvider class. The GetNonZeroBytes method uses $Crypto to populate the $Bytes array with a cryptographically strong sequence of random nonzero values. For each byte in the $Bytes array, the function performs a modulo operation (the remainder of dividing one number by another) to determine which character from the $Chars array is added to the $Password variable. The end result is a random password returned to the caller as a secure string.

The next code snippet contains the header for the ChangeLocalAdminPassword.ps1 script. This header includes information about what the script does, when it was updated, and the script's author. Just after the header is the script's parameter OUDN, shown here:

```
##################################################
# ChangeLocalAdminPassword.ps1
# Used to change the local admin passwords for machine
# acounts in Active Directory.
#
# Created: 11/2/2006
# Author: Tyson Kopczynski
##################################################
param([string] $OUDN)
```

Next, the script loads the Set-ChoiceMessage and New-PromptYesNo functions, as seen in the following code snippet:

```
##################################################
# Functions
##################################################
#------------------------------------------------
# Set-ChoiceMessage
#------------------------------------------------
# Usage:        Used to set yes and no choice options.
```

14

```
# $No:          The no message.
# $Yes:         The yes message.

function Set-ChoiceMessage{
    param ($No, $Yes)

    $N = ([System.Management.Automation.Host.ChoiceDescription]"&No")
    $N.HelpMessage = $No

    $Y = ([System.Management.Automation.Host.ChoiceDescription]"&Yes")
    $Y.HelpMessage = $Yes

    Return ($Y,$N)
    }

#-------------------------------------------------
# New-PromptYesNo
#-------------------------------------------------
# Usage:        Used to display a choice prompt.
# $Caption:     The prompt caption.
# $Message:     The prompt message.
# $Choices:     The object catagory.

function New-PromptYesNo{
    param ($Caption, $Message,
        [System.Management.Automation.Host.ChoiceDescription[]]$Choices)

    $Host.UI.PromptForChoice($Caption, $Message, $Choices, 0)
    }
```

In PowerShell, you're sometimes prompted to make a choice before a command continues. For example, as you learned in Chapter 5, "Understanding PowerShell Security,"
PowerShell might prompt for confirmation before running a script that isn't signed by a
trusted entity, depending on your execution policy setting, or PowerShell prompts you for
confirmation before running a command when a cmdlet is used with the confirm parameter, as shown in this example:

```
PS > get-process | stop-process —confirm

Confirm
Are you sure you want to perform this action?
Performing operation "Stop-Process" on Target "~e5d141.tmp (792)".
[Y] Yes  [A] Yes to All  [N] No  [L] No to All  [S] Suspend  [?] Help
(default is "Y"):
```

With the `Set-ChoiceMessage` and `New-PromptYesNo` functions, you can build a menu of Yes or No choices to display to users in the PowerShell console. The `Set-ChoiceMessage` function creates a collection of choice objects and is used with the `New-PromptYesNo` function to generate the choice menu. To generate this menu, `New-PromptYesNo` uses the `PromptForChoice` method from the `$host.UI` object, which is just an implementation of the `System.Management.Automation.Host.PSHostUserInterface` class.

In the following code snippet, variables that will be used later in the script are defined. In addition, two library files are dot sourced into the script's scope. The first file, `LibraryGen.ps1`, is a general library file that contains the script usage and Active Directory functions. The second file is the `LibraryCrypto.ps1` library, which, as mentioned previously in this section, contains the `New-RandomPassword` function, as shown in this example:

```
##################################################
# Main
##################################################
#--------------------
# Load Libraries
#--------------------
. .\LibraryGen.ps1
. .\LibraryCrypto.ps1


#--------------------
# Set Config Vars
#--------------------
$ScriptName = "ChangeLocalAdminPassword.ps1"
$ScriptUsage = "Used to change the local admin passwords on machines."
$ScriptCommand = "$ScriptName -OUDN value"
$ScriptParams = "OUDN = The distinguishedName of the OU where" `
    + "the machines are located."
$ScriptExamples = "$ScriptName ""OU=Accounts,DC=companyabc,DC=com"""
$ErrorLogName = $ScriptName + "_Errors.log"
$Date = Date
```

After defining the script's variables and dot sourcing any library files, the next step is to check if the user needs any usage help or if the required `OUDN` parameter was defined. This step is shown in the next code snippet:

```
#--------------------
# Verify Required Parameters
#--------------------
if ($args[0] -match '-(\?¦(h¦(help)))'){
    write-host
```

```
    Get-ScriptHeader $ScriptName $ScriptUsage
    Show-ScriptUsage $ScriptCommand $ScriptParams $ScriptExamples
    Return
    }

if (!$OUDN){
    write-host
    write-host "Please specify the OU machines are located in!" '
          -Foregroundcolor Red
    write-host
    Get-ScriptHeader $ScriptName $ScriptUsage
    Show-ScriptUsage $ScriptCommand $ScriptParams $ScriptExamples
    Return
    }
```

Next, the script creates a DataTable object. This is a new concept that uses a .NET DataTable object (from the System.Data.DataTable class, part of the ADO.NET architecture):

```
#---------------------
# Define DataTable
#---------------------
$ServersTable = new-object System.Data.DataTable
$ServersTable.TableName = "Servers"
[Void]$ServersTable.Columns.Add("Name")
[Void]$ServersTable.Columns.Add("Status")
```

DataTable objects are the equivalent of a database table, except the table is located in memory. Your scripts can use this table to hold data retrieved from other sources or data you specify manually.

In this script, a DataTable is used to hold status information about the servers queried from Active Directory. The script first creates a DataTable named $ServersTable by using the New-Object cmdlet and System.Data.DataTable class. When you first create a DataTable, it's empty and lacks structure, so you must define the structure before you can store data in it. For $ServersTable's structure, the script uses the Add method to add Name and Status columns to its Columns collection. Later in the script, the Add method is used to add rows of data to $ServersTable's Rows collection.

In the next code snippet, the Out-File cmdlet is used to create an error log and write header information to it. Then, the Get-ScriptHeader function is used to indicate to the script operator that the automation portion of the script has started:

```
#--------------------
# Begin Script
#--------------------
# Setup ErrorLog
$ScriptName + " Ran on: " + $Date | out-file $ErrorLogName

write-host
Get-ScriptHeader $ScriptName $ScriptUsage
write-host
```

The next step is for the script to verify that there is a valid domain connection. To accomplish this task, the script uses the Get-CurrentDomain function. If a valid domain connection doesn't exist, the script halts and returns the script status to the operator. If a connection does exist, the script continues execution and writes the domain name to the console. Then, the script uses the Get-ADObject function to validate if the string in the $OUDN variable is a valid distinguished name. If an object is returned from the function, the variable is valid; if no object is returned, the variable is considered invalid, and the script halts, as shown in the next code snippet:

```
.{
    trap{write-host 't "[ERROR]" -Foregroundcolor Red;
        throw write-host $_ -Foregroundcolor Red;
        Break}

    write-host "Domain Connection" -NoNewLine

    # You need to test for a domain connection
    $Domain = Get-CurrentDomain

    # You then return the domain's name
    write-host 't $Domain.Name -Foregroundcolor Green
}

write-host "Checking OU Name" -NoNewLine

if (!(Get-ADObject "distinguishedName" $OUDN "organizationalUnit")){
    write-host 't "Is not valid!" -Foregroundcolor Red
    write-host
    Break
    }
else{
    write-host 't "[OK]" -Foregroundcolor Green
    }
```

The following code snippet contains the logic for defining the password that will be used. First, the script asks the user if a password should be generated or specified by the user. If a password is to be generated, the script asks for the password length. Then, based on the defined length, a password is generated using the New-RandomPassword function. If the user chooses to specify the password, the script uses the Read-Host cmdlet with the AsSecureString switch to collect the password from the user:

```
#-------------------
# Get Password
#-------------------
$Choices = Set-ChoiceMessage "No" "Yes"
$Prompt = New-PromptYesNo "Question:" '
    "Do you want me to generate a random password?" $Choices

while(!$Password){

    trap{write-host "You need to input an integer!" '
        -Foregroundcolor Red; Continue}

    if ($Prompt -eq 0){
        write-host
        [int]$Length = read-host "Please enter the password length"

        if ($Length -gt 0){
            &{
                $Temp = New-RandomPassword $Length

                write-host
                write-host "Your new random password is:" '
                    -Foregroundcolor White

                [System.Runtime.InteropServices.Marshal]::PtrToStringAuto( '
                [System.Runtime.InteropServices.Marshal]::SecureStringToBSTR( '
                    $Temp))

                $Prompt = New-PromptYesNo "Question:" '
                    "Is this password ok?" $Choices

                if ($Prompt -eq 0){
                    $Script:Password = $Temp
                    }
                }
            }
        else{
            write-host "Password length needs to be longer then 0!" '
```

```
                    -Foregroundcolor Red
            }
        }
    else{
        write-host
        $Password = read-host "Then please enter a password" -AsSecureString
        }
    }
```

Now that the script has the password that will be used, it must next get a list of machines
that will have their passwords changed. The next code snippet contains the code that
accomplishes this task. In this code, you see usage of the DirectoryServices.
DirectorySearcher class to perform a search for computer objects (servers) under the
defined OU. Then, for each computer object that is returned from the search, the script
pings the server and adds a row to the $ServersTable DataTable that contains the server's
dNSHostName and its status:

```
#--------------------
# Get computers and status
#--------------------
write-host
write-host "Getting Server Info" -NoNewLine

&{
    trap{write-host 't "[ERROR]" -Foregroundcolor Red;
        throw write-host $_ -Foregroundcolor Red;
        Break}

    $Root =
        new-object DirectoryServices.DirectoryEntry "LDAP://$OUDN"

    $Searcher = new-object DirectoryServices.DirectorySearcher
    $Searcher.SearchRoot = $Root
    $Searcher.PageSize = 1000

    $SearchItem = "CN"
    $SearchValue = "*"
    $SearchClass = "Computer"
    $SearchCat = "*"

    $Searcher.Filter =
        "(&($($SearchItem)=$($SearchValue))(objectClass=$( '
        $SearchClass))(objectCategory=$($SearchCat)))"
```

```
    $Script:Computers = $Searcher.FindAll()
}

write-host 't "[DONE]" -Foregroundcolor Green

write-host "Getting Status Info" -NoNewLine

$Computers | foreach-object -Begin {$i=0;} '
    -Process {$Ping = new-object Net.NetworkInformation.Ping;
        &{$dNSHostName = $_.GetDirectoryEntry().dNSHostName.ToString();
        trap{"Ping [ERROR]: " + $dNSHostName + " $_" | out-file '
            $ErrorLogName -Append; Continue};
        $Result = $Ping.Send($dNSHostName);
        if ($Result.Status -eq "Success"){ '
            [Void]$ServersTable.Rows.Add($dNSHostName, "Online")} '
        else{[Void]$ServersTable.Rows.Add($dNSHostName, "Offline")};
        $i = $i+1;
        write-progress -Activity "Pinging Servers - $($dNSHostName)" '
            -Status "Progress:" '
            -PercentComplete ($i / $Computers.Count * 100)}}

write-host 't "[DONE]" -Foregroundcolor Green

# Write status info to ErrorLog
$ServersTable | out-file $ErrorLogName –Append
```

The next task is to change the passwords on all the online servers. First, the script converts the secure string in the $Password variable back to a regular string. Next, the script defines the $OnlineServers variable with all the server objects that have an online status using the DataTable Select method. The script uses WMI to connect to the server and figure out which account is the Administrator account. WMI then sets its password to the string that is in the $Password variable:

```
write-host "Changing Passwords"    -NoNewLine

$Password = [System.Runtime.InteropServices.Marshal]::PtrToStringAuto( '
    [System.Runtime.InteropServices.Marshal]::SecureStringToBSTR( '
    $Password))

$OnlineServers = $ServersTable.Select("Status = 'Online'")

foreach ($Server in $OnlineServers) {
    &{
```

```
        write-progress -Activity "Getting Users - $($Server.Name)" '
            -Status "Stand by..."

        $Users = get-wmiobject -ErrorVariable Err -ErrorAction '
                SilentlyContinue Win32_UserAccount -Computer $Server.Name

        write-progress -Activity "Getting Users - $($Server.Name)" '
            -Status "Done" -completed $True

        if ($Err.Count -ne 0){
            "Getting Users [ERROR]: " + $Server.Name + " " + $Err | out-file '
                $ErrorLogName -Append
            }
        else{
            foreach ($User in $Users){
                if ($User.SID.EndsWith("-500") -eq $True){
                    write-progress -Activity '
                        "Changing Password - '$($User.Name)" '
                        -Status "Stand by..."

                    trap{"Change Password [ERROR]: " + '
                        $Server.Name + " " + $_ | out-file '
                        $ErrorLogName -Append; Continue}

                    $WinNTUser =
                        new-object System.DirectoryServices.DirectoryEntry( '
                        "WinNT://" + $Server.Name + "/" + $User.Name)

                    $WinNTUser.SetPassword($Password)
                    $Null = $WinNTUser.SetInfo

                    write-progress -Activity '
                        "Changing Password - $($User.Name)" '
                        -Status "Done" -completed $True
                }
            }
        }
    }
    }

write-host 't "[DONE]" -Foregroundcolor Green
write-host
write-host "Script is now DONE!" -Foregroundcolor Green
write-host "Check the $ErrorLogName for errors." -Foregroundcolor Yellow
```

Summary

In this chapter, you explored many different aspects about how PowerShell interacts with Active Directory. Starting from its usage of the .Net Framework to understanding how to manage and search for objects, you saw firsthand what can be accomplished. In addition, you saw some of PowerShell's rough edges when it comes to support for the `DirectoryEntry` class.

Given time and maturity, the Active Directory support in PowerShell should get better, and it's even possible that improvements will make it into PowerShell 2.0 RTM. Until then, even with its shortcomings, PowerShell is a powerful tool for managing Active Directory. This power can even be further enhanced by utilizing additional cmdlets, functions, or scripts that others in the community or vendors created. Although these enhancements were not covered in this chapter, they exist, and if an administrator wants to quickly work past PowerShell's quirkiness, we suggest using these tools.

## CHAPTER 15

PowerShell and Exchange Server 2007

For years, Exchange administrators had two choices for performing repetitive tasks: Do them manually by using the graphical interface, or write scripts in complicated and time-consuming programming languages. Although these programming languages can be used to perform many routine tasks in an Exchange environment, they weren't developed specifically with that purpose in mind. Hence, even the simplest task could take hundreds of lines of code.

Over time, the inability to automate tasks easily has proved to be one of the most frustrating aspects of managing an Exchange environment. Windows automation in general wasn't sufficient because of Microsoft's reliance on GUIs and little support for CLIs. This frustration became the motivation for the PowerShell team, led by Jeffrey Snover, to develop a CLI shell interface that enables administrators to do everything from the command line.

Around the same time PowerShell was being developed, the Exchange product team was designing the specifications for the next version of Exchange (E12, which became Exchange Server 2007). Initially, it seemed the team would develop yet another limited Microsoft Management Console (MMC) GUI as the Exchange management interface. However, the Exchange team decided to take a different course by embracing the concept of PowerShell-based management.

The result is that in Exchange Server 2007, configuration and administration are done with two new administrative tools: the Exchange Management Shell (EMS) and the Exchange Management Console (EMC). Both utilities rely on PowerShell to access and modify information and configuration settings in an Exchange Server 2007 environment.

> **NOTE**
>
> Exchange Server 2007 is the first Microsoft product to use PowerShell exclusively to drive its management interfaces.

The EMS is a command-line management interface for performing server administration and configuration. Because it's built on a PowerShell platform, it can connect to the .NET runtime (also known as the Common Language Runtime, or CLR). So, tasks that previously had to be done manually in the management application can now be scripted, giving administrators more flexibility for repetitive tasks. Furthermore, administrators can manage every aspect of Exchange Server 2007, including creating and managing e-mail accounts, configuring Simple Mail Transport Protocol (SMTP) connectors and transport agents, and setting properties for database stores. Every management task in the Exchange environment can now be accomplished from the command line. In addition, the EMS can be used to check settings, create reports, provide information on the health of Exchange servers, and, best of all, automate tasks that need to be done frequently.

The EMC is an MMC 3.0 GUI utility for viewing and modifying the configuration of Exchange Server 2007 Organizations. Although similar to the Exchange System Manager (ESM) in previous Exchange versions, the EMC's interface has been redesigned to be more organized and easier to learn. The EMC is limited in the scope of modifications administrators can make, so some configuration settings can be accessed only by using the EMS.

The EMS and EMC rely on PowerShell to accomplish management tasks. The EMC is a graphical interface that calls the EMS to perform tasks, and the EMS is a snap-in for PowerShell. Therefore, no matter which utility administrators use to create a report or modify a setting, they're actually using PowerShell. While keeping with this concept, this chapter's goal is to explain how the EMS and PowerShell can be used to manage an Exchange Server 2007 environment. Additionally, you review three PowerShell scripts that can be used to manage an Exchange Server 2007 environment.

Accessing the Exchange Management Shell (EMS)

The EMS is nothing more than a collection cmdlets that are compiled into a DLL, which is used as a way to extend PowerShell's functionality. Typically, extending functionality is done to manage an application with PowerShell and can be accomplished easily by using snap-ins, much as you add snap-ins to the MMC to increase functionality. Because the EMS is just a PowerShell snap-in, accessing EMS cmdlets requires loading the EMS snap-in into your PowerShell session, as shown here:

```
PS C:\> add-pssnapin Microsoft.Exchange.Management.PowerShell.Admin
```

Additionally, you can also start the EMS using the Windows Start menu shortcut. However, some differences exist between just loading the EMS snap-in and starting the EMS using the Windows shortcut. If you just load the snap-in, you don't get the customized Exchange administration console. Your PowerShell session won't look and act like the EMS because the snap-in loads only the cmdlets for managing the Exchange environment. To make your PowerShell session resemble the EMS, you need to run the same configuration script that the Start menu shortcut runs to start the EMS. This script, Exchange.ps1, is in the default Exchange Server 2007 bin directory: C:\Program Files\Microsoft\Exchange Server\Bin.

When this script is executed, the resulting PowerShell console session is the EMS, as shown in Figure 15.1.

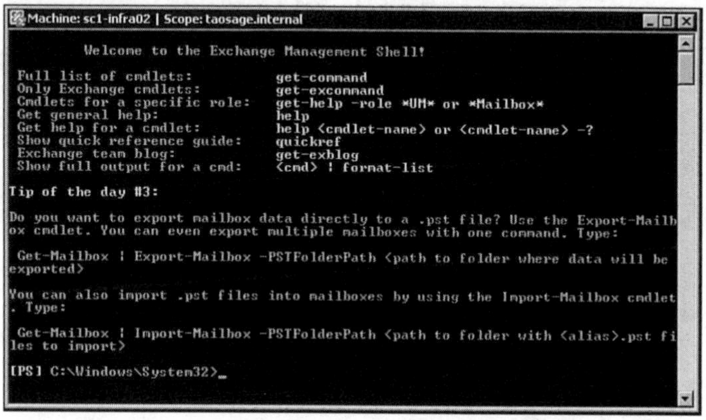

FIGURE 15.1   The Exchange Management Shell (EMS)

Using the Exchange Management Shell

The EMS consists of PowerShell's default set of cmdlets and several additional cmdlets that can be used to complete Exchange-oriented management activities. The following can be included in these activities:

- ▶ Management of an Exchange Organization
- ▶ Reporting on an Exchange Organization
- ▶ Performing bulk management operations

This section's goal is to gain a better understanding for some of the tasks that can be completed using the EMS. Note that the term "some" is being used. The purpose of this book is not to replay information that is readily available within help resources. Instead, the purpose is to explore PowerShell functionality and how it relates to the everyday needs of an IT professional. To accomplish this, you are shown details about some of the EMS cmdlets and how some of these cmdlets can be used to complete tasks.

To get started, you might want to become better aquatinted with the different ways you can gain access to EMS related help. For example, you can use the **Exchange Server 2007 Help File**, which contains all the EMS cmdlet help topics in a role-based and task-based hierarchy. Additionally, you might use **Microsoft Technet**, which also contains all the EMS cmdlet help topics in a role-based and task-based hierarchy. Or, you might take advantage of EMS's slightly enhanced `Get-Help` cmdlet, which provides you with the ability to get help information pertaining to Exchange-related roles, components, and functionalities. For example, to get help related to the Mailbox role, you might use the following command:

```
[PS] C:\> Get-Help -Role *mailbox*

Name                      Category          Synopsis
----                      --------          --------
Get-ExchangeServer        Cmdlet            Use the Get-ExchangeSe...
Set-ExchangeServer        Cmdlet            Use the Set-ExchangeSe...
Test-ServiceHealth        Cmdlet            Use the Test-ServiceHe...
Test-SystemHealth         Cmdlet            Use the Test-SystemHea...
...
```

Notice how the role name is enclosed using the wildcard characters (*). That is a requirement. Other resources also include the following:

- **Get-ExCommand**—This cmdlet behaves identically to the `Get-Command` cmdlet, but returns only Exchange Server 2007-related cmdlets.

- **Get-PSCommand**—This cmdlet behaves identically to the `Get-Command` cmdlet, but excludes all Exchange Server 2007-related cmdlets.

- **QuickRef**—This cmdlet behaves identically to the `Get-Command` cmdlet, but returns only Exchange Server 2007-related cmdlets.

- **Get-Tip**—This cmdlet generates a new Exchange Management Shell Tip of the Day.

- **Get-ExBlog**—This cmdlet opens Internet Explorer and navigates to the Exchange Team blog.

By using the previously listed resources, you should be able to gain insight into the different cmdlets that are available to manage an Exchange Server 2007 environment. Additionally, to further help you better understand how the EMS can be used to complete management tasks, the next few sections highlight some of the more important cmdlets, details about their usage by reviewing a number of working examples. Although not all cmdlets and usage scenarios are reviewed, the sections should provide a basis for better understanding how the EMS is used.

Working with Servers

To get information about Exchange servers within an organization, use the `Get-ExchangeServer` cmdlet. For example, executing just the cmdlet by itself returns a list of all the Exchange servers. Primarily, you use the `Get-ExchangeServer` cmdlet for reporting purposes. To manage or modify the properties of an Exchange server, use the `Set-ExchangeServer` cmdlet. If you wanted to report on or manage an Exchange server, you might use any of the cmdlets that are directly associated with a server role, as shown in Table 15.1:

TABLE 15.1   Exchange Server Cmdlets

Cmdlet	Usage
`Get-ClientAccessServer`	Used to get Client Access Server properties.
`Get-MailboxServer`	Used to get Mailbox Server properties.
`Get-TransportServer`	Used to get Transport Server properties.
`Set-ClientAccessServer`	Used to set Client Access Server properties.
`Set-MailboxServer`	Used to set Mailbox Server properties.
`Set-TransportServer`	Used to set Transport Server properties.

Working with Storage Groups

To report on or manage a storage group, you can use one of many storage group cmdlets. For example, to get information about all the storage groups in an organization, use the `Get-StorageGroup` cmdlet. To create a new storage group, use the `New-StorageGroup` cmdlet. All the storage group cmdlets and their usage information are shown in Table 15.2:

TABLE 15.2   Storage Group Cmdlets

Cmdlet	Usage
`New-StorageGroup`	Used to create a storage group.
`Get-StorageGroup`	Used to get storage group properties
`Set-StorageGroup`	Used to set storage group properties
`Move-StorageGroupPath`	Used to move a storage group path.
`Remove-StorageGroup`	Used to remove a storage group object from Active Directory.

Example: Managing Storage Groups

In this usage example, you use the EMS and some of the `*-StorageGroup` cmdlets to create and manage a storage group. To complete this example, start with the following steps:

1. Open the EMS using the following steps: **Start > All Programs > Microsoft Exchange Server 2007 > Exchange Management Shell**.

2. Use the following command to create the new storage group:

```
[PS] C:\> new-storagegroup –name "Sales"
```

The command that was just issued creates a new storage group in the default Storage Group path location. However, what if the indented path for the new storage group was supposed to be `C:\StorageGroups\Sales`? To correct this problem, use the `Move-StorageGroupPath` cmdlet, as shown in the following examples:

1. Get the properties for the storage group that was created:

```
[PS] C:\> get-storagegroup "EX01\Sales" | select *
```

2. Take note of the current values for the `SystemFolderPath` and `LogFolderPath` properties. Using EMS, create a new folder on the root of `C:\` drive, as shown here:

```
[PS] C:\> mkdir C:\StorageGroups
[PS] C:\> dir C:\
```

3. Move the storage group to another folder path using the following command:

```
[PS] C:\> get-storagegroup "EX01\Sales" | move-storagegrouppath
-logfolderpath "C:\StorageGroups\Sales" -systemfolderpath
"C:\StorageGroups\Sales" -ConfigurationOnly
[PS] C:\> get-storagegroup "EX01\Sales" | select *
```

Working with Databases

To report on or manage Exchange mailbox databases, use one of many database cmdlets. For example, to create a new mailbox database, use the `New-MailboxDatabase` cmdlet. Then, to manage that database, use the `Set-MailboxDatabase` cmdlet. More information about the mailbox database cmdlets and their usage is shown in Table 15.3.

TABLE 15.3   Database Cmdlets

Cmdlet	Usage
New-MailboxDatabase	Used to create a new mailbox database object in Active Directory.
Set-MailboxDatabase	Used to set the properties of a mailbox database.
Move-DatabasePath	Used to set a new path to the location of a mailbox database.
Mount-Database	Used to mount a database.
Dismount-Database	Used to dismount a database.
Remove-MailboxDatabase	Used to delete a mailbox database object from Active Directory.

Example: Managing Databases

In this usage example, you use the EMS and some of the `*-*Database` cmdlets to create and manage a database. To complete this example, use the following steps:

1. The following command creates the database:

```
[PS] C:\> new-mailboxdatabase -Name "Sales" -StorageGroup "EX01\Sales"
```

2. Mount the database using the following command:

```
[PS] C:\> mount-database "EX01\Sales"
```

3. Verify the database has been created using the following command:

```
[PS] C:\> get-mailboxdatabase "Sales" | select *
```

4. Now that the Sales database is created, the next step is to create the rest of the databases with the commands that you learned. The first step is to add all the database names into an array, as shown here:

```
[PS] C:\> $databases = "IT", "HR", "Exec"
```

5. Pipe the array you just created into a ForEach loop and use the New-MailboxDatabase cmdlet to create the desired databases, as shown here:

```
[PS] C:\> $databases | foreach{new-mailboxdatabase -Name "$_"
-StorageGroup "EX01\$_"}
```

NOTE

To correctly execute the previous command example, you would first need to have created storage groups named IT, HR, and Exec.

6. Using the same type of logic, mount each of the databases, as shown here:

```
[PS] C:\> $databases | foreach{mount-database "EX01\$_"}
```

15

Working with Recipients

A recipient in Exchange Server 2007 can be a mailbox user, a mail-enabled user, a mail contact, a distribution group, a security group, a dynamic distribution group, or a mail-enabled public folder. To manage Exchange recipients, the EMS has a collection of cmdlets that are related to the following tasks:

▶ Managing distribution groups and dynamic distribution groups

▶ Managing user and resource mailboxes

▶ Managing contacts and mail users

▶ Managing public folders

▶ Managing the Microsoft exchange recipient

To help better understand the recipient management cmdlets, the next few sections review how to use the EMS to create mailboxes and manage those mailboxes using these cmdelts.

Creating Mailboxes

You can use two primary methods to create a mailbox. The first method is to mail enable an existing user using the `Enable-Mailbox` cmdlet. The second method is to create a new user that has a mailbox using the `New-Mailbox` cmdlet. In this section of the chapter, you will understand the steps involved with using both of these cmdlets.

NOTE

You can also use the `New-MailUser` to create a user account that has a defined email address. However, this is typically used to create user accounts with email addresses that are outside of an Exchange Organization.

Example: Enabling Existing Users   When using the EMS, you can use the `Enable-Mailbox` cmdlet to mail enable existing users or an `InetOrgPerson`. The term mail enable refers to the creation of additional mailbox attributes on the Active Directory user against which you execute the cmdlet. However, a user's mailbox object in an Exchange database is not actually created until the user actually logs in or receives an email message.

When using the `Enable-Mailbox` cmdlet, you must define the required parameters `Identity` and `Database`. The `Identity` parameter specifies the user or `InetOrgPerson` that you wish to mail enable. An argument for this parameter can be any of the following values:

▶ GUID (Globally Unique Identifier)

▶ Distinguished Name (DN)

▶ Domain\Account

▶ User principal name (UPN)

The Database parameter is used to specify the Exchange database where the new mailbox is to be located. An argument for this parameter can be any of the following values:

- ► GUID of the database

- ► Database name

- ► Server name\database name

- ► Server name\storage group\database name

In addition to the two required parameters just described, several additional optional parameters can be used to define mailbox attributes, such as Alias, Share, Room, PrimarySmtpAddress, and so on. Use the Enable-Mailbox cmdlet help information for a complete list of optional parameters.

The following shows an example of the Enable-Mailbox cmdlet used to mail enable the user named Maiko:

```
[PS] C:\> enable-mailbox -Identity companyabc\Maiko -Database sc1
-ex01\SG1\Marketing
```

Additionally, like all PowerShell cmdlets, you can use the Enable-Mailbox cmdlet in conjunction with other cmdlets to complete complex automation tasks. An example of this follows:

```
[PS] C:\> $Users = get-qadgroup -name "All-IT" | foreach{$_.members}
[PS] C:\> $Users | foreach{enable-mailbox -identity $_ -Database
"sc1-ex01\SG1\Marketing"}
```

Here, the Enable-Mailbox cmdlet is used in conjunction with a Quest AD cmdlet to mail enable users who are a member of the All-IT security group.

Example: Creating New Users   The New-Mailbox cmdlet is used to create new mail enabled users. An example of using this cmdlet follows:

```
[PS] C:\> $Password = read-host "Enter password" -AsSecureString
[PS] C:\> new-mailbox -alias "jjones" -name "Jason Jones" -database
"sc1-ex01\Sales" -org "companyabc.com/APAC/Sales" -UserPrincipalName
jjones@companyabc.com -password $Password -firstname "Jason" -lastname
"Jones"
```

When using this cmdlet, several required parameters must be defined. These parameters are defined in Table 15.4:

15

TABLE 15.4   New-Mailbox Required Parameters

Parameter	Database
Database	Used to specify the Exchange database where the new mailbox is to be located. An argument for this parameter can be any of the following values: ▶ GUID of the database ▶ Database name ▶ Server name\database name ▶ Server name\storage group\database name
Name	Used to specify the name of the user. The string that you define for this parameter is the resulting CN for the user's object in Active Directory.
Password	Used to specify the initial password for the user. The argument for this parameter must be typed as system.Security.SecureString. Additionally, the Password parameter is not required when creating a linked mailbox, resource mailbox, or shared mailbox because these accounts are disabled.
UserPrincipalName	Used to specify the user principal name (UPN) for this mailbox that is also the logon name for the user. A UPN consists of a user name and a suffix. Typically, the suffix is the domain name where the user account resides.

Working with Mailboxes

To report on or manage Exchange mailboxes, you use one of many database cmdlets. For example, to create a new mailbox database, use the New-MailboxDatabase cmdlet. Then, to manage that database, use the Set-MailboxDatabase cmdlet. More information about the mailbox database cmdlets and their usage is shown in Table 15.5:

TABLE 15.5   Mailbox Cmdlets

Cmdlet	Usage
Connect-Mailbox	Used to connect a disconnect mailbox to a user object.
Disable-Mailbox	Used to disable a mailbox from a user or InetOrgPerson and remove that object"s Exchange attributes.
Export-Mailbox	Used to export contents of a mailbox to a specified mailbox folder (ExMerge for Exchange 2007).
Get-Mailbox	Used to retrieve and view attributes from a mailbox object.
Import-Mailbox	Used to import mailbox data from a .pst file to a mailbox.
Move-Mailbox	Used to move a mailbox between databases, servers, and even organizations.
Remove-Mailbox	Used to delete a user object associated with a mailbox and then remove the mailbox object from the Exchange database.
Restore-Mailbox	Used to restore mailbox data from a database restored to a recovery storage group.
Set-Mailbox	Used to modify the settings of an existing mailbox.

Example: Managing a Mailbox   In this usage example, you use the EMS and some of the `*-*Mailbox` cmdlets to report on and manage a group of mailboxes. To complete this example, use the following steps:

1. Using the same EMS console from the previous example, use the `Get-Mailbox` cmdlet to get information about the mailboxes that you just created, as shown here:

    ```
    [PS] C:\> $Users | get-mailbox | fl name, database
    ```

2. What if these users should have been in the `Sales` database? Use the `Move-Mailbox` cmdlet to move these mailboxes into the correct database, as shown here:

    ```
    [PS] C:\> $Users | get-mailbox | move-mailbox -TargetDatabase "sc1-
    ex01\SG1\IT"
    ```

3. Verify that the mailboxes have been moved by using the following command:

    ```
    [PS] C:\> get-mailbox | where{$_.database -eq "sc1-ex01\SG1\IT"}
    ```

Scripting Scenario: GetDatabaseSizeReport.ps1

The first Exchange Server 2007 script you examine in this chapter is the `GetDatabaseSizeReport.ps1` script, which produces a report on the size of a mailbox database in an Exchange organization. The report contains the following information:

▶ The mailbox server name

▶ The full database name, including the storage group name

▶ The drive where the database is located

▶ The free space on the drive in gigabytes

▶ The database size in gigabytes

Here's an example of the report `GetDatabaseSizeReport.ps1` produces:

```
Server,Database,Drive,FreeSpace,Size
SFEX01,SG1\DB1,C:,34.67,40.453
SFEX02,SG1\DB1,F:,40.56,20.232
SFEX02,SG1\DB2,F:,40.56,30.2144
SFEX02,SG2\DB1,F:,40.56,45.333
```

Any information about your network environment is helpful. However, when you're using Exchange, an understanding of mailbox database sizes, their growth, free space on the hosting drive, and an overall picture of how mailbox databases work in a network environment can help you prevent potential problems.

This script was developed for companyabc.com, a small manufacturing company with a network consisting of several hundred users and two Exchange servers. Because of budget constraints, the IT department is made up of only one person. The limited budget has also prevented companyabc.com from purchasing and installing monitoring and reporting software for IT systems. As a result, the IT employee has only manual methods for ensuring the systems' operational status and often doesn't have time to do any proactive monitoring.

As a result, the Exchange mailbox databases have grown to the point that offline maintenance can no longer be done, and database disks tend to run out of space. After several near disasters, companyabc.com's management has asked the IT employee to find a way to improve monitoring of the Exchange databases. Needing a quick, flexible, and cost-effective solution, the IT employee turned to scripting and requested the development of the `GetDatabaseSizeReport.ps1` script.

A working copy of this script can be downloaded from www.informit.com/title/ 9780672329883. Running this script doesn't require any parameters be defined. However, an optional parameter, `ExportFile`, should have its argument set to the name of the CSV file where you want to export report data. Here's the command to run the `GetDatabaseSizeReport.ps1` script:

```
PS D:\Scripts> .\GetDatabaseSizeReport.ps1
```

Figures 15.2 and 15.3 show the execution of the `GetDatabaseSizeReport.ps1` script.

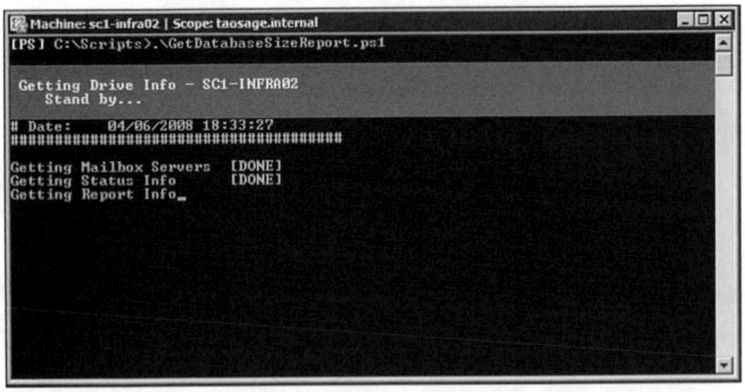

FIGURE 15.2   The `GetDatabaseSizeReport.ps1` script being executed

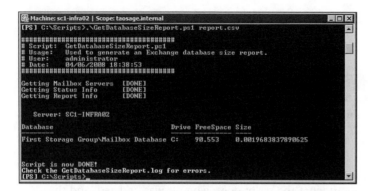

FIGURE 15.3   The GetDatabaseSizeReport.ps1 script after being executed

The GetDatabaseSizeReport.ps1 script performs the following sequence of actions:

1. The script creates two DataTable objects: $ServersTable, used to store status information for Exchange mailbox servers, and $ReportTable, used to store the Exchange database size report.

2. The script creates an error log named GetDatabaseSizeReport_Errors.log by using the Out-File cmdlet. This error log gives users detailed error information.

3. The script uses the Get-MailboxServer cmdlet to get a list of all Exchange mailbox servers. The list is then populated into the $MailboxServers variable.

4. The script uses the System.Net.NetworkInformation.Ping class to ping each server in the $MailboxServers object collection. If a server responds, a new row is created in $ServersTable consisting of the server's name and its status as "Online." If a server doesn't respond, a new row is created in $ServersTable with the server's status set to "Offline".

5. The listing of servers and their status information is sent to the script's error log for future reference by using the Out-File cmdlet.

6. For each server with an "Online" status in $ServersTable, the script does the following:

   ▶ The Get-MailboxDatabase cmdlet is used to get a listing of all mailbox databases on the server. Each mailbox database's Name, StorageGroupName, and EdbFilePath are populated into the $Databases variable.

   ▶ For each mailbox database in the $Databases object collection, the script uses the Get-WmiObject cmdlet to collect information about the database size and free drive space. The script then adds a row to the $ReportTable containing the mailbox server name ($Server.Name), database name ($DBName), drive letter of the database's location ($DBDriveName), free space ($DBDriveFreeSpace), and database size ($DBSize).

7. The script exports all data from the $ReportTable by using the Export-DataTable function.

The first code snippet contains the header for the GetDatabaseSizeReport.ps1 script. This header includes information about what the script does, when it was updated, and the script's author. Just after the header is the script's only parameter ExportFile, shown here:

```
##################################################
# GetDatabaseSizeReport.ps1
# Used to generate an Exchange database size report.
#
# Created: 10/26/2006
# Author: Tyson Kopczynski
##################################################
param([string] $ExportFile)
```

For the GetDatabaseSizeReport.ps1 script, only one function (Export-DataTable) is loaded, as shown in the next code snippet:

```
##################################################
# Functions
##################################################
#-------------------------------------------------
# Export-DataTable
#-------------------------------------------------
# Usage:        Used to export a DataSet to a CSV file.
# $Data:        A DataSet object.
# $FileName:    The name of the export CSV file.

function Export-DataTable{
    param ($Data, $FileName)

    $Null =
        [System.Reflection.Assembly]::LoadWithPartialName( '
            "System.Windows.Forms")

    trap{write-host "[ERROR] $_" -Foregroundcolor Red; Continue}
```

```
if ($FileName -eq ""){
    $exFileName = new-object System.Windows.Forms.saveFileDialog
    $exFileName.DefaultExt = "csv"
    $exFileName.Filter = "CSV (Comma delimited)(*.csv)|*.csv"
    $exFileName.ShowHelp = $True
    $exFileName.ShowDialog()

    $FileName = $exFileName.FileName
    }

if ($FileName -ne ""){
    $LogFile = new-object System.IO.StreamWriter($FileName, $False)

    for ($i=0; $i -le $Data.Columns.Count-1; $i++){
        $LogFile.Write($Data.Columns[$i].ColumnName)

        if ($i -lt $Data.Columns.Count-1){
            $LogFile.Write(",")
            }
        }

    $LogFile.WriteLine()

    foreach ($Row in $Data.Rows){
        for ($i=0; $i -le $Data.Columns.Count-1; $i++){
            $LogFile.Write($Row[$i].ToString())

            if ($i -lt $Data.Columns.Count-1){
                $LogFile.Write(",")
                }
            }

        $LogFile.WriteLine()
        }

    $LogFile.Close()
    }
}
```

To perform the data export, the Export-DataTable function uses the .NET
System.IO.StreamWriter class to create an object based on the .NET TextWriter class.
The resulting TextWriter object ($LogFile) can be used to write an object to a string,
write strings to a file, or serialize XML. In this script, $LogFile is used to dump the

DataTable's contents into the CSV export file (which is created along with $LogFile). To perform this task, the Export-DataTable function writes DataTable's column names, separated with a comma (,) delimiter, to the CSV export file. Then, the function loops through each value in DataTable's rows and writes these values to the CSV export file, separated with a comma (,) delimiter.

If Export-DataTable is called and a CSV export filename isn't specified, this function makes use of a .NET System.Windows.Forms.SaveFileDialog class to construct a Save As dialog box for collecting the export file's name and location (see Figure 15.4).

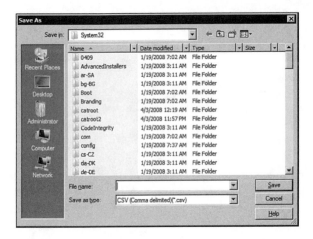

FIGURE 15.4   Windows Forms Save As dialog box

This example shows how PowerShell can use .NET-based Windows Forms to collect or display data.

In the next code snippet, variables that will be used later in the script are defined. In addition, the library file LibraryGen.ps1, which contains the script usage functions, is being dot sourced:

```
###############################################
# Main
###############################################
#--------------------
# Load Libraries
#--------------------
. .\LibraryGen.ps1


#--------------------
# Set Config Vars
#--------------------
$ScriptName = "GetDatabaseSizeReport.ps1"
```

```
$ScriptUsage = "Used to generate an Exchange database size report."
$ScriptCommand = "$ScriptName -ExportFile value"
$ScriptParams = "ExportFile = The export CSV file path/filename."
$ScriptExamples = "$ScriptName ""report.csv"""
$ErrorLogName = "GetDatabaseSizeReport.log"
$Date = Date
```

Next, the script checks to see if the user needed any usage help, as shown in the following code snippet:

```
#--------------------
# Verify Required Parameters
#--------------------
if ($args[0] -match '-(\?|(h|(help)))'){
    write-host
    Get-ScriptHeader $ScriptName $ScriptUsage
    Show-ScriptUsage $ScriptCommand $ScriptParams $ScriptExamples
    Return
    }
```

In the next code snippet, the two DataTable objects are created. The first DataTable is the $ServersTable, which stores server information. The second DataTable is the $ReportTable, which stores the report information:

```
#--------------------
# Define DataTables
#--------------------
$ServersTable = new-object System.Data.DataTable
$ServersTable.TableName = "Servers"
[Void]$ServersTable.Columns.Add("Name")
[Void]$ServersTable.Columns.Add("Status")

$ReportTable = new-object System.Data.DataTable
$ReportTable.TableName = "Servers"
[Void]$ReportTable.Columns.Add("Server")
[Void]$ReportTable.Columns.Add("Database")
[Void]$ReportTable.Columns.Add("Drive")
[Void]$ReportTable.Columns.Add("FreeSpace")
[Void]$ReportTable.Columns.Add("Size")
```

15

The Out-File cmdlet is used to create an error log and write header information to it. Then, the Get-ScriptHeader function is used to indicate to the script operator that the automation portion of the script has started, as shown here:

```
#- - - - - - - - - - - - - - - - - - -
# Begin Script
#- - - - - - - - - - - - - - - - - - -
# Setup ErrorLog
$ScriptName + " Ran on: " + $Date | out-file $ErrorLogName

write-host
Get-ScriptHeader $ScriptName $ScriptUsage
write-host
```

After displaying the script header to the user, the script's next task is to get a list of mailbox servers using the Get-MailboxServer cmdlet. Then, for each server object in $MailboxServers variable, the script pings that server to determine its status. During this task, both the resulting status and the server's name are written to a new row in the $ServersTable DataTable, as shown in the next code snippet:

```
#- - - - - - - - - - - - - - - - - - -
# Get Servers and Status
#- - - - - - - - - - - - - - - - - - -
write-host "Getting Mailbox Servers" -NoNewLine
$MailboxServers = get-mailboxserver
write-host 't "[DONE]" -Foregroundcolor Green

write-host "Getting Status Info" -NoNewLine

$MailboxServers | foreach-object -Begin {$i=0;} '
    -Process {&{$Ping = new-object Net.NetworkInformation.Ping;
        $MBServerName = $_.Name;
        trap{"Ping [ERROR]: " + $MBServerName + " $_" | out-file '
            $ErrorLogName -Append; Continue};
        $Result = $Ping.Send($MBServerName);
        if ($Result.Status -eq "Success"){ '
            [Void]$ServersTable.Rows.Add($MBServerName, "Online")} '
        else{[Void]$ServersTable.Rows.Add($MBServerName, "Offline")};
        $i = $i+1;
        write-progress -Activity "Pinging Servers - $($MBServerName)" '
            -Status "Progress:" '
            -PercentComplete ($i / $MailboxServers.Count * 100)}}
```

```
write-host 't "[DONE]" -Foregroundcolor Green

# Write status info to ErrorLog
$ServersTable | out-file $ErrorLogName –Append
```

The next task, as shown in the following code snippet, is to generate the final report. To do this, the script uses the `Get-MailboxDatabase` cmdlet to get the `EdbFilePath` for each Exchange server that is online. Then, for each mailbox database, the script uses WMI to collect the database size and free space for the drive on which the database is located. After collecting and formatting report information, the script then adds a new row to the `$ReportTable` DataTable that contains the database information, its size, and the drive free space:

```
#--------------------
# Get Report Info
#--------------------
write-host "Getting Report Info"   -NoNewLine

$OnlineServers = $ServersTable.Select("Status = 'Online'")

foreach ($Server in $OnlineServers) {
    &{
        trap{"Make Report [Error]: " + $Server.Name + " $_" | '
            out-file $ErrorLogName -Append; Continue}

        write-progress -Activity "Getting Database Info - $($Server.Name)" '
            -Status "Stand by..."

        $Databases = get-mailboxdatabase -Server $Server.Name | '
            select Name, StorageGroupName, EdbFilePath

        foreach ($Database in $Databases){
            &{
                write-progress '
                    -Activity "Getting Drive Info - $($Server.Name)" '
                    -Status "Stand by..."

                $DBDriveName = $Database.EdbFilePath.DriveName
                $DBDrive = '
                    get-wmiobject Win32_PerfRawData_PerfDisk_LogicalDisk '
                    -Computer $Server.Name -Filter "Name = '$DBDriveName'"

                write-progress -Activity '
```

15

```
                       "Getting Drive Size Info - $($Server.Name)" '
                       -Status "Stand by..."

               # Needed to replace \ with \\
               $DBPath = $Database.EdbFilePath.PathName.Replace("\","\\")
               $DBFile = get-wmiobject CIM_DataFile -Computer $Server.Name '
                   -Filter "Name = '$DBPath'"

               $DBName = $Database.StorageGroupName + "\" + $Database.Name

               # Needed to convert from MB to GB
               $DBDriveFreeSpace = $DBDrive.FreeMegabytes / 1000

               # Needed to convert Bytes to GB
               $DBSize = $DBFile.FileSize / 1073741824

               [Void]$ReportTable.Rows.Add($Server.Name, $DBName, '
                   $DBDriveName, $DBDriveFreeSpace, $DBSize)
           }
           }

       write-progress -Activity '
           "Getting Database Info - $($Server.Name)" '
           -Status "Done" -completed $True
   }
   }

write-host 't "[DONE]" -Foregroundcolor Green
```

Finally, the script writes the report to the PowerShell console using the `Format-Table`
cmdlet and then exports the data to a CSV file using the `Export-DataTable` function, as
shown here:

```
$ReportTable | format-table -groupBy Server Database, Drive, '
    FreeSpace, Size -autosize

$Null = Export-DataTable $ReportTable $ExportFile
```

Scripting Scenario: `GetEvent1221Info.ps1`

Administrators can use the `GetEvent1221Info.ps1` script to search the Application event
logs of Exchange Server 2007 mailbox servers and generate a report containing Event ID

1221 messages. Exchange administrators can use these messages to determine the amount of whitespace present in a database over a specified time span (number of days before the current day). Based on information gathered from Event ID 1221 messages, the report contains the following:

- ▶ The mailbox server name

- ▶ The date and time the event was written to the Application log

- ▶ The full database name, including the storage group name

- ▶ The amount of whitespace in megabytes

Here's an example of the report GetEvent1221Info.ps1 produces:

```
Server,TimeWritten,Database,MB
SFEX02,10/27/2006 1:00:02 AM,SG1\DB1,500
SFEX02,10/27/2006 1:00:06 AM,SG2\PF1,700
SFEX02,10/27/2006 2:00:00 AM,SG1\DB1,500
SFEX02,10/27/2006 2:00:01 AM,SG2\PF1,700
SFEX02,10/27/2006 3:00:00 AM,SG1\DB1,500
SFEX02,10/27/2006 3:00:32 AM,SG2\PF1,700
SFEX02,10/27/2006 4:00:00 AM,SG1\DB1,500
SFEX02,10/27/2006 4:00:00 AM,SG2\PF1,700
SFEX01,10/27/2006 1:00:04 AM,SG1\DB2,200
SFEX01,10/27/2006 1:00:04 AM,SG1\DB1,100
SFEX01,10/27/2006 2:00:00 AM,SG1\DB1,200
SFEX01,10/27/2006 2:00:00 AM,SG1\DB2,100
SFEX01,10/27/2006 3:15:00 AM,SG1\DB1,100
SFEX01,10/27/2006 3:15:00 AM,SG1\DB2,200
SFEX01,10/27/2006 4:00:00 AM,SG1\DB1,200
SFEX01,10/27/2006 4:00:00 AM,SG1\DB2,100
```

15

This script was developed for companyabc.com, a marketing firm of 50 users who have large (4GB and up) Exchange mailboxes. It produces marketing packages consisting of digital images, which result in an average package size of more than 20MB. Because companyabc.com's employees are scattered among many home offices and remote locations, they usually e-mail marketing packages to each other instead of posting them to a shared location.

Employees have been using their mailboxes as online file systems, so mailbox sizes have grown rapidly. Realizing that mailboxes of this size would be costly and difficult, companyabc.com's Exchange administrator has requested that marketing content be saved locally to users' hard drives and then deleted from their mailboxes. This practice has kept the Exchange databases from growing too quickly; however, the high deletion rate of large e-mail messages has created another problem: large areas of whitespace in Exchange databases.

The amount of whitespace is important because after an Exchange database grows, its size can't be decreased until the administrator does an offline defragmentation. For example, a database has grown to 12GB, but users have deleted 3GB of messages. After an online defragmentation, Event ID 1221 logs report 3GB of whitespace. New messages written to the database use this whitespace, and the database doesn't grow until that whitespace is exhausted.

The database still takes up 12GB on the hard drive, even though it contains only 9GB of data. A larger-than-necessary database can increase the time needed for backup and restore jobs. By reviewing Event ID 1221 messages, administrators can determine whether an offline defragmentation is needed to shrink the database in an effort to improve overall performance. Furthermore, with periodic review of Event ID 1221 logs, administrators can track a database's average whitespace amount, which helps determine the growth patterns of actual data in a database. This information can be helpful in deciding when additional space needs to be allocated for a database.

With no budget available to purchase a suite of Exchange tools, companyabc.com requested the development of a script for monitoring the amount of whitespace in Exchange databases. The resulting script is GetEvent1221Info.ps1.

A working copy of this script can be downloaded from www.informit.com/title/ 9780672329883. Running this script requires defining one parameter. The Days parameter should have its argument set to the time period (in number of days) for querying Event ID 1221 messages from mailbox servers. An optional parameter, ExportFile, should have its argument set to the name of the CSV file where you want to export report data. Here's the command to run the GetEvent1221Info.ps1 script:

```
PS D:\Scripts> .\GetEvent1221Info.ps1 5
```

Figures 15.5 and 15.6 show the execution of the GetEvent1221Info.ps1 script.

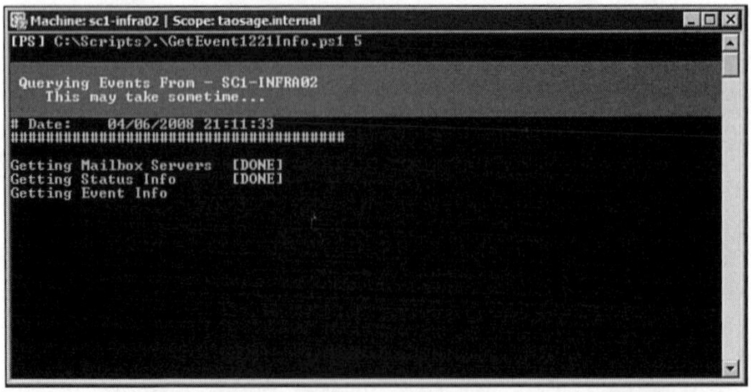

FIGURE 15.5   The GetEvent1221Info.ps1 script being executed

FIGURE 15.6   The `GetEvent1221Info.ps1` script after being executed

The `GetEvent1221Info.ps1` script performs the following sequence of actions:

1. The script creates two `DataTable` objects: `$ServersTable`, used to store status information for Exchange mailbox servers, and `$EventsTable`, used to store the Event ID 1221 report.

2. The script creates an error log named `GetEvent1221Info_Errors.log` by using the `Out-File` cmdlet. This error log gives users detailed error information.

3. The script uses the `Get-MailboxServer` cmdlet to get a list of all Exchange mailbox servers, which is then populated to the `$MailboxServers` variable.

4. The script uses the `System.Net.NetworkInformation.Ping` class to ping each server in the `$MailboxServers` object collection. If a server replies, a new row is added to `$ServersTable` consisting of the server's name and its `"Online"` status. If a server doesn't reply, a new row is added with the server's status set to `"Offline"`.

5. The listing of servers and their status information is sent to the script's error log for future reference by using the `Out-File` cmdlet.

6. For each server with an `"Online"` status in `$ServersTable`, the script does the following:

   ▶ The `Get-RemoteEventLog` function is used to create an object (`$Events`) bound to the server's Application log. To create the object, the function uses the .NET `System.Diagnostics.Eventlog` class, which allows an application or script to interact with a machine's event log.

   ▶ Next, the script uses the `Select-Object` cmdlet to select all the 1221 events from the `$Events` object's `Entries` property that fall within the specified period (`$Days`). The resulting collection of events is populated to the `$1221Events` variable.

   ▶ For each `$1221Event` in the `$1221Events` object collection, the script then uses the `get_timewritten` method of `$1221Events` to populate the `$TimeWritten` variable with the time the event was written. Next, a regular expression is used to strip the database's free space ($MB) and name ($Database) from the event message.

▶ A row is added to $EventsTable containing the server's name ($Server.Name), the time the event was written ($TimeWritten), the database name ($Database), and the free space in megabytes ($MB).

7. The script exports all data from $EventsTable by using the Export-DataTable function.

The first code snippet contains the header for the GetEvent1221Info.ps1 script. This header includes information about what the script does, when it was updated, and the script's author. Just after the header are the script's parameters, as shown here:

```
#################################################
# GetEvent1221Info.ps1
# Used to consolidate 1221 events from mailbox servers.
#
# Created: 10/26/2006
# Author: Tyson Kopczynski
#################################################
param([int] $Days, [string] $ExportFile)
```

Next, as shown in the following code snippet the Get-RemoteEventLog function is loaded. This function is used to collect remote EventLog information from a machine using the System.Diagnostics.Eventlog class. Then, the Export-DataTable function is loaded which was discussed in the previous section.

```
#################################################
# Functions
#################################################
#------------------------------------------------
# Get-RemoteEventLog
#------------------------------------------------
# Usage:        Used to collect remote EventLog information from a machine.
# $Machine:     The name of the machine. ("MyServer")
# $Log:         The name of the EventLog. ("Application")

function Get-RemoteEventLog{
    param ($Machine, $Log)

    trap{Continue}

    new-object System.Diagnostics.Eventlog $Log, $Machine
```

```
    }

#------------------------------------------------
# Export-DataTable
#------------------------------------------------
# Usage:        Used to export a DataSet to a CSV file.
# $Data:        A DataSet object.
# $FileName:    The name of the export CSV file.

function Export-DataTable{
    param ($Data, $FileName)

    $Null = '
        [System.Reflection.Assembly]::LoadWithPartialName( '
            "System.Windows.Forms")

    trap{write-host "[ERROR] $_" -Foregroundcolor Red; Continue}

    if ($FileName -eq ""){
        $exFileName = new-object System.Windows.Forms.saveFileDialog
        $exFileName.DefaultExt = "csv"
        $exFileName.Filter = "CSV (Comma delimited)(*.csv)|*.csv"
        $exFileName.ShowDialog()

        $FileName = $exFileName.FileName
        }

    if ($FileName -ne ""){
        $LogFile = new-object System.IO.StreamWriter($FileName, $False)

          for ($i=0; $i -le $Data.Columns.Count-1; $i++){
            $LogFile.Write($Data.Columns[$i].ColumnName)

            if ($i -lt $Data.Columns.Count-1){
                $LogFile.Write(",")
                }
            }

        $LogFile.WriteLine()

        foreach ($Row in $Data.Rows){
            for ($i=0; $i -le $Data.Columns.Count-1; $i++){
                $LogFile.Write($Row[$i].ToString())
```

```
                if ($i -lt $Data.Columns.Count-1){
                    $LogFile.Write(",")
                    }
                }

            $LogFile.WriteLine()
            }

        $LogFile.Close()
        }
    }
```

In the next code snippet, variables that will be used later in the script are defined. In addition, the library file LibraryGen.ps1, which contains the script usage functions, is being dot sourced:

```
###############################################
# Main
###############################################
#--------------------
# Load Libraries
#--------------------
. .\LibraryGen.ps1


#--------------------
# Set Config Vars
#--------------------
$ScriptName = "GetEvent1221Info.ps1"
$ScriptUsage = "Used to consolidate 1221 events from mailbox servers."
$ScriptCommand = "$ScriptName -Days value -ExportFile value"
$ScriptParams = "Days = The number of days to filter events by.", '
    "ExportFile = The export CSV file path/filename."
$ScriptExamples = "$ScriptName 5 ""report.csv"""
$ErrorLogName = "GetEvent1221Info.log"
$Date = Date
```

Next, the script checks to see if the script user needed any usage help. If no help is needed, the script then checks to see if the Days parameter has been defined. If this parameter has not been defined, the script then informs the script operator that the parameter is required and shows the script usage information, as shown in the following code snippet:

```
#-------------------
# Verify Required Parameters
#-------------------
if ($args[0] -match '-(\?|(h|(help)))'){
    write-host
    Get-ScriptHeader $ScriptName $ScriptUsage
    Show-ScriptUsage $ScriptCommand $ScriptParams $ScriptExamples
    Return
    }

if (!$Days){
    write-host
    write-host "Please specify the number of days!" -Foregroundcolor Red
    write-host
    Get-ScriptHeader $ScriptName $ScriptUsage
    Show-ScriptUsage $ScriptCommand $ScriptParams $ScriptExamples
    Return
    }
```

Then, in the next code snippet, the two DataTable objects are created. The first DataTable is the $ServersTable, which stores server information, and the second DataTable is the $EventsTable, which stores the report information:

```
#-------------------
# Define DataSets
#-------------------
$ServersTable = new-object System.Data.DataTable
$ServersTable.TableName = "Servers"
[Void]$ServersTable.Columns.Add("Name")
[Void]$ServersTable.Columns.Add("Status")

$EventsTable = new-object System.Data.DataTable
$EventsTable.TableName = "Servers"
[Void]$EventsTable.Columns.Add("Server")
[Void]$EventsTable.Columns.Add("TimeWritten",[DateTime])
[Void]$EventsTable.Columns.Add("Database")
[Void]$EventsTable.Columns.Add("MB")
```

The Out-File cmdlet is used to create an error log and write header information to it. Then, the Get-ScriptHeader function is used to indicate to the script operator that the automation portion of the script has started, as shown in the following:

```
#--------------------
# Begin Script
#--------------------
# Setup ErrorLog
$ScriptName + " Ran on: " + $Date | out-file $ErrorLogName

write-host
Get-ScriptHeader $ScriptName $ScriptUsage
write-host
```

The next task is to get a list of mailbox servers using the Get-MailboxServer cmdlet. Then, for each server object in $MailboxServers variable, the script pings that server to determine its status. During this task, both the resulting status and the server's name are written to a new row in the $ServersTable DataTable, as shown in the next code snippet:

```
#--------------------
# Get Servers and Status
#--------------------
write-host "Getting Mailbox Servers"  -NoNewLine
$MailboxServers = get-mailboxserver
write-host 't "[DONE]" -Foregroundcolor Green

write-host "Getting Status Info"  -NoNewLine

$MailboxServers | foreach-object -Begin {$i=0;} '
    -Process {&{$Ping = new-object Net.NetworkInformation.Ping;
        $MBServerName = $_.Name;
        trap{"Ping [ERROR]: " + $MBServerName + " $_" | out-file '
            $ErrorLogName -Append; Continue};
        $Result = $Ping.Send($MBServerName);
        if ($Result.Status -eq "Success"){  '
            [Void]$ServersTable.Rows.Add($MBServerName, "Online")} '
        else{[Void]$ServersTable.Rows.Add($MBServerName, "Offline")};
        $i = $i+1;
        write-progress -Activity "Pinging Servers - $($MBServerName)" '
            -Status "Progress:" '
            -PercentComplete ($i / $MailboxServers.Count * 100)}}

write-host 't "[DONE]" -Foregroundcolor Green

# Write status info to ErrorLog
$ServersTable | out-file $ErrorLogName –Append
```

In the next code snippet, the script generates the final report. To do this, the script uses the DataTable Select method to create a collection of online server objects ($OnlineServers). Then, for each server in $OnlineServers object collection, the script uses the Get-RemoteEventLog function to retrieve all the Application event messages from that server. For each event message retrieved with an event ID of 1221, a new row is added to the $EventsTable DataTable that contains formatted information from the event message and the server's name:

```
#--------------------
# Get Event Info
#--------------------
write-host "Getting Event Info"  -NoNewLine

$OnlineServers = $ServersTable.Select("Status = 'Online'")

foreach ($Server in $OnlineServers){
    &{
        trap{"Event Info [Error]: " + $Server.Name + " $_" | '
            out-file $ErrorLogName -Append; Continue}

        $Events = Get-RemoteEventLog $Server.Name "Application"

        # This may take a long time depending on the number of servers
        write-progress -Activity "Querying Events From - $($Server.Name)" '
            -Status "This may take sometime..."

        $1221Events = $Events.Entries | where {$_.EventID -eq "1221" -and '
            $_.TimeWritten -ge $Date.AddDays(-$Days)}

        foreach ($1221Event in $1221Events){
            &{
                $Message = $1221Event | select Message
                $TimeWritten = $1221Event.get_timewritten()

                # This RegEx strips out the database name from the message
                $Database = [Regex]::Match($Message, '"[^"\r\n]*"')
                $Database = $Database.Value.Replace('"', "")

                # This RegEx strips out size of the whitespace
                $MB = [Regex]::Match($Message, '[0-9]+')

                [Void]$EventsTable.Rows.Add($Server.Name, $TimeWritten, '
                    $Database, $MB)
            }
        }
    }
}
```

```
        write-progress -Activity "Querying Events From - $($Server.Name)" '
            -Status "Done" -completed $True
    }
    }

write-host 't "[DONE]" -Foregroundcolor Green
```

The script exports the report information from the $EventsTable DataTable using the
Export-DataTable function:

```
#--------------------
# Export Data to CSV File
#--------------------
$Null = Export-DataTable $EventsTable $ExportFile

write-host
write-host "Script is now DONE!" -Foregroundcolor Green
write-host "Check the $ErrorLogName for errors." -Foregroundcolor Yellow
```

Scripting Scenario: ProvisionExchangeUsers.ps1

With the ProvisionExchangeUsers.ps1 script, Exchange administrators can provision
mail-enabled user accounts in Exchange Server 2007 environments quickly and easily
based on information in a CSV import file. This file is structured as follows:

- The user's first name

- The user's last name

- The user's e-mail alias

- The fully qualified database name

Here's an example of the import file:

```
FName,LName,Alias,Database
Stu,Gronko,sgronko,SFEX01\SG1\DB1
Caelie,Hallauer,challauer,SFEX02\SG2\DB2
Duane,Putnam,dputnam,SFEX02\SG2\DB2
Essie,Fea,efea,SFEX02\SG1\DB1
Rona,Trovato,rtrovato,SFEX01\SG1\DB2
Gottfried,Leibniz,gleibniz,SFEx01\SG1\DB1
```

With some tweaking to the code in ProvisionExchangeUsers.ps1, the format of the CSV import file and the information for provisioning mail-enabled user accounts can be tailored to fit any environment. This flexibility is important to meet changing automation needs.

This script was requested by companyabc.com, a large technology company that's in the process of completing several mergers. The company needs to provision many new mail-enabled user accounts. Because of the number of accounts to create and the varying information for each merger's account-provisioning process, an automated method that could be changed to meet different needs is the best solution. To meet the flexibility requirements, companyabc.com's IT department developed the ProvisionExchangeUsers.ps1 script.

A working copy of this script can be downloaded from www.informit.com/title/9780672329883. Running this script requires defining three parameters:

- ▶ UPNSuffix should have its argument set to the universal principal name (UPN) suffix for new mail-enabled accounts.

- ▶ OUDN should have its argument set to the distinguishedName of the OU where new mail-enabled accounts should be stored.

- ▶ ImportFile should have its argument set to the name of the CSV import file containing the list of users to create.

Here's the command to run the ProvisionExchangeUsers.ps1 script:

```
PS D:\Scripts> .\ProvisionExchangeUsers.ps1 "companyabc.com"
"OU=Accounts,DC=companyabc,DC=com" users.csv
```

Figures 15.7 and 15.8 show the execution of the ProvisionExchangeUsers.ps1 script.

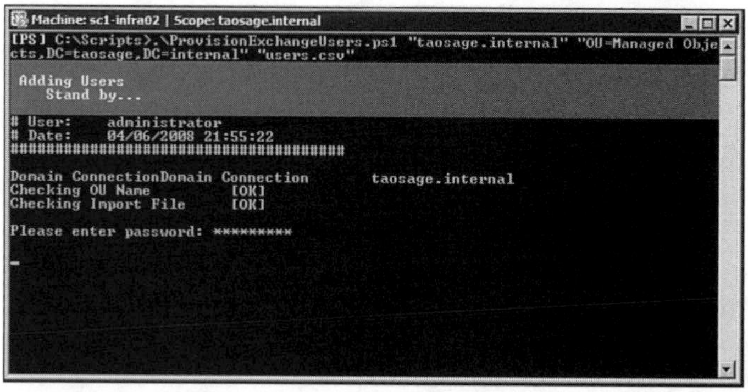

FIGURE 15.7   The ProvisionExchangeUsers.ps1 script being executed

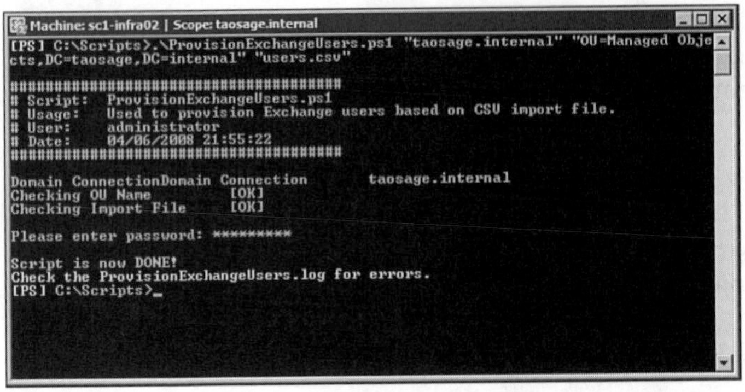

FIGURE 15.8   The `ProvisionExchangeUsers.ps1` script after being executed

The `ProvisionExchangeUsers.ps1` script performs the following sequence of actions:

1. The script creates an error log named `ProvisionExchangeUsers_Errors.log` by using the `Out-File` cmdlet. This error log gives users detailed error information.

2. The script connects to the current logon domain by using `Get-CurrentDomain` function. Using the object returned from this function, the script writes the domain's name to the PowerShell console. If this connection fails, the script halts.

3. The script verifies that the specified OU exists in the current domain by using the `Get-ADObject` function. If the OU isn't valid, the script halts.

4. The script uses the `Test-Path` cmdlet to verify that the import file is valid. If the file is invalid, the script halts.

5. The script uses the `Read-Host` cmdlet and its `AsSecureString` parameter to request the password for all new user accounts. The resulting secure string is then populated into the `$Password` variable.

6. The script uses the `Import-Csv` cmdlet to populate the `$Users` variable with the CSV import file's contents.

7. For each user in the `$Users` object collection, the script uses the `New-Mailbox` cmdlet to create a mail-enabled user account based on information in the CSV file and information provided by the user. Errors generated during account creation are sent to the script's error log by using the `Out-File` cmdlet.

The first code snippet contains the header for the `ProvisionExchangeUsers.ps1` script. This header includes information about what the script does, when it was updated, and the script's author. Just after the header are the script's parameters, as shown here:

```
###################################################
# ProvisionExchangeUsers.ps1
# Used to provision Exchange users based on CSV import file.
```

```
#
# Created: 10/21/2006
# Author: Tyson Kopczynski
################################################
param([string] $UPNSuffix, [string] $OUDN, [string] $ImportFile)
```

In the next code snippet, variables that will be used later in the script are defined. In addition, the library file LibraryGen.ps1, which contains the script usage functions, is being dot sourced, as shown here:

```
################################################
# Main
################################################
#-------------------
# Load Libraries
#-------------------
. .\LibraryGen.ps1


#-------------------
# Set Config Vars
#-------------------
$ScriptName = "ProvisionExchangeUsers.ps1"
$ScriptUsage = "Used to provision Exchange users based on CSV import file."
$ScriptCommand = "$ScriptName -UPNSuffix value -OUDN value -ImportFile value"
$ScriptParams = "UPNSuffix = The new users UPN suffix.", '
    "OUDN = The distinguishedName of the OU to create users in.", '
    "ImportFile = The import CSV file path/filename."
$ScriptExamples = "$ScriptName ""companyabc.com""" '
    + " ""OU=Accounts,DC=companyabc,DC=com""" '
    + " ""users.csv"""
$ErrorLogName = "ProvisionExchangeUsers.log"
$Date = Date
```

As shown in the following code snippet, the script next checks to see if the script user needed any usage help. If no help is needed, the script checks to see if the UPNSuffix, OUDN, and ImportFile parameters were defined. If these parameters are not defined, the script informs the script operator that the parameter is required and shows the script usage information:

```
#--------------------
# Verify Required Parameters
#--------------------
if ($args[0] -match '-(\?|(h|(help)))'){
    write-host
    Get-ScriptHeader $ScriptName $ScriptUsage
    Show-ScriptUsage $ScriptCommand $ScriptParams $ScriptExamples
    Return
    }


if (!$UPNSuffix){
    write-host
    write-host "Please specify the UPN suffix!" -Foregroundcolor Red
    write-host
    Get-ScriptHeader $ScriptName $ScriptUsage
    Show-ScriptUsage $ScriptCommand $ScriptParams $ScriptExamples
    Return
    }


if (!$OUDN){
    write-host
    write-host "Please specify the OU to create users in!" '
            -Foregroundcolor Red
    write-host
    Get-ScriptHeader $ScriptName $ScriptUsage
    Show-ScriptUsage $ScriptCommand $ScriptParams $ScriptExamples
    Return
    }


if (!$ImportFile){
    write-host
    write-host "Please specify the import CSV file name!" '
            -Foregroundcolor Red
    write-host
    Get-ScriptHeader $ScriptName $ScriptUsage
    Show-ScriptUsage $ScriptCommand $ScriptParams $ScriptExamples
    Return
    }
```

Next, the Out-File cmdlet creates an error log and writes header information to it. The Get-ScriptHeader function is used to indicate to the script operator that the automation portion of the script has started, as shown here:

```
#....................
# Begin Script
#....................
# Setup ErrorLog
$ScriptName + " Ran on: " + $Date | out-file $ErrorLogName

write-host
Get-ScriptHeader $ScriptName $ScriptUsage
write-host
write-host "Domain Connection" -NoNewLine
```

The script must verify that there is a valid domain connection. To accomplish task, the script uses the Get-CurrentDomain. If a valid domain connection doesn't exist, the script halts and returns the script status to the operator. If a connection does exist, the script continues execution and writes the domain name to the console, as shown in the next code snippet:

```
.{
    trap{write-host 't "[ERROR]" -Foregroundcolor Red;
        throw write-host $_ -Foregroundcolor Red;
        Break}

    write-host "Domain Connection" -NoNewLine

    # You need to test for a domain connection
    $Domain = Get-CurrentDomain

    # You then return the domain's name
    write-host 't $Domain.Name -Foregroundcolor Green
}
```

In the next code snippet, the distinguished name in the $OUDN variable is verified. To perform the verification, the script uses Get-ADObject function. This function connects to Active Directory and completes a search for the OU by its distinguished name. If an object is returned from the function, the OU is valid; if no object is returned, the OU is considered invalid, and the script halts:

```
write-host "Checking OU Name" -NoNewLine

if (!(Get-ADObject "distinguishedName" $OUDN "organizationalUnit")){
    write-host 't "Is not valid!" -Foregroundcolor Red
```

```
    write-host
    Break
    }
else{
    write-host 't "[OK]" -Foregroundcolor Green
    }
```

The script verifies that the import file is valid using the Test-Path cmdlet, as shown here:

```
write-host "Checking Import File" -NoNewLine

if (!(test-path $ImportFile -pathType Leaf)){
    throw write-host 't "Is not a valid file!" -Foregroundcolor Red
    }
else{
    write-host 't "[OK]" -Foregroundcolor Green
    }
```

Next, the script collects the password from the user using the Read-Host cmdlet with the AsSecureString switch, as shown in the next code snippet:

```
#- - - - - - - - - - - - - - - - - -
# Get Password
#- - - - - - - - - - - - - - - - - -
write-host
$Password = read-host "Please enter password" –AsSecureString
```

Finally, the script provisions the new user accounts using the New-Mailbox cmdlet, information from the import file, and information provided by the script user, as shown here:

```
#- - - - - - - - - - - - - - - - - -
# Create mailboxes
#- - - - - - - - - - - - - - - - - -
write-host
write-progress -Activity "Adding Users" -Status "Stand by..."

$Users = import-csv $ImportFile

$Users | foreach-object -Begin {$i=0;} '
```

```
    -Process {$FName = $_.FName;
        $LName = $_.LName;
        $Alias = $_.Alias;
        $Database = $_.Database;
        $UPN = $Alias + "@" + $UPNSuffix;
        $Name = $FName + " " + $LName;
        $Null = new-mailbox -Name $Name -Database $Database '
            -OrganizationalUnit $OUDN -UserPrincipalName $UPN '
            -Password $Password -ResetPasswordOnNextLogon $True '
            -Alias $Alias -DisplayName $Name -FirstName $FName '
            -LastName $LName -ErrorVariable Err -ErrorAction '
            SilentlyContinue;
        if ($Err.Count -ne 0){ '
            "Add User [ERROR]: " + $Alias + " " + $Err | '
            out-file $ErrorLogName -Append};
        $i = $i+1;
        write-progress -Activity "Adding Users" -Status "Progress:" '
            -PercentComplete ($i / $Users.Count * 100)}

write-host "Script is now DONE!" -Foregroundcolor Green
write-host "Check the $ErrorLogName for errors." -Foregroundcolor Yellow
```

Summary

In this chapter, you were introduced to how PowerShell is used to manage Exchange Server 2007 through a GUI using the EMC and the command line using the EMS. Exchange Server 2007 is the first application that uses PowerShell in this fashion. To accomplish this feat, Exchange Server 2007 makes use of PowerShell's capability to be extended through the use of snap-ins. By using a snap-in more, cmdlets are made available to a PowerShell user, further increasing the user's ability to manage an Exchange organization.

The scripts that were reviewed in this chapter served as a good demonstration of what can be accomplished using the Exchange Server 2007 snap-in. Thanks to these examples, you should now have an understanding about how to use PowerShell to gather Exchange database size information, calculate a database's whitespace, and quickly provision mail enabled users. However, the limits to what can be accomplished around Exchange management don't stop there. The limits to what can be done with PowerShell should in many respects be bounded only by your own scripting talent and imagination.

## CHAPTER 16

PowerShell and System Center Operations Manager 2007

One of the serious shortcomings of the early releases of the Microsoft Operations Management (MOM) product was the lack of a good scripting shell. This forced administrators to either use the GUI for all operations or become developers to leverage the APIs. The release of Microsoft System Center Operations Manager (SCOM) 2007 introduced a host of new features to the platform, including PowerShell integration. This gives administrators a powerful new set of tools to script and automate complex tasks without having to become developers.

The Operations Manager PowerShell interface is truly integrated in the sense that it defaults to the Operations Manger object tree rather than the directory structure. This enables the administrator and scripts to interact directly with the objects rather than use a complex set of command-line options or arguments.

Operations Manager PowerShell Integration

The Operations Manager command shell is a customized PowerShell environment that loads the Operations Manager PowerShell snap-in, sets the location to the root of the Operations Manager Monitoring Object, and completes several other tasks. This lets an Operations Manager administrator execute management-specific commands easily and execute ad-hoc scripts natively in Operations Manager.

We explore the command shell in this section to familiarize you with the features, navigation around in the shell, and how to get help.

The Command Shell

The command shell is installed when you install a SCOM management server. You launch it separately from the standard Windows PowerShell. To launch the Operations Manager command shell, execute the following steps:

1. Select **Start**.

2. Select **All Programs**.

3. Select **System Center Operations Manager 2007**.

4. Select **Command Shell**.

This opens the Operations Manager command shell. On launching the command shell, you get the following customized message:

```
Welcome to the Operations Manager 2007 Command Shell.This command shell is
designed to provide interactive and script based access to Operations Manager
data and operations.This functionality is provided by a set of Operations
Manager commands.
To list all commands, type: Get-Command
To list all Operations Manager commands, type: Get-OperationsManagerCommand
To get help for a command, type: Get-Help [command name]
Connecting to Operations Manager Management Server 'om2.cco.com'.
PS Monitoring:\om2.cco.com
>
```

This is the customized shell that enables you to execute the Operations Manager cmdlets and scripts. It is a little bit different from the standard Windows PowerShell, so the next sections explore how to navigate and use the customized shell. The prompt shows us that we are using the command shell and that we are connected to the om2.cco.com management server.

> **NOTE**
>
> The command shell displays a lot of information, and the default width of the command shell window is only 80 characters wide by default. You can adjust the properties of the command shell to show more information and make it easier to work with.
>
> After launching the command shell, right-click on the window and select Properties. Select the Layout tab and change the Screen Buffer size width to 120 and the height to 300. Change the Window Size to 120 and 90. You can adjust these sizes to fit your screen. Click OK and select Modify shortcut that started this window to preserve the settings. Click OK to save.

The Object Tree

After launching the command shell, you can get a list of the current location by executing the dir cmdlet, as shown here:

```
PS Monitoring:\om2.cco.com
>dir
```

The cmdlet produces a stream of information of over a hundred objects depending on the Management Packs you have installed. To control this stream of information, you can display the results page by page:

```
PS Monitoring:\om2.cco.com
>dir | more
```

Reviewing the results page by page, the objects shown are not files and folders, but Operations Manager objects. This is because the dir cmdlet is really just an alias for the select-object cmdlet, so the dir command returns objects from the current location. In the case of the standard Windows PowerShell prompt, this is the folder tree. In the case of the Operations Manager command shell, this is the Operations Manager Monitoring Object tree.

For each of the objects returned, the cmdlet shows the following:

- ▶ ID
- ▶ PathName
- ▶ DisplayName
- ▶ ManagmentMode
- ▶ ManagementGroup
- ▶ HealthState
- ▶ OperationalState

You can show just the DisplayName and the PathName by using the following command:

```
PS Monitoring:\om2.cco.com
>dir | select-object DisplayName, PathName
```

This still returns a large number of objects. You can narrow the results even further by using the where cmdlet (where-object) to filter the objects returned, as shown in the following:

```
PS Monitoring:\om2.cco.com
>dir | select-object DisplayName, PathName | where {$_.DisplayName
-like "*Windows Server*"}
DisplayName                                                    PathName
-----------                                                    --------
Windows Server Computer Group                                  Microsoft.
Windows.Server.ComputerGroup
Microsoft Windows Servers with Print Service Computer Group    Microsoft.
Windows.Server.PrintServer.Microsoft_Windows_S...
Windows Server Instances Group                                 Microsoft.
Windows.Server.InstanceGroup
Windows Server 2003 Computer Group                             Microsoft.
Windows.Server.2003.ComputerGroup
Windows Server 2000 Computer Group                             Microsoft.
Windows.Server.2000.ComputerGroup
PS Monitoring:\om2.cco.com
>
```

Now we can see the path to the Windows Server Computer Group, which contains all the monitored Windows Server computer objects. To list the Windows Server computer objects, execute the following command dir Microsoft.Windows.Server.ComputerGroup with the following result:

```
>dir Microsoft.Windows.Server.ComputerGroup
Id                    : 25c83bfd-abc9-36c2-a123-a9c24fa43c02
PathName              : GP.cco.com
DisplayName           : GP.cco.com
ManagementMode        :
ManagementGroup       : CCO
HealthState           : Warning
OperationalState      :


Id                    : 3117612d-af1e-adb0-22fe-6bea70d82b70
PathName              : RMS.cco.com
DisplayName           : RMS.cco.com
ManagementMode        :
ManagementGroup       : CCO
HealthState           : Error
```

```
OperationalState :

Id                : e68f754e-27f5-1254-b5f9-f63cbff01ae9
PathName          : archive.cco.com
DisplayName       : archive.cco.com
ManagementMode    :
ManagementGroup   : CCO
HealthState       : Success
OperationalState  :

. . . . . . .
```

The list was truncated after the first three computers. You can see that the health state for the gps.cco.com server is in a warning state, the rms.cco.com server is in an error state, and the archive.cco.com server is in a success state (which means it is healthy).

Similarly, we can quickly find the health state of Exchange 2007 servers using the following command:

```
PS Monitoring:\om2.cco.com
>dir microsoft.exchange.2007.basecomputergroup | select-object
DisplayName, HealthState
```

This command shows the health state of all the Exchange 2007 servers.

The Operations Manager 2007 follows an object-contain model, meaning that objects contain other objects. You can also drill further into the objects to explore the objects that are contained within. To navigate the object tree, use the familiar cd cmdlet, which is an alias for the set-location cmdlet. We can navigate to the Windows Server Computer Group object using the following command:

```
PS Monitoring:\om2.cco.com
>cd Microsoft.Windows.Server.ComputerGroup
PS Monitoring:\om2.cco.com\Microsoft.Windows.Server.ComputerGroup
>
```

Note that the prompt now shows where in the object tree we are located. We can use the dir cmdlet to explore the error state of the rms.cco.com server. Recalling that the pathname was rms.cco.com, we can use the following command to navigate to the rms.cco.com object:

```
PS Monitoring:\om2.cco.com\Microsoft.Windows.Server.ComputerGroup
>cd rms.cco.com
PS
Monitoring:\om2.cco.com\Microsoft.Windows.Server.ComputerGroup\RMS.cco.com
>
```

Once again, note that the prompt shows where in the object tree we are located. We can quickly get the health state of the objects contained in the rms.cco.com computer object by executing the following command:

```
PS Monitoring:\om2.cco.com\Microsoft.Windows.Server.ComputerGroup\RMS.cco.com
>dir | select-object DisplayName, HealthState
```

We can even return only the objects where the state is in error by using the where cmdlet in the following command:

```
PS Monitoring:\om2.cco.com\Microsoft.Windows.Server.ComputerGroup\RMS.cco.com
>dir | select-object DisplayName, HealthState | where {$_.HealthState -eq
"Error"}
```

Now we have the list of objects that are in an error state in the rms.cco.com Windows Server Computer Group object.

We can also move to the top of the tree by using the cd cmdlet. For example, to move up one level in the tree you can use the following command:

```
PS Monitoring:\om2.cco.com\Microsoft.Windows.Server.ComputerGroup\RMS.cco.com
>cd ..
PS Monitoring:\om2.cco.com\Microsoft.Windows.Server.ComputerGroup
>
```

You can also move to the top of the tree using the following command:

```
PS Monitoring:\om2.cco.com\Microsoft.Windows.Server.ComputerGroup
>cd \
PS Monitoring:\
>
```

This takes you all the way to the top of the tree, even above the management server where the console originally defaulted to (which in the case of the examples was om2.cco.com). You can navigate back to the management server by using the cd cmdlet, as shown in the following:

```
PS Monitoring:\
>cd om2.cco.com
PS Monitoring:\om2.cco.com
>
```

Now the location is back to the original location when the command shell was launched. You can use the dir and cd cmdlets to navigate around the operations management object tree and even between management servers.

Getting Help

The Operations Manager 2007 PowerShell snap-in loads a large number of new cmdlets to manipulate the management objects.

The Get-OperationsManagerCommand cmdlet shows all the cmdlets:

```
Get-OperationsManagerCommand
```

Executing this gives you a list of the 87 cmdlets added by the Operations Manager PowerShell snap-in. The cmdlet helpfully shows the name and the basic syntax for the cmdlet on a single line. You can narrow the results of the cmdlet by using the where cmdlet. The code that follows would return the five cmdlets that relate to alerts:

```
Get-OperationsManagerCommand | where {$_.Name –like "*Alert*"}
```

After you have identified a cmdlet, you can get additional help using the standard get-help cmdlet. The three levels of help provided by the cmdlet are shown in the three commands that follow:

```
get-help get-alert
get-help get-alert –detailed
get-help get-alert - full
```

This chapter covers the most common cmdlets and their uses, but it does not exhaustively cover all 87 of the cmdlets. At the end of the chapter, all the Operations Manager cmdlets are listed for reference along with their descriptions.

Operations Manager 2007 PowerShell Scripts

The command shell loads the Operations Manager snap-in and sets the location. However, when automating scripts, the shell that is launched is the default Windows PowerShell. Without a couple of lines of code, any scripts with Operations Manager cmdlets will fail.

For the purposes of creating automated scripts, there are two commands that will start all of your Operations Manager PowerShell scripts. These are shown in the code box that follows:

```
add-pssnapin "Microsoft.EnterpriseManagement.OperationsManager.Client";
set-location "OperationsManagerMonitoring::";
```

The first command adds the PowerShell snap-in that contains all the cmdlets for Operations Manager 2007. Without this, PowerShell does not recognize any of the Operations Manager cmdlets. The second command sets the location to the Operations Manager Monitoring Object, which allows management objects to be referenced directly.

Agent Cmdlets

The agent cmdlets enable you to get information about agents, install agents, and uninstall agents. These cmdlets are useful for doing bulk operations on agents that are tedious to do in the Operations Manager Console. They even enable you set some parameters that cannot be accessed in the console, such as specifying the failover management servers.

get-Agent

The get-agent cmdlet returns the agents that are contained in a management server. You can get the syntax of the get-agent cmdlet using get-help:

```
PS Monitoring:\om2.cco.com
>get-help get-agent

NAME
    Get-Agent
SYNOPSIS
    Gets the agents associated with the specified management server.
SYNTAX
    Get-Agent [[-Path] [<String[]>]] [<CommonParameters>]
    Get-Agent [-ManagementServer] <ManagementServer>
[<CommonParameters>]
DETAILED DESCRIPTION
    Gets the agents associated with the specified management server.
RELATED LINKS
```

```
     Approve-AgentPendingAction
     Reject-AgentPendingAction
REMARKS
     For more information, type: "get-help Get-Agent -detailed".
     For technical information, type: "get-help Get-Agent -full"
```

The basic command shown in the following returns all the agents associated with the current management server.

```
PS Monitoring:\om2.cco.com
>get-agent
```

This returns all agents and might be a long list. We can select a single agent using the where cmdlet, as shown in the example that follows:

```
PS Monitoring:\om2.cco.com
>get-agent | where {$_.DisplayName -eq "rms.cco.com"}
PrimaryManagementServerName            : om2.cco.com
Id                                     : 3117612d-af1e-adb0-22fe-
                                         6bea70d82b70
LastModified                           : 1/6/2008 11:30:07 PM
Name                                   : RMS.cco.com
DisplayName                            : RMS.cco.com
HostComputer                           : RMS.cco.com
HostedHealthService                    : RMS.cco.com
HealthState                            : Success
PrincipalName                          : RMS.cco.com
NetworkName                            : RMS.cco.com
ComputerName                           : RMS
Domain                                 : CCO
IPAddress                              : 10.12.1.23
Version                                : 6.0.6278.0
RequestCompression                     : True
CommunicationPort                      : 5723
MaximumSizeOfAllTransferredFilesBytes  : 0
MaximumQueueSizeBytes                  : 104857600
ManuallyInstalled                      : False
InstallTime                            : 1/6/2008 10:46:25 PM
InstalledBy                            : CCO\administrator
CreateListener                         : False
AuthenticationName                     :
```

16

```
ActionAccountIdentity        : SYSTEM
HeartbeatInterval            : 60
ProxyingEnabled              : True
ManagementGroup              : CCO
ManagementGroupId            : 00000000-0000-0000-0000-000000000000
```

You can see some useful information such as the IPAddress, InstallTime, or if it was manually installed. For a large number of agents, you can find all manually installed agents in the management group using the following command:

```
get-agent -path "\" | where {$_.ManuallyInstalled}
```

This command would return agents from all management servers and filter it based on the ManuallyInstalled attribute being true.

install-agent

The install-agent cmdlet installs agents on computers to be managed. This command is useful for scripting the install of agents onto computers. The syntax for the cmdlet using get-help is shown in the following:

```
PS Monitoring:\om2.cco.com
>get-help install-agent
NAME
    Install-Agent
SYNOPSIS
    Installs agents.
SYNTAX
    Install-Agent [[-ManagementServer] [<ManagementServer>]][-Agent
ManagedComputer] <CustomMonitoringObject[]> [[-Inst
    allAgentConfiguration] [<InstallAgentConfiguration>]][[-Failover
Servers] [<ManagementServer[]>]] [-WhatIf] [-Confi
    rm] [<CommonParameters>]
DETAILED DESCRIPTION
    Installs agents on managed computers specified by the
AgentManagedComputer parameter.
RELATED LINKS
    Uninstall-Agent
    Start-Discovery
    Get-ManagementServer
    New-LdapQueryDiscoveryCriteria
    New-WindowsDiscoveryConfiguration
```

```
New-DeviceDiscoveryConfiguration
REMARKS
    For more information, type: "get-help Install-Agent -detailed".
    For technical information, type: "get-help Install-Agent -full".
```

The tricky part about the `install-agent` cmdlet is that before an agent can be installed on a computer to be managed, the computer must be discovered by the Operations Manager infrastructure. This requires a three-step process to install the agent, which is to configure the discovery of computers, to discover the computers, and to install the agent on the discovered computers. In the next set of examples, an agent is installed on a computer named webtest by its primary management server om2.cco.com.

The first step is to specify the computer to be discovered (that is, webtest) using the `new-WindowsDiscoveryConfiguration` cmdlet, as shown in the following command:

```
$windows_discovery_config = new-WindowsDiscoveryConfiguration '
    -ComputerName "webtest"
```

The results of the `new-WindowsDiscoveryConfiguration` cmdlet are stored in the `$windows_discovery_config` variable.

Using the results from the `new-WindowsDiscoveryConfiguration` enables the actual discovery of the webtest computer to be initiated with the `start-discovery` cmdlet. The command to do that is shown in the following:

```
$discovery_results = start-discovery -managementserver om2.cco.com '
    -windowsdiscoveryconfiguration $windows_discovery_config
```

The discovery results are stored in the `$discovery_results` variable to be used in the actual agent install. The `agent-install` cmdlet is used to initiate installation of the agent on the discovered computer webtest. The command is shown in the following:

```
Install-agent -managementserver om2.cco.com '
    -agentmanagedcomputer $discovery_results.custommonitoringobjects
```

The agent displays in the Operations Manager 2007 console as a managed computer.

uninstall-agent

The `uninstall-agent` cmdlet does the opposite of the `install-agent` cmdlet, which is to say it removes the agent from a managed computer. This would not be used to move a managed computer from one management server to another, which is done using the set-ManagementServer cmdlet and is covered later in the chapter. The uninstall-agent cmdlet is useful for automating the removal of agents from managed computers. The syntax for the cmdlet using get-help is shown in the following:

```
PS Monitoring:\om2.cco.com
>get-help uninstall-agent
NAME
    Uninstall-Agent
SYNOPSIS
    Uninstalls the Operations Manager agent from managed computers.
SYNTAX
    Uninstall-Agent [-AgentManagedComputer] <AgentManagedComputer[]>
[[-AgentConfiguration] [<UninstallAgentConfigurati
    on>]] [-WhatIf] [-Confirm] [<CommonParameters>]
DETAILED DESCRIPTION
    Uninstalls the Operations Manager agent from managed computers.
RELATED LINKS
    Install-Agent
    Uninstall-Agent
REMARKS
    For more information, type: "get-help Uninstall-Agent -detailed".
    For technical information, type: "get-help Uninstall-Agent -full".
```

The command requires the agent objects to be passed in as parameters, rather than the agent names. Fortunately, you can use the aforementioned get-agent cmdlet to get the agent object to pass into the uninstall-agent cmdlet. The commands to uninstall the agent from webtest.cco.com managed computer are shown in the following.

```
$agent = get-agent | where {$_.Name -eq "webtest.cco.com"}
uninstall-agent -AgentManagedComputer $agent
```

The agent will be gone in the Operations Manager 2007 Console as a managed computer.

Task Cmdlets

The task cmdlets are useful for running tasks automatically. This provides a way of triggering the task available in Operations Manager and returning the status of those tasks. This is a huge benefit, as it allows these tasks to be started from outside of the Operations Manager 2007 environment and facilitates integration with other platforms and systems.

get-Task

The get-Task cmdlet returns the tasks available in the management group. Given that there are potentially hundreds of tasks available in a given management group and more are added each time a management pack is installed, it is important to locate a specific task. The get-Task cmdlet makes this possible. The syntax for the cmdlet using get-help is shown in the following:

```
PS Monitoring:\om2.cco.com
>get-help get-Task
NAME
    Get-Task
SYNOPSIS
    Gets monitoring tasks.
SYNTAX
    Get-Task [[-Path] [<String[]>]] [[-Criteria] [<String>]]
[<CommonParameters>]
    Get-Task [-Id] <Guid> [[-Path] [<String[]>]] [<CommonParameters>]
    Get-Task [-MonitoringObject] <MonitoringObject> [[-Criteria]
[<String>]] [<CommonParameters>]
DETAILED DESCRIPTION
    Gets monitoring tasks.
RELATED LINKS
    Start-Task
REMARKS
    For more information, type: "get-help Get-Task -detailed".
    For technical information, type: "get-help Get-Task -full".
```

The work of the get-Task cmdlet is complicated by the architecture of Operations Manager. For example, if you wanted to run the IPConfig task against a specific computer in the Operations Console, you simply select the computer object and click on the IPConfig action. For this example, we select a Windows Server 2003 computer named rms.cco.com. The IPConfig task is listed under the Actions for the rms.cco.com computer. Mission accomplished.

To locate the IPConfig task, we use the get-Task cmdlet. The first thing to try is to run the get-Task with no parameters, as shown in the following:

```
get-Task
```

After a lot of scrolling, it becomes clear that this is not going to work as a way of locating a task. Given that there are hundreds of tasks, this list is far too long to search manually.

The next step is to use the where cmdlet to filter for the IPConfig task. The resulting command looks like this:

```
get-task | where {$_.DisplayName -eq "IPConfig"}
```

The list is much shorter, with only four task objects returned. However, we need to find the correct one to run against the rms.cco.com computer. The reason for the multiplicity of IPConfig tasks is that each one is associated with a different path, which is dependent on the operating system of the computer. The path can be seen in the name of the task object, as shown in the four paths listed here:

- Microsoft.Windows.Client.XP.Computer.IPConfig.Task

- Microsoft.Windows.Server.2000.Computer.IPConfig.Task

- Microsoft.Windows.Server.2003.Computer.IPConfig.Task

- Microsoft.Windows.Client.2000.Computer.IPConfig.Task

To return the correct task for the rms.cco.com computer, simply match the name to the operating system (Windows Server 2003) of the computer. The resulting command is:

```
get-task | where {$_.Name -eq "Microsoft.Windows.Server.2003.Computer.IPConfig.
Task"}
```

This command will return the appropriate task for the rms.cco.com server. This task object can now be used with the start-Task cmdlet to execute a task.

start-Task

The start-Task cmdlet starts an Operations Manager 2007 task. This enables an administrator to start a task programmatically and automate task execution. The syntax for the cmdlet using get-help is shown in the following:

```
PS Monitoring:\om2.cco.com
>get-help start-Task
NAME
    Start-Task
SYNOPSIS
    Starts a task.
SYNTAX
    Start-Task [-Task] <MonitoringTask> [[-Overrides] [<Hashtable>]]
[[-Credential] [<PSCredential>]] [[-Asynchronous]]
        [[-Path] [<String[]>]] [-WhatIf] [-Confirm] [<CommonParameters>]
```

```
    Start-Task [-Task] <MonitoringTask> [-TargetMonitoringObject]
<MonitoringObject> [[-Overrides] [<Hashtable>]]
    [[-Credential] [<PSCredential>]] [[-Asynchronous]] [-WhatIf]
[-Confirm] [<CommonParameters>]
DETAILED DESCRIPTION
    Starts a task.
RELATED LINKS
    Get-Task
    Get-TaskResult
REMARKS
    For more information, type: "get-help Start-Task -detailed".
    For technical information, type: "get-help Start-Task -full".
```

Leveraging the work from the previous section on the get-Task cmdlet, we know the command to return the IPConfig task object that targets the rms.cco.com Windows Server 2003 computer. The following commands capture that IPConfig task object and then use the start-Task cmdlet to start the task:

```
$tasktorun = get-task | where {$_.Name -eq
"Microsoft.Windows.Server.2003.Computer.IPConfig.Task"}
start-task -task $tasktorun -asynchronous '
    -path \om2.cco.com\Microsoft.Windows.Server.ComputerGroup\rms.cco.com
```

The task status can be reviewed in the Operations Console in the Monitoring section in the Task Status view. The task status includes the output of the task.

If you want to run the command on a single command line in PowerShell, you can also nest the get-Task cmdlet in parentheses to have it executed inline as shown in the following command:

```
start-task -task (get-task | where {$_.Name -eq '
    "Microsoft.Windows.Server.2003.Computer.IPConfig.Task"}) -asynchronous '
    -path \om2.cco.com\Microsoft.Windows.Server.ComputerGroup\rms.cco.com
```

get-TaskResult

Rather than use the Operations Console to check the results of a task, you can use the get-TaskResult cmdlet to get that status. This enables the results to be captured automatically and logged in line with the script. The syntax for the cmdlet using get-help is shown in the following:

```
PS Monitoring:\om2.cco.com
>get-help get-TaskResult

NAME
    Get-TaskResult
SYNOPSIS
    Gets monitoring task results.
SYNTAX
    Get-TaskResult [[-Criteria] [<String>]] [[-Path] [<String[]>]]
[<CommonParameters>]
    Get-TaskResult [-Id] <Guid> [[-Path] [<String[]>]]
[<CommonParameters>]
    Get-TaskResult [-BatchId] <Guid> [[-Path] [<String[]>]]
[<CommonParameters>]
DETAILED DESCRIPTION
    Gets monitoring task results.
RELATED LINKS
    Start-Task
REMARKS
    For more information, type: "get-help Get-TaskResult -detailed".
    For technical information, type: "get-help Get-TaskResult -full".
```

When the start-Task cmdlet is run, it returns the task result object. This can be captured to a variable and then used with the get-TaskResult cmdlet to check the results.

```
$taskresult = start-task -task (get-task | where {$_.Name -eq '
    "Microsoft.Windows.Server.2003.Computer.IPConfig.Task"}) -asynchronous '
    -path \om2.cco.com\Microsoft.Windows.Server.ComputerGroup\rms.cco.com
get-TaskResult $taskresult.ID
```

This shows the task results object, which includes the task status, who submitted it, the time started and finished, and the output of the task. You can select just the task status, Succeeded in this case, using the following simple change to the command using the select cmdlet:

```
$taskresult = start-task -task (get-task | where {$_.Name -eq '
    "Microsoft.Windows.Server.2003.Computer.IPConfig.Task"}) -asynchronous '
    -path \om2.cco.com\Microsoft.Windows.Server.ComputerGroup\rms.cco.com
get-TaskResult $taskresult.ID | select Status
```

Management Server Cmdlets

The management server cmdlets enable administrators to manage management servers and their settings. These cmdlets are useful for moving agents between management servers and configuring the failover management servers for agents.

get-ManagementServer

The get-ManagementServer returns management servers for the Operations Manager 2007 management group.

The syntax for the cmdlet using get-help is shown in the following:

```
PS Monitoring:\om2.cco.com
>get-help get-ManagementServer
NAME
    Get-ManagementServer
SYNOPSIS
    Gets management servers.
SYNTAX
    Get-ManagementServer [[-Path] [<String[]>]] [<CommonParameters>]
DETAILED DESCRIPTION
    Gets management servers for all connected management groups by
default. You can use the Path parameter to limit the
    set of management groups for which to retrieve management
servers. Specify the Root parameter to retrieve only the
    root management servers.
RELATED LINKS
    Set-ManagementServer
REMARKS
    For more information, type: "get-help Get-ManagementServer
-detailed".
    For technical information, type: "get-help Get-ManagementServer
-full".
```

By default, the get-ManagementServer cmdlet with no parameters returns all the management server objects in the management group. So, the command that follows returns all the management servers in the CCO management group:

```
get-ManagementServer
```

These results can be filtered to select a specific management server or set of management servers. For example, the command that follows would return just the object for the om2.cco.com management server:

```
get-ManagementServer | where {$_.DisplayName -eq "om2.cco.com"}
```

Finally, the command can also return the special case of the root management server for the management group. The command to return the root management server is:

```
get-ManagementServer | where {$_.IsRootManagementServer}
```

The help text incorrectly references a -root parameter for the get-ManagementServer cmdlet, which does not exist. The previous command will correctly return the root management server.

set-ManagementServer

The set-ManagementServer cmdlet enables an administrator to specify or change the primary and failover management servers for an agent or group of agents. The syntax for the cmdlet using get-help is shown in the following:

```
PS Monitoring:\om2.cco.com
>get-help set-ManagementServer
NAME
    Set-ManagementServer

SYNOPSIS
    Sets the management server of an agent.
SYNTAX
    Set-ManagementServer [-PrimaryManagementServer] <ManagementServer>
[-AgentManagedComputer]
        <AgentManagedComputer[]> [[-FailoverServer] [<ManagementServer[]>]]
[<CommonParameters>]
    Set-ManagementServer [-PrimaryManagementServer] <ManagementServer>
[-GatewayManagementServer]
        <ManagementServer[]> [[-FailoverServer] [<ManagementServer[]>]]
[<CommonParameters>]
DETAILED DESCRIPTION
    Sets the management server of an agent.
RELATED LINKS
    Get-ManagementServer
    Get-Agent
REMARKS
    For more information, type: "get-help Set-ManagementServer -detailed".
    For technical information, type: "get-help Set-ManagementServer
-full".
```

The cmdlet takes a management server and agent object, so pathnames will not work. The commands to get the agent object (rms.cco.com), get the management server object (om3.cco.com), and then set the primary management server on the agent are shown in the following:

```
$agent = get-agent | where {$_.DisplayName -eq "rms.cco.com"}
$managementserver = get-ManagementServer | where {$_.DisplayName -eq "om3.cco.com"}
set-ManagementServer –AgentManagedComputer $agent –PrimaryManagementServer
$managementserver
```

The –AgentManagedComputer parameter can take multiple objects, so a single command can change the primary management server for a number of objects at once.

Another common task is setting the failover management server for agents. By default, the agents randomly select a management server to fail over to if they cannot connect to their primary management server. In many organizations, there may be a designated failover management server. However, the UI does not have an option to set this. The set-ManagementServer cmdlet enables administrators to set this using the following command:

```
$agent = get-agent | where {$_.DisplayName -eq "rms.cco.com"}
$failovermanagementserver = get-ManagementServer | where {$_.DisplayName -eq
"om4.cco.com"}
set-ManagementServer –AgentManagedComputer $agent –FailoverServer
$failovermanagementserver
```

In the case of the previous code, the commands set the failover management server on the rms.cco.com agent managed computer to om4.cco.com. Multiple management server objects can be passed in the $failovermanagementserver variable, allowing there to be multiple failover management servers specified.

get-DefaultSetting

The get-DefaultSetting cmdlet returns the settings for the management group. These are the settings that are exposed in the Operations Console, in the Administration section under the Settings folder. The cmdlet enables the settings to be queried programmatically. The syntax for the cmdlet using get-help is shown here:

```
PS Monitoring:\om2.cco.com
>get-help get-DefaultSetting
NAME
    Get-DefaultSetting
```

```
SYNOPSIS
    Gets the default settings for a management group.
SYNTAX
    Get-DefaultSetting [[-Path] [<String[]>]] [<CommonParameters>]
DETAILED DESCRIPTION
    Gets the default  settings for a management group.
RELATED LINKS
    Set-DefaultSetting
REMARKS
    For more information, type: "get-help Get-DefaultSetting -detailed".
    For technical information, type: "get-help Get-DefaultSetting -full".
```

The command returns the name of the path to the setting and its current value. To return all 49 settings, execute the following command:

```
get-DefaultSetting
```

To return just a single value, use the where cmdlet to filter the objects returned. The following commands return the agent heartbeats interval:

```
get-defaultsetting | where {$_.Name -eq "Agent\Heartbeats\Interval"}
```

The default Settings Paths section in this chapter has tables with the complete listing of all paths.

set-DefaultSetting

The set-DefaultSetting cmdlet sets the default settings for the management group. These are the settings that are exposed in the SCOM Operations Console, in the Administration section under the Settings folder. The cmdlet enables the settings to be changed programmatically, rather than relying on the graphical user interface. The syntax for the cmdlet using get-help is shown here:

```
PS Monitoring:\om2.cco.com
>get-help set-DefaultSetting
NAME
    Set-DefaultSetting
SYNOPSIS
    Sets default settings.
```

```
SYNTAX
    Set-DefaultSetting [-Name] <String> [-Value] <String> [[-Path]
[<String[]>]] [-WhatIf] [-Confirm]
    [<CommonParameters>]
    Set-DefaultSetting [-Setting] <DefaultSettingBase[]> [[-Path]
[<String[]>]] [-WhatIf] [-Confirm]
    [<CommonParameters>]
DETAILED DESCRIPTION
    Sets default settings.
RELATED LINKS
    Get-DefaultSetting
REMARKS
    For more information, type: "get-help Set-DefaultSetting -detailed".
    For technical information, type: "get-help Set-DefaultSetting -full".
```

The set-DefaultSetting cmdlet requires that you know the setting that you want to change. These can be listed using the get-DefaultSetting cmdlet or in the next section that contains a complete list of all the paths.

For example, to change the number of days to keep task status to 14 days, execute the following command:

```
set-defaultsetting -Name
"ManagementGroup\PartitioningAndGroomingSettings\JobStatusDaysToKeep" '
    -Value 14
```

The setting can be viewed in the Operations Console by selecting the Administration section, the Settings folder, and then by opening the Database Grooming and looking at the Task history setting.

> **NOTE**
>
> If you have the Operations Console open, you may need to close and reopen the console to see the changes. The console has a local cache that can cause changes to seem delayed. This is a known problem with the console, but the settings are in effect as soon as the set-DefaultSetting command is completed.

Default Setting Paths

The paths for the 49 default settings are listed in this section. They are used with the get-DefaultSetting and the set-DefaultSetting cmdlets. See the sections on those cmdlets for information on how to use these paths.

Listing 16.1 lists a set of miscellaneous paths that address the default settings for the agents and the management group.

LISTING 16.1   Miscellaneous Default Setting Paths

```
HealthService\ProxyingEnabled
Agent\Heartbeats\Interval
NotificationServer\WebAddresses\WebConsole
ManagementGroup\AlertResolution\AlertAutoResolveDays
ManagementGroup\AlertResolution\HealthyAlertAutoResolveDays
ManagementGroup\CustomerExperienceImprovementProgramEnabled
ManagementGroup\SendOperationalDataReports
ManagementGroup\ErrorReporting\SendErrorReports
ManagementGroup\ErrorReporting\QueueErrorReports
ManagementGroup\WebAddresses\OnlineProductKnowledge
```

Listing 16.2 lists the paths for the default settings on management servers. These do not affect the settings on existing management servers, but change what the default settings would be for new management servers.

LISTING 16.2   Management Server Default Setting Paths

```
ManagementServer\AutoApproveManuallyInstalledAgents
ManagementServer\RejectManuallyInstalledAgents
ManagementServer\MissingHeartbeatThreshold
ManagementServer\ProxyAddress
ManagementServer\ProxyPort
ManagementServer\UseProxyServer
```

Listing 16.3 shows the paths that affect the settings for the data warehouse.

LISTING 16.3   Data Warehouse Default Setting Paths

```
ManagementGroup\DataWarehouse\DataWarehouseDatabaseName
ManagementGroup\DataWarehouse\DataWarehouseServerName
ManagementGroup\DataWarehouse\ReportingServerUrl
```

Listing 16.4 lists the client monitoring default settings paths.

LISTING 16.4   Client Monitoring Default Setting Paths

```
ManagementGroup\ClientMonitoringSettings\MaxNumberOfCabsToCollect
ManagementGroup\ClientMonitoringSettings\ErrorTransmissionFilters
ManagementGroup\ClientMonitoringSettings\ExceptionFolders
ManagementGroup\ClientMonitoringSettings\PublishMicrosoftSolutionLinks
ManagementGroup\ClientMonitoringSettings\PublishMicrosoftSurveyLinks
```

LISTING 16.4   Continued

```
ManagementGroup\ClientMonitoringSettings\PublishMicrosoftDataCollectionRequests
ManagementGroup\ClientMonitoringSettings\PublishMicrosoftFileCollectionRequests
ManagementGroup\ClientMonitoringSettings\PublishMicrosoftRegistryCollectionRequests
ManagementGroup\ClientMonitoringSettings\PublishMicrosoftWMIQueryRequests
ManagementGroup\ClientMonitoringSettings\PublishMicrosoftMemoryDumpRequests
ManagementGroup\ClientMonitoringSettings\PolicyResponseUrl
```

Listing 16.5 lists the paths to the custom alert fields. These are populated into alerts if specified.

LISTING 16.5   Alert Custom Field Default Setting Paths

```
ManagementGroup\AlertCustomFieldSettings\CustomField1
ManagementGroup\AlertCustomFieldSettings\CustomField2
ManagementGroup\AlertCustomFieldSettings\CustomField3
ManagementGroup\AlertCustomFieldSettings\CustomField4
ManagementGroup\AlertCustomFieldSettings\CustomField5
ManagementGroup\AlertCustomFieldSettings\CustomField6
ManagementGroup\AlertCustomFieldSettings\CustomField7
ManagementGroup\AlertCustomFieldSettings\CustomField8
ManagementGroup\AlertCustomFieldSettings\CustomField9
ManagementGroup\AlertCustomFieldSettings\CustomField10
```

The grooming settings paths are listed in Listing 16.6. These set the retention times for the data in the Operations database.

LISTING 16.6   Grooming Default Setting Paths

```
ManagementGroup\PartitioningAndGroomingSettings\EventDaysToKeep
ManagementGroup\PartitioningAndGroomingSettings\PerformanceDataDaysToKeep
ManagementGroup\PartitioningAndGroomingSettings\AlertDaysToKeep
ManagementGroup\PartitioningAndGroomingSettings\StateChangeEventDaysToKeep
ManagementGroup\PartitioningAndGroomingSettings\MaintenanceModeHistoryDaysToKeep
ManagementGroup\PartitioningAndGroomingSettings\AvailabilityHistoryDaysToKeep
ManagementGroup\PartitioningAndGroomingSettings\JobStatusDaysToKeep
ManagementGroup\PartitioningAndGroomingSettings\MonitoringJobDaysToKeep
ManagementGroup\PartitioningAndGroomingSettings\PerformanceSignatureDaysToKeep
```

16

Maintenance Mode Cmdlets

Maintenance mode is one of the favorite targets of Operations Manager 2007 automation. Maintenance mode prevents the object or objects from generating alerts or notifications. This set of cmdlets enables an administrator to automate the setting of maintenance mode windows for objects. The PowerShell maintenance cmdlets enable administrators to integrate the setting of Operations Manager maintenance windows with other automated tasks being run.

The new-MaintenanceWindow and set-MaintenanceWindow cmdlets accept only specific reason codes. These are displayed differently than in the Operations Manager Console, though they represent the same values. Table 16.1 shows the planned and unplanned reason codes.

TABLE 16.1   Maintenance Window Reason Codes

Planned Reason Codes	Unplanned Reason Codes
PlannedOther	UnplannedOther
PlannedHardwareMaintenance	UnplannedHardwareMaintenance
PlannedHardwareInstallation	UnplannedHardwareInstallation
PlannedOperatingSystemReconfiguration	UnplannedOperatingSystem Reconfiguration
PlannedApplicationMaintenance	ApplicationUnresponsive
ApplicationInstallation	ApplicationUnstable
SecurityIssue	LossOfNetworkConnectivity

new-MaintenanceWindow

The new-MaintenanceWindow cmdlet puts an object or objects into maintenance mode, creating a new maintenance mode window. The new-MaintenanceWindow cmdlet is useful for automating the placement of an object into maintenance mode. The syntax for the cmdlet using get-help is shown here:

```
PS Monitoring:\om2.cco.com
>get-help new-MaintenanceWindow
NAME
    New-MaintenanceWindow
SYNOPSIS
    Puts the specified monitoring object into maintenance mode.
SYNTAX
    New-MaintenanceWindow [-StartTime] <DateTime> [-EndTime] <DateTime>
[[-Reason] [<MaintenanceModeReason>]]
    [-Comment] <String> [[-Path] [<String[]>]] [-WhatIf] [-Confirm]
[<CommonParameters>]
    New-MaintenanceWindow [-StartTime] <DateTime> [-EndTime] <DateTime>
[[-Reason] [<MaintenanceModeReason>]]
```

```
    [-Comment] <String> [-MonitoringObject] <MonitoringObject>
[-WhatIf] [-Confirm] [<CommonParameters>]
DETAILED DESCRIPTION
    Puts the specified monitoring object into maintenance mode.
RELATED LINKS
    Set-MaintenanceWindow
    Get-MaintenanceWindow
REMARKS
    For more information, type: "get-help New-MaintenanceWindow -detailed".
    For technical information, type: "get-help New-MaintenanceWindow -full".
```

The new-MaintenanceWindow cmdlet accepts either a monitoring object or path to the object. A sample command to put the rms.cco.com Windows Server Computer object into maintenance mode for two hours is shown in the following:

```
new-MaintenanceWindow –StartTime ([DateTime]::Now) '
    –EndTime ([DateTime]::Now.AddHours(2)) '
    –Comment "Updates to the software." '
    –Reason ApplicationInstallation '
    –Path \om2.cco.com\Microsoft.Windows.Server.ComputerGroup\rms.cco.com
```

The start time for the window is now, will last for two hours, and the reason is a planned application installation. The full path to rms.cco.com object is specified. After executing this command, the rms.cco.com computer would go into maintenance mode and exit automatically after two hours have passed.

If you get the health state of the object in maintenance mode, you will find that it shows as Uninitialized. For example:

```
dir Microsoft.Windows.Server.ComputerGroup | where {$_.DisplayName -eq
"rms.cco.com"}
```

This returns the rms.cco.com computer object and shows the health state as Uninitialized.

get-MaintenanceWindow

The get-MaintenanceWindow returns the parameters of an existing or historical maintenance mode window. The get-MaintenanceWindow cmdlet is useful for automating the querying of the object in maintenance mode or reviewing the history. The syntax for the cmdlet using get-help is shown here:

16

```
PS Monitoring:\om2.cco.com
>get-help get-MaintenanceWindow
NAME
    Get-MaintenanceWindow
SYNOPSIS
    Gets maintenance window information.
SYNTAX
    Get-MaintenanceWindow [[-History]] [[-Path] [<String[]>]]
[<CommonParameters>]
    Get-MaintenanceWindow [-MonitoringObject] <MonitoringObject> [[-History]]
[<CommonParameters>]
DETAILED DESCRIPTION
    Gets maintenance window information for a monitoring object that is
currently in maintenance mode. The cmdlet can r
    etrieve maintenance windows for top-level items, items at the current
location or for specified monitoring objects.
RELATED LINKS
    Set-MaintenanceWindow
    New-MaintenanceWindow
REMARKS
    For more information, type: "get-help Get-MaintenanceWindow -detailed".
    For technical information, type: "get-help Get-MaintenanceWindow -full".
```

The command is straightforward to run. To get the information on the maintenance window for the rms.cco.com, the following command can be used:

```
PS Monitoring:\om2.cco.com
>get-maintenancewindow -path
\om2.cco.com\Microsoft.Windows.Server.ComputerGroup\rms.cco.com
MonitoringObjectId      : 3117612d-af1e-adb0-22fe-6bea70d82b70
StartTime               : 4/20/2008 10:54:33 PM
ScheduledEndTime        : 4/21/2008 12:54:33 AM
EndTime                 :
Reason                  : ApplicationInstallation
Comments                : Updates to the software.
User                    : CCO\administrator
LastModified            : 4/20/2008 10:54:38 PM
ManagementGroup         : CCO
ManagementGroupId       : 5ba16cb4-a63d-031c-89cb-5864892d38c6
```

This command shows the status of the maintenance mode window for the object, including the user who placed the object in maintenance mode.

If the object is not in maintenance mode, then the command generates an error. However, the maintenance mode history can be returned by adding the `-history` parameter to the command. The resulting command is shown in the following:

```
get-maintenancewindow -path
\om2.cco.com\Microsoft.Windows.Server.ComputerGroup\rms.cco.com -history
```

set-MaintenanceWindow

Sometimes it is necessary to extend or modify the maintenance mode window, which is where the `set-MaintenceWindow` cmdlet comes into play. The syntax for the cmdlet using `get-help` is shown in the following:

```
PS Monitoring:\om2.cco.com
>get-help set-MaintenanceWindow
NAME
    Set-MaintenanceWindow
SYNOPSIS
    Sets properties of a maintenance window.
SYNTAX
    Set-MaintenanceWindow [-EndTime] <DateTime> [[-Reason]
[<MaintenanceModeReason>]] [[-Comment] [<String>]] [[-Path]
    [<String[]>]] [-WhatIf] [-Confirm] [<CommonParameters>]
    Set-MaintenanceWindow [-EndTime] <DateTime> [[-Reason]
[<MaintenanceModeReason>]] [[-Comment] [<String>]] [-Monito
    ringObject] <MonitoringObject> [-WhatIf] [-Confirm] [<CommonParameters>]
DETAILED DESCRIPTION
    Sets properties of a maintenance window. It can be used to update end time,
reason and comments on the current main
    tenance mode for the monitoring object specified by the MonitoringObject or
Path parameters.
RELATED LINKS
    New-MaintenanceWindow
    Get-MaintenanceWindow
REMARKS
    For more information, type: "get-help Set-MaintenanceWindow -detailed".
    For technical information, type: "get-help Set-MaintenanceWindow -full".
```

The cmdlet enables an administrator to adjust some of the parameters of the maintenance window, including the end time, the reason, and the comment.

16

```
set-MaintenanceWindow -EndTime ([DateTime]::Now.AddMinutes(1)) '
    -Path \om2.cco.com\Microsoft.Windows.Server.ComputerGroup\rms.cco.com
```

The command sets the maintenance window to end one minute from now. The end time cannot be set to now, as the system interprets that as occurring in the past and generates an error. Unfortunately, the start time cannot be adjusted even if it is in the future.

> **NOTE**
>
> The set-MaintenanceWindow cmdlet with the -EndTime ([DateTime]::Now.
> AddMinutes(1)) parameter is useful for closing out the maintenance mode window
> after all IT tasks have wrapped up early. For example, maybe a planned maintenance
> window was scheduled to last four hours for patching. However, patching completes in
> one hour. The cmdlet can be used to close all the maintenance mode windows and put
> the object back into management at the time the patching is complete rather than wait
> for the window to expire.

Comprehensive Operations Manager Cmdlet List

It is difficult to get a complete listing of all the Operations Manager cmdlets and what they do. Microsoft does not list this information on its Web site, and there are few other resources on Operations Manager 2007 and PowerShell. To help address that gap, this section gives a comprehensive alphabetical listing of all the Operations Manager 2007 cmdlets.

Some of the cmdlets are explored in this chapter. For the others, get-help cmdlet provides a wealth of information.

Get/Set Cmdlets

Table 16.2 lists the get and set verb cmdlets that are available in the Operations Manager 2007 command shell.

TABLE 16.2   Operations Manager Get/Set Cmdlets

Cmdlet	Description
Get-Agent	Gets the agents associated with the specified management server.
Get-AgentPendingAction	Gets agent-pending actions.
Get-Alert	Gets the specified alerts.
Get-AlertDestination	Gets the connector to which the alert is forwarded.
Get-AlertHistory	Gets the history for the specified alerts.
Get-Connector	Gets the connectors for a management group.
Get-DefaultSetting	Gets the default settings for a management group.
Get-Diagnostic	Returns the available diagnostics.

TABLE 16.2   Continued

Cmdlet	Description
Get-Discovery	Returns available discoveries.
Get-Event	Gets events.
Get-FailoverManagementServer	Returns the failover management servers.
Get-GatewayManagementServer	Returns the gateway management servers.
Get-MaintenanceWindow	Gets maintenance window information.
Get-ManagementGroupConnection	Gets all open Management Group connections.
Get-ManagementPack	Gets imported management packs.
Get-ManagementServer	Gets management servers.
Get-Monitor	Gets management pack monitors.
Get-MonitorHierarchy	Retrieves the hierarchy of monitors for a particular monitoring object.
Get-MonitoringClass	Gets monitoring classes.
Get-MonitoringClassProperty	Gets the properties of a specified monitoring class.
Get-MonitoringObject	Gets monitoring objects.
Get-MonitoringObjectGroup	Returns the list of monitoring object groups.
Get-MonitoringObjectPath	Gets the path to a monitoring object.
Get-MonitoringObjectProperty	Gets properties and associated values of monitoring objects.
Get-NotificationAction	Gets notification actions.
Get-NotificationEndpoint	Gets notification end points.
Get-NotificationRecipient	Gets notification recipients.
Get-NotificationSubscription	Gets notification subscriptions.
Get-OperationsManagerCommand	Returns all cmdlets that are provided by Operations Manager.
Get-Override	Gets management pack overrides.
Get-PerformanceCounter	Gets performance counters.
Get-PerformanceCounterValue	Gets data associated with a specified performance counter.
Get-PrimaryManagementServer	Returns the primary management server.
Get-Recovery	Returns available recovery objects.
Get-RelationshipClass	Gets monitoring relationship classes.
Get-RelationshipObject	Gets monitoring relationship objects.
Get-RemotelyManagedComputer	Gets remotely managed computers.
Get-RemotelyManagedDevice	Gets remotely managed devices.
Get-ResultantCategoryOverride	Gets resultant category overrides.
Get-ResultantRuleOverride	Gets resultant rule overrides.
Get-ResultantUnitMonitorOverride	Gets resultant monitor overrides.
Get-RootManagementServer	Returns the root management server.
Get-Rule	Gets monitoring rules.

16

TABLE 16.2   Continued

Cmdlet	Description
Get-RunAsAccount	Gets run as accounts.
Get-State	Gets the monitoring state for specified monitoring objects.
Get-Task	Gets monitoring tasks.
Get-TaskResult	Gets monitoring task results.
Get-Tier	Gets tiered management groups.
Get-UserRole	Gets user roles.
Set-AlertDestination	Sets the Operations Manager Connector Framework connector to which the specified alert will be forwarded.
Set-DefaultSetting	Sets default settings.
Set-MaintenanceWindow	Sets properties of a maintenance window.
Set-ManagementServer	Sets the management server of an agent.
Set-ProxyAgent	Sets the proxy agent for a remotely managed computer or device.

Add/Remove Cmdlets

Table 16.3 lists the add and remove verb cmdlets that are available in the Operations Manager 2007 command shell.

TABLE 16.3   Operations Manager Add/Remove Cmdlets

Cmdlet	Description
Add-ConnectorToTier	Configures an Operations Manager Connector Framework connector for a specified tier.
Add-RemotelyManagedComputer	Adds a remotely-managed computer to an agent.
Add-RemotelyManagedDevice	Adds a remotely managed device to an agent.
Add-UserToUserRole	Adds the specified user to an Operations Manager role.
Remove-ConnectorFromTier	Removes an Operations Manager Connector Framework connector from a specified tier.
Remove-DisabledMonitoringObject	Removes all monitoring objects for which discovery is disabled.
Remove-ManagementGroup	Removes a connection to a Connection management group.
Remove-RemotelyManaged	Removes a remotely managed Computer computer from an agent.
Remove-RemotelyManagedDevice	Removes a remotely managed device from an agent.
Remove-Tier	Removes a tier.

Enable/Disable Cmdlets

Table 16.4 lists the enable and disable verb cmdlets that are available in the Operations Manager 2007 command shell.

TABLE 16.4   Operations Manager Enable/Disable Cmdlets

Cmdlet	Description
Disable-NotificationSubscription	Disables a notification subscription.
Disable-Rule	Disables a rule.
Enable-NotificationSubscription	Enables a notification subscription.
Enable-Rule	Enables a rule.

Install/Uninstall Cmdlets

Table 16.5 lists the install and uninstall verb cmdlets that are available in the Operations Manager 2007 command shell.

TABLE 16.5   Operations Manager Install/Uninstall Cmdlets

Cmdlet	Description
Install-Agent	Installs agents.
Install-AgentByName	Installs an Operations Manager agent on the specified computer.
Install-ManagementPack	Installs a management pack.
Uninstall-Agent	Uninstalls the Operations Manager agent from managed computers.
Uninstall-ManagementPack	Uninstalls a management pack.

Various Cmdlets

Table 16.6 lists various cmdlets that are available in the Operations Manager 2007 command shell that are not listed in other sections.

TABLE 16.6   Operations Manager Various Cmdlets

Cmdlet	Description
Approve-AgentPendingAction	Approves the specified agent pending action.
Export-ManagementPack	Exports a management pack to a file.
New-CustomMonitoringObject	Creates a custom monitoring object.
New-DeviceDiscoveryConfiguration	Creates an object that represents settings to use to discover devices.
New-LdapQueryDiscoveryCriteria	Creates a new LdapQueryDiscoveryCriteria object used to discover computers.
New-MaintenanceWindow	Puts the specified monitoring object into maintenance mode.

16

TABLE 16.6   Continued

Cmdlet	Description
New-ManagementGroupConnection	Creates a new connection to a management group or tiered management group.
New-MonitoringPropertyValuePair	Creates a new monitoring property-value pair object.
New-Tier	Creates a new tier connection.
New-WindowsDiscoveryConfiguration	Creates an object that describes computers to discover.
Reject-AgentPendingAction	Rejects the specified agent pending action.
Resolve-Alert	Resolves an alert.
Start-Discovery	Starts a discovery task for discovering devices or computers.
Start-Task	Starts a task.

Summary

The Operations Manager PowerShell integration brings the scripting capabilities of the product to a whole new level. The PowerShell integration in Operations Manager 2007 in the command shell enables administrators to automate all Operations Manager 2007 administration tasks, from installing agents to changing management servers, to executing tasks, and to setting the maintenance windows for objects.

The command shell is a powerful new tool in the arsenal of the Operations Manager 2007 administrator.

## CHAPTER 17

PowerShell 2.0 Features

In previous chapters of this book, aspects of PowerShell 2.0 were explored along with topics about PowerShell 1.0. A number of new features were not touched upon in the earlier chapters, nor was a chapter solely dedicated to just a PowerShell 2.0 feature. Additionally, an attempt was made to keep PowerShell 2.0 clearly labeled and identified.

The reason behind this separation is because at the time of writing this book, PowerShell 2.0 was still a Community Technology Preview (CTP). A CTP version of software is considered pre-beta, which means that features and functionality are still not fully defined, fully functional, and in some cases, they are fully documented. The purpose of this chapter is to discuss the PowerShell 2.0 features that where either not discussed or briefly touched on earlier chapters. As part of the discussion, effort has been made to provide as much information as possible. However, in some cases, because of the possible volatility of a feature, missing documentation, or limited usage scenarios, the details about a feature may have been shortened or not discussed.

Why was this done? As mentioned, PowerShell 2.0 is still a CTP version. It can't be stressed enough that there will be changes from the CTP version to the RTM version of PowerShell 2.0. However, regardless of its current state, PowerShell 2.0 is a giant step forward for PowerShell. A number of the new features are powerful and should be discussed because of the benefits they might provide current PowerShell users. The most important of these new features is called *remoting*, which is discussed in the next section.

Remoting

In PowerShell 1.0, a major disadvantage is the lack of an interface to execute commands on a remote machine. You can use Windows Management Instrumentation (WMI) to accomplish this, but the allure of a native-based "remoting" interface was sorely missing when PowerShell was first released. In fact, the lack of remote command execution was a glaring lack of functionality that needed to be addressed. Naturally, the PowerShell product team took this functionality limitation to heart and addressed it by introducing a new feature in PowerShell 2.0: "remoting."

> **NOTE**
>
> For the sake of conformity, a command in this chapter is a summary, a cmdlet, expression, script, and so on. In other words, a command is something that can be executed.

Remoting, as its name suggests, is a new feature that is designed to facilitate command (or script) execution on remote machines. This could mean execution of a command or commands on one remote machine or thousands of remote machines (provided you have the infrastructure to support this). Additionally, commands can be issued synchronously or asynchronously, one at time or through a persistent connection called a *runspace*, and even scheduled or throttled.

To use remoting, you must have the appropriate permissions to connect to a remote machine, execute PowerShell, and execute the desired command(s). In addition, the remote machine must have PowerShell 2.0 and Windows Remote Management (WSMAN) installed, and PowerShell must be configured for remoting.

> **NOTE**
>
> At the time this chapter was written, PowerShell remoting was supported only with WSMAN 2.0 CTP2 and on Windows Vista SP1 to Windows Server 2008 machines.

Additionally, when using remoting, the remote PowerShell session that is used to execute commands determines the execution environment. Therefore, the commands you attempt to execute are subject to a remote machine's execution policies, profiles, and preferences.

> **WARNING**
>
> Commands that are executed against a remote machine do not have access to information defined in your local profile. Commands that use a function or alias defined on your local machine will fail unless they are defined on the remote machine as well.

Understanding Remoting

In its most basic form, PowerShell remoting works using the following conversation flow between "a client" (most likely the machine with your PowerShell session) and "a server" (remote host) that you want to execute command(s) against:

1. A command is executed on the client.

2. That command is transmitted to the server.

3. The server executes the command and then returns the output to the client.

4. The client displays or uses the returned output.

At a deeper level, PowerShell remoting is dependent on WSMAN for facilitating the command and output exchange between a "client" and "server." WSMAN, which is a component of Windows Hardware Management, is a Web-based service that enables Administrators to enumerate information on and manipulate remote machines. To handle remote sessions, WSMAN is built around a SOAP-based standards protocol called WS-Management. This protocol is firewall-friendly and primarily developed for the exchange of management information between systems that may be based on a variety of operating systems on various hardware platforms.

When PowerShell uses WSMAN to ship commands and output between a client and server, that exchange is done using a series of XML messages. The first XML message that is exchanged is a request to the server, which contains the desired command to be executed. This message is submitted to the server using the SOAP protocol. The server, in return, executes the command using a new instance of PowerShell called a runspace. After execution of the command is complete, the output from the command is returned to the requesting client as the second XML message. This second message, like the first, is also communicated using the SOAP protocol.

> **NOTE**
>
> By default, `Configure-WSMan.ps1` script configures WSMAN to operate over port 80. However, that doesn't mean traffic is unencrypted. In this mode, WSMAN will accept only a connection encrypted using Negotiate or Kerberos SSP.

This translation into an XML message is performed because you cannot ship "live" .NET objects (how PowerShell relates to programs or system components) across the network. So, to perform the transmission, objects are serialized into a series of XML (CliXML) data elements. When the server or client receives the transmission, it converts the received XML message into a deserialized object type. The resulting object is no longer "live." Instead, it is a record of properties based on a point in time, and it no longer possesses any methods.

17

Executing Commands on a Remote Machine

The Universal Code Execution Model is a theme (or set of features) that was introduced in PowerShell 2.0. This model is defined so that any command, expression, and ScriptBlock is executable:

▶ In the foreground or background.

▶ On one or more machines.

▶ Over any network connection (LAN or a WAN).

▶ Within unrestricted or restricted environments.

▶ Over short or long connections.

▶ Using impersonation or supplied credentials.

▶ Initiated by user input or by events.

Needless to say, remoting is an aspect of this model in that it meets many, if not all, of these definitions. However, at its core, remoting is a feature that enables commands to be executed on a single machine or many machines.

When using remoting, there are three different modes that can be used to execute commands. These modes are as follows:

▶ **1 to 1**—Referred to as the "Interactive" mode, this mode enables you to remotely manage a machine in much the same way you would an SSH session.

▶ **Many to 1**—Referred to as the "Fan-In" mode, this mode enables multiple administrators to manage a single host using an interactive session.

▶ **1 to Many**—Referred to as the "Fan-Out" mode, this mode enables a command to execute across a large number of machines.

More information about each mode is provided in the following sections.

Interactive Remoting

With interactive remoting, the PowerShell session you execute commands in looks and feels much like an SSH session, as shown in Figure 17.1. The key to achieving this mode of remoting is a PowerShell feature called a runspace. Runspaces, by definition, are instances of the System.Management.Automation class, which defines the PowerShell session and its host program (Windows PowerShell host, cmd.exe, and so on). In other words, a runspace is an execution environment in which PowerShell runs.

Not widely discussed in Powershell 1.0, runspaces in PowerShell 2.0 are the method by which commands are executed on local and remote machines. When a runspace is created, it resides in the global scope and it is an environment to itself that includes its own properties, execution polices, and profiles. This environment persists for the lifetime of the runspace, regardless of the volatility of the host machine's environment.

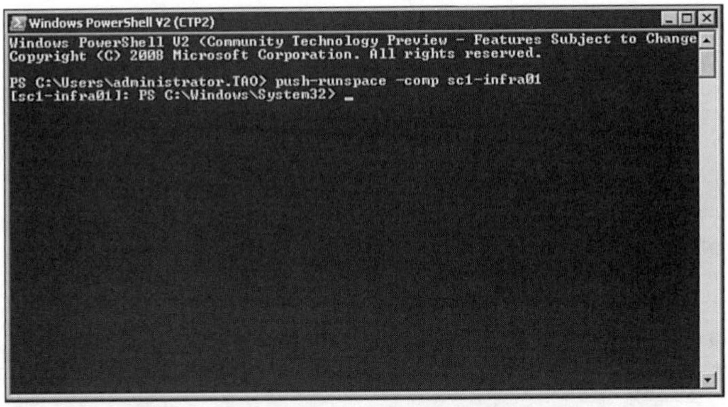

FIGURE 17.1   Interactive remote PowerShell session

Being tied to the host program that created it, a runspace ceases to exist when the host program is closed. When this happens, all aspects of the runspace are gone, and you can no longer retrieve or use the runspace. However, when created on a remote machine, a runspace can remain until it is stopped.

To create a runspace on a machine, there are two cmdlets that can be used. The Push-Runspace cmdlet is used to create an interactive PowerShell session. This is the cmdlet that was shown in Figure 17.1. When this cmdlet is used against a remote machine, a new runspace (PowerShell process) is created and a connection is established from the local machine to the runspace on the remote computer. If executed against the local machine, a new runspace (PowerShell process) is created and connection is established back to a local machine. To close the interactive session, you use the Pop-Runspace cmdlet or the quit alias.

Fan-In Remoting

Fan-In remoting is named in reference to the abilities of multiple administrators to open their own runspaces at the same time. In other words, many administrators can "fan in" from many machines into a single machine. When connected, each administrator is then limited to the scope of his own runspace. This partitioning of access can be achieved thanks to the new PowerShell 2.0 security model that enables the creation of restricted shells and cmdlets.

The steps needed to fully utilize the new security model require some software development using the .NET Framework. The ability to provide secure partitioned remote management access on a single host to a number of different administrators is a powerful feature. Usage can range from a Web-hosting company that wants to partition remote management access to each customer for each of its Web sites to internal IT departments that want to consolidate their management consoles on a single server.

Fan-Out Remoting

Fan-Out remoting is named in reference to the ability to issue commands to a number of remote machines at one time. When using this method or remoting, command(s) are issued on your machine. These commands then "fan out" and are executed on each of the remote machines that have been specified. The results from each remote machine are then returned to your machine in the form an object, which you can then work with or review.

Ironically enough, PowerShell has always supported the concept of Fan-Out remoting. In PowerShell 1.0, Fan-Out remoting was achieved using WMI. For example, you could always import a list of machine names and then use WMI to remotely manage those machines:

```
[PS] C:\> import-csv machineList.csv | foreach {Get-WmiObject
Win32_NetworkAdapterConfiguration -computer $_.MachineName}
```

Although the ability to perform Fan-Out remoting in PowerShell 1.0 using WMI is a powerful feature, this form of remoting suffers in usability because it is synchronous in nature. In other words, after a command has been issued, it is executed on each remote machine one at a time. Although this happens, further command execution has to wait until the command issued has finished being executed on all of the specified remote machines.

Attempting to synchronously manage a large number of remote machines can prove to be a challenging task. To address this challenge in PowerShell 2.0, the product team tweaked the remoting experience so that Fan-Out remoting could be done asynchronously. With these changes, you can still perform remote WMI management as shown in the previous example; however, you can also asynchronously execute remote commands using the following methods:

▶ Executing the command as a background job

▶ Using the Invoke-Command cmdlet

▶ Using the Invoke-Command cmdlet with a reusable runspace

The first method, a background job, as its name might suggest, enables commands to be executed in the background. This is not truly asynchronously, but a command that is executed as a background job allows you to continue executing additional commands while the job is being completed. For example, to run the previously shown WMI example as a background job, you simply add the AsJob parameter for the Get-WmiObject cmdlet, as shown in the following:

```
[PS] C:\> import-csv machineList.csv | foreach {Get-WmiObject
Win32_NetworkAdapterConfiguration -computer $_.MachineName -asjob}
```

With the AsJob parameter (new in PowerShell 2.0) being used, each time the Get-WmiObject cmdet is called in the foreach loop, a new background job is created to complete execution of the cmdlet. More details about background jobs are provided later in this chapter; this example shows how background jobs can be used to achieve asynchronous remote command execution when using WMI.

The second method to asynchronously execute remote commands is to use the new cmdlet called Invoke-Command. This cmdlet is new in PowerShell 2.0 and it enables you to execute commands both locally and remotely on machines. Unlike WMI, which uses remote procedure call (RPC) connections to remotely manage machines, the Invoke-Command cmdlet utilizes WSMAN to push the commands out to each of the specified "targets" in an asynchronous manner.

To use the cmdlet, there are two primary parameters that need to be defined. The first parameter, ScriptBlock, is used to specify a scriptblock that contains the command to be executed. The second parameter, ComputerName (NetBIOS name or IP address), is used to specify the machine or machines to execute the command that is defined in the script-block. For example:

```
[PS] C:\> invoke-command -scriptblock {get-process} -computer
sc1-infra01,sc1-infra02
```

> **NOTE**
>
> You can specify a script file to be executed using the ScriptBlock parameter. However, the script must be present in the specified location on all of the machines specified using the ComputerName parameter.

Additionally, the Invoke-Command cmdlet also supports a set of parameters that make it an even more powerful vehicle to conduct remote automation tasks. These parameters are described in Table 17.1.

TABLE 17.1   Important Invoke-Command Parameters

Parameters	Details
AsJob	Used to execute the command as a background job.
Credential	Used to specify alternate credentials that are used to execute the specified command.
ThrottleLimit	Used to specify the maximum number of connections that can be established by the Invoke-Command cmdlet.
Runspace	Used to execute the command in the specified runspaces.

As discussed previously, the AsJob parameter is used to execute the specified command as a background job. However, unlike the Get-WmiObject cmdlet, when the AsJob parameter is used with the Invoke-Command cmdlet, a background job is created on the client machine that then spawns a number of child background job(s) on each of the specified remote machine(s). After execution of a child background is finished, the result(s) are returned to parent background job on the "client" machine.

Needless to say, if a large number of remote machines are defined using the ComputerName parameter, the client machine might become overwhelmed. To help prevent the client machine or your network from drowning in an asynchronous connection storm, the Invoke-Command cmdlet will by default limit the number of concurrent remote connections for an issued "command" to 32. If you want to "tweak" the number of concurrent connections allowed, you can use the ThrottleLimit parameter.

> **NOTE**
>
> The ThrottleLimit parameter can also be used with the New-Runspace and Start-PsJob cmdlets.

An important concept to understand when using the Invoke-Command cmdlet is how it actually executes commands on a remote machine. By default, this cmdlet sets up a temporary runspace for each of the targeted remote machine(s). After execution of the specified command has finished, both the runspace and the connection resulting from that runspace are closed. This means that no matter how the ThrottleLimit parameter is used, if you execute a number of different commands using the Invoke-Command cmdlet at the same time, the actual number of concurrent connections to a remote machine is the total number of times you invoked the Invoke-Command cmdlet.

Needless to say, if you want to reuse the same existing connection and runspace, you need to use the Invoke-Command cmdlet's Runspace parameter. However, to make use of the parameter requires an already existing runspace on the targeted remote machine(s). To create a persistent runspace on a remote machine, use the New-Runspace cmdlet shown in the following example:

```
[PS] C:\> new-runspace -computer "scl-infra01","scl-ad01"
```

After executing the previous command, two persistent runspaces on each the specified targets are created. These runspaces can then be used to complete multiple commands and even share data between those commands. To use these runspaces, you need to retrieve the resulting runspace object(s) using the Get-Runspace cmdlet, and then pass it into the Invoke-Command cmdlet. For example:

```
[PS] C:\> $Runner = new-runspace -computer "scl-infra01","scl-ad01"
[PS] C:\> invoke-command -scriptblock {get-service "W32Time"} -run $Runner
| select ComputerName, Name, Status

ComputerName                    Name                    Status
------------                    ----                    ------
scl-ad01                        W32Time                 Running
scl-infra01                     W32Time                 Running
```

First, the $Runner variable is used to store the two resulting runspace objects that are created using the New-Runspace cmdlet. Next, the $Runner variable is defined as the argument for the Runspace parameter of the Invoke-Command cmdlet. By doing this, the command that is defined as the argument for the ScriptBlock parameter is executed in each of the runspaces represented by the $Runner variable. Finally, the results from the command executed in each of the runspaces is returned and piped into Select-Object cmdlet to format the output. In this case, the output shows the current status of the W32Time service on each of the specified remote machines.

After you have finished executing commands, it's important to understand that the runspaces that where created will remain open until you close the current PowerShell Console. To free up the resources being consumed by a runspace, you need to delete it using the Remove-Runspace cmdlet. For example, to remove the runspaces contained in the $Runner variable, pass that variable into the Remove-Runspace cmdlet, as shown here:

```
[PS] C:\> $Runner

SessionId Name               ComputerName    State    Shell
--------- ----               ------------    -----    -----
        7 Runspace7          scl-ad01        Opened   Microsoft.PowerShell
        8 Runspace8          scl-infra01     Opened   Microsoft.PowerShell


[PS] C:\> $Runner | remove-runspace
[PS] C:\> $Runner

SessionId Name               ComputerName    State    Shell
--------- ----               ------------    -----    -----
        7 Runspace7          scl-ad01        Closed   Microsoft.PowerShell
        8 Runspace8          scl-infra01     Closed   Microsoft.PowerShell
```

Workgroups and Different Domains
You can manage machines in a workgroup using remoting. However, some Windows security settings need to be modified or verified before attempting to remotely manage these machines. These settings are discussed in the following sections.

Windows XP SP2 or Greater and Windows Server 2003   For Windows XP SP2 or greater and Windows Server 2003 machines, you need to ensure that the "Network Access: Sharing and security model for local accounts" policy in Security Settings\Local Policies\Security Options is set to Classic.

Windows Vista and Windows Server 2008   On Windows Vista and Windows Server 2008 machines, you need to execute the following PowerShell command:

```
[PS] C:\> new-itemproperty —path
HKLM:\SOFTWARE\Microsoft\Windows\CurrentVersion \Policies\System —name
LocalAccountTokenFilterPolicy —propertyType DWord —value 1
```

For machines that are in another domain, if that domain trusts your domain, then you should be able to almost always remotely execute commands against these machines without issue. However, as a general "best-practice," you should use the Credential parameter for the Invoke-Command, New-Runspace, or Start-PsJob cmdlets to authenticate as a member of the Administrators group on the remote machine.

In instances in which the remote machine's domain doesn't trust your domain, you need to add your machine as a trusted WSMAN trusted host. To complete this task, use the following command:

```
[PS] C:\> winrmWSMAN s winrmWSMAN/config/client
'@{TrustedHosts="<Remote-computer-name>"}'
```

Background Jobs

By default, the PowerShell Console completes commands only in a synchronous manner. This means that when a command is executed, the command prompt is suppressed until execution of the issued command has completed. To address the impact of a command that takes a long time to complete execution might have on the usability of a console session, background jobs were introduced in PowerShell 2.0. When used, a background job (PsJob) executes a command "in the background" within its own runspace, so that additional commands can then be issued using the PowerShell Console. In other words, by using a background job, you can complete automation tasks that take an extended period of time to run without impacting the usability of your PowerShell Console session.

> **NOTE**
>
> To use background jobs (local or remote), PowerShell must be configured for remoting.

The Start-PsJob cmdlet is used to start a background job on the local machine. For example, to execute a script file as a background job you would use the following command:

```
[PS] C:\> start-psjob "C:\scripts\VM_Backup.ps1"
```

After it is executed, the command starts a background that executes the VM_Backup.ps1 script file. To see the current or resulting status of a job or jobs, you need to use the Get-PsJob cmdlet shown in the next example:

```
[PS] C:\> get-psjob

SessionId        Name           State         HasMoreData     Location
---------        ----           -----         -----------     --------
1                Job1           Completed     True            localhostCX
```

When executed, the Get-PsJob cmdlet returns an object or objects that represent all of the jobs that have been executed or are being executed in the current PowerShell Console. However, while the resulting objects may contain all of the related information about jobs, they don't contain the results from any of the jobs. To get the results from a background job, you must use the Receive-PsJob cmdlet, as shown in the following example:

```
[PS] C:\> receive-psjob -sessionid 1

---- Yeah, the script was executed and the VM was backed up. :>0
```

To delete jobs, you can either close your PowerShell Console or use the Remove-PsJob cmdlet, as shown in the following example:

```
[PS] C:\> remove-psjob -sessionid 1
```

Additional background job cmdlets are listed in Table 17.2:

TABLE 17.2   Additional Background Job Cmdlets

Cmdlet	Summary	Description
Stop-PSJob	Stops a Windows PowerShell background job (PsJob).	The Stop-PsJob cmdlet stops Windows PowerShell background jobs that are in progress. You can use this cmdlet to stop all jobs or stop selected jobs based on their name, session ID, instance ID, or state, or by passing a job object to Stop-PsJob.
Wait-PSJob	Suppresses the command prompt until one or all of Windows PowerShell background jobs (PsJobs) running in the console are complete.	The Wait-PsJob cmdlet waits for Windows PowerShell background jobs (PsJobs) executing in the specified before it displays the command prompt. You can use this command to determine when the complete results of a command are available.

17

Graphical PowerShell

Introduced in PowerShell 2.0 is an interactive GUI-based shell called Graphical PowerShell. To run Graphical PowerShell, you can either click **Start > All Programs > Windows PowerShell V2 > Graphical Windows PowerShell** or, from the command line, you can also execute **gpowershell.exe**.

Some of Graphical PowerShell's features are as follows:

▶ The shell provides syntax coloring and supports Unicode.

▶ There is an interactive **Input** pane that enables the execution of commands from within the shell. Results from executed commands are shown in an **Output** pane.

▶ There is also a multitabbed scripting pane used for editing or loading different ps1 files.

▶ Loaded script files can be dot-sourced by either pressing <F5> or by clicking the "Run" option on the toolbar.

▶ In addition, you can open up to eight runspaces from within the shell.

NOTE

Graphical PowerShell is installed when you install PowerShell 2.0. However, to use it, you must also have the NET Framework 3.0 installed.

In the Graphical PowerShell GUI, you will find an interactive prompt at the bottom of the shell that can be used to execute commands. This prompt is similar to the prompt found in the PowerShell Console. To complete a task, compose the command you want to execute and press **Enter** or click the green **Run** bottom. As the command is executed, the output is streamed into a separate Output pane above the interactive prompt. Also, to open up an additional runspace to execute commands, you can use the **Runspace > New Runspace** menu option. Both the Input and Output panes are shown in Figure 17.2.

To compose, edit, and execute scripts, you can either open the desired script or activate the Script pane by clicking the **Script** pane toggle button or using the **File > New Script** menu option. After the Script pane has been opened, you can compose a new script or edit the script that you opened. This pane is multitabbed, which means you can create or edit additional scripts in additional tabs in the Script pane. Additionally, the script you compose or edit can be executed by clicking the green **Run** button, pressing **F5**, or selecting the **File > Run** menu option. To execute only part of the script, select the portion of the script to be executed and use any of the execution methods mentioned previously.

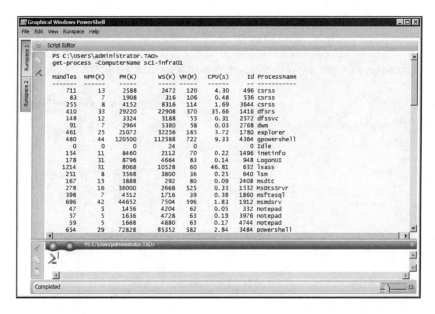

FIGURE 17.2   Graphical PowerShell

Graphical PowerShell is an interesting new edition to PowerShell functionality. However, at the time this book was written, Graphical PowerShell was considered an early alpha to beta version. As such, there are a couple known issues on top of being a limited integrated development environment (IDE). These include:

▶ No support for commands that require user input. For example, `netsh`, `telnet`, `ftp`, and `nslookup` are not supported.

▶ No support for `PSHost` functionality.

▶ Output formatting still has ellipses (…).

▶ The script editor is not fully optimized and may seem slow for scripts over a 1,000 lines.

Script Cmdlets

As defined earlier in this book, cmdlets are instances of reusable code that are based on the .NET Framework. All cmdlets are compiled into a DLL and must be loaded into a PowerShell session either during startup or by executing a series of commands. Although developing a series of cmdlets can be a great way to extend PowerShell functionality, the aspect of writing a bunch of code and then compiling that code and loading it into PowerShell may seem like daunting work to individuals who are not application developers (scripters and IT professionals).

To empower these individuals with the many of the same benefits that cmdlets provide to application developers, the PowerShell product team introduced a new PowerShell 2.0 feature called **script cmdlets**. In contrast to cmdlets, script cmdlets are written using the PowerShell script language, just like any other script, but in a specialized script block. For example:

```
Cmdlet Get-DayMessage
{
   Process
   {"Today is: $(get-date)"}
}
```

Script cmdlets come in two flavors: unnamed script cmdlets and named script cmdlets, which use the same Verb-Noun naming format as compiled cmdlets. In either case, both types of script cmdlets make use of the cmdlet keyword, which is used to identify them as cmdlets. With unnamed script cmdlets, the cmdlet keyword is declared in the script block using the following structure:

```
{
  cmdlet
  {
    Param ()
    Begin{}
    Process{}
    End{}
  }
}
```

As shown in the previous example, like compiled cmdlets, script cmdlets can declare their own mandatory and optional parameters while also having access to common parameters (such as -verbose and -debug). Furthermore, script cmdlets also support the usage of the same input processing methods (Begin, Process, and End) used in compiled cmdlets. Script cmdlets can also accept values from the pipeline while their output can also be piped to other compiled and script cmdlets.

With named script cmdlets, the structure is similar and supported methods, attributes, and parameters are the same as unnamed script cmdlets. The primary difference is that the script block is declared using the cmdlet keyword as shown in the following example:

```
cmdlet <Verb-Noun>
  {
    Param ()
    Begin{}
    Process{}
    End{}
  }
```

Besides the minor differences in structure, the only real difference between named and unnamed script cmdlets is in how they are invoked. Unnamed script cmdlets are invoked either as they are composed in the PowerShell Console or when the script file that contains them is executed. Conversely, named script cmdlets are invoked only when they are called. For example, if you were to execute a script file that contained a named script cmdlet called Get-MyMessage. The Get-MyMessage script cmdlet is only declared and must be explicitly called in order to be executed.

Out-GridView **Cmdlet**

The Out-GridView cmdlet is a new feature in PowerShell 2.0. This cmdlet allows output from any PowerShell command to be sent to a fully rendered and interactive grid window. When executed, the resulting Grid View window can then be used to search, sort, group, filter, and export the output data. For example, the following command creates an instance of the Grid View window:

```
[PS] C:\> get-process | out-gridview
```

The resulting Grid View window, shown in Figure 17.3, contains the output from the Get-Process cmdelt. By using the interactive interface created by the Out-GridView cmdlet, you can manipulate the output as needed.

> **NOTE**
>
> Like Graphical PowerShell, to use the Out-GridView cmdlet, you must also have the NET Framework 3.0 installed.

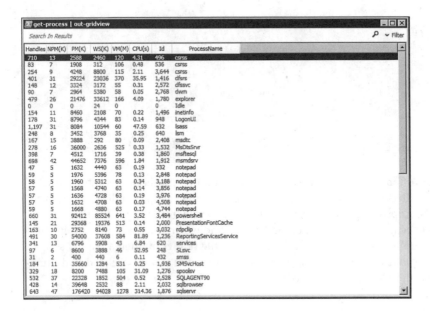

FIGURE 17.3   Resulting Grid View window

Script Internationalization

The primary goal of the script internationalization features in PowerShell 2.0 is to make it easier to display messages in a script user's native language. To accomplish this goal, when a script is executed (and provided the internationalization features are being used), PowerShell queries the user interface (UI) culture of the operating system and imports the appropriate predefiend text strings that are stored separately from script code in a DATA section.

> **NOTE**
>
> Script internationalization is not supported in PowerShell 1.0. If these features are defined in a script that is executed using PowerShell 1.0, the script will not run.

A breakdown of the script international features follows:

- ▶ Support for the new `.psd1` file type. These types of files store translated text strings and are located in language-specific subdirectories.

- ▶ The capability to use the DATA section feature, which allows text strings to be separated from script logic.

- ▶ A new variable called `$Culture`, which stores the name of the UI language used for elements such as date, time, and currency.

▶ A new variable called $UICulture, which stores the name of the UI language used for user interface elements such as menus and text strings.

▶ A new cmdlet named ConvertFrom-StringData, which is used to convert text strings into dictionary-like hash tables.

▶ A new cmdlet named Import-LocalizedData, which is used to import translated text strings for a specified language into a script at runtime.

DATA Sections

Taken from the page of modularity found with **Dynamic-Link Libraries (DLL)**, another new feature introduced in PowerShell 2.0 is called **DATA sections**. The primary goal with this feature is to make the task of separating data from execution code easier to manage by providing a means to isolate data (text strings and other read-only elements) from script logic.

> **NOTE**
>
> DATA sections is not supported in PowerShell 1.0. If this feature is used in a script that is executed using PowerShell 1.0, the script will not run.

When data is separated from script logic, you are able to start modularizing a script's components. For example, using DATA sections, you can create a separate resource file (as explained in the "Script Internationalization" section) for text, error messages, help strings, and so on. Thus, dumping "data" into separate resource files makes not only isolating and locating strings that need to be translated easier, but it also makes performing validation testing on script logic easier.

To create a DATA section, you need to use the following syntax:

```
DATA <variable> [-supportedCommand <cmdlet-name>] {
 <Permitted content>
}
```

Based on the syntax from the previous code box, a valid DATA section might look as follows:

```
DATA ErrorMsg {
 "Warning, task didn''t complete because host was shutdown!"
}
```

Notice the usage of the DATA keyword (not case sensitive) to designate that this is a DATA section. In addition, the variable name is required, but the $ prefix is omitted. As for content in a DATA section, you are limited to the elements shown in Table 17.3.

TABLE 17.3   Allowed DATA Section Elements

Elements	Notes
All Windows PowerShell operators, except match.	For a list, type "get-help about_operator".
If, Else, and ElseIf statements.	For details, type "get-help about_if".
$Culture $UICulture $True $False $Null	For descriptions of these variables, type "get-help about_automatic_variable".
Comments	
Pipelines	
Statements separated by semicolons (;).	
Literals, such as the following: a 1 1,2,3 Windows PowerShell 2.0" @("red", "green", "blue") @{ a = 0x1; b = "great"; c ="script" } [XML] @' <p> Hello, World	

Additionally, you many only use the following cmdlets in a DATA section:

▶ ConvertFrom-StringData

▶ Cmdlets you "permitted" using the supportedCommand parameter

For example, the following code box shows the ConvertFrom-StringData being used:

```
DATA ErrorMsgs {
 ConvertFrom-StringData @'
   Err1 = "Warning, task didn't complete because host was shutdown!"
   Err2 = "Warning, maybe you don't have access - try a different account!"
   '@
}
```

> **NOTE**
>
> When using the `ConvertFrom-StringData` in a DATA section, content that contains prohibited elements must be enclosed in single-quoted strings.

Modules

Modulization is a concept that was touched upon during the explanation of the DATA sections feature. Interestingly enough, a **module** is also new PowerShell 2.0 feature that is focused purely on supporting the modularizing of a script's components. In other words, modules enable scripts to be divided and organized into self-contained, independent, reusable units of code or resources.

A primary characteristic of a module is that it is self contained. When a module is used, code is executed in its own context, which prevents conflicts with any existing variables, functions, aliases, and other resources. In other words, a key aspect of a module is the capability to be portable. Thanks to this portability, modules can be easily used to build complex automation tools by bringing together and/or sharing existing resources.

These reusable components can either be DLLs or script files. To create a script-based module, you just need to take PowerShell code (like a function) and save it as a `.psm1` file. Then, to load a module into PowerShell, use the `Add-Module` cmdlet. When referring to the module, you can either use an absolute path, or place the module in either of the following directories and refer to it using the file name:

▶ `pshome\packages`

▶ `~\Documents\WindowsPowerShell\packages`

> **NOTE**
>
> Other module cmdlets include `Get-Module`, `Remove-Module`, and `Export-Module`.

Script Debugging

Debugging code is often an import task that any programmer or scripter has to do both during the development and support cycle of any type of software. To debug code, you often use a debugging tool or features in a programming language. Depending on the tools or features available for a programming language, the debugging process can either be easy a difficult task, as is the case with lower-level programming languages.

In PowerShell 1.0, debugging is accomplished by using either an IDE tool, such as **Powershell Analyzer**, by making use of internal PowerShell debug settings, by writing code to insert pseudo breakpoints, or by making use of PowerShell's exception-handling methods. Needless to say, there is much to be desired from the PowerShell engine in terms of language-based debugging features.

17

The PowerShell product creators were aware of the pain associated with attempting to perform debugging in PowerShell 1.0. That's why in PowerShell 2.0, a series of debugging cmdlets were introduced to enable you to actively debug a script, script cmdlet, function, command, or expression. Using these cmdlets, you can set breakpoints, step through script logic, examine the values of variables, run diagnostics and log commands, and even display the call stack. Details about the new debugging cmdlets are shown in Table 17.4:

TABLE 17.4   PowerShell Debugging Cmdlets

Debugging Cmdlets	Cmdlet Details
New-PsBreakpoint	The New-PsBreakPoint cmdlet establishes a point in a script at which Windows PowerShell stops executing. At the breakpoint, Windows PowerShell stops executing the script and gives control to the debugger.
Get-PsBreakpoint	A breakpoint is a point in a script at which execution stops temporarily so that you can examine the instructions in the script. Get-PsBreakpoint is one of several cmdlets designed for debugging Windows PowerShell scripts.
Enable-PsBreakpoint	The Enable-PsBreakpoint cmdlet re-enables a disabled breakpoint. You can use it to enable all breakpoints or to specify a breakpoint by submitting a breakpoint object or a breakpoint ID.
Disable-PsBreakpoint	The Disable-PsBreakpoint cmdlet disables a breakpoint, which ensures that it is not hit when the script runs. You can use it to disable all breakpoints or to specify a breakpoint by submitting a breakpoint object or a breakpoint ID.
Remove-PsBreakpoint	The Remove-PsBreakpoint cmdlet deletes a breakpoint, which ensures that it is not hit when the script runs. You can use it to disable all breakpoints or to specify a breakpoint by submitting a breakpoint object or a breakpoint ID.
Get-PsCallStack	The Get-PsCallStack cmdlet displays the current call stack. Although it is designed to be used with the Windows PowerShell debugger, you can use this cmdlet to display the call stack in a script or function outside of the debugger.
Step-Into	The Step-Into cmdlet executes a script one statement at a time. As it executes each statement, it displays a preview of the next statement in the debug message. Unlike Step-Over, Step-Into executes the next statement, even if that statement is in a function or in another script.
Step-Out	The Step-Out cmdlet exits the current breakpoint and resumes execution of the script until completion or the next breakpoint. If you use Step-Out while stepping through a function or invoked script, it exits the function or invoked script and steps back into the main script.

TABLE 17.4   Continued

Debugging Cmdlets	Cmdlet Details
Step-Over	The Step-Over cmdlet executes the script one statement at a time. However, unlike Step-Into, it executes and does not stop at the statements in functions and script invocations. Instead, it steps to the statement that follows the function or invoked script. If used before a function call, a Step-Over command steps over the function. However, if used while already stepping through a function, it continues to step through the function one statement at a time.

Summary

When released, PowerShell 1.0 was a major step forward in the manageability of Microsoft technologies. PowerShell 2.0 looks to continue with that trend by introducing many new features that further improve the ability for people to manage Microsoft products and environments. In other words, PowerShell has a bright future and some of that future—in the form of new features—was reviewed in this chapter.

Although these features range from remoting to script internationalization, and in appearance seem disconnected, they are, in fact, part of a series of themes that the PowerShell product group has decided to focus on for PowerShell 2.0. These themes are as follows:

- ▶ Universal Code Execution Model
- ▶ Production scripting
- ▶ GUI over PowerShell
- ▶ Community Feedback

As mentioned before in this chapter, the Universal Code Execution Model is a theme in PowerShell 2.0 aimed at ensuring that commands can traverse environments located in the foreground, background, or even on remote machines. With features like remoting and background jobs, Universal Code Execution Model is a primary theme in the 2.0 release of PowerShell.

Production scripting is also another important theme; it is aimed at making PowerShell scripting easier and more portable. Central to this theme is the script cmdlets feature, but also the concept of making PowerShell scripts modular in nature. This modularization can either be in the form of actual modules that can be shared among scripts or other scripters. Or, it can simply be the capability to support multiple different languages, much like a compiled application does.

GUI over PowerShell is another theme. It is more developer focused, but two obvious features that are part of this theme are the Graphical PowerShell and the Out-GridView cmdlet. Graphical PowerShell should provide the most benefit to an IT professional who needs not only a good PowerShell console, but also an IDE to write scripts with.

The final theme is Community Feedback. With PowerShell 2.0, the product team has gone out of its way to listen to the user community. As such, the community drives and dictates the product roadmap and the continued PowerShell improvements.

APPENDIX A

The `PSShell.ps1` Script

`PSShell.ps1` can be used as a secure shell solution for kiosk workstations. A working copy is in the `Scripts\Chapter 10\PSShell` folder on the source CD. This script requires an understanding of Windows Shell Replacement. Make sure you read the following sections about the script components to ensure that you know how to deploy and use the script effectively. First, however, you should review why this script is needed.

Companyabc.com manufactures processors for the general public and the U.S. government. Employees working on processors intended for government use must have special security clearance, and any data related to manufacturing of these processors must be secured to prevent exposure to unauthorized entities, both inside and outside the company.

These security requirements pose a challenge for companyabc.com. Its IT department has to support business procedures for both the retail and government contract divisions. Also, companyabc.com's CEO has issued a directive that all computer use must take place on a centralized system, which means any users at any location can access the company's data and applications. A centralized system further complicates security measures.

The IT department's solution to meet these requirements involves deploying Windows Terminal Service (WTS) server farms. Users working on the retail side have one set of WTS farms with a lower level of security. Users working in the government contract division have a different set of WTS farms isolated from retail users and with a high degree of security.

The IT department has decided to use thin clients for the WTS farms for quick deployment and a high degree of control over access and data security. However, although companyabc.com has the budget to build the WTS farms, funds to purchase thin clients and thin client software for all users aren't available. Further complicating matters is a recent company-wide Windows XP desktop refresh. In addition, desktop hardware that was just purchased must be used for another few years until it can be replaced.

To stay within the budget, the IT department has searched for an inexpensive way to turn the existing Windows XP desktops into thin clients. One systems administrator read a technical article about using Windows Shell Replacement to turn a Windows XP desktop into a secure kiosk, but it involves replacing Windows Explorer with Internet Explorer to create the kiosk interface. Although this method is fine for a simple Web browsing kiosk, the IT department needs complete control over the user interface shell.

To meet this need, the IT department has decided to use PowerShell and its support of .NET Windows Forms as a way to provide a customizable shell replacement for Windows Explorer. After development and testing, the final solution to companyabc.com's thin-client need is a hybrid of several different components. These components include Windows Shell Replacement, which uses cmd.exe as the base shell, and a PowerShell script that uses Windows Forms to present a secure, Windows Explorer–like desktop to logged on users. The following sections explain the components of PSShell.ps1 (named PSShell Kiosk) in more detail.

Component One: Shell Replacement

PSShell Kiosk's first component is the shell replacement. Windows, by default, uses the Windows Explorer shell (explorer.exe) as an interface for interacting with the operating system. However, this shell is not required to run Windows. Sometimes users want more functionality than Windows Explorer offers, or they want to decrease functionality as a way to improve security, as is the case with companyabc.com.

Windows users and administrators can modify explorer.exe or replace it with another shell (although it might not be supported by Microsoft). This process is called Windows Shell Replacement. Shells that can be used with Windows Shell Replacement range from GUI-based shells, such as Internet Explorer (iexplore.exe), Geoshell, and LiteStep to CLI-based shells, such as cmd.exe, command.com, and even PowerShell.

You can use two methods to replace explorer.exe. One is modifying the Windows Registry and specifying your replacement shell in the Shell value found in the HKEY_LOCAL_MACHINE\Software\Microsoft\Windows NT\CurrentVersion\Winlogon key.

For companyabc.com, changing the Registry on every Windows XP desktop isn't an option. Furthermore, getting rid of the shell for the entire Windows XP installation isn't wise. Suppose IT technicians need to log on to machines to perform system maintenance. If the default shell for the entire machine has been replaced by using the Registry method, the technicians are stuck with using the limited replacement shell because the shell has been changed for all users. Although there are ways to enable user-based shell replacement in the Registry, changing the Registry isn't a user-friendly or effective way to manage the deployment of replacement shells, as companyabc.com's IT department has discovered.

The second method for replacing `explorer.exe`, which requires Active Directory, is using the Group Policy Object (GPO) setting called Custom user interface. This setting enables you to specify the shell for users when they log on to a machine. The benefits of using GPOs include centralization and ease of management. In addition, you can have different shell settings based on the user, not the machine the user is logging on to. Because companyabc.com is looking for this type of control, the IT department has chosen the GPO method to manage PSShell Kiosk. The following sections explain the steps to set up this solution.

Step One: Creating the PSShell Secure Kiosk GPO

To create the GPO for configuring the Windows Shell Replacement, follow these steps:

1. Using the Group Policy Management Console (GPMC), create a GPO called **PSShell Kiosk Desktop GPO**.

2. Next, disable the Computer Configuration settings.

3. Remove **Authenticated Users** from the security filter settings for the PSShell Kiosk Desktop GPO.

4. In the Active Directory Users and Computers console, create a Domain Local group called **PSShell Kiosk Desktop GPO - Apply** and add a test user account to the group.

5. Add the PSShell Kiosk Desktop GPO - Apply group to the security filter settings for the PSShell Kiosk Desktop GPO.

6. Finally, link the PSShell Kiosk Desktop GPO to the top-level organizational unit (OU) containing all your user accounts, and make sure the linking orders of any other GPOs don't override the PSShell Kiosk Desktop GPO.

> **NOTE**
>
> Linking the PSShell Kiosk Desktop GPO to the top-level OU containing user accounts assumes there are no other GPOs linked to child OUs that might override this GPO. Furthermore, the GPO is applied to a group of users instead of a group of machines to prevent users with a higher security clearance from having a nonsecured desktop.

Step Two: Configuring the Windows Shell Replacement Settings

Next, you configure the Windows Shell Replacement settings by following these steps:

1. In the Group Policy Management Console (GPMC), edit the **PSShell Kiosk Desktop GPO**.

2. In the GPMC, click to expand **User Configuration**, **Administrative Templates**, and then click **System**. Then click to select the **Custom user interface** setting.

3. Right-click **Custom user interface** and click **Properties**.

4. In the Custom user interface Properties dialog box, click to select the **Enabled** option, type **cmd /c "C:\PSShell\Launch.bat"** in the Interface file name text box, as shown in Figure A.1, and then click **OK**.

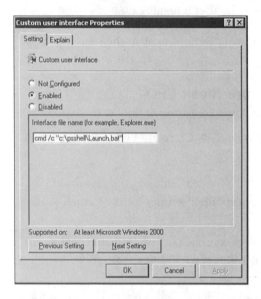

FIGURE A.1   Custom user interface Properties dialog box

Setting the interface filename to cmd forces Windows to use cmd.exe as the replacement shell. The /c switch forces cmd to carry out the C:\PSShell\Launch.bat command and then stop, which closes the cmd window after the Launch.bat file has finished running.

> **NOTE**
>
> Using the C:\PSShell path assumes that the files for PSShell Kiosk have been copied to this location. However, these files don't necessarily need to be copied to this location. They can be located on clients or a Windows network share.

Component Two: PSShell.exe

You might be wondering why cmd is used as the replacement shell instead of PowerShell. Unfortunately, when you're running a PowerShell script, there's no way to do so without displaying the PowerShell console. If explorer.exe is replaced with PowerShell, the resulting desktop contains the PowerShell console.

However, companyabc.com wants users to have a desktop similar to explorer.exe, not a desktop containing the PowerShell console. The solution involves the second component, PSShell.exe. PSShell.exe is a C# Windows application that hides the PowerShell console when PSShell.ps1 runs. The following code snippet shows the source code for this application:

```
using System;
using System.Diagnostics;

namespace PSShell
{
    static class Program
    {
        static void Main()
        {
            Process Process = new Process ();

            Process.StartInfo.FileName = "powershell.exe ";
            Process.StartInfo.Arguments = "-Command \"C:\\PSShell\\PSShell.ps1\"";
            Process.StartInfo.CreateNoWindow = true;
            Process.StartInfo.WindowStyle = ProcessWindowStyle.Hidden;
            Process.Start();
        }
    }
}
```

To hide the PowerShell console, PSShell.exe makes use of the .NET System.Diagnostics. Process class. By using this class with the .NET ProcessWindowStyle enumeration, you can define how a process's window should display when it starts. The style (appearance) can be Hidden, Normal, Minimized, or Maximized. For this example, you want the PowerShell window's style to be defined as Hidden. After starting the PowerShell process by using the Start() method with the specified arguments to run PSShell.ps1, Windows doesn't draw (display) the PowerShell console.

> **NOTE**
>
> Again, the C:\PSShell path in the PSShell.exe source code is only a suggestion. If you change the deployment path for PSShell Kiosk, you need to update the code and build a new executable. If you're familiar with C#, however, a better solution is modifying PSShell.exe so that it can take arguments to define the path to the PSShell.ps1 script.

To understand why cmd is used as the replacement shell, remember that PSShell.exe is not a shell, but an application written to suppress the PowerShell console when running a script. It's also needed to start PowerShell and run `PSShell.ps1` so that the PowerShell console is hidden. To start `PSShell.exe`, however, you need to call it from another shell, such as cmd. The interface filename you entered for the Custom user interface setting specified a batch file named `Launch.bat`, which is used to start `PSShell.exe`.

The result is that cmd is used to run `Launch.bat`, which then starts `PSShell.exe`. `PSShell.exe`, in turn, starts PowerShell, which finally runs the `PSShell.ps1` script. This workaround is a bit convoluted but necessary to compensate for a feature PowerShell lacks. With this workaround, you can still use PowerShell to generate a secure desktop.

Component Three: `PSShell.ps1`

The last component of PSShell Kiosk is `PSShell.ps1`, which generates the PSShell Kiosk desktop for logged on users. This desktop is generated by a Windows Form, which is possible because of PowerShell's capability to use .NET Windows Forms. The sole purpose of this script is to give users the illusion of seeing the default Windows desktop, when they're actually using a custom desktop with limited functionality.

The PSShell Kiosk solution determines what users see and what programs they can run from the desktop. Companyabc.com wants high-security users to be able to perform these tasks on a secure desktop:

▶ Starting the Microsoft Remote Desktop (RDP) client, which is configured to connect to the secure WTS farm

▶ Starting a limited instance (by GPO) of Internet Explorer that navigates to companyabc.com's Web-based e-mail site

▶ Logging off the PSShell Kiosk when they're finished using it

The first code snippet contains the header for the PSShell.ps1 script. This header includes information about what the script does, when it was updated, and the script's author:

```
##################################################
# PSShell.ps1
# Used as a shell replacement for explorer.exe.
#
# Created: 10/17/2006
# Author: Tyson Kopczynski
##################################################
```

In next code snippet, there are two long, complex statements involving the .NET `System.Reflection.Assembly` class:

```
$Null=[System.Reflection.Assembly]::LoadWithPartialName("System.Windows.Forms")
$Null=[System.Reflection.Assembly]::LoadWithPartialName("System.Drawing")
```

These two statements are necessary because PowerShell loads only a few .NET assemblies into its AppDomain. For example, if you try to create a Windows Forms object with the New-Object cmdlet, you would get the following error:

```
PS C:\> $Form = new-object System.Windows.Forms.Form
New-Object : Cannot find type [System.Windows.Forms.Form]: make sure
the assembly containing this type is loaded.
At line:1 char:19
+ $Form = new-object  <<<< System.Windows.Forms.Form
PS C:\>
```

To use the System.Windows.Forms.Form class, you need to load the assembly into PowerShell first by using the LoadWithPartialName() method. Assemblies must also be loaded into PowerShell for.NET-based DLLs included with Microsoft SDKs, third-party vendors, or your custom DLLs. For example, say you develop a .NET-based DLL to manage xyz application. To use that DLL in PowerShell, you use the LoadFrom() or LoadFile() methods from the System.Reflection.Assembly class, as shown in this example:

```
PS C:\> [System.Reflection.Assembly]::LoadFrom("C:\Stuff\myfirst.dll")
0
PS C:\>
```

> **NOTE**
>
> Microsoft has made the LoadWithPartialName() method obsolete. The replacement is the Load() method, which is meant to prevent partial binds when .NET assemblies are loaded. Using the Load() method requires more work. However, if you don't mind the implications of a partial bind (such as your script failing), you can continue using LoadWithPartialName() until it's removed from the .NET Framework.

Now that the required assemblies for Windows Forms objects have been loaded, the next task is to finish configuring the runtime environment for the script. The first step, as shown in the following code snippet, is to define a set of launch command strings that will be used to control the applications users can launch from the PSShell Kiosk desktop. These command strings are discussed in more depth later in this section:

```
# Launch command strings
$LaunchIE = {$IE = new-object -com InternetExplorer.Application; '
    $IE.navigate("webmail.companyabc.com"); $IE.visible = $True; $IE}
$LaunchRemoteDesktop = {mstsc /v:earth.companyabc.com /f}
```

Then, after defining the launch command strings, the next task is to create a PowerShell Runspace, as demonstrated in the next code snippet:

```
#-------------------
# Create Runspace
#-------------------
# For more info on Runspaces see:
# http://windowssdk.msdn.microsoft.com/en-us/library/ms714459(VS.80).aspx

$Runspace =
    [System.Management.Automation.Runspaces.RunspaceFactory]::CreateRunspace()
$RunspaceInvoke =
    new-object System.Management.Automation.RunspaceInvoke($Runspace)
$Runspace.Open()
```

This code shows a PowerShell runspace, which is represented by the PowerShell System.Management.Automation.Runspaces namespace. A **runspace** is an abstraction of the PowerShell runtime that enables a hosting application to run PowerShell commands to perform tasks or gather information. Although powershell.exe is a hosting application and uses its own runspace to process commands, runspaces are most beneficial when used in applications outside PowerShell.

Runspaces are needed to support PowerShell, but they were developed mainly to create an easy way for other applications to call the PowerShell runtime and have it run PowerShell commands. In a sense, the Windows Form that PSShell.ps1 creates is an application, so it makes sense for it to interact with a PowerShell runspace to perform tasks. By taking advantage of PowerShell runspaces, you then don't have to spend time adding logic to the Windows Form to make it perform tasks for users.

Creating a runspace ($Runspace) for the Windows Form simply involves using the CreateRunspace() method from the PowerShell System.Management.Automation. Runspaces.RunspaceFactory class. Next, you create a RunspaceInvoke object that enables the Windows Form to run commands via the runspace. Last, you open the runspace by using the Open() method so that it can be used by the Windows Form.

After defining the Runspace, the next task is to construct the form itself as shown in the following code snippet. In the section that is titled "Define Images," a series of Drawing.Image objects are created. These objects are used later in the form to represent such items are the PSShell Kiosk desktop start menu and application icons. Then in the code section, titled "Create Form," the form object is created using a set of predefined properties used to make the form look like the default Windows desktop.

```
#--------------------
# Define Images
#--------------------
$ImagePath = Split-Path -Parent $MyInvocation.MyCommand.Path
$ImgStart = [Drawing.Image]::FromFile("$Imagepath\Images\Start.png")
$ImgRDP = [Drawing.Image]::FromFile("$Imagepath\Images\RDP.png")
$ImgIE = [Drawing.Image]::FromFile("$Imagepath\Images\IE.png")


#--------------------
# Create Form
#--------------------
$Form = new-object System.Windows.Forms.Form
$Form.Size = new-object System.Drawing.Size @(1,1)
$Form.DesktopLocation = new-object System.Drawing.Point @(0,0)
$Form.WindowState = "Maximized"
$Form.StartPosition = "CenterScreen"
$Form.ControlBox = $False
$Form.FormBorderStyle = "FixedSingle"
$Form.BackColor = "#647258"
```

Having constructed the form, the final task before activating the form and showing it to the user is to add the menu items. This task is completed in the next code snippet.

The following code adds several MenuItems to the ToolStripMenu that acts as the Start menu for the PSShell Kiosk desktop:

```
#--------------------
# Build Menu
#--------------------
$MenuStrip = new-object System.Windows.Forms.MenuStrip
$MenuStrip.Dock = "Bottom"
$MenuStrip.BackColor = "#292929"


# Start Menu
$StartMenuItem = new-object System.Windows.Forms.ToolStripMenuItem("")
$StartMenuItem.Padding = 0
$StartMenuItem.Image = $ImgStart
$StartMenuItem.ImageScaling = "None"


# Menu Item 1
$MenuItem1 = new-object System.Windows.Forms.ToolStripMenuItem("&Webmail")
$MenuItem1.Image = $ImgIE
$MenuItem1.ImageScaling = "None"
```

A

```
$MenuItem1.add_Click({$RunspaceInvoke.Invoke($LaunchIE)})


$StartMenuItem.DropDownItems.Add($MenuItem1)

# Menu Item 2
$MenuItem2 = new-object System.Windows.Forms.ToolStripMenuItem("&Remote Desktop")
$MenuItem2.Image = $ImgRDP
$MenuItem2.ImageScaling = "None"
$MenuItem2.add_Click({$RunspaceInvoke.invoke($LaunchRemoteDesktop)})


$StartMenuItem.DropDownItems.Add($MenuItem2)

# Menu Item 3
$MenuItem3 = new-object System.Windows.Forms.ToolStripMenuItem("&Log Off")
$MenuItem3.add_Click({'
    $RunspaceInvoke.invoke({Get-WmiObject Win32_OperatingSystem | '
    foreach-object {$_.Win32Shutdown(0)}})})


$StartMenuItem.DropDownItems.Add($MenuItem3)
```

Basically, the preceding code snippet shows several MenuItems being added to the
ToolStripMenu, which is acting as the start menu for the PSShell Kiosk desktop. These
menu items are the way users start applications or log off the PSShell Kiosk desktop. Each
menu item is assigned a click event that uses the $RunspaceInvoke object and its
invoke() method to run a specified PowerShell command. The following list describes the
action each menu item performs:

▶ $MenuItem1—Uses the command specified in the $LaunchIE variable to start Internet
  Explorer

▶ $MenuItem2—Uses the command specified in the $LaunchRemoteDesktop variable to
  start mstsc.exe (the Microsoft RDP client)

▶ $MenuItem3—Uses the Get-WmiObject cmdlet to log off Windows

Finally, the script needs to activate the form and show it to the user using the ShowDialog
method. This is shown in the final code snippet:

```
#-------------------
# Show Form
#-------------------
$MenuStrip.Items.Add($StartMenuItem)
$Form.Controls.Add($MenuStrip)
$Form.Add_Shown({$Form.Activate()})
$Form.ShowDialog()
```

Putting It All Together

After the PSShell Kiosk Desktop GPO is configured and ready to be applied to users, the next step is to deploy the following PSShell Kiosk files to the desktops used as secure thin clients:

- ▶ Launch.bat—The batch file used to start PSShell.exe
- ▶ PSShell.exe—The C# application used to run the PSShell.ps1 script
- ▶ PSShell.ps1—The PowerShell script that creates the PSShell Kiosk
- ▶ Images folder—The folder containing images used on the PSShell Kiosk desktop

As discussed earlier, the PSShell Kiosk solution is currently configured to reside in the C:\PSShell path. So, after you have deployed these files to this location on each desktop, you can place users who need a secure desktop in the PSShell Kiosk Desktop GPO - Apply group. Figure A.2 shows the PSShell Kiosk desktop with the three menu items.

FIGURE A.2   The PSShell Kiosk desktop

Symbols

A

E

How can we make this index more useful? Email us at indexes@samspublishing.com

Q-R

How can we make this index more useful? Email us at indexes@samspublishing.com

X-Y-Z

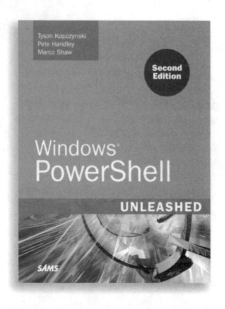

FREE Online Edition

Your purchase of **Windows PowerShell Unleashed** includes access to a free online edition for 45 days through the Safari Books Online subscription service. Nearly every Sams book is available online through Safari Books Online, along with more than 5,000 other technical books and videos from publishers such as Addison-Wesley Professional, Cisco Press, Exam Cram, IBM Press, O'Reilly, Prentice Hall, and Que.

SAFARI BOOKS ONLINE allows you to search for a specific answer, cut and paste code, download chapters, and stay current with emerging technologies.

Activate your FREE Online Edition at
www.informit.com/safarifree

> **STEP 1:** Enter the coupon code: 7VQA-MDDP-IIEE-F9PF-1KWV.

> **STEP 2:** New Safari users, complete the brief registration form.
> Safari subscribers, just log in.

If you have difficulty registering on Safari or accessing the online edition, please e-mail customer-service@safaribooksonline.com